Nathan H. Dole

Complete Works of Lyof N. Tolstoï

Vol. 2

Nathan H. Dole

Complete Works of Lyof N. Tolstoï
Vol. 2

ISBN/EAN: 9783337319519

Printed in Europe, USA, Canada, Australia, Japan

Cover: Foto ©Thomas Meinert / pixelio.de

More available books at **www.hansebooks.com**

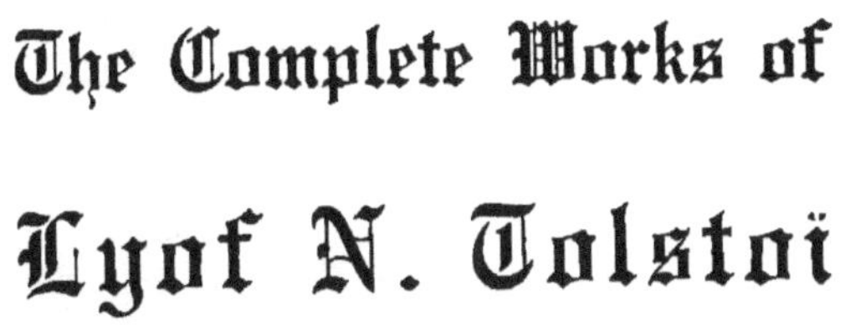

The Complete Works of Lyof N. Tolstoï

My Confession
My Religion
The Gospel in Brief

THE KELMSCOTT SOCIETY
PUBLISHERS NEW YORK

MY CONFESSION

MY RELIGION

THE GOSPEL IN BRIEF

INTRODUCTION

Count Tolstoï's religious teachings are not allowed by the censorship to be published complete in Russia, but they are issued in a cheap pamphlet form printed in Geneva, Switzerland. This so-called Elpidin edition has been used in preparing the present translation of "My Confession," and "My Religion," — or as it is called in the original, *F Chom Moya Viera*, "In What my Faith?"[1] If it varies in any material respect from the English translation made some years ago through the medium of the French, it is in the line of greater simplicity. Count Tolstoï can hardly be called a stylist; he writes earnestly, convincingly, often eloquently, but never hesitates to repeat, so that the word or set of words will be found recurring again and again even in the same sentence. The French are stylists, and they modify, condense, and amplify till the semblance of form is sometimes lost, and the thought is transferred in a paraphrase. The plain figure is embroidered and covered with filigree.

Nevertheless, the main thing in these essays is the thought. It is that which Count Tolstoï so earnestly wishes to make known. As he says, he was in the same condition as the thief on the cross, and was saved by

[1] The "Short Exposition of the Gospels," published separately in the same form, is only a part of Count Tolstoï's "Gospel in Brief" which is included in the present volume.

his faith. If the thief on the cross could have lived to preach he might have been a prototype of Paul; but Count Tolstoï was not condemned to die without speaking, and he felt it his duty to tell the world what brought him happiness and peace. It was not to be supposed that his arraignment of a Church, which preached one thing and practised its opposite, would be permitted. The Orthodox Church of his own land stopped it easily enough by forbidding his book to be published and sold. Personally he was let alone, because he preached the gospel of non-resistance and disapproved of nihilistic violence. Elsewhere the reverend critics, avoiding the real question at issue, attacked him with more or less violence, or tried to minimize the effect of his prophet's word by calling him names. In fact, he has been treated with the same spirit as has animated the persecutors of the prophets since the beginning of the world.

Count Tolstoï tells in his "Confession" how he was led from nihilism in the real sense of the word to faith in the literal interpretation of Christ's words, and how he was saved from despair and brought to a joyful knowledge of the meaning of life. In "My Religion" he shows how he threw aside the Church interpretation and went to the original Greek, to Christ's own words, and how he was amazed to find how perfectly they answered the needs of his soul, when once they were stripped of fictitious and extraneous notions. Mr. Huntington Smith, the former translator of "My Confession," in his preface said: —

"The interpretation is not new in theory, but never before has it been carried out with so much zeal, so much determination, so much sincerity, and, granting the premises, with logic so unanswerable, as in this beautiful confession of faith. How movingly does he depict the doubts and fears of the searcher after the better life; how impressive his earnest inquiry for truth; how inspiring his confidence in the natural goodness as opposed to the natural depravity of man; how convincing his argument that the doctrine of Jesus is simple, practicable, and conducive to the highest happiness; how terrifying his enumeration of the sufferings of 'the martyrs to the doctrine of the world'; how pitiless his arraignment of the Church for its complacent indifference to the welfare of humanity here in this present stage of existence; how sublime his prophecy of the golden age when men shall dwell together in the bonds of love, and sin and suffering shall be no more the common lot of mankind! We read, and are thrilled with a divine emotion, but which of us is willing to accept the truth here unfolded as the veritable secret of life?

"Shall we take seriously this eloquent enunciation of faith in humility, in self-denial, in fraternal love, or shall we regard it only as a beautiful and peaceful phase in the career of a man of genius who, after the storm and stress of a life of sin and suffering, has turned back to the ideals of youth and innocence, and sought to make them once more the objects of desire? Fanaticism, do you say? Ah, yes; but did not Jesus and his disciples practise just such fanaticism as this? Does any one deny that all that is best in this modern world (and there is so much of the best, after all), that all that is best has come from the great moral impulse generated by a little group of fanatics in an obscure corner of Asia eighteen centuries ago? That impulse we still feel, in spite of all the obstructions that have been put in its way to nullify its action; and if any would seek for strength from the primary source of power, who shall say him nay? And so although we may smile at the artlessness of this Russian evangelist in his determination to find in the Gospels the categorical imperative of self-renunciation, although we may regard with wonder the magnificent audacity of his exegetical speculations, we cannot refuse to admire a faith so sincere, so intense, and, in many respects, so elevating and so noble."

Count Tolstoï makes several references to a "Criticism of Dogmatic Theology" and a translation of the Four Gospels accompanied by a Concordance on which he has been laboring for a number of years. As these works are thoroughly technical and repeat much of what has already been given, and however valuable to the special student and the controversial theologian, are not likely to be of interest to the general reader, it has been decided to omit them from this edition.

CONTENTS

MY CONFESSION

INTRODUCTION TO "MY RELIGION"

CHAPTER I

I WAS christened and educated in the Orthodox Christian Faith; I was taught it in my childhood, and in my boyhood and youth. Nevertheless, when, at eighteen years of age, I left the university in the second year, I had discarded all belief in anything I had been taught.

To judge by what I can now remember, I never had a serious belief; I merely trusted in what my elders made their profession of faith, but even this trust was very precarious.

I remember once in my twelfth year, a boy, now long since dead, Volodinka M——, a pupil in the gymnasium, spent a Sunday with us, and brought us the news of the last discovery in the gymnasium. This discovery was that there was no God, and that all we were taught on the subject was a mere invention (this was in 1838). I remember well how interested my elder brothers were in this news; I was admitted to their deliberations, and we all eagerly accepted the theory as something particularly attractive and possibly quite true.

I remember, also, that when my elder brother, Dmitri, then at the university, with the impulsiveness natural to his character, gave himself up to a passionate faith, began to attend the church services regularly, to fast, and to lead a pure and moral life, we all of us, and some older than ourselves, never ceased to hold him up to ridicule, and for some incomprehensible reason gave him the nickname of Noah. I remember that Musin-Pushkin, then curator of the University of Kazan, having invited us to a ball, tried to persuade my brother, who had refused the invitation, by the jeering argument that even David danced before the Ark.

I sympathized then with these jokes of my elders, and drew from them this conclusion, — that I was bound to learn my catechism, and go to church, but that it was not necessary to take all this too seriously.

I also remember that I read Voltaire when I was very young, and that his tone of mockery amused without disgusting me.

This estrangement from all belief went on in me, as it does now, and always has done, in those of the same social position and culture. This falling off, as it seems to me, for the most part goes on thus: people live as others live, and their lives are guided, not by the principles of the faith that is taught them, but by their very opposite; belief has no influence on life, nor on the relations among men — it is relegated to some other sphere apart from life and independent of it; if the two ever come into contact at all, belief is only one of the outward phenomena, and not one of the constituent parts of life.

By a man's life, by his acts, it was then, as it is now, impossible to know whether he was a believer or not. If there be a difference between one who openly professes the doctrines of the Orthodox Church, and one who denies them, the difference is to the advantage of the former. Then, as now, the open profession of the Orthodox doctrines was found mostly among dull, stern, immoral men, and those who think much of their own importance. Intellect, honor, frankness, good nature, and morality are oftener met with among those who call themselves disbelievers.

The school-boy is taught his catechism and sent to church; chinovniks, or functionaries, are required to show a certificate of having taken the holy communion. But the man belonging to our class, who is done with school and does not enter the public service, may now live a dozen years — still more was this the case formerly — without being once reminded of the fact that he lives among Christians, and is reckoned as a member of the Orthodox Christian Church.

Thus it happens that now, as formerly, the influence of early religious teaching, accepted merely on trust and upheld by authority, gradually fades away under the knowledge and practical experience of life, which is opposed to all its principles, and that a man often believes for years that his early faith is still intact, while all the time not a trace of it remains in him.

A certain S——, a clever and veracious man, once related to me how he came to give up his belief.

Twenty-six years ago, while he was off on a hunting expedition, he knelt down to pray before he lay down to rest, according to a habit of his from childhood. His elder brother, who was of the party, lay on some straw and watched him. When S—— had finished, and was preparing to lie down, his brother said to him:—

"Ah, so you still keep that up?"

Nothing more passed between them, but from that day S—— ceased to pray and to go to church. For thirty years S—— has not said a prayer, has not taken the communion, has not been in a church, — not because he shared the convictions of his brother, or even knew them, — not because he had come to any conclusions of his own, — but because his brother's words were like the push of a finger against a wall ready to tumble over with its own weight; they proved to him that what he had taken for belief was an empty form, and that consequently every word he uttered, every sign of the cross he made, every time he bowed his head during his prayers, his act was unmeaning. When he once admitted to himself that such acts had no meaning in them, he could not continue them.

Thus it has been, and is, I believe, with the large majority of men. I am speaking of men of our class, I am speaking of men who are true to themselves, and not of those who make of religion a means of obtaining some temporal advantage. (These men are truly absolute unbelievers; for if faith be to them a means of obtaining any worldly end, it is most certainly no faith at all.) Such men of our own class are in this position: the light of knowledge and life has melted the artificially constructed edifice of belief within, and they have either observed that and cleared away the superincumbent ruins, or they have remained unconscious of it.

The belief instilled from childhood in me, as in so many others, gradually disappeared, but with this difference; that as from fifteen years of age I had begun to read philosophical works, I became very early conscious of my own disbelief. From the age of sixteen I ceased to pray, and ceased, from conviction, to attend the services of the church and to fast. I no longer accepted the faith of my childhood, but I believed in something, though I could not exactly explain in what. I believed in a God, — or rather, I did not deny the existence of a God, — but what kind of God I could not have told; I denied neither Christ nor His teaching, but in what that teaching consisted I could not have said.

Now, when I think over that time, I see clearly that all the faith I had, the only belief which, apart from mere animal instinct, swayed my life, was a belief in the possibility of perfection, though what it was in itself, or what would be its results, I could not have said.

I tried to reach intellectual perfection; my studies were extended in every direction of which my life afforded me a chance; I strove to strengthen my will, forming for myself rules which I forced myself to follow; I did my best to develop my physical powers by every exercise calculated to give strength and agility, and by way of accustoming myself to patient endurance; I subjected myself to many voluntary hardships and trials of privation. All this I looked on as necessary to obtain the perfection at which I aimed.

At first, of course, moral perfection seemed to me the main end, but I soon found myself contemplating in its stead an ideal of general perfectibility; in other words, I wished to be better, not in my own eyes nor in God's, but in the sight of other men. And very soon this striving to be better in the sight of men feeling again changed into another, — the desire to have more power than others, to secure for myself a greater share of fame, of social distinction, and of wealth.

CHAPTER II

At some future time I may relate the story of my life, and dwell in detail on the pathetic and instructive incidents of my youth. I think that many and many have had the same experiences as I did. I desired with all my soul to be good; but I was young, I had passions, and I was alone, wholly alone, in my search after goodness. Every time I tried to express the longings of my heart to be morally good, I was met with contempt and ridicule, but as soon as I gave way to low passions, I was praised and encouraged.

Ambition, love of power, love of gain, lechery, pride, anger, vengeance, were held in high esteem.

As I gave way to these passions, I became like my elders, and I felt that they were satisfied with me. A kind-hearted aunt of mine, a really good woman with whom I lived, used to say to me that there was one thing above all others which she wished for me — an intrigue with a married woman: "*Rien ne forme un jeune homme, comme une liaison avec une femme comme il faut.*" Another of her wishes for my happiness was that I should become an adjutant, and, if possible, to the Emperor; the greatest piece of good fortune of all she thought would be that I should find a very wealthy bride, who would bring me as her dowry as many slaves as could be.

I cannot now recall those years without a painful feeling of horror and loathing.

I put men to death in war, I fought duels to slay others, I lost at cards, wasted my substance wrung from the sweat of peasants, punished the latter cruelly, rioted with loose women, and deceived men. Lying, robbery, adultery of all kinds, drunkenness, violence, murder..... There was not one crime which I did not commit, and yet I was not the less considered by my equals a comparatively moral man.

Such was my life during ten years.

During that time I began to write, out of vanity, love of gain, and pride. I followed as a writer the same path which I had chosen as a man. In order to obtain the fame and the money for which I wrote, I was obliged to hide what was good and to say what was evil. Thus I did. How often while writing have I cudgeled my brains to conceal under the mask of indifference or pleasantry those yearnings for something better which formed the real thought of my life. I succeeded in this also, and was praised.

At twenty-six years of age, on the close of the war, I came to Petersburg and made the acquaintance of the authors of the day. I met with a hearty reception and much flattery.

Before I had time to look around, the prejudices and views of life common to the writers of the class with which I associated became my own, and completely put an end to all my former struggles after a better life. These views, under the influence of the dissipation of my life, supplied a theory which justified it.

The view of life taken by these my fellow-writers was that life is a development, and the principal part in that development is played by ourselves, the thinkers, while among the thinkers the chief influence is again due to us, the artists, the poets. Our vocation is to teach men.

In order to avoid answering the very natural question, "What do I know, and what can I teach?" the theory in question is made to contain the formula that it is not necessary to know this, but that the artist and the poet teach unconsciously.

I was myself considered a marvelous artist and poet, and I therefore very naturally adopted this theory. I, an artist and poet, wrote and taught I knew not what. For doing this I received money; I kept a splendid table, had excellent lodgings, women, society; I had fame. Naturally what I taught was very good.

The faith in poetry and the development of life was a true faith, and I was one of its priests. To be one of its priests was very advantageous and agreeable. I long remained in this belief, and never once doubted its truth.

But in the second, and especially in the third year of

this way of life, I began to doubt the infallibility of the doctrine, and to examine it more closely. What first led me to doubt was the fact that I began to notice the priests of this belief did not agree among themselves. Some said: —

"We are the best and most useful teachers; we teach what is needful, and all others teach wrong."

They disputed, quarreled, abused, deceived, and cheated one another. Moreover, there were many among us who, quite indifferent to the question who was right or who was wrong, advanced only their own private interests by the aid of our activity. All this forced on me doubts as to the truth of our belief.

Again, having begun to doubt the truth of our literary faith, I began to study its priests more closely, and became convinced that almost all the priests of this faith were immoral men, most of them worthless and insignificant, and beneath the moral level of those with whom I associated during my former dissipated and military career; but conceited and self-satisfied as only those can be who are wholly saints, or those who know not what holiness is.

I grew disgusted with mankind and with myself, and I understood that this belief was a delusion. The strangest thing in all this was that, though I soon saw the falseness of this belief and renounced it, I did not renounce the rank given me by these men, — the rank of artist, poet, teacher. I was simple enough to imagine that I was a poet and artist, and could teach all men without knowing what I was teaching. But so I did.

By my companionship with these men I had gained a new vice, — a pride developed to a morbid extreme, and an insane self-confidence in teaching men what I myself did not know.

When I now think over that time, and remember my own state of mind and that of these men (a state of mind common enough among thousands still), it seems to me pitiful, terrible, and ridiculous; it excites the feelings which overcome us as we pass through a madhouse.

We were all then convinced that it behooved us to

speak, to write, and to print as fast as we could, as much as we could, and that on this depended the welfare of the human race. And thousands of us wrote, printed, and taught, and all the while confuted and abused one another. Quite unconscious that we ourselves knew nothing, that to the simplest of all problems in life — what is right and what is wrong — we had no answer, we all went on talking together without one to listen, at times abetting and praising one another on condition that we were abetted and praised in turn, and again turning upon one another in wrath — in short, we reproduced the scenes in a madhouse.

Thousands of laborers worked day and night, to the limit of their strength, setting up the type and printing millions of words to be spread by the post all over Russia, and still we continued to teach, unable to teach enough, angrily complaining the while that we were not much listened to.

A strange state of things indeed, but now it is comprehensible to me. The real motive that inspired all our reasoning was the desire for money and praise, to obtain which we knew of no other means than writing books and newspapers, and so we did. But in order to hold fast to the conviction that while thus uselessly employed we were very important men, it was necessary to justify our occupation to ourselves by another theory, and the following was the one we adopted: —

Whatever is, is right; everything that is, is due to development; development comes from civilization; the measure of civilization is the diffusion of books and newspapers; we are paid and honored for the books and newspapers which we write, and we are therefore the most useful and best of men!

This reasoning might have been conclusive had we all been agreed; but, as for every opinion expressed by one of us there instantly appeared from another one diametrically opposite, we had to hesitate before accepting it. But we did not notice this; we received money, and were praised by those of our party, consequently we — each one of us — considered that we were in the right.

It is now clear to me that between ourselves and the inhabitants of a madhouse there was no difference: at the time I only vaguely suspected this, and, like all madmen, thought all were mad except myself.

CHAPTER III

I LIVED in this senseless manner another six years, up to the time of my marriage. During this time I went abroad. My life in Europe, and my acquaintance with many eminent and learned foreigners, confirmed my belief in the doctrine of general perfectibility, as I found the same theory prevailed among them. This belief took the form which is common among most of the cultivated men of our day. This belief was expressed in the word "progress." It then appeared to me this word had a real meaning. I did not as yet understand that, tormented like every other man by the question, "How was I to live better?" when I answered that I must live for progress, I was only repeating the answer of a man carried away in a boat by the waves and the wind, who to the one important question for him, "Where are we to steer?" should answer, "We are being carried somewhere."

I did not see this then; only at rare intervals my feelings, and not my reason, were roused against the common superstition of our age, which leads men to ignore their own ignorance of life.

Thus, during my stay in Paris, the sight of a public execution revealed to me the weakness of my superstitious belief in progress. When I saw the head divided from the body, and heard the sound with which they fell separately into the box, I understood, not with my reason, but with my whole being, that no theory of the wisdom of all established things, nor of progress, could justify such an act; and that if all the men in the world from the day of creation, by whatever theory, had found this thing necessary, I knew it was not necessary, it was a bad thing, and that therefore I must judge of what was right and necessary, not by what men said and did, not by progress, but what I felt to be true in my heart.

Another instance of the insufficiency of this superstition of progress as a rule for life was the death of my brother. He fell ill while still young, suffered much during a whole year, and died in great pain. He was a man of good abilities, of a kind heart, and of a serious temper, but he died without understanding why he had lived, and still less what his death meant for him. No theories could give an answer to these questions, either to him or to me, during the whole period of his long and painful lingering.

But these occasions for doubt were few and far between; on the whole, I continued to live in the profession of the faith of progress. "Everything develops, and I myself am developing; and why this is so will one day be apparent," was the formula I was obliged to adopt.

On my return from abroad I settled in the country, and occupied myself with the organization of schools for the peasantry. This occupation was especially dear to my heart, because it was free from the spirit of falseness so evident to me in the career of a literary teacher.

Here again I acted in the name of progress, but this time I brought a spirit of critical inquiry to the system on which the progress rested. I said to myself that progress was often attempted in an irrational manner, and that it was necessary to leave a primitive people and the children of peasants perfectly free to choose the way of progress which they thought best. In reality I was still bent on the solution of the same impossible problem, — how to teach without knowing what I had to teach. In the highest spheres of literature I had understood that it was impossible to do this because I had seen that each taught differently, and that the teachers quarreled among themselves, and scarcely succeeded in concealing their ignorance from one another. Having now to deal with peasants' children, I thought that I could get over this difficulty by allowing the children to learn what they liked. It seems now absurd when I remember the expedients by which I carried out this whim of mine to teach, though I knew in my heart that I could teach nothing useful, because I myself did not know what was necessary.[1]

After a year spent in this employment with the school I again went abroad, for the purpose of finding out how I was to teach without knowing anything.

I believed that I had found a solution abroad, and, armed with all that essence of wisdom, I returned to Russia, the same year in which the peasants were freed from serfdom; and, accepting the office of arbitrator,[2] I began to teach the uneducated people in the schools, and the educated classes in the journal which I began to publish. Things seemed to be going on well, but I felt that my mind was not in a normal state and that a change was near. I might even then, perhaps, have come to that state of despair to which I was brought fifteen years later, if it had not been for a new experience in life which promised me safety — family life.

For a year I was occupied with arbitration, with the schools, and with my newspaper, and got so involved that I was harassed to death; the struggle over the arbitration was so hard for me, my activity in the schools was so dubious to me, my shuffling in the newspaper became so repugnant to me, consisting as it did in forever the same thing, — in the desire to teach all people and to hide the fact that I did not know how or what to teach, — that I fell ill, more with a mental than physical sickness, gave up everything, and started for the steppes to the Bashkirs to breathe a fresher air, to drink kumiss, and live an animal life.

After I returned I married. The new circumstances of a happy family life completely led me away from the search after the meaning of life as a whole. My life was concentrated at this time in my family, my wife and children, and consequently in the care for increasing the means of life. The effort to effect my own individual perfection, already replaced by the striving

[1] See "School Scenes from Yasnaya Polyana," Vol. XV.

[2] *Posrednik*, sometimes translated Justice of the Peace.

after general progress, was again changed into an effort to secure the particular happiness of my family.

In this way fifteen years passed.

Notwithstanding that during these fifteen years I looked upon the craft of authorship as a very trifling thing, I continued all the time to write. I had experienced the seductions of authorship, the temptations of an enormous pecuniary reward and of great applause for valueless work, and gave myself up to it as a means of improving my material position, and of stifling in my soul all questions regarding my own life and life in general. In my writings I taught what for me was the only truth, — that the object of life should be our highest happiness and that of our family.

Thus I lived; but, five years ago, a strange state of mind began to grow upon me: I had moments of perplexity, of a stoppage, as it were, of life, as if I did not know how I was to live, what I was to do, and I began to wander, and was a victim to low spirits. But this passed, and I continued to live as before. Later, these periods of perplexity began to return more and more frequently, and invariably took the same form. These stoppages of life always presented themselves to me with the same questions: "Why?" and "What after?"

At first it seemed to me that these were aimless, unmeaning questions; it seemed to me that all they asked about was well known, and that if at any time when I wished to find answers to them I could do so without much trouble — that just at that time I could not be bothered with this, but whenever I should stop to think them over I should find an answer. But these questions presented themselves to my mind with ever increasing frequency, demanding an answer with still greater and greater persistence, and like dots grouped themselves into one black spot.

It was with me as it happens in the case of every mortal internal ailment — at first appear the insignificant symptoms of indisposition, disregarded by the patient; then these symptoms are repeated more and more frequently, till they merge in uninterrupted suffering. The sufferings increase, and the patient, before he has time to look around, is confronted with the fact that what he took for a mere indisposition has become more important to him than anything else on earth, that it is death!

This is exactly what happened to me. I became aware that this was not a chance indisposition, but something very serious, and that if all these questions continued to recur, I should have to find an answer to them. And I tried to answer them. The questions seemed so foolish, so simple, so childish; but no sooner had I taken hold of them and attempted to decide them than I was convinced, first, that they were neither childish nor silly, but were concerned with the deepest problems of life; and, in the second place, that I could not decide them — could not decide them, however I put my mind upon them.

Before occupying myself with my Samara estate, with the education of my son, with the writing of books, I was bound to know why I did these things. As long as I do not know the reason "why" I cannot do anything, I cannot live. While thinking about the management of my household and estate,[1] which in these days occupied much of my time, suddenly this question came into my head: —

"Well and good, I have now six thousand desyatins in the government of Samara, and three hundred horses — what then?"

I was perfectly disconcerted, and knew not what to think. Another time, dwelling on the thought of how I should educate my children, I asked myself, "*Why?*" Again, when considering by what means the well-being of the people might best be promoted, I suddenly exclaimed, "But what concern have I with it?" When I thought of the fame which my works were gaining me, I said to myself: —

"Well, what if I should be more famous than Gogol, Pushkin, Shakespear, Molière — than all the writers of the world — well, and what then?"....

I could find no reply. Such questions will not wait:

[1] All this expressed in the one word *khozyaïstvo*.

they demand an immediate answer; without one it is impossible to live; but answer there was none.

I felt that the ground on which I stood was crumbling, that there was nothing for me to stand on, that what I had been living for was nothing, that I had no reason for living.

CHAPTER IV

My life had come to a stop. I was able to breathe, to eat, to drink, to sleep, and I could not help breathing, eating, drinking, sleeping; but there was no real life in me because I had not a single desire, the fulfilment of which I could feel to be reasonable. If I wished for anything, I knew beforehand that, were I to satisfy the wish, or were I not to satisfy it, nothing would come of it. Had a fairy appeared and offered me all I desired, I should not have known what to say. If I had, in moments of excitement, I will not say wishes, but the habits of former wishes, at calmer moments I knew that it was a delusion, that I really wished for nothing. I could not even wish to know the truth, because I guessed in what it consisted.

The truth was, that life was meaningless. Every day of life, every step in it, brought me, as it were, nearer the precipice, and I saw clearly that before me there was nothing but ruin. And to stop was impossible; to go back was impossible; and it was impossible to shut my eyes so as not to see that there was nothing before me but suffering and actual death, absolute annihilation.

Thus I, a healthy and a happy man, was brought to feel that I could live no longer, — some irresistible force was dragging me onward to escape from life. I do not mean that I wanted to kill myself.

The force that drew me away from life was stronger, fuller, and more universal than any wish; it was a force like that of my previous attachment to life, only in a contrary direction. With all my force I struggled away from life. The idea of suicide came as naturally to me as formerly that of bettering my life. This thought was so attractive to me that I was compelled to practise upon myself a species of self-deception in order to avoid carrying it out too hastily. I was unwilling to act hastily, only because I wanted to employ all my powers in clearing away the confusion of my thoughts; if I should not clear them away, I could at any time kill myself. And here was I, a man fortunately situated, hiding away a cord, to avoid being tempted to hang myself by it to the transom between the closets of my room, where I undressed alone every evening; and I ceased to go hunting with a gun because it offered too easy a way of getting rid of life. I knew not what I wanted; I was afraid of life; I struggled to get away from it, and yet there *was* something I hoped for from it.

Such was the condition I had to come to, at a time when all the circumstances of my life were pre-eminently happy ones, and when I had not reached my fiftieth year. I had a good, loving, and beloved wife, good children, and a large estate, which, without much trouble on my part, was growing and increasing; I was more than ever respected by my friends and acquaintances; I was praised by strangers, and could lay claim to having made my name famous without much self-deception. Moreover, I was not mad or in an unhealthy mental state; on the contrary, I enjoyed a mental and physical strength which I have seldom found in men of my class and pursuits; I could keep up with a peasant in mowing, and could continue mental labor for eight or ten hours at a stretch, without any evil consequences. And in this state of things it came to this, — that I could not live, and as I feared death I was obliged to employ ruses against myself so as not to put an end to my life.

The mental state in which I then was seemed to me summed up in the following: My life was a foolish and wicked joke played on me by some one. Notwithstanding the fact that I did not recognize a "Some one," who may have created me, this conclusion that some one had wickedly and foolishly made a joke of me in bringing me into the world seemed to me the most natural of all conclusions.

I could not help reasoning that *there*, somewhere, is some one who is now diverting himself at my expense, as he watches me, as after from thirty to forty years of a life of study and development, of mental and bodily growth, with all my powers matured and having reached that summit of life from which it is seen in its completeness, I stand like a fool on this height, understanding clearly that there is nothing in life, that there never was anything, and never will be. To him it must seem ridiculous.

But whether there is, or is not, such a being, in either case it did not help me. I could not attribute a reasonable motive to any single act in my whole life. I was only astonished that I could not have realized this at the very beginning. All this had so long been known to me! Illness and death would come (indeed, they had come), if not to-day, then to-morrow, to those whom I loved, to myself, and nothing remains but stench and worms. All my acts, whatever I did, would sooner or later be forgotten, and I myself be nowhere. Why, then, busy one's self with anything? How could men fail to see this, and live? How wonderful this is! It is possible to live only as long as life intoxicates us; as soon as we are sober again we see that it is all a delusion, and a stupid delusion! In this, indeed, there is nothing either ludicrous or amusing; it is only cruel and stupid!

There is an old Eastern fable about a traveler in the steppes who is attacked by a furious wild beast. To save himself the traveler gets into a waterless well; but at the bottom of it he sees a dragon with its jaws wide open to devour him. The unhappy man dares not get out for fear of the wild beast, and dares not descend for fear of the dragon, so he catches hold of the branch of a wild plant growing in a crevice of the well. His arms grow tired, and he feels that he must soon perish, death awaiting him on either side, but he still holds on; and he sees two mice, one black and one white, gradually making their way round the stem of the wild plant on which he is hanging, nibbling it through. The plant will soon give way and break off, and he will fall into the jaws of the dragon. The traveler sees this, and knows that he must inevitably perish; but, while still hanging, he looks around him, and, finding some drops of honey on the leaves of the wild plant, he stretches out his tongue and licks them.

Thus do I cling to the branch of life, knowing that the dragon of death inevitably awaits me, ready to tear me to pieces, and I cannot understand why such tortures have fallen to my lot. I also strive to suck the honey which once comforted me, but this honey no longer rejoices me, while the white mouse and the black, day and night, gnaw through the branch to which I cling. I see the dragon plainly, and the honey is no longer sweet. I see the dragon, from which there is no escape, and the mice, and I cannot turn my eyes away from them. It is no fable, but a living, undeniable truth, to be understood of all men.

The former delusion of happiness in life which hid from me the horror of the dragon no longer deceives me. However I may reason with myself that I cannot understand the meaning of life, that I must live without thinking, I cannot do this, because I have done so too long already. Now I cannot help seeing the days and nights hurrying by and bringing me nearer to death. I can see but this, because this alone is true — all the rest is a lie. The two drops of honey, which more than anything else drew my eyes away from the cruel truth, my love for my family and for my writings, to which latter I gave the name of art, were no longer sweet to me.

"My family," I said to myself; "but a family — a wife and children — are also human beings, and subject to the same conditions as I myself; they must either be living in a lie, or they must see the terrible truth. Why should they live? Why should I love them, care for them, bring them up, and watch over them? To bring them to the despair which fills myself, or to make dolts of them? As I love them, I cannot conceal from them the truth — every step they take in knowledge leads them to it, and that truth is death."

"Art, poetry?" ....

Under the influence of success, and flattered by praise, I had long been persuading myself that this was a work which must be done notwithstanding the approach of death, which would destroy everything — my writings, and the memory of them; but I soon saw that this was only another delusion, I saw clearly that art is only the ornament and charm of life. Life having lost its charm for me, how could I make others see a charm in it? While I was not living my own life, but one that was external to me was bearing me away on its billows, while I believed that life had a meaning, though I could not say what it was, the reflections of life of every kind in poetry and art gave me delight, it was pleasant to me to look at life in the mirror of art; but when I tried to discover the meaning of life, when I felt the necessity of living myself, the mirror became either unnecessary, superfluous, and ridiculous, or painful. I could no longer take comfort from what I saw in the mirror — that my position was stupid and desperate.

It was a genuine cause of rejoicing when in the depths of my soul I believed that my life had a meaning. Then this play of lights, the comic, the tragic, the pathetic, the beautiful, and the terrible in life, amused me. But when I knew that life was meaningless and terrible, the play in the mirror could no longer entertain me. No sweetness could be sweet to me when I saw the dragon, and the mice nibbling away my support.

Nor was that all. Had I simply come to know that life has no meaning, I might have quietly accepted it, might have known that was my allotted portion. But I could not rest calmly on this. Had I been like a man living in a forest, out of which he knows that there is no issue, I could have lived on; but I was like a man lost in a forest, and who, terrified by the thought that he is lost, rushes about trying to find a way out, and, though he knows each step leads him still farther astray, cannot help rushing about.

It was this that was terrible! And to get free from this horror, I was ready to kill myself. I felt a horror of what awaited me; I knew that this horror was more horrible than the position itself, but I could not patiently await the end. However persuasive the argument might be that all the same a blood-vessel in the heart would be ruptured or something would burst and all be over, still I could not patiently await the end. The horror of the darkness was too great to bear, and I longed to free myself from it as speedily as possible by a rope or a pistol ball. This was the feeling that, above all, drew me to think of suicide.

CHAPTER V.

"BUT is it possible that I have overlooked something, that I have failed to understand something," I asked myself; "may it not be that this state of despair is common among men?"

And in every branch of human knowledge I sought an explanation of the questions that tormented me; I sought that explanation painfully and long, not out of mere curiosity; I did not seek it indolently, but painfully, obstinately, day and night; I sought it as a perishing man seeks safety, and I found nothing.

I sought it in all branches of knowledge, and not only did I fail, but, moreover, I convinced myself that all those who had searched like myself had likewise found nothing; and not only had found nothing, but had come, as I had, to the despairing conviction, that the only absolute knowledge man can possess is this, — that life is without meaning.

I sought in all directions, and thanks to a life spent in study, and also to my connections with the learned world, the most accomplished scholars in all the various branches of knowledge were accessible to me, and they did not refuse to open to me all the sources of knowledge both in books and through personal intercourse. I knew all that learning could answer to the question, "What is life?"

It was long before I could believe that human learning had no clear answer to this question. For a long time it seemed to me, as I listened to the gravity and seriousness of tone wherewith Science affirmed its positions on matters unconnected with the problem of life, that I must have misunderstood something. For a long time I was timid in the presence of learning, and I fancied that the insufficiency of the answers which I received was not its fault, but was owing to my own gross ignorance; but this thing was not a joke or pastime with me, but the business of my life, and I was at last forced, willy-nilly, to the conclusion that these questions of mine were the only legitimate questions underlying all knowledge, and that it was not I that was in fault in putting them, but science in pretending to have an answer to them.

The question, which in my fiftieth year had brought me to the notion of suicide, was the simplest of all questions, lying in the soul of every man, from the undeveloped child to wisest sage; a question without which, as I had myself experienced, life was impossible. That question was as follows: —

"What will come from what I am doing now, and may do to-morrow? what will come from my whole life?"

Otherwise expressed, the question will be this: —

"Why should I live? why should I wish for anything? why should I do anything?"

Again, in other words, it is: —

"Is there any meaning in my life which will not be destroyed by the inevitable death awaiting me?"

To this question, one and the same though variously expressed, I sought an answer in human knowledge, and I found that with respect to this question all human knowledge may be divided as it were into two opposite hemispheres with their two opposite poles, the one negative, the other positive; but that at neither pole is to be found any answer to the problems of life.

One system of knowledge seems to deny that there is such a question, but, on the other hand, has a clear and exact answer to all its own independent inquiries; this is the system of experimental science, at the extreme end of which is mathematics. Another system accepts the question, but does not answer it; it is that of abstract philosophy, and at its extremity is metaphysics.

I had been addicted from my early youth to abstract studies, but later, mathematics and the natural sciences attracted me; and till I came to put clearly to myself this question as to the meaning of life, until it grew up in me, as it were, of itself, and demanded an immediate answer, I was content with the artificial and conventional answers given by learning.

In the domain of experience I said to myself: —

"Everything develops and becomes differentiated, tends to complication and perfection, and there are laws which govern this process. You are a part of the whole. If you learn as much as possible of this whole, and if you learn the law of its development, you will then know your own place in the great unity, and know yourself as well."

I am ashamed to confess it, but there was a time when I was satisfied with this. It was the very time when I was myself developing, — when my muscles were growing stronger, my memory was becoming enriched, my powers of thinking and understanding were on the increase, — and I, being conscious of this growth, very naturally thought that the law of my own growth was the law of the universe and explained the meaning of my own life.

But the time came when I had ceased to grow, and I felt that I was not developing, but drying up; my muscles grew weaker, my teeth began to fall out, and I saw that this law of growth not only explained nothing, but that such a law did not and could not exist; that I had taken for a general law what only affected myself at a certain age.

I looked more closely into the nature of this law and it became clear to me that there could be no laws of eternal development; it became clear to me, that to say everything in infinite space and time is developed, complicated, differentiated, and perfected, is to talk nonsense. Such words have no meaning, for in the infinite there can be no simple or compound, or past or future, or better or worse.

The main thing was that my personal question, "What am I with my desires?" remained absolutely without an answer. I understood that these branches of knowledge were very interesting, very attractive, but that they were clear and exact in inverse proportion to their applicability to the questions of life. The less they had to do with these questions, the clearer and more exact they were; the more they attempted to answer these questions, the obscurer and less attractive they became. If we turn to those branches of knowledge which have attempted to answer the problems of life, to physiology, psychology, biology, sociology, we meet with a striking poverty of thought, with the greatest obscurity, with an utterly unjustifiable pretension to decide questions beyond their competence, and a constant contradiction of one thinker by another, and even by himself. If we turn to the branches of knowledge which are not concerned with the problems of life, but find an answer to their own particular scientific questions, we are lost in admiration of human intellect; but we know beforehand that we shall get no answer to our questions about life itself, for these branches of knowledge directly ignore the question of life.

They say: —

"We cannot tell you what you are and why you live; such questions we do not study. But if you wish to know the laws of light, of chemical affinities, of the development of organisms; if you wish to know the laws that govern different bodies, their forms, and relations to number and size; if you wish to know the laws of your own mind, — we can give you clear, exact, and absolutely certain answers."

The relation of experimental science to the question of the meaning of life may be put thus: —

Question. "Why do I live?"

Answer. "Infinitely small particles, in infinite combinations, in infinite space and infinite time, change their forms in infinite combinations, and when you have learned the laws of these changes, you will know why you live."

I used to say to myself when theorizing, "Spiritual causes lie at the root of man's life and development, and they are the ideals which govern him. These ideals find expression in religion, in the sciences, in the arts, and in the forms of government. These ideals rise ever higher and higher from one stage to another, till man at last reaches his highest good. I am a part of humanity, and am therefore called upon to assist in making the ideals of humanity known and accepted."

In the days of my mental weakness I was satisfied with this reasoning; but as soon as the problem of life really, as it were, arose within me, the whole theory fell to pieces at once. Not to speak of the dishonest inaccuracy, by which learning of this kind is made to give as general results those due to the study of but a small part of mankind; not to speak of the many contradictions among the various champions of this theory, as to what are the ideals of humanity, — the strangeness, if it be not the silliness, of this way of thinking is that, in order to answer the question which occurs to every man, — "What am I?" or "Why do I live?" or "What am I to do?" — a man must first answer this other question: —

"What is the life of that humanity, to us unknown, mankind, of which we are acquainted with but one minute part in one minute period of time?"

In order to understand what he himself is, a man must first know what that mysterious humanity is which is formed of other men like himself, ignorant of what they are.

I must confess there was a time when I believed this. That was the time when I had my own cherished ideals which determined my caprices, and I strove to evolve a theory which should enable me to look on my fancies as a law of humanity. But as soon as the question of the meaning of life made itself clearly felt within me, this answer was scattered in dust. And I understood that, as in the experimental sciences there are real sciences and semi-sciences which try to give answers to questions not appropriate to them, so in the domain of theoretical knowledge is there a whole series of widely diffused philosophies which attempt to answer questions not appropriate to them. The semi-sciences of this domain, jurisprudence and historical sociology, endeavor to decide the questions concerning man and his life, by deciding, each in his own way, another question, that of the life of humanity as a whole.

But, as in the domain of the experimental sciences, a man who earnestly asks, "How am I to live?" cannot be satisfied with the answer, "Study in infinite space and time the infinite combinations and changes of infinite particles, and thou wilt know what thy own life means;" so a sincere man cannot be satisfied with this other answer, "Study the life of humanity as a whole, and then, though we know neither its beginning nor its end, and are ignorant of its parts, thou wilt know what thy life means."

It is the same with these semi-sciences as with the semi-experimental ones; they are full of obscurities, inaccuracies, stupidities, and contradictions, exactly in proportion to their divergence from their proper sphere. The problem of experimental science is the succession of cause and effect in material phenomena. If the question of a finite cause is raised, experimental science stumbles against an absurdity. The problem of speculative science is the conception of the uncaused existence of life. If the question of the cause of phenomena is raised, — as, for instance, of social and historical phenomena, — speculative science lands also in an absurdity.

Experimental science has positive significance, and shows the greatness of man's intellect, only when it does not inquire into finite causes; while, on the contrary, speculative science shows the greatness of man's

Intellect, is a science at all only when it entirely puts aside all questions of the succession of phenomena, and looks upon man only in relation to finite causes. Such in this department of science, constituting its pole, is metaphysics, or philosophy.

This science puts the question clearly, "What am I, and what is the whole universe? Why do I and the universe exist?" and it has always answered it in the same way. Whatever name the philosopher may give to the principle of life existing in me and in all other living beings, whether he call it an idea, a substance, a spirit, or a will, he still says ever that it is a reality, and that I have a real existence; but why this is so he does not know, and does not try to explain if he is an exact thinker.

I ask: "Why should this reality be? What comes of the fact that it is and will be?" Philosophy not only cannot answer, but it can only put the same question. And if it be a true philosophy, then its whole labor consists in this,—that it should put this question clearly. And if it keep firmly to its proper sphere, it can only answer the question, "What am I and the whole universe?" by saying, "All and nothing," and to the question, "Why?" by adding, "I do not know."

Thus, however I examine and twist the speculative replies of philosophy, I never receive an answer to my question; and that, not as in the sphere of experimental knowledge, because the answer does not relate to the question, but because here, although great mental labor has been applied directly to the question, there *is* no answer, and instead of an answer I get back my own question repeated in a complicated form.

CHAPTER VI

In my search for a solution of the problem of life, I experienced the same feeling as a man who is lost in a forest. He comes to an open plain, climbs up a tree, and sees around him a space without end, but nowhere a house—he sees clearly that there can be none; he goes into the thick of the wood, into the darkness, and sees darkness, but again no house.

Thus had I lost my way in the forest of human knowledge, in the light of the mathematical and experimental sciences which opened out for me clear horizons where there could be no house, and in the darkness of philosophy, plunging me into a greater gloom with every step I took, until I was at last persuaded that there was, and could be, no issue.

When I followed what seemed the bright light of learning, I saw that I had only turned aside from the real question. However alluring and clear were the horizons unfolded before me, however alluring it was to plunge into the infinity of these kinds of knowledge, I saw that the clearer they were the less did I need them, the less did they give me an answer to my question.

"Well," said I to myself, "I know now all that science so obstinately seeks to learn; but an answer to my question as to the meaning of my life is not to be obtained in this way."

I saw that philosophy, notwithstanding that, or perhaps because an answer to my question had become the direct object of its inquiries, gave no answer but the one I had given to myself: —

"What is the meaning of my life?"

"It has none."

Or, "What will come of my life?"

"Nothing."

Or, "Why does all that is exist, and why do I exist?"

"Because it does exist."

When I turned to one branch of human science, I obtained an endless number of exact answers to questions I had not asked: about the chemical elements of the stars, about the movement of the sun toward the constellation Hercules, on the origin of species and of man, about the infinitely small and imponderable particles of ether; but the only answer to my question as to the meaning of my life was this: —

"You are what you call your life; that is, a temporary and accidental agglomeration of particles. The mutual action and reaction of these particles on one another has produced what you call your life. This agglomeration will continue during a certain time, then the reciprocal action of these particles will cease, and with it will end what you call your life, and with it will end all your questions as well. You are an accidentally combined lump of something. The lump undergoes decomposition, this decomposition men call life; the lump falls asunder, decomposition ceases, and with it all doubting."

This is the answer from the clear and positive side of human knowledge, and if true to its own principles it can give no other.

Such an answer proves that the answer does not answer the question. I want to know the meaning of my life; but that it is a particle of the infinite not only does not give a meaning to it, but destroys any possibility of a meaning.

The obscure compromises which this branch of experimental exact science makes with speculative science, when it is said that the meaning of life consists in development, and the concurrent efforts made toward this development from their obscurity and inaccuracy cannot be considered an answer.

The speculative side of human knowledge, when it keeps firmly to its own principles, has everywhere and through all time given and still gives one and the same answer: —

"The world is something eternal and incomprehensible. The life of man is an inconceivable part of this inconceivable *whole*."

Again I set aside all the compromises between the speculative and experimental sciences that constitute all the ballast of the semi-sciences, of so-called jurisprudence, of political economy, and of history. In these sciences we have again a false conception of development and perfection, with this difference, that formerly it was a development of everything, and now it is a development of human life. The inaccuracy is again the same; development and perfection in infinity can have no object, no direction, and therefore can give no answer to my question.

Whenever speculative science is exact, where philosophy is true to itself, and does not simply serve, after the manner of what Schopenhauer calls "professorial philosophy," to divide all existing phenomena into new columns, and give to them new names — wherever the philosopher does not overlook the great question of all, the answer is always the same, the answer given by Socrates, Schopenhauer, Solomon, and Buddha.

"We approach truth only in the proportion as we are farther from life," said Socrates, when preparing to die. Why do we who love truth strive for death? In order to be free from the body and all the ills that accompany life in it. If so, then, how shall we not be glad of the approach of death?

A wise man seeks death all his life, and therefore death has no terrors for him.

This is what Schopenhauer says: —

"Accept the ultimate principle of the universe as will, and in all phenomena, from the unconscious tendencies of the obscure forces of nature to the conscious activity of man, acknowledge only the objectivity of that will, and still we can never get rid of this logical consequence, that with the free denial and annihilation of that will, all phenomena also disappear, there is an end to the constant efforts and impulses now going on, without aim and without intermission, in every degree of the objectivity in which and through which the universe exists, there is an end to the varieties of successive forms, and with form vanish its postulates, space and time, even to the last and fundamental elements of form, the subject and the object. If there is no will, no phenomenal appearance, then there is no universe. The only thing that remains to us is nothing. But this passage to annihilation is opposed by our own nature, by our will to live — *Wille zum Leben* — which causes our own existence and that of the universe. That we so fear annihilation, or, what is the same, that we so wish to live, only shows that we ourselves are nothing but that wish — life —

and know nothing beyond it. Consequently, after the perfect annihilation of will, what remains to us who are full of wishes is assuredly nothing; on the other hand, for those in whom will has transformed itself and repudiated itself, the whole of this too material universe of ours, with all its suns and milky ways, is *nothing*."

"Vanity of vanities," says Solomon, "vanity of vanities; all is vanity. What profit hath a man of all his labor which he taketh under the sun? One generation passeth away, and another generation cometh: but the earth abideth forever. .... The thing that hath been, it is that which shall be; and that which is done is that which shall be done: and there is no new thing under the sun. Is there anything whereof it may be said, See, this is new? it hath been already of old time, which was before us. There is no remembrance of former things; neither shall there be any remembrance of things that are to come with those that shall come after.

"I the Preacher was king over Israel in Jerusalem. And I gave my heart to seek and search out by wisdom concerning all things that are done under heaven: this sore travail hath God given to the sons of man to be exercised therewith. I have seen all the works that are done under the sun; and behold, all is vanity and vexation of spirit. .... I communed with mine own heart, saying, Lo, I am come to great estate, and have gotten more wisdom than all they that have been before me in Jerusalem: yea, my heart had great experience of wisdom and knowledge. And I gave my heart to know wisdom, and to know madness and folly: I perceived that this also is vexation of spirit. For in much wisdom is much grief: and he that increaseth knowledge increaseth sorrow.

"I said in mine heart, Go to now, I will prove thee with mirth, therefore enjoy pleasure: and, behold, this also is vanity. I said of laughter, It is mad: and of mirth, What doeth it? I sought in mine heart to give myself unto wine (yet acquainting mine heart with wisdom), and to lay hold on folly, till I might see what was that good for the sons of men, which they should do under the heaven all the days of their life. I made me great works; I builded me houses; I planted me vineyards; I made me gardens and orchards, and I planted trees in them of all kind of fruits; I made me pools of water, to water therewith the wood that bringeth forth trees: I got me servants and maidens, and had servants born in my house; also I had great possessions of great and small cattle above all that were in Jerusalem before me: I gathered me also silver and gold, and the peculiar treasure of kings and of the provinces: I gat me men singers and women singers, and the delights of the sons of men, as musical instruments, and that of all sorts. So I was great, and increased more than all that were before me in Jerusalem: also my wisdom remained with me. And whatsoever mine eyes desired I kept not from them, I withheld not mine heart from any joy..... Then I looked on all the works my hands had wrought, and on the labor that I had labored to do: and behold, all was vanity and vexation of spirit, and there was no profit under the sun.

"And I turned myself to behold wisdom, and madness, and folly..... And I myself perceived also that one event happeneth to them all. Then said I in my heart, As it happeneth to the fool, so it happeneth even to me; and why was I then more wise? Then I said in my heart, that this also is vanity. For there is no remembrance of the wise more than of the fool forever; seeing that which now is in the days to come shall be forgotten. And how dieth the wise man? as the fool.

"Therefore I hated life; because the work that is wrought under the sun is grievous unto me: for all is vanity and vexation of spirit. Yea, I hated all my labor which I had taken under the sun: because I should leave it unto the man that shall be after me..... For what hath man of all his labor, and of the vexation of his heart, wherein he hath labored under the sun? For all his days are sorrows, and his travail grief; yea, his heart taketh not rest in the night. This is also vanity. There is nothing better for a man than that he should eat and drink, and that he should make his soul enjoy good in his labor. This also I saw, that it was from the hand of God. ....

"All things come alike to all: there is one event to the righteous, and to the wicked; to the good, and to the clean, and to the unclean; to him that sacrificeth, and to him that sacrificeth not: as is the good, so is the sinner; and he that sweareth, as he that feareth an oath. This is an evil among all things that are done under the sun, that there is one event unto all: yea, also the heart of the sons of men is full of evil, and madness is in their heart while they live, and after that they go to the dead.

"For to him that is joined to all the living there is hope: for a living dog is better than a dead lion. For the living know that they shall die: but the dead know not anything, neither have they any more a reward; for the memory of them is forgotten. Also their love, and their hatred, and their envy, is now perished; neither have they any more a portion forever in anything that is done under the sun."

Thus speaks Solomon, or the one who wrote those words; and this is what an Indian sage says: —

"Sakya Muni, the young and happy heir to a great throne, from whom had been kept the sight of illness, old age, and death, once while out driving saw a horrible-looking, toothless, slavering old man. The prince from whom till then old age had been concealed was much astonished, and asked the driver what it meant, and why the man was in such a pitiable and disgusting state. When he learned that this was the common lot of all men, and that he himself, prince and young though he was, must inevitably one day be the same, he was unable to continue his drive, and ordered the carriage to be driven home, that he might have time to think it all over. He shut himself up alone and thought it over. He probably thought of something which consoled him, for again he went out for a drive, merry and happy. This time he was met by a sick man. He sees a worn-out, tottering man, who is quite blue in the face, and has dim eyes. The prince, from whom all sicknesses had been concealed, stopped and asked what it was. When he was told that it was illness, that old men are subject to it, and he himself, sound and happy prince though he was, might fall ill the next day, he again lost all desire for amusement, and gave orders to drive home. There he again sought peace of mind, and probably found it, for soon after he started again, for the third time, in his carriage. This time, however, he saw something new also — some men were carrying something by.

"'What is that?'

"'A dead man.'

"'What does dead mean?' asked the prince; and he was told that to become one meant to become what the man before him now was.

"The prince descended and approached the body, uncovered it, and looked at it.

"'What will become of him?' asked the prince.

"He was told that the body would be buried in the earth.

"'Why?'

"'Because he will never be alive again, and only stench and worms can come from him.'

"'And that is the lot of all men? And it will be so with me? I shall be put underground to stink and have worms come from me?'

"'Yes.'

"'Back! I will not go for the drive, and never will go again.'"

So Sakya Muni could find no comfort in life, and he decided that life was a very great evil, and applied all his energies to freeing himself and others from it, so that after death life should in no way be renewed, and the very root of life should be destroyed. Thus speak all the Indian sages.

Here we have the only direct answers which human wisdom can give to the problem of life.

"The life of the body is evil and a lie, and so the annihilation of that life is a good for which we ought to wish," says Socrates.

"Life is what it ought not to be, an evil; and a passage from it into nothingness is the only good in life," says Schopenhauer.

"Everything in the world, both folly and wisdom, both riches and poverty, rejoicing and grief, — all is vanity and worthless. Man dies and nothing is left of him, and this again is vanity," says Solomon.

"To live, knowing that sufferings, illness, old age, and death are inevitable, is not possible; we must get rid of life, get rid of the possibility of living," says Buddha.

And what these powerful intellects have said, millions on millions of men have thought and felt. I also have thought and felt the same.

Thus my wanderings over the fields of knowledge not only failed to cure me of my despair, but increased it. One branch of knowledge gave no answer at all to the problem of life; another gave a direct answer which confirmed my despair, and showed that the state to which I had come was not the result of my going astray, of any mental disorder, but, on the contrary, it assured me that I was thinking rightly, that I was in agreement with the conclusions of the most powerful intellects among mankind.

I could not be deceived. All is vanity. A misfortune to be born. Death is better than life; life's burden must be got rid of.

CHAPTER VII

HAVING failed to find an explanation in knowledge, I began to seek it in life itself, hoping to find it in the men who surrounded me; and I began to watch men like myself, to observe how they lived, and how they practically treated the question that had brought me to despair.

And this is what I found among those of the same social position and culture as myself.

I found that for the people of my class there were

four means of escape from the terrible state in which we all were.

The first means of escape is through ignorance. It consists in not perceiving and understanding that life is an evil and an absurdity. People of this class — for the greater part women, or very young or very stupid men — have not understood the problem of life as it presented itself to Schopenhauer, to Solomon, and to Buddha. They see neither the dragon awaiting them, nor the mice eating through the plant to which they cling, and they lick the drops of honey. But they only lick the honey for a time; something directs their attention to the dragon and the mice, and then there is an end to their tasting. From these I could learn nothing: we cannot unknow what we do know.

The second means of escape is the Epicurean. It consists, even while we know the hopelessness of taking advantage of every good there is in life, in avoiding the sight of the dragon and mice, and in the meantime in seeking the honey as best we can, especially wherever there is most of it. Solomon points out this issue from the difficulty thus: —

"Then I commended mirth, because a man hath no better thing under the sun, than to eat, and to drink, and to be merry: for that shall abide with him of his labor the days of his life, which God giveth him under the sun..... Go thy way, eat thy bread with joy, and drink thy wine with a merry heart..... Live joyfully with the wife whom thou lovest all the days of the life of thy vanity, which he hath given thee under the sun, all the days of thy vanity: for that is thy portion in this life, and in thy labor which thou takest under the sun. Whatsoever thy hand findeth to do, do it with thy might; for there is no work, nor device, nor knowledge, nor wisdom, in the grave, whither thou goest."

Thus most of the people of our circle maintain the possibility of living. The conditions in which they are placed cause them to know more of the good than the evil of life, and their moral obtuseness enables them to forget that all the advantages of their position are accidental, and that not all men can have harems and palaces, like Solomon; that for one man who has a thousand wives, there are a thousand men who have none, and for each palace there must be thousands of men to build it in the sweat of their brow, and that the same chance which has made me a Solomon to-day may make me Solomon's slave to-morrow. The dullness of their imagination enables these men to forget what destroyed the peace of Buddha, the inevitable sickness, old age, and death, which if not to-day, then to-morrow, must be the end of all their pleasures.

Thus think and feel the majority of the men of our time and class. That some of them call their dullness of thought and imagination by the name of positive philosophy, does not, in my opinion, separate them from those who, in order not to see the real question, lick the honey. I could not imitate such as these; not having their obtuseness of imagination, I could not artificially prevent its action. Like every man who really lives, I could not turn my eyes aside from the mice and the dragon, when I had once seen them.

The third means of escape is through strength and energy. It consists in destroying life when we have perceived that it is an evil and an absurdity. Only the rare men, strong and logical, act thus. Understanding all the stupidity of the joke that is played on us, and understanding that the happiness of the dead is more than the happiness of the living, and that it is better not to be, they thus act and put an end at once to the stupid joke, using any means of doing it—a rope round the neck, water, a knife in the heart, or a railway train. The number of those in my own class acting thus continually increases, and those that do this are for the most part in the very prime of life, with their intellectual powers in their flower, and with but few of the habits that undermine man's reason as yet formed.

I saw that this means of escape was the worthiest, and wished to make use of it.

The fourth means of escape is through weakness. It

consists, though the evil and absurdity of life are well known, in continuing to drag it out, though aware that nothing can come of it. People of this class know that death is better than life, but have not the strength of character to act as their reason dictates, to have done with deceit and kill themselves; they seem to be waiting for something to happen. This way of escape is due solely to weakness, for if I know what is better, and it is within my reach, why not seize it?.... To this class of men I myself belonged.

Thus do people of my own class, in four different ways, save themselves from a terrible contradiction. However earnestly I strained my reasoning faculties I could not find any other than these four ways. The first way is to ignore the fact that life is absurdity, vanity, and evil, — is not to know that it is better not to live. For me not to know this was impossible, and when I once saw the truth, I could not shut my eyes to it.

The second way is to make the best of life as it is, without thinking of the future. This, again, I could not do. Like Sakya Muni, I could not drive for pleasure, when I knew there were such things as old age, suffering, and death. My imagination was too lively for that. Moreover, I could not enjoy chance pleasures which fell for a few rare instants to my lot.

The third way is, knowing that life is an evil and a foolish thing, to put an end to it, to kill one's self. I understood this, but still for some reason I did not kill myself.

The fourth way is to accept life as described by Solomon and Schopenhauer, to know that it is a stupid and ridiculous joke played on one, and yet live on, to wash, dress, dine, talk, and even write books. This position was revolting and painful to me, but I remained in it.

I now see that I did not kill myself because I had, in a confused sort of way, an inkling that my ideas were wrong. However plausible and unanswerable appeared to me the idea, which I shared with the wisest on earth, that life has no meaning, I still felt a confused doubt of the truth of my conclusions, which formed itself thus:—

"My reason tells me that life is contrary to reason. If there is nothing higher than reason — and there is nothing, and nothing can prove it — then reason is the creator of life for me; were there no reason there would be no life for me. How can this reason deny life, and at the same time be its creator? Again, from the other side, if there were no life, I should have no reason, consequently reason is the son of life. Life is all. Reason is the fruit of life, and this same reason denies life itself."

I felt that something here was wrong. I said to myself:—

"Life undoubtedly has no meaning, and is evil, but I have lived and am still alive, and so also have lived and are living the whole human race. How is this? Why do all men live when all men are able to die? Is it that I and Schopenhauer alone are wise enough to have understood the unmeaning emptiness and evil of life?"

To see the inanity of life is a simple matter enough, and it has long been apparent to the simplest, but men have lived and still live on. Why is it men live on, and never think of calling in question the reasonableness of life?

My acquired knowledge, confirmed by the wisdom of the wisest in the world, showed me that everything on earth, organic or inorganic, was arranged with extraordinary wisdom, and that my own position alone was a foolish one. But those fools, the enormous masses of simple people, know nothing of the organic and inorganic structure of the world, but live on, and it seems to them that their lives are subjected to perfectly reasonable conditions!....

Then I thought to myself: "But what if there be something more for me to know? Surely this is the way in which Ignorance acts. Ignorance always says exactly what I do now! When Ignorance does not know anything it calls that which it does not know stupid! It really comes to this, that mankind as a whole have always lived, and are living, as if they understood the meaning of life, for not doing so they could not live at all; whereas I say that all this life is meaningless, and that I cannot live."

No one prevents us from denying life by suicide, but, then, kill yourself and you will no longer argue about it. If you dislike life, kill yourself. If you live and cannot comprehend the meaning of life, put an end to it, and do not go on talking and writing about being unable to understand life. You have got into a gay company, in which all are well satisfied, all know what they are doing, and you alone are wearied and repelled; then get out of it!

And after all, then, what are we who, persuaded of the necessity of suicide, still cannot bring ourselves to the act, but weak, inconsistent men, — to speak more plainly, stupid men, who carry about with them their stupidity, like the fool with the placarded basket?

Our wisdom, indeed, however firmly it be grounded on truth, has not imparted to us a knowledge of the meaning of life, yet all humanity sharing in life — millions — doubt not that life has a meaning.

It is certainly true that, from the far, far distant time when that life began of which I know something, men have lived who, though they knew all the arguments about the inanity of life such as proved to me that life had no meaning, still lived on, and gave to life a meaning of their own.

Since any sort of life began for men, they have had some conception of their own about it, and have so lived down to my own time. All that is in and around me, physical or immaterial, it is all the fruit of their knowledge of life.[1] The very tools of thought with which I have judged life, and condemned it, were fashioned, not by me, but by them. I was born, and bred, and have grown up, thanks to them. They dug out the iron, taught how to hew down the forests, to tame the cows and the horses, to sow corn, to live one with another;

[1] An untranslatable pun: *plotskoye i nyeplotskoye, vsyo eto-plod* (pronounced *plot*): "Material and immaterial is all the material;" literally, "fleshly and unfleshly is all the fruit." — Ed.

they gave order and form to our life; moreover, they taught me how to think and how to speak. And I, the work of their hands, their foster-child, the pupil of their thoughts and sayings, have proved to them they themselves had no meaning!

"There must be something wrong here," said I. "I have made some mistake."

I could not, however, discover where the mistake lay.

CHAPTER VIII

ALL these doubts, which I am now able to express more or less clearly, I could not then explain. Then I only felt that, however logical and unavoidable were my conclusions as to the inanity of life, confirmed as they were by the greatest thinkers, there was something wrong in them. Whether in the conclusion itself, or in the way of putting the question, I did not know; I only felt that, though my reason was entirely convinced, that was not enough.

All my reasoning could not induce me to act in accordance with my convictions, *i.e.* to kill myself.

I should not speak the truth, if I said that my reason alone brought me to the position in which I was and prevented me from suicide. Reason had been at work, no doubt, but something else had worked too, something which I can only call the consciousness of life. There also worked in me a force, which determined my attention to one thing rather than to another, and it was this that drew me out of my desperate position, and completely changed the current of my thoughts. This force led me to the idea that I, with hundreds of other men like me, did not form the whole of mankind,—that I was still ignorant of what human life was.

When I watched the narrow circle of those who were my equals in social position, I saw only people who did not understand the question, people who understood the question but kept down their understanding of it by the intoxication of life, people who understood it and put an end to life, and people who, understanding, lived on through weakness, in despair. And I saw no others. It seemed to me that the narrow circle of learned, rich, and idle people, to which I myself belonged, formed the whole of humanity, and that the milliards living outside it were animals, not men.

However strange, improbable, and inconceivable it now seems to me, that I, reasoning about life, could over-look the life of mankind surrounding me on all sides, and fall into such an error as to think that the life of a Solomon, a Schopenhauer, and my own, was the real normal life, and the life lived by unconsidered milliards a circumstance unworthy of attention — however strange this appears to me now, I see that it was so. Led away by intellectual pride, it seemed to me beyond a doubt that I, with Solomon and Schopenhauer, had put the question so exactly and truly that there could be no other form of it; it seemed unquestionable that all these milliards of men had failed to conceive the depth of the question, that I had sought the meaning of my life; and it never once occurred to me to think: —

"But what meaning has been given, what meaning is given now, by the milliards of those who have lived and are living in the world?"

I long lived in this state of mental aberration, which, though not always openly expressed in words, is not the less common among the most learned and most liberal men. But whether, owing to my strange kind of instinctive affection for the laboring classes, which impelled me to understand them, and to see that they are not so stupid as we think, or owing to the sincerity of my conviction that I could know nothing beyond the advisability of hanging myself, I felt that, if I wished to live and understand the meaning of life, I must seek it not amongst those who have lost the meaning of life, and wish to kill themselves, but amongst the milliards of the living and the dead who have made our life what it is, and on whom now rests the burden of our life and their own.

So I watched the life common to such enormous numbers of the dead and the living, the life of simple, unlearned, and poor men, and found something quite different. I saw that all these milliards, who are alive and have lived, with rare exceptions, did not come into my classification; I could not count them among those who do not understand the question, because they not only put it, but answer it, with extraordinary clearness. I could not call them Epicureans, because their life has far more of privation and suffering than of enjoyment; to count them amongst those who, against their reason, live through a life without meaning, was still less possible, because every act of their lives, and death itself, is explained by them. Self-murder they regard as the greatest of crimes. It appeared that throughout mankind there is a knowledge of the meaning of life which I had neglected and despised. It resulted, that the knowledge based on reason denies a meaning to life, and excludes life; while the meaning given to life by the milliards that form the great whole of humanity is founded on a despised and fallacious knowledge.

The knowledge based on reason, the knowledge of the learned and the wise, denies a meaning in life, while the great mass of men, all humanity, have an unreasoning knowledge of life which gives a meaning to it.

This unreasoning knowledge is the faith which I could not but reject. This is a God, one and yet three; this is the creation in six days, devils and angels, — and all that I cannot accept while I keep my senses!

My position was terrible. I knew that from the knowledge which reason has given man, I could get nothing but the denial of life, and from faith nothing but the denial of reason, which last was even more impossible than the denial of life. By the knowledge founded on reason it was proved that life is an evil and that men know it to be so, that men may cease to live if they will, but that they have lived and they go on living — I myself lived on, though I had long known that life was meaningless and evil. If I went by faith it resulted that, in order to understand the meaning of life, I should have to abandon reason, the very part of me that required a meaning in life!

CHAPTER IX

I WAS stopped by a contradiction from which there were only two ways of escape: either what I called reasonable was not so reasonable as I thought it, or what I called unreasonable was not so unreasonable as I thought it. I began to verify the process of thinking through which I had been led to the conclusions of reasoning knowledge.

On doing this, I found the process complete and flawless. The conclusion that life was nothing was unavoidable; but I discovered a mistake. The mistake was that I had not confined my thoughts to the question proposed. The question was, why should I live, *i.e.* what of real and imperishable will come of my shadowy and perishable life—what meaning has my finite existence in the infinite universe? And I had tried to answer this by studying life.

It was evident that the decision of any number of questions concerning life could not satisfy me, because my question, however simple it seemed at first, included the necessity of explaining the finite by infinity, and the contrary.

I asked myself what meaning my life had apart from time, causation, and space. But I replied to my question: what is the meaning of life in respect to time, causation, and space? The result was that after long and earnest efforts of thinking, I could only answer—none at all.

Through all my reasoning with myself I constantly compared, and I could not do otherwise, the finite with the finite, and the infinite with the infinite, and the conclusion was consequently inevitable: a force is a force, matter is matter, will is will, infinity is infinity, nothing is nothing,—and there was no getting beyond that. It was like what happens in mathematics, when thinking to resolve an equation we get identical terms. The process of solution is correct, but our answer is $a = a$, or $x = x$, or $0 = 0$. This happened to me in my inquiries into the meaning of my life. The answers given by all science to the question were "identity."

And in reality knowledge founded strictly on reason, which, like that carried on by Descartes, begins with absolute doubt of everything, throws aside all knowledge founded on faith, and reconstructs all in accordance with the laws of reason and experience, and it can give no other answer to the question about the meaning of life than the one which I myself obtained — an indefinite one.

It seemed to me at first that science did give a positive answer, the answer of Schopenhauer: life has no meaning, it is an evil; but, when I inquired more closely into the matter, I perceived that the answer was not positive, that it was my own feeling alone made me think it so. The answer boldly expressed in the same terms as that given by the Brahmins, and Solomon, and Schopenhauer, is only an indefinite one, — the identity of 0 and 0, life is nothing. Thus philosophical knowledge denies nothing, but merely answers that the question cannot be decided by it, — that the matter remains indefinite.

When I had come to this conclusion, I understood that it was useless to seek an answer to my question from knowledge founded on reason, and that the answer given by this form of knowledge is only an indication that no answer can be obtained till the question is put differently, — till the question be made to include the relation between the finite and the infinite. I also understood that, however unreasonable and monstrous the answers given by faith, they have the advantage of bringing into every question the relation of the finite to the infinite, without which there can be no answer.

However I may put the question, How am I to live? the answer is, "By the law of God."

Will anything real and positive come of my life, and what?

Eternal torment, or eternal bliss.

What meaning is there not to be destroyed by death?

Union with an infinite God, paradise.

In this way I was compelled to admit that, besides the reasoning knowledge, which I once thought the only true knowledge, there was in every living man another kind of knowledge, an unreasoning one, — faith, — which gives a possibility of living.

All the unreasonableness of faith remained for me the same as ever, but I could not help acknowledging that faith alone gave man answers as to the questions of life, and consequently the possibility of living.

Reasoning knowledge brought me to the conclusion that life was meaningless, and my life stood still, and I wished to put an end to myself. When I looked at the men around me, at humanity as a whole, I saw that men lived, and that they know the meaning of life. For other men, as for myself, faith gave a meaning to life and a possibility of living.

On examining farther into life in other countries than my own, as well among my contemporaries as among those who have passed away, I found the same thing. From the beginning of the human race, wherever there is life there is faith which makes life possible, and everywhere the leading characteristics of faith are the same.

Whatever answers any kind of faith ever gives to any one, every one of these answers gives an infinite meaning to the finite life of man, a meaning which is not destroyed by suffering, privation, and death. In faith, therefore, alone is found the possibility of living and a meaning in life. What is this faith? I understood that faith is not only the manifestation of things unseen, is not only a revelation (that is only a description of one of the signs of faith), is not the relation of man to God (faith must first be determined, and then God, and not faith through God), and is not only acquiescence with what has been told to man, as faith is most frequently understood to be, — but faith is the knowledge of the meaning of human life, in consequence of which man does not destroy himself, but lives. Faith is the force of life.

If a man lives, he believes in something. If he did not believe that there was something to live for, he would not live. If he does not see and understand the unreality of the finite, he believes in the finite; if he sees that unreality, he must believe in the infinite. Without faith it is impossible to live.

I then went back over all the past stages of my mental state, and was terrified. It was now clear to me that for any one to live, it was necessary for him either not to see infinity, or to accept an explanation of the meaning of life which should equalize the finite and the infinite. Such an explanation I had, but I had no need of it while I believed in the finite, and I began to apply to my explanation the tests of reason, and in the light of reason all former explanations were shown to be worthless. But the time when I ceased to believe in the finite passed, even then I tried to raise on the foundations of reason and out of what I knew an explanation which should give a meaning to life, but I tried in vain. In company with the greatest intellects among men I came only to the conclusion that o = o, and, though nothing else could have come of it, I was much astonished to have obtained such an answer to my problem.

What did I do when I sought an answer in the study of experimental science? I wanted to know why I lived, and to that end I studied everything outside myself. Clearly in this way I might learn much, but nothing of that which I needed.

What did I do when I sought an answer in the study of philosophy? I studied the thoughts of others in the same position as myself, and who had no answer to the question — "Why do I live?" Clearly I could in this way learn nothing but what I myself knew, namely, that it was impossible to know anything.

What am I? — a part of the infinite. In those few words lay the whole problem.

Could it be that mankind had only now begun to put this question? Could it be that no one before myself had asked this simple question, that must occur to the mind of every intelligent child?

Why! since men have been this question has been put, and since men have been it has been assuredly understood that the decision of this question is equally unsatisfactory, whether the finite be compared with the finite, and the infinite with the infinite, and since men have been, the relations of the finite to the infinite have been sought and expressed.

All these conceptions of the equality of the finite and the infinite, through which we receive the ideas of life, of God, of freedom, of good, we submit to logical analysis. And these conceptions will not bear the tests of reason.

If it were not so terrible, it would be laughable to think of the pride and self-confidence with which we, like children, pull out our watches, take away the spring, make a plaything of them, and are then astonished that they will no longer keep time.

The decision of the contradiction between the finite and the infinite, and such an answer to the question of what is life as shall enable us to live, is essential and precious to us. The only answer is the one to be found everywhere, always, and among all nations, an answer which has come down to us from the times in which the origin of human life is lost, an answer so difficult that we could never ourselves have come to it — this answer we in our careless indifference get rid of, by again raising the question which presents itself to every one, but which no one can answer.

The conception of an infinite God, of the divinity of the soul, of the way in which the affairs of men are related to God, of the unity and reality of the spirit, man's conception of moral good and evil, — these are conceptions worked out through the infinite mental labors of mankind; conceptions without which there would be no life, without which I should not myself exist, and yet I reject all this, the labor of the whole human race, and venture on working out the problem again in my own way alone.

I did not at the time think so, but the germs of these thoughts were already within me. I understood (1) that the position assumed by Schopenhauer, Solomon, and myself, notwithstanding all our wisdom, was foolish: we understand that life is an evil, and yet we live. This is clearly foolish, because if life is foolish, and I care so much for reason, life should be put an end to, and then there would be no one to deny it.

(2) I understood that all our arguments turned in a charmed circle, like a cog-wheel the teeth of which no longer catch in another. However much and however well we reason, we get no answer to our question; it will always be $0 = 0$, and consequently our method is probably wrong.

(3) I began to understand that in the answers given by faith was to be found the deepest source of human wisdom, that I had no reasonable right to reject them on the ground of reason, and that these principle answers alone solved the problem of life.

CHAPTER X

I UNDERSTOOD this, but it did not make it any easier for me.

I was now ready to accept any faith that did not require of me a direct denial of reason, for that would be to act a lie; and I studied Buddhism and Mohammedanism in their books, and especially also Christianity, both in its writings and in the lives of its professors around me.

I naturally turned my attention at first to the believers in my own immediate circle, to learned men, to orthodox divines, to the older monks, to the orthodox divines of a new shade of doctrine, the so-called New Christians, who preach salvation through faith in a Redeemer. I seized upon these believers, and asked them what they believed in, and what for them gave a meaning to life.

Notwithstanding that I made every possible concession, that I avoided all disputes, I could not accept the faith of these men. I saw that what they called their faith did not explain, but obscured, the meaning of life, and that they professed it, not in order to answer the questions as to life which had attracted me toward faith, but for some other purpose to which I was a stranger.

I remember the painful feeling of horror with which I returned to the old feeling of despair, after the hopes which I experienced many, many times in my relations with these people.

The more minutely they laid their doctrines before me, the more clearly I perceived their error, the more I lost all hope of finding in their faith an explanation of the meaning of life.

I was not so much revolted by the unnecessary and unreasonable doctrines which they mingled with the Christian truths always so dear to me, as by the fact that their lives were like my own, the only difference being that they did not live according to the principles which they professed. I was clearly conscious that they deceived themselves, and that for them, as for myself, there was no other meaning to life than to live while they lived, and take each for himself all that his hands could lay hold on. I saw this, because if the ideas of life which they conceived had done away with the fear of privation, suffering, and death, they would not have feared them. But these believers of our class, the same as I myself, lived in comfort and abundance, struggled to increase and preserve it, were afraid of privation, suffering, and death; and again, like myself and all the rest of us unbelievers, satisfied the lusts of the flesh, and led lives as evil as, if not worse than, those of infidels themselves.

No arguments were able to convince me of the sincerity of the faith of these men. Only actions, proving their conception of life to have destroyed the fear of poverty, illness, and death, so strong in myself, could have convinced me, and such actions I could not see among the various believers of our class. Such actions,

I saw, indeed, among the open infidels of my own class in life, but never among the so-called believers of our class.

I understood, then, that the faith of these men was not the faith which I sought; that it was no faith at all, but only one of the Epicurean consolations of life. I understood that this faith, if it could not really console, could at least soothe the repentant mind of a Solomon on his deathbed; but that it could not serve the enormous majority of mankind, who are born, not to be comforted by the labors of others, but to create a life for themselves. For mankind to live, for it to continue to live and be conscious of the meaning of its life, all these milliards must have another and a true conception of faith. It was not, then, the fact that Solomon, Schopenhauer, and I had not killed ourselves, which convinced me that faith existed, but the fact that these milliards have lived and are now living, carrying along with them on the impulse of their life both Solomon and ourselves.

I began to draw nearer to the believers among the poor, the simple, and the ignorant, the pilgrims, the monks, the raskolniks, and the peasants. The doctrines of these men of the people, like those of the pretended believers of my own class, were Christian. Here also much that was superstitious was mingled with the truths of Christianity, but with this difference, that the superstition of the believers of our class was entirely unnecessary to them, and never influenced their lives beyond serving as a kind of Epicurean distraction; while the superstition of the believing laboring class was so interwoven with their lives that it was impossible to conceive them without it — it was a necessary condition of their living at all. The whole life of the believers of our class was in flat contradiction with their faith, and the whole life of the believers of the people was a confirmation of the meaning of life which their faith gave them.

Thus I began to study the lives and the doctrines of the people, and the more I studied the more I became convinced that a true faith was among them, that their faith was for them a necessary thing, and alone gave them a meaning in life and a possibility of living. In direct opposition to what I saw in our circle — where life without faith was possible, and where not one in a thousand professed himself a believer — amongst the people there was not a single unbeliever in a thousand. In direct opposition to what I saw in our circle — where a whole life is spent in idleness, amusement, and dissatisfaction with life — I saw among the people whole lives passed in heavy labor and unrepining content. In direct opposition to what I saw in our circle — men resisting and indignant with the privations and sufferings of their lot — the people unhesitatingly and unresistingly accepting illness and sorrow, in the quiet and firm conviction that all these must be and could not be otherwise, and that all was for the best. In contradiction to the theory that the less learned we are the less we understand the meaning of life, and see in our sufferings and death but an evil joke, these men of the people live, suffer, and draw near to death, in quiet confidence and oftenest with joy. In contradiction to the fact that an easy death, without terror or despair, is a rare exception in our class, a death which is uneasy, rebellious, and sorrowful is among the people the rarest exception of all.

These people, deprived of all that for us and for Solomon makes the only good in life, and experiencing at the same time the highest happiness, form the great majority of mankind. I looked more widely around me, I studied the lives of the past and contemporary masses of humanity, and I saw that, not two or three, or ten, but hundreds, thousands, millions had so understood the meaning of life that they were able both to live and to die. All these men, infinitely divided by manners, powers of mind, education, and position, all alike in opposition to my ignorance, were well acquainted with the meaning of life and of death, quietly labored, endured privation and suffering, lived and died, and saw in all this, not a vain, but a good thing,

I began to grow attached to these men. The more I learned of their lives, the lives of the living and of the dead of whom I read and heard, the more I liked them, and the easier I felt it so to live. I lived in this way during two years, and then there came a change which had long been preparing in me, and the symptoms of which I had always dimly felt: the life of our circle of rich and learned men, not only became repulsive, but lost all meaning. All our actions, our reasoning, our science and art, all appeared to me in a new light. I understood that it was all child's play, that it was useless to seek a meaning in it. The life of the working-classes, of the whole of mankind, of those that create life, appeared to me in its true significance. I understood that this was life itself, and that the meaning given to this life was true, and I accepted it.

CHAPTER XI

When I remembered how these very doctrines had repelled me, how senseless they had seemed when professed by men whose lives were spent in opposition to them, and how these same doctrines had attracted me and seemed reasonable when I saw men living in accordance with them, I understood why I had once rejected them and thought them unmeaning, why I now adopted them and thought them full of meaning. I understood that I had erred, and how I had erred. I had erred, not so much through having thought incorrectly, as through having lived ill. I understood that the truth had been hidden from me, not so much because I had erred in my reasoning, as because I had led the exceptional life of an epicure bent on satisfying the lusts of the flesh. I understood that my question, "What is my life," and the answer, "An evil," were in accordance with the truth of things. The mistake lay in my having applied to life in general an answer which only concerned myself. I had asked what my own life was, and the answer was "An evil and absurdity." Exactly so, my life — a life of indulgence, of sensuality — was an absurdity and an evil; and the answer, "Life is meaningless and evil," therefore, referred only to my own life, and not to human life in general.

I understood the truth which I afterwards found in the Gospel: "That men loved darkness rather than light because their deeds were evil. For every man that doeth evil hateth the light, neither cometh to the light, lest his deeds should be reproved."

I understood that, for the meaning of life to be understood, it was necessary first that life should be something more than evil and meaningless, and afterwards that there should be the light of reason to understand it. I understood why I had so long been circling round this self-evident truth without apprehending it, and that if we would think and speak of the life of mankind, we must think and speak of that life as a whole, and not merely of the life of certain parasites on it.

This truth was always a truth, as $2 \times 2 = 4$, but I had not accepted it, because, besides acknowledging $2 \times 2 = 4$, I should have been obliged to acknowledge that I was evil. It was of more importance to me to feel that I was good, more binding on me, than to believe $2 \times 2 = 4$. I loved good men, I hated myself, and I accepted truth. Now it was all clear to me.

Now if the question, "What is life?" were asked of himself by an executioner, who passes his life in torturing and cutting off heads, or by a confirmed drunkard, or by a crazy man who has spent his whole life in a darkened chamber, hating that chamber and imagining that he would perish if he left it, evidently he could get no other answer to his question, "What is life?" than that life is the greatest of evils, and the crazy man's answer would be a true one, but only for himself. Here, then, was I such a crazy man? Were all of us rich, clever, idle men, crazy like this?....

I understood at last that we actually were; that I, at any rate, was. In fact the bird is so constituted that it must fly, pick up its food, build its nest, and when I see the bird doing this I rejoice in its joy. The goat, the hare, the wolf, are so constituted that they must feed and multiply, and bring up their young; and when they do this, I have a firm conviction that they are happy, and that their life is reasonable.

What, then, must man do? He also must gain his living like the animals, but with this difference, that he will perish if he attempt it alone; he must labor, not for himself, but for all. And when he does so, I am firmly convinced he is happy, and his life is reasonable.

What had I done during my thirty years of conscious life? I had not only not helped the life of others, I had done nothing for my own. I had lived the life of a parasite, and when I asked myself why I lived at all I received the answer, "There is no reason why." If the meaning of the life of man lies in his having to work out his life himself, how could I, who during thirty years had done my best to ruin my own life and that of others, expect to receive any other answer than this, — that my life was an evil and an absurdity? ....

It was an evil, an absurdity.

The life of the world goes on through the will of some one. Some one makes our own life and that of the universe his own inscrutable care. To have a hope of understanding what that will means, we must first fulfil it, we must do what is required of us. Unless I do what is required of me, I can never know what that may be, and much less know what is required of us all and of the whole universe.

If a naked, hungry beggar be taken from the cross-roads into an enclosed space in a splendid establishment, to be well clothed and fed, and made to work a handle up and down, it is evident that the beggar, before seeking to know why he has been taken, why he must work the handle, whether the arrangements of the establishment are reasonable or not, must first move the handle. If he move the handle he will find that the handle works a pump, the pump draws up water, and the water flows over garden beds. Then he will be taken from the covered well and set to other work; he will gather fruits and enter into the joy of his lord, and as he passes from less to more important labors, he will understand better and better the arrangements of the whole establishment; and he will take his share in them without once stopping to ask why he is there, nor will he ever think of reproaching the lord of that place.

And thus it is with those that do the will of their master; no reproaches come from simple untaught working-men, from those we regard as brutes. But we the while, wise men that we are, devour the goods of the master, and do nothing of that which he wills us to do; but instead, seat ourselves in a circle to argue why we should move the handle, for that seems to us stupid. And when we have thought it all out, what is our conclusion? Why, that the master is stupid, or that there is none, while we ourselves are wise, only we feel that we are fit for nothing, and that we must somehow or other get rid of ourselves.

CHAPTER XII

My conviction of the error into which all knowledge based on reason must fall assisted me in freeing myself from the seductions of idle reasoning. The conviction that a knowledge of truth can be gained only by living, led me to doubt the justness of my own life; but I had only to get out of my own particular groove, and look around me, to observe the simple life of the real working-class, to understand that such a life was the only real one. I understood that, if I wished to understand life and its meaning, I must live, not the life of a parasite, but a real life; and, accepting the meaning given to it by the combined lives of those that really form the great human whole, submit it to a close examination.

At the time I am speaking of, the following was my position:—

During the whole of that year, when I was asking myself almost every minute whether I should or should not put an end to it all with a cord or a pistol, during the time my mind was occupied with the thoughts which I have described, my heart was oppressed by a tormenting feeling. This feeling I cannot describe otherwise than as a searching after God.

This search after a God was not an act of my reason, but a feeling, and I say this advisedly, because it was opposed to my way of thinking; it came from the heart. It was a feeling of dread, or orphanhood, of isolation amid things all apart from me, and of hope in a help I knew not from whom.

Though I was well convinced of the impossibility of proving the existence of God — Kant had shown me, and I had thoroughly grasped his reasoning, that this did not admit of proof — I still sought to find a God, still hoped to do so, and still, from the force of former habits, addressed myself to one in prayer, whom I sought, and did not find.

At times I went over in my mind the arguments of Kant and of Schopenhauer, showing the impossibility of proving the existence of the Deity; at times I began to test their arguments and refute them.

I would say to myself that causation is not in the same category of thought as space and time. If I am, there is a cause of my being, and that the cause of all causes. That cause of all things is what is called God; and I dwelt on this idea, and strove with all my being to reach a consciousness of the presence of this cause.

As soon as I became conscious that there is such a power over me, I felt a possibility of living. Then I asked myself: —

"What is this cause, this power? How am I to think of it? What is my relation to what I call God?"

And only the old familiar answer came into my mind, "He is the creator, the giver of all."

This answer did not satisfy me, and I felt that what was necessary for life was failing me, a great horror came over me, and I began to pray to Him whom I sought, that He would help me. But the more I prayed, the clearer it became that I was not heard, that there was no one to whom one could turn. With despair in my heart that there was no God, I cried: —

"Lord, have mercy on me, and save! O Lord, my God, teach me!"

But no one had mercy on me, and I felt that my life had come to a standstill.

But again and again, from various other directions, I came back to the same conviction that I could not have appeared on earth without any motive or meaning,— that I could not be such a fledgling dropped from a nest as I felt myself to be. What if I cry, as the fallen fledgling does on its back in the high grass? It is because I know that a mother bore me, cared for me, fed me, and loved me. Where is she, where is that mother? If I have been thrown out, then who threw me? I cannot help seeing that some one who loved me brought me into being. Who is that some one? Again the same answer — God. He knows and sees my search, my despair, my struggle. "He is," I said to myself. I had only to admit that for an instant to feel that life rearose in me, to feel the possibility of existing and the joy of it.

Then, again, from the conviction of the existence of God, I passed to the consideration of our relation toward Him, and again I had before me the triune God, our Creator, who sent His Son, the Redeemer. Again, this God, apart from me and from the world, melted from before my eyes as ice melts; again there was nothing left, again the source of life dried up. I fell once more into despair, and felt that I had nothing to do but to kill myself, while, worst of all, I felt also that I should never do it.

Not twice, not three times, but tens, hundreds, of times did I pass through these alternations, — now of joy and excitement, now of despair and of consciousness of the impossibility of life.

I remember one day in the early springtime I was alone in the forest listening to the woodland sounds, and thinking only of one thing, the same of which I had constantly thought for two years — I was again seeking for a God.

I said to myself: —

"Very good, there is no God, there is none with a reality apart from my own imaginings, none as real as my own life — there is none such. Nothing, no miracles can prove there is, for miracles only exist in my own unreasonable imagination."

And then I asked myself: —

"But my idea of the God whom I seek, whence comes it?"

And again at this thought arose the joyous billows of life. All around me seemed to revive, to have a new meaning. My joy, though, did not last long. Reason continued its work: —

"The idea of a God is not God. The idea is what goes on within myself; the idea of God is an idea which I am able to rouse in my mind or not as I choose; it is not what I seek, something without which life could not be."

Then again all seemed to die around and within me, and again I wished to kill myself.

After this I began to retrace the process which had gone on within myself, the hundred times repeated discouragement and revival. I remembered that I had lived only when I believed in a God. As it was before, so it was now; I had only to know God, and I lived; I had only to forget Him, not to believe in Him, and I died.

What was this discouragement and revival? I do not live when I lose faith in the existence of a God; I should long ago have killed myself, if I had not had a dim hope of finding Him. I really live only when I am conscious of Him and seek Him. "What more, then, do I seek?" A voice seemed to cry within me, "This is He, He without whom there is no life. To know God and to live are one. God is life."

Live to seek God, and life will not be without God. And stronger than ever rose up life within and around me, and the light that then shone never left me again.

Thus I was saved from self-murder. When and how this change in me took place I could not say. As gradually, imperceptibly as life had decayed in me, till I reached the impossibility of living, till life stood still, and I longed to kill myself, so gradually and imperceptibly I felt the glow and strength of life return to me.

And strangely enough this power of life which came back to me was not new; it was old enough, for I had been led away by it in the earlier part of my life.

I returned, as it were, to the past, to childhood and my youth. I returned to faith in that Will which brought me into being and which required something of me; I returned to the belief that the one single aim of life should be to become better, that is, to live in accordance with that Will; I returned to the idea that the expression of that Will was to be found in what, in the dim obscurity of the past, the great human unity had fashioned for its own guidance; in other words, I returned to a belief in God, in moral perfectibility, and in the tradition which gives a meaning to life. The difference was that formerly I had unconsciously accepted this, whereas now I knew that without it I could not live.

The state of mind in which I then was may be likened to the following: It was as if I had suddenly found myself sitting in a boat which had been pushed off from some shore unknown to me, had been shown the direction of the opposite shore, had had oars put into my inexperienced hands, and had been left alone. I had used the oars as best I could and rowed on; but the farther I went toward the center, the stronger became the current which carried me out of my course, and the oftener I met other navigators, like myself, carried away by the stream. There were here and there solitary navigators who had continued to row hard, there were others who had thrown down their oars, there were large boats, and enormous ships crowded with men; some struggled against the stream, others glided on with it. The farther I got, the more, as I watched the long line floating down the current, I forgot the course pointed out to me as my own.

In the very middle of the stream, amid the crowd of boats and vessels floating down, I had altogether lost the course and thrown down my oars. From all sides the joyful and exulting navigators, as they rowed or sailed down-stream, with one voice assured me and one another that there could be no other direction. And I believed them, and let myself go with them. I was carried far, so far that I heard the roar of the rapids in which I was bound to perish, and I already saw boats that had been broken up within them.

Then I came to myself. It was long before I clearly comprehended what had happened. I saw before me nothing but the destruction toward which I was hurrying, which I dreaded, and I saw no salvation and knew not what I was to do! But on looking back, I saw a countless multitude of boats engaged in a ceaseless struggle against the force of the torrent, and then I remembered all about the shore, the oars, and the course, and at once I began to row hard up the stream and again toward the shore.

That shore was God, that course was tradition, those oars were the free will given me to make for the shore to seek union with the Deity.

CHAPTER XIII

And thus the vital force was renewed in me, and I began again to live. I renounced the life of our class, for I had come to confess that it was not life, but only the semblance of life, that its superfluous luxuries prevent the possibility of understanding life, and that in order to understand life, I must understand not the life of exceptional people, the parasites, but the life of the simple working-classes, the life that fashions life, and gives it the meaning which the working-classes accept. The simple laboring men around me were the Russian people, and I turned to this people and to the meaning which it gives to life.

This meaning, if it can be expressed, was as follows: —

Every man has come into this world by the will of God, and God has so created man that every man is able to ruin or to save his soul. The problem of man's life being to save his soul, in order to save his soul, he must live after God's word: to live after God's word, he must renounce all the pleasures of life, must labor, be humble, endure, and be meek. This, to the people, is the meaning of the whole system of faith, as it has come down to them through, and is now given them by, the pastors of their Church and the traditions which exist among them.

This meaning was clear to me, and dear to my heart. This popular faith, however, among the non-dissenting communities in which I lived, was inextricably bound up with something else so incapable of being explained that it repelled me: the sacraments, the services of the Church, the fasts, and the bowing before relics and images. The people were unable to separate these things, and no more could I. Though many things belonging to the faith of the people appeared strange to me, I accepted everything, I attended the church services, prayed morning and evening, fasted, prepared for the communion; and, while doing all this, for the first time felt that my reason found nothing to object to. What had formerly seemed to me impossible, now roused no opposition in me.

The position which I occupied with relation to questions of faith had become quite different to what it once was. Formerly, life itself had seemed to me full of meaning, and faith an arbitrary assertion of certain useless and unreasonable propositions which had no direct bearing on life. I had tried to find out their meaning; and once convinced they had none, had thrown them aside. Now, on the contrary, I knew for certain that my life had not and could not have any meaning, and that the propositions of faith not only appeared no longer useless to me, but had been shown beyond dispute by my own experience to be that which alone gave a meaning to life. Formerly I looked on them as a worthless, illegible scrawl; but now if I did not understand them, still I knew that they had a meaning, and I said to myself that I must learn to understand them.

I reasoned thus: —

"Faith springs, like man and his reason, from the mysterious first cause. That first cause is God, the cause of the body and the mind of man. As my body proceeded through successive gradations from God to me, so have my reason and my conception of life proceeded from Him, and consequently the steps of this process of development cannot be false. All that men sincerely believe in must be true; it may be differently expressed, but it cannot be a lie, and consequently, if it seem to me a lie, that must be because I do not understand it."

Again, I said to myself: —

"The true office of any faith is to give to life a meaning which death cannot destroy. It is only natural that for faith to give an answer to the question of the king dying amid every luxury, of the old and labor-worn slave, of the unthinking child, of the aged sage, of the half-witted old crone, of the happy woman full of the strong passions of youth, of all men under all possible differences of position and education, — it is only natural that, if there be but one answer to the one eternally repeated question — 'Why do I live, and what will come of my life?' — the answer, though one and the same in reality, should be infinitely varied in its phenomena; that, in exact proportion to its unvarying unity, to its truth, and its depth, it should appear strange, and even monstrous, in the attempts to find due expression, which are owing to the bringing-up and the social state of each individual answerer."

But these arguments, which justified the oddities of the ritual side of faith, were still insufficient to make me feel that I had a right, in a matter like faith, now become the one business of my life, to take part in acts of which I was still doubtful. I desired, with all the powers of my soul, to be in a condition to unite with the people, conforming to the rites which they practised, but I could not do it. I felt that I should lie to myself, and mock what I held most sacred, if I did this thing.

At this point our new Russian theologians came to my assistance.

According to the explanation of these divines, the fundamental dogma of faith is the infallibility of the Church. From the acceptance of this dogma follows, as a necessary consequence, the truth of all that is taught by the Church. The Church, as the assembly of believers united in love, and consequently possessing true knowledge, became the foundation of my faith. I said to myself: "Divine truth cannot be attained by any one man,—it can be reached only by the union of all men through love. In order to attain the truth, we must not go each his own way; and, to avoid division, we must have love one to the other, and bear with things which we do not agree with. Truth is revealed in love, and, therefore, if we do not obey the ordinances of the Church, we destroy love; but if love is destroyed we are deprived of the possibility of knowing the truth."

At the time I did not perceive the sophism involved in this reasoning. I did not then see that union through love may develop love to the highest degree, but can never give the Divine Truth, as stated in the words of the Nicene Creed,—I did not see that love can never make any particular form of creed binding on all believers. I did not then see error in this reasoning, and, thanks to it, I was able to accept and practise all the rites of the Orthodox Church, but without understanding the greater part of them. I struggled then, with all the powers of my soul, to avoid all discussions, all contradictions, and endeavored to explain, as reasonably as I could, all the Church doctrines that presented any difficulty.

While thus fulfilling the ordinances of the Church, I submitted my reason to the tradition adopted by the mass of my fellow-men. I united myself to my ancestors,—to those I loved,—my father, mother, and grandparents. They and all before them lived, and believed, and brought me into being. I joined the millions of the people whom I respect. Moreover, there was nothing bad in all this, for bad with me meant the indulgence of the lusts of the flesh. When I got up early to attend divine service, I knew that I was doing well, if it were only because I tamed my intellectual pride for the sake of a closer union with my ancestors and contemporaries, and, in order to seek for a meaning in life, sacrificed my bodily comfort.

It was the same with preparing for the communion, the daily reading of prayers, with genuflections, and the observance of all the fasts. However insignificant the sacrifices were, they were made in a good cause. I prepared for the communion, fasted, and observed regular hours for prayer both at home and at church. While listening to the church service, I weighed every word, and gave it a meaning whenever I could. At mass the words which appeared to me to have most importance were the following:—

"*Let us love one another in unity.*" What follows—the confession of belief in the unity of the Father, the Son, and the Holy Ghost—I passed over, because I could not understand it.

CHAPTER XIV

It was so necessary for me at that time to believe in order to live, that I unconsciously concealed from myself the contradictions and the obscurities in the doctrines.

But this interpretation of the ritual had its limits. If the Liturgy became clearer and clearer to me in its principal expressions; if I gave a kind of meaning to such expressions as "Remembering our Sovereign Lady, the most Holy Mother of God, and all the Saints, let us devote ourselves, each other, and our whole lives to the Christ God"; if I explained the frequent repetition of prayers for the Tsar and his family by the fact that they were more exposed to temptation than others, and were therefore more in need of prayer, and the prayers for victory over our enemies and opponents to mean victory over the principle of evil; these prayers and others like the hymn of the Cherubim, and all the mystery of the bread and wine, the adoration of the Virgin and others — in short, two-thirds of the whole service — either remained for me without an explanation at all, or made me feel that the only one I could apply to them was false, while to lie was to break off my connection with God, and lose utterly the possibility of believing.

I felt the same at the celebration of the principal Church holidays. To "remember the Sabbath day," that is, to consecrate one day to communion with God, was comprehensible to me. The great holiday, however, was in remembrance of the Resurrection, the reality of which I could neither imagine nor understand. This gave a name to the holiday in each week, to the Sunday. And on this day the sacrament of the Eucharist was celebrated, a mystery which to me was utterly inconceivable. The other twelve holidays, with the exception of Christmas, were all in remembrance of miracles, which I tried not to think of in order not to deny: the Ascension, Pentecost, Epiphany, the Intercession of the Virgin, and so on.

On these holidays I felt that the greatest importance was given to what I believed to be of the least, and I either held fast to the explanation that quieted me most, or else shut my eyes so as not to see what disquieted me.

This feeling came upon me strongest whenever I took part in the most ordinary, and, generally considered, the most important, sacraments, as christening and the holy communion. Here I had to do with nothing incomprehensible, but with what was easy to understand: such acts appeared to me a delusion, and I was on the horns of a dilemma — to lie, or to reject.

I shall never forget the painful feeling I experienced when I took the communion for the first time after many years. The service, the confession, the collects, all this was understood by me, and produced the glad conviction that the meaning of life lay open to me. The communion I explained to myself as an action done in remembrance of Christ, and as signifying a cleansing from sin and a complete acceptance of Christ's teaching. If this explanation was artificial, I, at least, was not troubled by its artificiality. It was such happiness for me to humble myself with a quiet heart before the confessor, a simple and mild priest, and, repenting of my sins, to lay bare all the mire of my soul; it was such happiness to be united in spirit with the meek Fathers of the Church who composed these prayers; such happiness to be one with all who have believed and who do believe, that I could not feel my explanation was artificial.

But when I drew near to the *tsarskiya dveri*, "the holy gates," and the priest called on me to repeat that I believed that what I was about to swallow was the real body and blood, it cut me to the heart; it was a false note, though small; it was no unconsidered word; it was the cruel demand of one who had evidently never known what faith was.

I now allow myself to say that it was a cruel demand, but then I did not think so; it was only unspeakably painful. I was no longer in that position where I had been in my youth, thinking that all was clear in life; I had been drawn toward faith because outside it I had found nothing, assuredly nothing but ruin; and as I could not throw faith aside, I had submitted. I had found in my soul a feeling which had helped me to do this. It was a feeling of self-abasement and submission. I humbled myself, I swallowed the blood and the body without any mocking thoughts in the wish to believe, but the shock had been received, and knowing beforehand what awaited me, I could never go a second time.

I still continued an exact observance of the rites of the Church, and I still believe that there was truth in the doctrines I followed; and then there happened to me a thing which now is clear enough, but which then appeared to me very strange.

I was at one time listening to the discourse of an unlettered muzhik, a pilgrim. He spoke of God, of faith, of life, and of salvation, and a knowledge of what faith was seemed open to me.

I went amongst the people, familiarizing myself with

their ideas of life and faith, and the truth became clearer and clearer to me. It was the same when I read the "Martyrology" and "Prologues"; they be came my favorite books. With the exception of the miracles, and looking on these as fables to bring out forcibly the thought, the reading of these books revealed to me the meaning of life. There I found the lives of Macarius the Great; of Ioasaph the Prince (the story of Buddha); the discourses of St. John Chrysostom; the story of the traveler in the well; of the Monk who found gold; of Peter the Publican; — this is the history of the martyrs, of those who have all testified the same, that life does not end with death; here we have the story of unlettered foolish men, who knew nothing of the doctrines of the Church.

But no sooner did I mix with learned believers, or consult their books, than doubts, uneasiness, and irritation came over me once more, and I felt that the more I studied their discourses the more I wandered from the truth, the nearer I came to the precipice.

CHAPTER XV

How often have I envied muzhiks their inability to read and write, their lack of learning. The very doctrines of faith which to me were manifest nonsense contained for them nothing that was false; they were able to accept them and to believe in truth, the same truth in which I also believed; only to me, unhappy, it was clear that truth was connected with falsehood by the finest threads of difference, and that I could not receive it in such a form.

In this condition I lived for three years, and when I first, like a new convert, little by little drew nearer to truth, and, led by an instinct, groped my way to the light, these obstacles seemed to me less formidable. When I failed to understand anything, I said, "I am wrong, I am wicked." But the more I became imbued with the spirit of the truths which I studied, the more surely I saw them to be the substratum of life, the greater and more formidable became the obstacles, the more clearly defined the line between what I did not understand; and because I was unable to understand, I could understand only through lying unto myself.

Notwithstanding all my doubts and sufferings, I still clung to Orthodoxy; but practical questions arose and had to be settled, and the decisions of these questions by the Church, contrary to the elementary principles of the faith by which I lived, compelled me finally to abandon all communion with it.

The questions were, in the first place, the relation of the Orthodox Church to other churches, to Catholicism and the so-called Raskolniks or Dissenters. The interest which I took in this great question of faith led me at this time to form acquaintance with the professors of different creeds, Catholics, Protestants, Old Believers, Molokans[1] and others, and among them I found many who sincerely believed and obeyed the highest moral standard. I desired to be a brother to these men, and what came of it? The doctrines which had seemed to promise me the union of all men in one faith and love, these doctrines, in the persons of their best representatives, told me that all these men were living in a lie; that what gives them strength to live is a temptation of the devil, that we alone possess the possibility of knowing truth.

And I saw that the members of the Orthodox Church consider all those who do not profess the same faith as themselves to be heretics, exactly as Catholics and others account our Orthodoxy to be heresy; I saw that Orthodoxy considers others who do not adopt the same outward symbols and the same formulas of faith as herself as her enemies, though she tries to conceal it; and it must be so, in the first place, because the assertion that you live a lie and I am in the truth is the hardest thing that one man can say to another; in the second place, because a man who loves his children and his brethren cannot but feel at enmity with those who

[1] "Milk-drinkers," who do not believe in fasting.

desire to convert his children and brethren to a false faith. Moreover, this enmity increases as men learn more of the -particular doctrines which they adopt Even I, who had believed faith was to be found in the union of love, was unwillingly forced to see that the doctrines of faith destroy the very thing which they should produce.

This snare is so evident, to men living like ourselves in countries where differing faiths are professed, and witnessing the contemptuous and self-confident exclusiveness with which the Catholic treats the Protestant and Orthodox, repaid by the scorn of the Orthodox for the Catholic and the Protestant, and that of the latter for both the others, while the same relation of enmity includes the Old Believers, the Revivalists, the Shakers, and all other creeds, that at first it perplexes us.

We say to ourselves: —

"No, it cannot be so simple as that, and yet these men have not seen that when two propositions contradict each other they cannot both have the one truth on which faith should rest. There was some cause for this, there was some explanation."

I myself thought there was, and sought for it; and with this object in view I read everything I could get on the subject, and consulted with as many as I could, but the only explanation I obtained was that in accordance with which "Sumsky" hussars account their "Sumsky" regiment the first in the world, while the yellow Uhlans consider that the first regiment in the world is that of the yellow Uhlans.

Clergymen of all the different religions, the best representatives of them, without exception, all told me of their belief that they alone were right and all others wrong, and that all they could do for those who were in error was to pray for them. I went to archimandrites, bishops, priors, and ascetic monks, and asked them; but no one made the slightest attempt to explain this snare to me. Only one among them all explained everything for me, but his explanation was such that I asked nothing more of any one.

I said that, for every unbeliever who returns to belief (in which category I place the whole of the present young generation) the principal question is, Why is truth to be found in the Orthodox Church and not in the Lutheran or the Catholic Church? He is taught in his gymnasium, and he cannot but know what the peasant is ignorant of, that Protestants and Catholics equally affirm their own faith to be the only true one.

Historical proofs, twisted by each sect to serve their own purpose, are insufficient. Is it not possible, as I have already said, for a higher knowledge to issue from the disappearance of these differences, as they do already disappear for those who sincerely believe? Can we not go farther on the way on which we and the Old Believers start out together? They affirm that our way of signing the cross, of singing hallelujah, and of moving round the altar, is not the same as theirs. We say:—

"You believe in the Nicene Creed, in the seven sacraments, and we also believe. Keep to that, and for the rest do as you will."

We shall then be united to them by this, that we both place the essential points of faith above the unessential. Again, can we not say to Catholics:—

"You believe in this and in that, in certain things which are essential, but in what concerns the dispute about the procession of the Trinity and the Pope, do as you please"?

Can we not say the same to the Protestant, and unite with him in what is really important?

My fellow-disputant agreed with me, but added that such concessions draw down the reproach that the clergy have receded from the faith of their forefathers and favor dissent, while the office of those in authority in the Church is to preserve the purity of the Russian Greek Orthodox faith as handed down from our ancestors.

Then I understood it all. I am in search of faith, the staff and strength of life, while these men seek the best means of fulfilling in the sight of men certain human obligations, and having to deal with human affairs, they fulfil them as ordinary men ever do. However much they may talk of their pity for the errors of their brethren, of praying for them at the throne of the Most High, for the accomplishment of earthly affairs force is needed, and force always has been, is, and will be, applied.

If two religious sects each believe that truth resides in themselves, and that the faith of the other is a lie, they will preach their doctrines in the hope of converting their brethren to the truth, and, if false doctrines are taught to the inexperienced sons of the Church who still tread in the ways of truth, she cannot but burn the books and banish the man who seduces her sons. What can be done with the Sectary, who in his fiery enthusiasm for a faith which the Church pronounces false, seduces her sons? What can be done with him, but to cut off his head or imprison him? In the time of Alexis Mikhaïlovitch men were burnt at the stake; in other words, the severest punishment of the time was applied, and in our days also the severest punishment is applied; men are condemned to solitary confinement. When I looked around me at all that was done in the name of religion, I was horrified, and almost entirely withdrew from the Orthodox Church.

The second point which concerned the relations of the Church to the problems of life was her connection with war and executions. At this time Russia was engaged in war, and, in the name of Christian love, Russians were engaged in slaying their brethren. Not to think of this was impossible. Not to see that murder is an evil, contrary to the very first principles of every faith, was impossible. But at the same time in the churches men were praying for the success of our arms, and the teachers of religion were accepting these murders as acts which were the consequence of faith. Not only murder in actual warfare was approved, but, during the troubles which ensued, I saw members of the Church, her teachers, monks, and ascetics, approving of the murder of erring and helpless youths. I looked round on all that was done by men who professed to be Christians, and I was horrified.

CHAPTER XVI

I CEASED from this time to doubt, and became firmly convinced that not all was truth in the faith which I had joined. Formerly I should have said that all in this faith was false, but now it was impossible to say so.

The people as a whole had a knowledge of truth; this was incontestable, for otherwise they could not live. Moreover, this knowledge of truth was open to me; I was already living by it, and felt all its force, but in that same knowledge there was also error. Of that again I could not doubt. All, however, that had formerly repelled me now presented itself in a vivid light. Although I saw that there was less of what had repelled me as false among the people than among the representatives of the Church, I also saw that in the belief of the people what was false was mingled with what was true.

Whence, then, came this truth and this falsehood? Both the falsehood and the truth came to them from what is called the Church; both the falsehood and the truth are included in the traditions, the so-called sacred traditions and writings.

I was thus, whether I would or not, brought to the study and analysis of these writings and traditions, a study which up to that time I had feared, and I turned to the study of theology, which I had once thrown aside with such contempt as useless. Then theology had seemed to me but profitless trifling with nonsense; then I was surrounded by the phenomena of life, which seemed to me clear and full of meaning; now I should have been glad to throw off ideas unsuited to a healthy state of mind, but I could not.

On this doctrinal basis was founded, or at least with it was very intimately bound up, the only explanation of the meaning of the life I had so lately discovered. However strange it might seem to my old practised intellect, it was the only hope of salvation. To be understood, it must be cautiously and carefully examined, even though the result might not be the certain knowledge of science, which, aware as I was of the special character of religious inquiry, I did not and could not seek to obtain.

I could not attempt to explain everything. I knew that the explanation of the whole, like the beginning of all things, was hidden in infinity. I wished to be brought to the inevitable limit where the incomprehensible begins; I wished that what remained uncomprehended should be so, not because the mental impulse to inquiry was not just and natural (all such impulses are just and without them I could understand nothing), but because I had learned the limits of my own mind. I wished to understand so that every unexplained proposition should appear to my reason necessarily unexplainable, and not an obligatory part of belief.

That the doctrines contained truth was unquestionable; but it was also unquestionable that they contained also falsehood, and I was bound to find the truth and the falsehood and separate the one from the other. I began to do this. What I found of false, what I found of true, and to what results I came, forms the following part of this work,[1] which, if it be thought worth while, and if it can be useful to any one, will probably be some day published.

1879.

The above was written by me three years ago.

The other day, on looking over this part again, on returning to the train of thought and to the feelings through which I had passed while writing it, I saw a dream.

This dream repeated for me in a condensed form all that I had lived through and described, and I therefore think that a description of it may, for those who have understood me, serve to render clearer, to refresh the remembrance of, and to collect into one whole, all that has been described at so much length in these pages. The dream was as follows.

[1] My Religion.

I see myself lying in bed, and I feel neither particularly well and comfortable, nor the contrary. I am lying on my back. I begin to think whether it is well for me to lie, and something makes me feel uncomfortable in the legs; if the bed be too short or ill-made, I know not, but something is not right. I move my legs about, and at the same time begin to think how and on what I am lying, a thing which previously had never troubled me. I examine my bed, and see that I am lying on a network of cords fashioned to the sides of the bedstead. My heels lie on one of these cords, my legs on another, and this is uncomfortable. I am somehow aware that the cords can be moved, and with my legs I push the cord away, and it seems to me that thus it will be easier.

But I had pushed the cord too far; I tried to catch it with my legs, but this movement causes another cord to slip from under me, and my legs hang down. I move my body to get right again, convinced that it will be easy, but this movement causes other cords to slip and change their places beneath me, and I perceive that my position is altogether worse; my whole body sinks and hangs, without my legs touching the ground. I hold myself up only by the upper part of the back, and I feel now not only discomfort, but horror. I now begin to ask myself what I had not thought of before. I ask myself where I am, and on what I am lying. I begin to look round, and first I look below, to the place toward which my body sank, and where I feel it must soon fall. I look below, and I cannot believe my eyes.

I am on a height far above that of the highest tower or mountain, a height beyond all my previous powers of conception. I cannot even make out whether I see anything or not below me, in the depths of that bottomless abyss over which I am hanging, and into which I feel drawn. My heart ceases to beat, and horror fills my mind. To look down is horrible. I feel that if I look down I shall slip from the last cord, and perish. I stop looking, but not to look is still worse, for then I think of what will at once happen to me when the last cord breaks. I feel that I am losing, in my terror, the last remnant of my strength, and that my back is gradually sinking lower and lower. Another instant, and I shall fall.

Then all at once comes into my mind the thought that this cannot be true — it is a dream — I will awake.

I strive to wake myself, and cannot. "What can I do? what can I do?" I ask myself, and as I put the question I look above.

Above stretches another gulf. I look into this abyss of heaven, and try to forget the abyss below, and I do actually forget it. The infinite depth repels and horrifies me; the infinite height attracts and satisfies me. I still hang on the last cords which have not yet slipped from under me, over the abyss; I know that I am hanging thus, but I look only upwards, and my terror leaves me. As happens in dreams, I hear a voice saying, "Look well; it is there!" My eyes pierce farther and farther into the infinity above, and I feel that it calms me. I remember all that has happened, and I remember how it happened — how I moved my legs, how I was left hanging in air, how I was horrified, and how I was saved from my horror by looking above. I ask myself, "And now, am I not hanging still?" and I feel in all my limbs, without looking, the support by which I am held. I perceive that I no longer hang, and that I do not fall, but have a fast hold. I question myself how it is that I hold on. I touch myself, I look around, and I see that under the middle of my body there passes a stay, and on looking up I find that I am lying perfectly balanced, and that it was this stay alone that held me up before.

As happens in dreams, the mechanism by which I am supported appears perfectly natural to me, a thing to be easily understood, and not to be doubted, although this mechanism has no apparent sense when I am awake. In my sleep I was even astonished that I had not understood this before. At my bedside stands a pillar, the solidity of which is beyond doubt, though there is nothing for it to stand on. From this pillar runs a cord, somehow cunningly and at the same time simply fixed, and if I lie across this cord and look upward, there cannot be even a question of my falling. All this was clear to me, and I was glad and easy in my mind. It seemed as if some one said to me, "See that you remember!"

And I awoke.

1882.

MY RELIGION

I HAVE lived in the world fifty-five years, and after the fourteen or fifteen years of my childhood, for thirty-five years of my life I was, in the proper acceptation of the word, a nihilist, — not a socialist and revolutionist, as is generally understood by that word, but a nihilist in the sense of one who believed in nothing. Five years ago I came to believe in the doctrine of Christ, and my whole life underwent a sudden transformation. What I had once wished for I wished for no longer. What had once appeared to me good now became evil, and the evil of the past I beheld as good.

My condition was like that of a man who goes forth on some errand, and suddenly on the way decides that the matter is of no importance, and returns home. What was at first on his right hand is now on his left, and what was at his left hand is now on his right; his former desire to be as far as possible from home has changed into a desire to be as near to it as possible. The direction of my life and my desires were completely changed; good and evil had changed places. All this resulted from the fact that I understood the doctrine of Christ in a different way from that in which I had understood it before.

I do not care to expound the doctrine of Christ; I wish only to tell how it was that I came to understand what in this doctrine is most simple, clear, evident, indisputable, and appeals most to all men, and how this understanding refreshed my soul and gave me happiness and peace.

I do not care to expound the doctrine of Christ; I should wish only one thing: to do away with all exposition.

Entrance to the Park of Yasnaya Polyana.

All the Christian Churches have always maintained that all men, however unequal in education and intellect, — the wise and the foolish, — are equal before God; that divine truth is accessible to every one. Christ has even declared it to be the will of God that what is concealed from the wise shall be revealed to the simple.

Not every one is able to understand the mysteries of dogmatics, homiletics, patristics, liturgics, hermeneutics, apologetics; but every one is able and ought to understand what Christ said to the millions of simple and ignorant people who have lived, and who are living to-day. Now, the things that Christ said to all these simple people who could not avail themselves of the comments of Paul, of Clement, of Chrysostom, and of others, are just what I did not understand, and which, now that I have come to understand them, I wish to make plain to all.

The thief on the cross believed in Christ, and was saved. Would it have been bad or injurious to any one if the thief had not died on the cross, but had descended from it, and told all men how he believed in Christ?

Like the thief on the cross, I believed in the doctrine of Christ, and was saved. This is not a vain comparison, but a most accurate expression of my spiritual condition of horror and despair in the presence of life and death, in which I found myself formerly, and of that condition of happiness and peace in which I find myself now.

Like the thief, I knew that my past and present life was vile; I saw that the majority of men about me lived in the same way. I knew, like the thief, that I was wretched and suffering, that all those about me suffered and were wretched; and I saw before me no escape from this condition but in death. As the thief was nailed to his cross, so was I nailed to this life of suffering and evil by an incomprehensible power. And as the thief saw before him, after the senseless and evil sufferings of life, the horrible shadows of death, so did I behold the same prospect.

In all this I was absolutely like the thief. But there

was a difference in our conditions; he was about to die, and I was still alive. The thief might believe that his salvation would be beyond the grave, while I had not only that before me, but also life this side the grave. I understood nothing of this life, it seemed to me frightful; and then suddenly I heard the words of Christ, and understood them; life and death ceased to seem evil, and instead of despair I tasted the joy and happiness that death could not take away.

Can it be harmful to any one, then, if I tell how this came about?

CHAPTER I

I HAVE written two large works explaining why I did not understand the doctrine of Christ, and why it became clear to me. "A Criticism of Dogmatic Theology" and a new translation of the four Gospels, followed by a Concordance. In these writings I seek methodically, step by step, to disentangle everything that conceals the truth from men; I translate the four Gospels anew, verse by verse, and I bring them together in a new concordance.

This work has lasted more than five years. Each year, each month, I discover new explanations and corroborations of the fundamental idea; I correct the errors which have crept in through haste and impulse, and I put the last touches to what I have already written. My life, of which only a small portion is before me, will doubtless end before I have finished my work; but I am convinced that the work will be of great service; so I shall do all that I can as long as I live.

Such was my prolonged outward work on theology and the Gospels, but my inward work, that which I propose to tell about in these pages, was of a very different nature. It was not a methodical exposition of theology and the text of the Gospels; it was an instantaneous removal of all that had hidden the meaning of the teaching, and an instantaneous illumination with the light of Truth.

It was an experience similar to that which might happen to a man who, following an erroneous model, should try to find the meaning of a heap of intermingled fragments, and should suddenly, by means of one large fragment, come to the conclusion that it was an entirely different statue from what he had supposed it to be; then beginning to fashion it anew, instead of the former incoherent mass of pieces, he would find, as he observed the outlines of each fragment, that all fitted well together, and formed one consistent whole, and he would be amazed at the confirmation of his thought

This is exactly what happened to me, and this is what I wish to relate. I wish to tell how I found the key to the true meaning of the doctrine of Christ, which revealed to me the truth clearly and convincingly, so that doubt was out of the question. The discovery came about in this way: —

Almost from the first period of my childhood, when I began to read the New Testament, I was touched and stirred most of all by that portion of the doctrine of Christ which inculcates love, humility, self-denial, and the duty of returning good for evil. This, to me, has always been the substance of Christianity; it was what I loved in it with all my heart, it was that in the name of which, after despair and disbelief, caused me to accept as true the meaning found in the Christian life by the working people, and in the name of which I submitted myself to those doctrines professed by these same working people — in other words, the Orthodox Church.

But in making my submission to the Church, I soon saw that I should not find in its creed the confirmation, the explanation of those principles of Christianity which seemed to me essential; I observed that the essence of Christianity, dear though it was to me, did not constitute the chief element in the doctrine of the Church. I observed that what seemed to me essential in Christ's teaching was not recognized by the Church as most important. Something else was regarded by the Church as most important. At first I did not appreciate the significance of this peculiarity of the Church teaching. "Well now," — I thought — "the Church sees in Christianity, aside from its inner meaning of love, humility, and self-denial, an outer, dogmatic meaning. This meaning is strange and even repulsive to me, but it is not in itself pernicious."

But the longer I continued to live in submission to the doctrine of the Church, the more clearly I saw this particular point was not so unimportant as it had seemed to me at first. I was driven from the Church by the strangeness of its dogmas, and the approval and the support which it gave to persecutions, to the death penalty, to wars, and by the intolerance common to all sects; but my faith was chiefly shattered by the indifference of the Church to what seemed to me essential in the teachings of Jesus, and by its avidity for what seemed to me not essential. I felt that something was wrong; but I could not discover what was wrong. I could not discover, because the doctrine of the Church did not deny, what seemed to me essential in the doctrine of Christ; it fully recognized it, yet recognized it in such a way that what was chief in the teaching of Christ was not given the first place. I could not blame the Church because she denied the essence of the doctrine of Jesus, but because she recognized it in a way which did not satisfy me. The Church did not give me what I expected from her.

I had passed from nihilism to the Church simply because I felt it to be impossible to live without religion, without a knowledge of good and evil beyond the animal instincts. I hoped to find this knowledge in Christianity; but Christianity, as it then presented itself to me, was only a very indeterminate spiritual tendency, from which it was impossible to deduce any clear and obligatory principles of life. For these rules I turned to the Church. The Church offered me certain rules, but they not only did not attract me to the Christian dispensation now so dear to me, but rather repelled me from it. I could not follow the Church. A life based on Christian truth was precious and indispensable to me, and the Church offered me rules completely at variance with the truth I loved. The rules of the Church touching belief in dogmas, the observance of the sacrament, fasts, prayers, were not necessary to me, and did not seem to be based on Christian truth. Moreover, the rules of the Church weakened and sometimes destroyed the desire for Christian truth which alone gave meaning to my life.

I was troubled most by the fact that all human evil, the habit of judging private persons, of judging whole nations, of judging other religions, and the wars and massacres that were the consequence of such judgments, all went on with the approbation of the Church. Christ's teaching — judge not, be humble, forgive offenses, deny self, love, — this doctrine was extolled by the Church in words, but at the same time the Church approved what was incompatible with the doctrine. Was it possible that Christ's teaching admitted of such contradiction? I could not believe so.

Moreover, it always seemed to me astonishing that, as far as I knew the Gospels, the passages on which the Church based affirmation of its dogmas were those that were most obscure, while the passages from which came the fulfilment of its teaching were the most clear and precise. And yet the dogmas and the obligations depending on them were definitely formulated by the Church, while the recommendation to obey the moral law was put in the most obscure, vague, and mystical terms. Was this the intention of Jesus in teaching His doctrine? A resolution of my doubts I could find only in the Gospels, and I read them, and reread them.

Of everything in the Gospels, the Sermon on the Mount always had for me an exceptional importance. I now read it more frequently than ever. Nowhere else does Christ speak with so great solemnity as in these passages, nowhere else does He give so many clear and comprehensible moral laws, appealing to every man's heart; nowhere else does He address Himself to a larger multitude of the common people. If there are any clear and precise Christian principles, one ought to find them here. I therefore sought the solution of my doubts in these three[1] chapters of Matthew. I read the Sermon

[1] v., vi., and vii.

on the Mount many, many times, and I always experienced the same feelings of enthusiasm and emotion, as I read the verses that exhort the hearer to turn the other cheek, to give up his cloak, to be at peace with all men, to love his enemies, — but each time with the same disappointment. The divine words — addressed to all men — were not clear. They exhorted to an absolute renunciation of everything, such as entirely stifled life, as I understood it; to renounce everything, therefore, could not, it seemed to me, be an absolute condition of salvation. But the moment this ceased to be an absolute condition, clearness and precision were at an end.

I read not only the Sermon on the Mount; I read all the Gospels, and all the theological commentaries on them. I was not satisfied with the declarations of the theologians that the Sermon on the Mount was only an indication of the degree of perfection to which man should aspire; but that fallen man, weighed down by sin, could not reach such an ideal; and that the salvation of humanity was in faith and prayer and grace.

I could not admit the truth of these propositions, because it seemed to me strange that Christ, knowing beforehand that it was impossible for man, with his own powers, to carry his teaching into practice, should propound rules so clear and admirable, addressed to the understanding of every one. But as I read these maxims it always seemed to me that they applied directly to me, that their fulfilment was demanded of me. As I read these maxims I was filled with the joyous assurance that I might that very hour, that very moment, begin to practice them. I desired to do so, I tried to do so, but as soon as I began to enter upon the struggle I could not help remembering the teaching of the Church — *Man is weak, and to this he cannot attain* — and my strength failed. I was told, "You must believe and pray;" but I was conscious that I had small faith, and so I could not pray. I was told, "You must pray, and God will give you faith; this faith will inspire prayer, which in turn will invoke faith that will inspire more prayer, and so on, indefinitely."

But reason and experience alike convinced me that such methods were useless. It seemed to me that the only true way was for me to try to follow the teaching of Christ.

And so, after all this fruitless search, study of all that had been written for and against the divinity of this doctrine, after all this doubt and suffering, I remained alone with my heart and with the mysterious book before me. I could not give to it the meanings that others gave, neither could I discover what I sought nor could I get away from it. Only after I had gone through alike all the interpretations of the wise critics and all the interpretations of the wise theologians and had rejected them all according to the words of Jesus, "*Except ye....become as little children, ye shall not enter into the kingdom of heaven*"[1] — I suddenly understood what I had not understood before. I understood, not because I made any artificial combination of texts, or any profound and ingenious misinterpretations; on the contrary, I understood everything because I put all commentaries out of my mind. The passage that gave me the key to the whole was from the fifth chapter of Matthew, verses thirty-eight and thirty-nine: —

"*It has been said unto you, An eye for an eye, and a tooth for a tooth: But I say unto you, That you resist not evil.*"

Suddenly, for the first time, I understood the exact and simple meaning of those words; I understood that Jesus said exactly what he said. Immediately — not that I saw anything new; only the veil that had hidden the truth from me fell away, and the truth was revealed in all its significance.

"*It has been said unto you, An eye for an eye, and a tooth for a tooth: But I say unto you, That you resist not evil.*"

These words suddenly appeared to me absolutely new, as if I had never read them before. Always before, when I had read this passage, I had, singularly enough, allowed certain words to escape me, "*But I say unto*

[1] Matt. xviii. 3.

you, that you resist not evil." To me it had always been as if the words just quoted had never existed, or had never possessed a definite meaning.

Later on, as I talked with many Christians familiar with the Gospel, I noticed frequently the same blindness with regard to these words. No one remembered them, and often, in speaking of this passage, Christians took up the Gospel to see for themselves if the words were really there. Through a similar neglect of these words I had failed to understand the words that follow: —

"*But whosoever shall smite thee on thy right cheek, turn to him the other also,*" etc.[1]

Always these words had seemed to me to demand long-suffering and privation contrary to human nature. These words touched me; I felt that it would be noble to follow them, but I also felt that I should never have the strength to put them into practice, only to put them into practice so as to suffer. I said to myself, "If I turn the other cheek, I shall get another blow; if I give, all that I have will be taken away. Life would be an impossibility. Since life is given to me, why should I deprive myself of it? Christ cannot demand that." Thus I reasoned, persuaded that Christ in these words exalted suffering and deprivation, and in exalting them, made use of exaggerated terms lacking in clearness and precision; but when I understood the words "*Resist not evil,*" it became clear to me that Jesus did not exaggerate, that he did not demand suffering for suffering, but that he said with great clearness and precision exactly what he wished to say.

He said "*Resist not evil,* and if you do so you will know beforehand that you may meet with those who, when they have struck you on one cheek and met with no resistance, will strike you on the other; who, having taken away your coat, will take away your cloak also; who, having profited by your labor, will force you to labor still more without reward. And yet, though all this should happen to you, '*Resist not evil*'; do good to them that injure you."

[1] Matt. v. 39, *et seq.*

When I understood these words as they were said, all that had been obscure became clear to me, and what had seemed exaggerated I saw to be perfectly reasonable. For the first time I saw that the center of gravity of the whole idea lay in the words "*Resist not evil*"; and that what followed was only a development of this command; I saw that Jesus did not exhort us to turn the other cheek and give up the cloak that we might endure suffering, but that his exhortation was, "*Resist not evil*," and that he afterward declared suffering to be the possible consequence of the practice of this maxim.

Exactly as a father who is sending his son on a far journey does not command him to pass his nights without shelter, to go without food, to expose himself to rain and cold when he says to him, "Go thy way, and tarry not, even though thou should'st be wet or cold," so Jesus does not say, "Turn the other cheek and suffer." He says, "*Resist not evil*"; no matter what happens, "*Resist not evil*."

These words, "*Resist not evil or the evil man*," understood in their direct significance, were to me truly the key that opened all the rest. And I began to be astonished that I could have miscomprehended words so clear and precise.

"*It has been said unto you, An eye for an eye, and a tooth for a tooth: but I say unto you, That you resist not evil or the evil man.*"

Whatever injury the evil-disposed may inflict upon you, bear it, give all that you have, but resist not evil or the evil one. Could anything be more clear, more definite, more intelligible than that? I had only to grasp the simple and exact meaning of these words, just as they were spoken, when the whole teaching of Christ, not only as set forth in the Sermon on the Mount, but in the entire Gospels, became clear to me; what had seemed contradictory was now in harmony; above all, what had seemed superfluous was now indispensable. Each portion fell into harmonious unison and filled its proper part, like the fragments of a broken statue when put together as they should be. In the

Sermon on the Mount, as well as throughout the whole Gospel, I found everywhere affirmation of the same doctrine, "*Resist not evil.*"

In the Sermon on the Mount, as well as in all other places, Christ presents Himself to His disciples, in other words, to those that observe the rule of non-resistance to evil, as turning the other cheek, giving up their cloaks, persecuted, used despitefully, and in want. Elsewhere, many times Christ says that he who does not take up his cross, who does not renounce worldly advantage, he who is not ready to bear all the consequences of the commandment, "*Resist not evil,*" cannot become His disciple.

To His disciples Jesus says, Choose to be poor; be ready to bear persecution, suffering, and death, without resistance to evil.

He himself was ready to bear suffering and death rather than resist evil, and He reproved Peter for wishing to avenge Him, and He died forbidding His followers to resist, nor did He make any modification in His doctrine. All His early disciples observed this rule, and passed their lives in poverty and persecution, and never rendered evil for evil.

Christ must have said what He said. We may declare the universal practice of such a rule is very difficult; we may deny that he who follows it will find happiness; we may say with the unbelievers that it is stupid, that Christ was a dreamer, an idealist who propounded impracticable maxims which His disciples followed out of sheer stupidity; but it is impossible not to admit that Christ expressed in a manner at once clear and precise what He wished to say; that is, that according to His doctrine a man must not resist evil, and, consequently, that whoever adopts His doctrine cannot resist evil. And yet neither believers nor unbelievers will admit this simple and clear interpretation of Christ's words.

CHAPTER II

WHEN I understood that the words "*Resist not evil,*" meant *resist not evil,* my whole former conception of Christ's teaching suddenly changed; and I was horrified, not that I had failed to understand it before, but that I had misunderstood it so strangely. I knew, as we all know, that the true significance of the Christian doctrine was comprised in the injunction to love one's neighbor. When we say, "*Turn the other cheek,*" "*Love your enemies,*" we express the very essence of Christianity. I knew all that from my childhood; but why had I failed to understand aright these simple words? Why had I always sought for some ulterior meaning? "*Resist not evil*" means never resist, never oppose violence; or, in other words, never do anything contrary to the law of love. If any one takes advantage of this disposition and affronts you, bear the affront, and do not, above all, have recourse to violence. Christ said this in words so clear and simple that it would be impossible to express the idea more clearly. How was it, then, that believing or trying to believe that He who said this was God, I still maintained that it is beyond my power to obey them? If my master says to me, "Go; cut some wood," and I reply, "I cannot do this: it is beyond my strength," I say one of two things: either I do not believe what my master says, or I do not wish to do what my master commands. Should I, without having made the slightest effort of my own to obey, then say of God's commandment that I could not obey it without the aid of a supernatural power? Should I say this of a commandment which He gave us to obey, concerning which He said that whoever obeyed it and taught it should be called great, concerning which He declared that only those that obey it shall have life, which He Himself obeyed, and which He expressed so clearly and simply that it leaves no room for doubt as to its meaning!

God descended to earth to save mankind; salvation was secured by the second person of the Trinity, God-the-Son, who suffered for men, thereby redeeming them from sin, and gave them the Church as the shrine for the transmission of grace to all believers; but aside from this, Person God-the-Son gave to men a doctrine and the example of a life for their salvation. How, then, could I say that the rules of life formulated by Him so clearly and simply for every one — were so difficult to obey that it was impossible to obey them without supernatural aid? He not only did not say, but He distinctly declared, that those that did not obey could not enter into the kingdom of God. Nowhere did He say that obedience would be difficult; on the contrary, He said, "*My yoke is easy and my burden is light.*"[1] And John, His evangelist, says, "*His commandments are not grievous.*"[2] Since God laid down His command and defined so accurately the conditions of its fulfilment and obedience to it to be easy, and Himself practised it in human form, as did also His disciples, how could I say it was hard or impossible to obey without supernatural aid?

If a man should bend all the energies of his mind to overthrow any law, what could this man say of greater force than that the law was essentially impracticable, and that the maker of the law knew that it was impracticable, and that to obey it required supernatural aid.

Yet that is exactly what I had been thinking of the command, "*Resist not evil.*" I endeavored to find out how and when I got the strange idea that Christ's law was divine, but could not be obeyed; and as I reviewed my past history, I perceived that the idea had not been communicated to me in all its crudeness, — it would then have been revolting to me, — but that I had drunk it in with my mother's milk insensibly from earliest childhood, and all my after life had only confirmed me in this strange error.

From my childhood I had been taught that Christ was God, and that His doctrine was divine, but at the same

[1] Matt. xi. 30. [2] 1 John v. 3.

time, I was taught to respect the institutions that protected me from violence and evil, and to regard them as sacred. I was taught to resist evil; I was inspired with the idea that it was humiliating to submit to evil, and that resistance to it was praiseworthy. I was taught to judge, and to inflict punishment. Then I was taught the soldier's trade, that is, to resist evil by homicide; the army to which I belonged was called "The Christophile Army,"[1] and it was sent forth with a Christian benediction. Moreover, from infancy to manhood I learned to venerate what was in direct contradiction to Christ's law, —to meet an aggressor with his own weapons, to avenge myself by violence for all offenses against my person, my family, or my people. Not only was I not blamed for this, but I was led to regard it as fine, and not contrary to Christ's law.

All that surrounded me, my comfort, my personal security, and that of my family and my property, depended then on a law which Christ repudiated, — the law of "a tooth for a tooth."

My Church instructors taught me that Christ's teaching was divine, but, because of human weakness, impossible of practice, and that the grace of Christ alone could aid us to follow its precepts. My secular teachers and the whole organization of life agreed in calling Christ's teaching impracticable and visionary, and by words and deeds taught what was opposed to it. I was so thoroughly possessed with this idea of the impracticability of the divine doctrine, it had gradually become such a habit with me, the idea conformed so well with my desires, that I had never noticed the contradiction in which I had become involved. I did not see how impossible it was to confess Christ as God, the basis of whose teaching is the law of the non-resistance of evil, and at the same time deliberately to assist in the organization of property, of tribunals, of the government, of the army; to arrange my life in a manner entirely contrary to the doctrine of Jesus, and at the same time to pray to this same Christ to help us to obey His com-

[1] *Khristoliubivoye voïnstvo.*

mands, to forgive our sins, and to aid us that we resist not evil. It did not enter my head, clear as it is to me now, how much more simple it would be to arrange and organize life conformably to Christ's law, and then to pray for tribunals, and massacres, and wars, if these things are so indispensable to our happiness.

Thus I came to understand how my error arose. It arose from my confessing Christ in words and rejecting Him in reality.

The position concerning the resistance of evil is a position which unites the whole teaching into one whole, nor only because it is not a mere verbal affirmation; it is a rule the practice of which is obligatory, since it is a law.

It is exactly like a key which opens everything, but only when the key is thrust into the lock. When we regard it as a verbal affirmation impossible of performance without supernatural aid, it amounts to the nullification of the entire doctrine. Why should not a doctrine seem impracticable, when we have suppressed its fundamental proposition? Unbelievers look on it as totally absurd — they cannot look on it in any other way. To set up an engine, to heat the boiler, to start it, but not to attach the belt — that is what is done with Christ's teaching when it is taught that one may be a Christian without observing the commandment, "*Resist not evil.*"

Not long ago I was reading the fifth chapter of Matthew with a Hebrew rabbi. At nearly every verse the rabbi said, "That is in the Bible," or "That is in the Talmud," and he showed me in the Bible and in the Talmud sentences very like the declarations of the Sermon on the Mount. But when we reached the verse about non-resistance of evil the rabbi did not say, "This also is in the Talmud," but he asked me, with a cynical smile, "Do the Christians obey this command? Do they turn the other cheek?"

I had nothing to say in reply, especially as at that particular time Christians not only were not turning the other cheek, but were smiting the Jews on both cheeks. But I was interested to know if there were anything similar in the Bible or in the Talmud, and I asked him about it.

"No," he replied, "there is nothing like it; but tell me, do the Christians obey this law?"

By this question he told me that the presence in the Christian doctrine of a commandment which no one observed, and which Christians themselves regarded as impracticable, is simply an avowal of the foolishness and nullity of that law. I could say nothing in reply to the rabbi.

Now that I understand the exact meaning of the doctrine, I see clearly the strangely contradictory position in which I was placed. Having recognized Christ as God, and His doctrine as divine, and having at the same time organized my life wholly contrary to that doctrine, what remained for me but to regard the doctrine as impracticable? In words I had recognized Christ's teaching as sacred; in actions I had professed a doctrine not at all Christian, and I had recognized and reverenced the unchristian customs which hampered my life on every side.

The Old Testament, throughout, teaches that misfortunes came upon the people of Judæa because they believed in false gods, and not in the true God. Samuel, in the eighth and twelfth chapters of the first book, accuses the people of adding to their other apostasies a new one: in place of God, who was their King, they had raised up a man for a king, who, they thought, would deliver them. "*Turn not aside after* tohu, *after vain things*," Samuel says to the people; "*turn not aside after vain things, which cannot profit nor deliver; for they are* tohu, *are vain.*" "*Fear Jehovah and serve him. .... But if ye shall still do wickedly, ye shall be consumed, both ye and your king.*"[1]

And so with me, faith in *tohu*, in vain things, in empty idols, had concealed the truth from me. Across the path which led to the truth, *tohu*, the idol of vain things, rose before me, cutting off the light, and I had not the strength to beat it down.

[1] 1 Sam. xii. 21, 24, 25.

One day I was walking (in Moscow) in the Borovitskiya Gates. At the gates an old lame beggar was sitting, with a dirty cloth wrapped about his ears. I was just taking out my purse to give him something. At the same moment down from the Kremlin ran a gallant ruddy-faced young soldier, a grenadier in the crown tulup. The beggar, on perceiving the soldier, arose in fear, and ran with all his might toward the Alexandrovsky Park. The grenadier chased him for a time, but not overtaking him, stopped and began to curse the poor wretch because he had established himself under the gateway contrary to regulations. I waited for the soldier. When he approached me, I asked him if he knew how to read.

"Yes; why do you ask?"

"Have you read the New Testament?"

"I have."

"And do you remember the words, 'If thine enemy hunger, feed him'....?"

I repeated the passage. He remembered it, and heard me to the end, and I saw that he was uneasy. Two passers-by stopped and listened. The grenadier seemed to be troubled that he should be condemned for doing his duty in driving persons away as he was ordered to drive them away. He was confused, and evidently sought for an excuse. Suddenly a light flashed in his intelligent dark eyes; he looked at me over his shoulder, as if he were about to move away.

"And have you read the military regulation?" he asked.

I said that I had not read it.

"Then don't speak to me," said the grenadier, with a triumphant wag of the head, and buttoning up his tulup he marched gallantly away to his post.

He was the only man that I ever met who had solved, with an inflexible logic, the question which eternally confronted me in social relations, and which rises continually before every man who calls himself a Christian.

CHAPTER III

We are wrong when we say that the Christian doctrine is concerned only with the salvation of the individual, and has nothing to do with questions of State. Such an assertion is simply a bold and proofless affirmation of a most manifest untruth, which, when we examine it seriously, falls of itself to the ground. It is well, I said to myself; I will not resist evil; I will turn the other cheek in private life; but if the enemy comes, or here is an oppressed nation, and I am called upon to do my part in the struggle against evil men, to go forth and kill them, I must decide the question, to serve God or *tohu*, to go to war or not to go. I am a peasant; I am appointed starshina of a village, a judge, a juryman; I am obliged to take the oath of office, to judge, to condemn. What ought I to do? Again I must choose between God's law and the human law. I am a monk, I live in a monastery; the neighboring peasants trespass on our pasturage, and I am appointed to take part in the struggle with the evil doers, to plead for justice against the muzhiks. Again I must choose. No man can escape the decision of this question.

I do not speak of those, the largest part of whose activity is spent in resisting evil: military men, judges, governors. No one is so obscure as not to be obliged to choose between God's service, the fulfilment of His commandments, and the service of *tohu*, in his relation to the State. My personal existence is entangled with that of the State, but the State exacts from me an unchristian activity directly contrary to Christ's commands. Now, with general military conscription and the part that every man, in his quality as juror, must take in judicial affairs, this dilemma arises before every one with remarkable definiteness. Every man is forced to take up murderous weapons — the gun, the sword; and even if he does not get as far as murder, his carbine must be loaded, and his sword keen of edge; that is, he must be ready for murder. Every citizen is forced into the ser vice of the courts to take part in meting out judgment and sentence; that is, to deny Christ's command regarding non-resistance of evil, in acts as well as in words.

Mankind to-day faces the grenadier's problem: the gospel or military regulations, divine law or human law, exactly as Samuel faced it. Christ Himself faced it, and so did His disciples; and those that would be Christians now face it; and I also faced it.

Christ's law, with its doctrine of love, humility, and self-denial, had always long before touched my heart and attracted me to it. But everywhere, in history, in the events that were going on about me, in my individual life, I saw a contrary law revolting to my heart, my conscience, and my reason, and encouraging to my animal instincts. I felt that if I adopted Christ's law, I should be alone; I might be unhappy; I was likely to be persecuted and afflicted as Christ had said. But if I adopted the human law, every one would approve; I should be in peace and safety, with all the capabilities of intellect at my command to put my conscience at ease. As Christ said, I should laugh and be glad. I felt this, and so I did not analyze the meaning of Christ's law, but sought to understand it in such a way that it might not interfere with my life as an animal. But it was impossible to understand it in that way, and so I did not understand it at all.

Through this lack of understanding, I reached a degree of blindness which now astounds me. As an instance in point, I will adduce my former understanding of these words, —

"*Judge not, that ye be not judged.*" [1]

"*Judge not, and ye shall not be judged; condemn not, and ye shall not be condemned.*" [2]

The courts in which I served, and which insured the safety of my property and my person, seemed to be institutions so indubitably sacred and so entirely in accord with the divine law, it had never entered into my head that the words I have quoted could have any other meaning than an injunction not to speak ill of one's neighbor.

[1] Matt. vii. 1. [2] Luke vi. 37.

It never entered into my head that Christ spoke in these words of the court of the zemstvo, of the criminal tribunal, of the circuit court, and all the senates and departments. Only when I understood the true meaning of the words, "*Resist not evil*," did the question arise as to Christ's relation to all these courts and departments; and when I understood that Christ would renounce them, I asked myself, "Is not this the real meaning: Not only do not judge your neighbor, do not speak ill of him; but do not judge him in the courts, do not judge him in any of the tribunals that you have instituted?"

Now in Luke (vi. 37-49) these words follow immediately the doctrine that exhorts us to resist not evil and to render for evil, good. And after the injunction, "*Be ye therefore merciful, as your Father also is merciful*," it says, "*Judge not, and ye shall not be judged; condemn not, and ye shall not be condemned.*"

"*Judge not;*" I asked myself, "does not this mean, Institute no tribunals for the judgment of your neighbor"? I had only to put this question boldly, when heart and reason united in an affirmative reply.

I know how surprising at first such an understanding of these words must be. It also surprised me. In order to show how far I was before from the true interpretation, I shall confess a shameful pleasantry. Even after I had become a believer, and was reading the New Testament as a divine book, on meeting such of my friends as were judges or attorneys, I was in the habit of saying, "And you still judge, although it is said, 'Judge not, and ye shall not be judged'?" I was so sure that these words could have no other meaning than a condemnation of evil speaking that I did not comprehend the horrible blasphemy I thus committed. I was so thoroughly convinced that these words did not mean what they did mean, that I quoted them in their true sense in the form of a pleasantry.

I shall relate in detail how it was that all doubt with regard to the true meaning of these words was effaced from my mind, and how I saw their purport to be that Christ denounced the institution of all human tribunals, of whatever sort; that he meant to say so, and could not have expressed himself otherwise.

When I understood the command, "*Resist not evil,*" in its proper sense, the first thing that occurred to me was that human tribunals, instead of conforming to this law, were directly opposed to it, and indeed to the entire doctrine; and therefore that if Christ had thought of tribunals at all, He would have condemned them.

Christ said, "*Resist not evil.*" The aim of tribunals is to resist evil. Christ exhorted us to *return good for evil;* tribunals return evil for evil. Christ said, Make no distinction between the good and the evil; tribunals do nothing else. Christ said, *Forgive; forgive not once or seven times*, but without limit; *love your enemies, do good to them that hate you*, — but tribunals do not forgive, they punish; they return not good but evil to those whom they regard as the enemies of society. It would seem, then, that Christ denounced judicial institutions.

But perhaps, said I to myself, Christ never had anything to do with courts of justice, and so did not think of them. But I saw that such a theory was not tenable. Jesus, from His childhood to His death, was concerned with the tribunals of Herod, of the Sanhedrim, and of the High Priests. I saw that Jesus must really have spoken many times of the courts of justice as of an evil. He told His disciples that they would be dragged before the judges, and He Himself told them how to behave in court. He said of Himself that He should be condemned by a tribunal, and He showed what the attitude toward judges ought to be. Christ then must have had in mind the judicial institutions that condemned Him and His disciples; that have condemned and continue to condemn millions of men.

Christ saw the wrong, and pointed it out. When the sentence against the woman taken in adultery was about to be carried into execution, He absolutely repudiated the judgment, and demonstrated that man could not be the judge, since man himself was guilty. And this idea He propounded many times, as where it is declared that the man with a beam in his eye cannot see the mote in another's eye, or that the blind cannot lead the blind. He even pointed out the consequences of such misconceptions, — the disciple would be the same as his Master.

But, perhaps, after having said this in regard to the judgment of the woman taken in adultery, and illustrated the general weakness of humanity by the parable of the beam; perhaps, after all, Christ would admit of an appeal to the justice of men where it was necessary for protection against evil men; but I soon saw that this is inadmissible. In the Sermon on the Mount, he says, addressing the multitude, —

"*And if any man will sue thee at the law, and take away thy coat, let him have thy cloak also.*"[1]

Of course He forbids all men to go to law.

Once more, perhaps, Christ spoke only of the personal bearing which a man should have when brought before judicial institutions, and did not condemn justice, but admitted the necessity in a Christian society of individuals who judge others in properly constituted forms. But I saw that this view also is inadmissible. In the Lord's prayer all men, without exception, are commanded to forgive others, that their own trespasses may be forgiven. This thought Christ often expresses. He who brings his gift to the altar with prayer must first forgive all men. How, then, can a man judge and condemn when his religion commands him to forgive all trespasses without limit? So I saw that according to Christ's teaching no Christian judge could pass sentence of condemnation.

But might not the relation between the words "*Judge not, and ye shall not be judged*" and the preceding or subsequent passages permit us to conclude that Christ, in saying, "*Judge not,*" had no reference to human tribunals? No; this could not be so: on the contrary, it is clear from the relation of the phrases that in saying "*Judge not,*" Christ did actually speak of judicial institutions. According to Matthew and Luke, before saying "*Judge not, condemn not,*" He said, "*Resist not evil; endure evil; do good to all men.*" And prior to this, as

[1] Matt. v. 40.

Matthew tells us, He repeated the ancient criminal law of the Jews, "*An eye for an eye, and a tooth for a tooth.*" Then, after this reference to the old criminal law, He added, "*But I say unto you, That ye resist not evil;*" and, after that, "*Judge not.*" Jesus did, then, refer directly to human criminal law, and repudiated it in the words, "*Judge not.*"

Moreover, according to Luke, He not only said, "*Judge not,*" but also, "*Condemn not.*" He had some purpose in adding this almost synonymous word; the addition of this word can have only one object: it shows clearly what meaning should be attributed to the other.

If He had wished to say "Judge not your neighbor," He would have said "neighbor"; but He added the words which are translated "*Condemn not,*" and then completed the sentence, "*And ye shall not be condemned; forgive, and ye shall be forgiven.*"

But some may still insist that Christ, in expressing Himself in this way, did not refer at all to the tribunals, and that I have read my own thoughts into words of His that have a different significance. I will ask how Christ's first disciples, the apostles, regarded courts of justice, — whether they recognized and approved of them. The apostle James says: —[1]

"*Speak not evil one of another, brethren. He that speaketh evil of his brother, and judgeth his brother, speaketh evil of the law, and judgeth the law: but if thou judge the law, thou art not a doer of the law, but a judge. There is one lawgiver, who is able to save and to destroy: who art thou that judgest another?*"

The word translated "speak evil" is the verb καταλαλέω. It may be seen, without consulting a lexicon, that this word ought to mean "to speak against, to accuse"; and this is its true meaning, as any one may find out for himself by opening a lexicon. In the translation we read, "*He that speaketh evil of his brother, ... speaketh evil of the law.*" Why so? is the question that involuntarily arises. I may speak evil of my brother, but I do not thereby speak evil of the law; but if I *accuse*

[1] James iv. 11, 12.

my brother, if I bring him to court, it is plain that I thereby accuse Christ's law; in other words, I consider Christ's law inadequate: I accuse and judge the law. It is clear, then, that I do not practise His law, but that I make myself a judge of the law. The judge, says Christ, is he who can save. How then shall I, who cannot save, become a judge and punish?

The entire passage refers to human justice, and repudiates it. The whole epistle is permeated with the same idea. In the second chapter we read: —

"(1) *My brethren, faith in our Lord Jesus Christ the glorified should be without respect of persons.*

"(2) *For if there come into your synagogue a man with a gold ring, in rich apparel, and there come in also a poor man in vile raiment* (3) *and you have respect to him that wears the rich apparel and you say to him: 'It is seemly for you to sit here,' and you say to the poor man: 'You stand there or sit here under my foot-stool';* (4) *are you not then partial among yourselves, and are you not become judges with evil thoughts?*

"(5) *Hearken, my beloved brethren, has not God chosen the poor of this world to be rich in faith and heirs of the kingdom which He promised to those that love Him?* (6) *But you despised the poor! Do not the rich oppress you, and do they not draw you before the judgment-seat?* (7) *Do they not dishonor the worthy name by which you are called?*

"(8) *If you fulfil the royal law according to the Scripture, — Thou shalt love thy neighbor as thyself,*[1] *— you do well.* (9) *But if you have respect to persons, you commit sin, and are convicted as transgressors before the law.* (10) *For whosoever shall keep the whole law and offend in one point, he is guilty in all.* (11) *For he that said, 'Do not commit adultery' said also 'Do not kill.' Now if thou commit no adultery, yet if thou kill, thou art become a transgressor of the law.*[2]

"(12) *So speak and so do as men that shall be judged by the law of liberty.*

"(13) *For he shall have judgment without mercy, that*

[1] Lev. xix. 18. [2] Deut. xxii. 22; Lev. xviii. 17–25.

hath shewed no mercy; and mercy shall triumph over judgment."[1]

(The last phrase, "*mercy shall triumph over judgment,*" has been frequently translated "*mercy is exalted above judgment,*" and cited thus in the sense that there can be such a thing as Christian judgment, but that it ought to be merciful.)

James exhorts his brethren to have no respect of persons. If you διασκρίβιτε — have respect of the condition of persons, — you discriminate; you are like the untrustworthy judges of the tribunals. You regard the beggar as worse, while on the contrary the rich man is worse. He oppresses you and draws you before the judgment-seats. If you live according to the law of love for your neighbor, according to the law of mercy (which James calls "*the law of liberty,*" to distinguish it from all others) — if you live according to this law, it is well. But if you have respect of persons, if you make discriminations among men, you transgress the law of mercy. Then, doubtless thinking of the case of the woman taken in adultery, who was brought before Jesus, about to be stoned to death according to the law, or thinking of the crime of adultery in general, James says that he who inflicts death on the adulterous woman would himself be guilty of murder, and thereby transgress the eternal law; for the eternal law forbids both adultery and murder. He says: —

"*So speak ye, and so do, as they that shall be judged by the law of liberty. For he shall have judgment without mercy, that hath shewed no mercy; and therefore mercy blots out judgment.*"[2]

Could the idea be expressed in terms more clear and precise? All discrimination among men is forbidden, as well as any judgment that shall classify persons as good or bad; human judgment is declared to be inevitably defective, and such judgment is denounced as criminal when it condemns for crime; judgment is blotted out by the law of God, the law of mercy.

[1] Jas. ii. 13. (Count Tolstoï's rendering.)
[2] Jas. ii. 12, 13.

I open the epistles of the Apostle Paul, who had been a victim of tribunals, and in the first chapter of Romans I read the admonitions of the apostle for the vices and errors of those to whom his words are addressed; among other matters he speaks of courts of justice: —

"*Who, knowing the righteous judgment of God, that they which commit such things are worthy of death, not only do the same, but have pleasure in them that do them.*"[1]

"*Therefore thou art inexcusable, O man, whosoever thou art that judgest another: for wherein thou judgest another, thou condemnest thyself; for thou that judgest another doest the same things.*

"*But we know that the judgment of God against those that do such things is righteous.*

"*And thinkest thou, O man, to escape the judgment of God, when thou judgest those that do such things, and yet doest them thyself?*

"*Or despisest thou the riches of His goodness and forbearance and longsuffering: not knowing that the goodness of God leadeth thee to repentance?*"[2]

The Apostle Paul says that they who know the righteous judgment of God, themselves act unjustly and teach others to do the same, and therefore it is impossible to absolve a man who judges.

Such an opinion regarding tribunals I find in the epistles of the apostles, and we know that human justice was among the trials and sufferings that they endured with resignation to the will of God. When we think of the situation of the early Christians, in the midst of heathen, we can easily understand that it could never have occurred to the Christians persecuted by human tribunals to defend human tribunals. Only on occasion could they touch upon this evil, denying that on which it is based, and thus they did. The apostles speak of this evil.

I consulted with the early Fathers of the Church, and found that they all invariably had distinct teaching which distinguishes them from all others — in this re

[1] Rom. i. 32.
[2] Rom. ii. 1-4.

spect, that they laid no obligation on any one, they did not judge[1] or condemn any one, and that they endured the tortures inflicted by human justice. The martyrs, by their acts, declared themselves to be of the same mind. I saw that Christianity before Constantine regarded tribunals only as an evil which was to be endured with patience; but it never could have occurred to any early Christian that a Christian could take part in the administration of the courts of justice.

I saw that Christ's words, "*Judge not, condemn not,*" were understood by His first disciples exactly as I understood them now, in their direct and literal meaning: judge not in courts of justice; take no part in them.

All this seemed absolutely to corroborate my conviction that the words, "*Judge not, condemn not,*" referred to the justice of tribunals. Yet the meaning, "Speak not evil of your neighbor," is so firmly established, and courts of justice flaunt their decrees with so much assurance and audacity in all Christian countries, with the support even of the Church, that for a long time still I doubted the correctness of my interpretation.

"If men have understood the words in this way," I said to myself, "and have instituted Christian tribunals, they must certainly have some reason for so doing; there must be a good reason for regarding these words as a denunciation of evil speaking, and there must be a basis of some sort for the institution of Christian tribunals."

I turned to the Church commentaries. In all, from the fifth century onward, I found the invariable interpretation to be, "Accuse not your neighbor;" that is, avoid evil speaking. As the words came to be understood exclusively in this sense, a difficulty arose, — How to refrain from judgment? It is impossible not to condemn evil; and so all the commentators discussed the question, What is blamable, and what is not blamable? Some, such as Chrysostom and Theophylact, said that, as far as servants of the Church were concerned,

[1] Athenagoras, Origen.

the phrase could not be construed as a prohibition of judgment, since the apostles themselves judged men. Others said that Christ doubtless referred to the Jews, who accused their neighbors of shortcomings, and were themselves guilty of great sins.

Nowhere a word about human institutions, about tribunals, to show how they were affected by the warning, "*Judge not.*" Did Jesus sanction courts of justice, or did he not?

To this natural question I found no reply—as if it was evident that from the moment a Christian took his seat on the judge's bench he might not only judge his neighbor, but condemn him to death.

I turned to other writers, Greek, Catholic, Protestant, —to the Tübingen school, to the historical school. All, even the most liberal commentators, interpreted the words in question as an injunction against evil speaking.

But why, contrary to the spirit of the whole doctrine of Christ, are these words interpreted in such a narrow way as to exclude courts of justice from the injunction, "*Judge not*"? Why is it supposed that Christ, in forbidding as an offense the judgment of a neighbor which may involuntarily slip from the tongue, did not forbid, did not even consider, the more deliberate judgment that results in punishment inflicted upon the condemned? To this there is no response; not even an allusion to the least possibility that the words "to judge" could be used as referring to a court of justice, to the tribunals from whose punishments millions have suffered.

Moreover, when the words, "*Judge not, condemn not,*" are under discussion, the cruelty of judging in courts of justice is passed over in silence, or else commended. The commentators and theologians all declare that in Christian countries tribunals are necessary, and are not contrary to the law of Christ.

Realizing this, I began to doubt the sincerity of the commentators, and I did what I should have done in the first place; I turned to the translation of the words rendered "to judge" and "to condemn." In the original these words are *κρίνω* and *καταδικάζω*. The defective translation in the Epistle of James of the word καταλαλέω which is rendered "to speak evil," strengthened my doubts as to the correct translation of the others. When I looked through different versions of the Gospels, I found καταδικάζω rendered in the Vulgate by *condemnare*, "to condemn"; in the French it is the same; in the Slavonian the rendering is *asuzhdaïte*, "condemn." Luther has *verdammen*, "to curse."

The divergency of these renderings increased my doubts, and I propounded to myself this question: What is and what must be the meaning of the Greek word κρίνω, as used by the two evangelists, and of καταδικάζω, as used by Luke, who, scholars tell us, wrote very correct Greek.

How would these words be translated by a man who knew nothing of the evangelical creed and its commentators, and who had before him only this sentence?

I consulted the general lexicon, and found that the word κρίνω has several different meanings, the one most used being "to condemn in a court of justice," and even "to condemn to death," but in no instance does it signify "to speak evil." I consulted a lexicon of New Testament Greek, and found that it was often used in the sense "to condemn in a court of justice," sometimes in the sense "to choose," never as meaning "to speak evil." And so I inferred that the word κρίνω might be translated in different ways, but that the rendering "to speak evil" was the most forced and far-fetched.

I looked for the word καταδικάζω, which follows κρίνω, evidently to define more closely the sense in which the first word is understood by the writer. I looked for καταδικάζω in the general lexicon, and found that it never had any other signification than "to condemn in judgment," or "to judge worthy of death." I examined the contents and found that the word was used four times in the New Testament, each time in the sense "to condemn under sentence, to judge worthy of death." In James (v. 6) we read, "*Ye have condemned and killed the just.*" The word rendered "condemned" is this same καταδικάζω, and is used with reference to Christ, who was judged. The word is never used in any other sense in the New Testament or in any other writing in the Greek language.

What, then, are we to say to all this? To what degree is my conclusion lame? Are not all of us who live in our circle, whenever we consider the fate of humanity, filled with horror at the sufferings and the evil inflicted on mankind by the enforcement of criminal codes, — a scourge to those who condemn as well as to the condemned, — from the slaughters of Genghis Khan to those of the French Revolution and the executions of our own times? He would indeed be without compassion who could refrain from feeling horror and repulsion, not only at the sight of human beings thus treated by their kind, but at the simple recital of death inflicted by the knout, the guillotine, or the gibbet.

The Gospel, every word of which we regard as sacred, declares distinctly and without equivocation: "You have a criminal law, a tooth for a tooth; but I give you a new law, That you resist not evil. Obey this law; render not evil for evil, but do good to every one, forgive every one, under all circumstances."

Further on comes the injunction, "*Judge not*"; and that these words might not be misunderstood, Christ added, "*Condemn not;* condemn not to punishment."

My heart said clearly, distinctly, "Punish not with death." "Punish not with death," said Science; "the more you kill, the more evil increases." Reason said, "Punish not with death; evil cannot suppress evil." The Word of God, in which I believed, said the same thing. And when, in reading the doctrine, I came to the words, "*Condemn not, and ye shall not be condemned; forgive, and ye shall be forgiven,*" I confessed that this was God's Word, and I declared that it meant that I was not to indulge in gossip and evil speaking, and yet I continued to regard tribunals as a Christian institution, and myself as a Christian judge!

I was overwhelmed with horror at the grossness of the error into which I had fallen.

CHAPTER IV

I NOW understood what Christ said when he said: "*Ye have heard that it hath been said, An eye for an eye, and a tooth for a tooth: but I say unto you, That ye resist not evil, but endure it.*"

Christ says: "You have thought that you were acting in a reasonable manner in defending yourself by violence against evil, in tearing out an eye for an eye, by establishing criminal tribunals, guardians of the peace, armies; by resisting your enemies; but I say unto you: Do no violence; have no share in violence; do harm to no one, not even to those that you consider your enemies."

I understood now that on the ground Christ took with regard to the non-resistance of evil, He not only told us what would result from the observance of this rule, but established a new basis for society conformable to His doctrine, and opposed to the social basis established by the law of Moses, by Roman law, and by the different codes in force to-day. He formulated a new law, the effect of which would be to deliver humanity from the evil which it has brought on itself.

He said: "You believe that your laws correct evil; as a matter of fact, they only increase it. There is only one way to suppress evil, and that is to return good for evil, without distinction. For thousands of years you have tried that method; now try mine, try the reverse."

A strange fact: in these later days, I have often talked with different persons about this commandment of Christ, "*Resist not evil,*" and rarely have I found any one to agree with me! Two classes of men would never, even in principle, admit the literal interpretation of this law, always hotly defended the justice of resisting evil. These men were at two opposite poles, — they were the conservative Christian patriots who called their Church the true one, and the atheistic revolutionists.

Neither of these two classes is willing to renounce the right to resist by violence what they regard as evil

And the wisest and most intelligent among them will never acknowledge the simple and evident truth, that if we once admit the right of any man to resist by violence what he regards as evil, every other man has equally the right to resist by violence what he regards as evil.

Not long ago I had in my hands an interesting correspondence between an orthodox Slavyanophile and a Christian revolutionist. The one advocated the violence of war in the name of the oppressed Slav brethren; the other, the violence of revolution in the name of our brethren, the oppressed Russian peasantry. Both invoked violence, and both rested on the doctrine of Christ.

Christ's doctrine is understood in a hundred different ways, but never in the simple and direct way which harmonizes with the inevitable meaning of His words.

We have arranged our entire social fabric on the very principles that Jesus repudiated; we do not wish to understand His doctrine in its simple and direct acceptation, and yet we assure ourselves and others, either that we follow His doctrine, or else that His doctrine is not expedient for us.

So-called believers believe that Christ-God, the second person of the Trinity, descended upon earth to teach men by His example how to live; they go through the most elaborate ceremonies for the consummation of the sacraments, the building of churches, the sending out of missionaries, the establishment of priesthoods, for parochial administration, for the performance of rituals; but they forget one little detail, — to do what He said.

Unbelievers endeavor in every possible way to organize their existence independent of the Christ's law, having decided that this law is not expedient for them. But to endeavor to put His teachings in practice, this no one wishes to do; and moreover, without any attempt to put them in practice, both believers and unbelievers have decided in advance that it is impossible.

He said, simply and clearly, this law of resistance to evil by violence, which you have made the basis of your life, is false and wrong; and He gave another basis, that of non-resistance to evil, a law which, according to His doctrine, would deliver man from evil. He says: —

"You believe that your laws, which resort to violence, correct evil; they only augment it. For thousands of years you have tried to destroy evil by evil, and you have not destroyed it; you have only augmented it. Do as I command you, as I do, and you will know that this is true."

Not only in words, but by His whole life and by His death, did He carry out His doctrine of the non-resistance of evil.

Believers listen to all this. They hear it in their churches, persuaded that the words are divine; they call Him God, but they say: —

"All this is very good, but it is impossible as society is now organized; it would derange our whole life, which we are accustomed to, and love! And so we believe it all, but only in this sense: That it is the ideal toward which humanity ought to strive; the ideal which is to be attained by prayer, and by believing in the sacraments, in the redemption, and in the resurrection of the dead."

The others, the unbelievers, the free-thinkers, who comment on Christ's doctrine, the historians of religions, the Strausses, the Renans, — completely imbued with the teachings of the Church, which says that Christ's teaching has no direct application to life, but is a visionary doctrine, the consolation of feeble minds, tell us that it was all very well preached in the fishermen's huts by Galilee; but that for us it is only the sweet dream *du charmant docteur*, as Renan calls Him.

In their opinion Christ could not rise to the height of comprehending all the wisdom attained by our civilization and culture. If He had stood on that height of cultivation whereon stand these learned men, He never would have uttered His charming nonsense about the birds of the air, the turning of the other cheek, the taking no thought for the morrow. These learned historians judge of the value of Christianity by what they see of it in our society. The Christianity of our society and our time regards life, with its present organization, as true and sacred; with its prison-cells and solitary confinement, its alcazars, its factories, its newspapers, its houses of infamy, its parliaments; and only as much of Christ's teaching is accepted as does not interfere with this life. Since Christ's teaching is opposed to all this life, then nothing of it is accepted except the empty words. The historical critics see this, and, unlike the so-called believers, having no motives for concealment, submit this empty form of Christ's teaching to a profound analysis; they refute it systematically, and prove that Christianity is made up of nothing but chimerical ideas.

It would seem that before criticising Christ's teaching, it would be necessary to understand what it consisted of; and to decide whether His doctrine is reasonable or not, it would be well first to realize that He said exactly what He said. And this none of us do — either Church commentators or free-thinkers — and we know very well why we do not.

We know perfectly well that Christ's teaching repudiates and has always repudiated all human errors, all *tohu*, all the empty idols that we try to except from the category of errors, by dubbing them "Church," "State," "Culture," "Science," "Art," "Civilization." But Jesus spoke against all these, not excusing any form of *tohu*.

Not only Jesus, but all the Hebrew prophets, and John the Baptist, and all the true sages of the world, have denounced the Church and State and culture and civilization of their times as sources of man's perdition.

Imagine an architect who says to a house-owner, "Your house is good for nothing; it needs to be entirely rebuilt," and then describes how the supports are to be cut and where they are to be fastened. The proprietor turns a deaf ear to the words, "Your house is good for nothing, and needs to be rebuilt," and pretends to listen respectfully when the architect begins to discuss the internal changes and arrangements. Evidently, in this case, all the architect's advice will seem to be impracticable; and a less respectful house-owner would call it nonsensical. Precisely in this way we treat Christ's teaching.

I give this illustration for want of a better. I remember now that Jesus, in teaching His doctrine, made use of the same comparison. "*Destroy this temple,*" He said, "*and in three days I will raise it up.*" And for this they crucified Him; and for this they now crucify His doctrine.

The least that can be asked of men who pass judgment upon any doctrine is that they shall judge of it as the teacher himself understood it. Jesus understood His doctrine, not as a distant ideal impossible of attainment, not as a collection of fantastic and poetical reveries with which to charm the simple-hearted inhabitants of Galilee; He understood it as a reality, a reality which should be the salvation of mankind. He was not dreaming as He hung on the cross, but He cried out and He died for His doctrine. And thus many men have died, and still die. It is impossible to say that such a doctrine is a dream.

All teaching of the truth is chimerical to those lost in error. We have gone so far that many people — and I was of the number — say that this teaching is chimerical because it is contrary to human nature. It is against nature, they say, to turn the other cheek when we have been struck, to give our own to others, to toil, not for ourselves, but for others. It is natural, they say, for a man to defend his person, his family, his property; that is to say, it is the nature of man to struggle for existence. A learned lawyer has proved scientifically that the most sacred duty of man is to defend his rights; that is, to fight.

But the moment we detach ourselves from the idea that the existing organization established by man is the best — is sacred, — the moment we do this, the objection that Christ's teaching is contrary to human nature is immediately turned against him who makes it. No one will deny that not only to kill or torture a man, but to torture a dog, to kill a fowl or a calf, is repugnant and painful to human nature. (I know men living by agricultural labor who have ceased to eat meat solely because it had fallen to their lot to slaughter their animals.) And yet the whole organization of our life is such that every personal enjoyment is purchased at the price of human suffering contrary to human nature.

The whole organization of our life, all the complicated mechanism of our institutions, which are based on violence, testifies that violence is contrary to human nature.

No judge, though he has condemned the criminal to death according to the code, is willing to hang him with his own hands; no nachalnik would tear a muzhik from his weeping family and cast him into prison; no general or soldier, untrained by discipline and service in war, would slay a hundred Turks or Germans or destroy their village, or even wound a single man. Yet all these things are done, thanks to the complicated administrative and social machinery, the task of which is to divide responsibility for misdeeds in such a way that no one feels them to be contrary to nature.

One class of men makes the laws; another executes them; a third trains men to habits of discipline, that is, to automatic and unquestioning obedience; a fourth class — and these are the most severely trained of all — does all kinds of violence, even slay their fellows without knowing why or to what end. But let a man free himself in thought for a moment from this network of human organization in which he is entangled, and he will readily see that it is contrary to his nature.

Let us abstain from affirming that organized violence, of which we make use to our own profit, is a divine, immutable truth, and we shall see clearly which is most in harmony with human nature, — violence or the Christ's teaching.

What is the law of nature? Is it to know that my security and that of my family, all my amusements and pleasures, are purchased by the poverty, corruption, and suffering of millions, by the annual crop of criminals, by hundreds of thousands of suffering prisoners; by millions of soldiers and guardians of civilization, torn from their homes and stupefied by discipline, to protect our pleasures with loaded revolvers against famishing men? Is it to purchase every fragment of bread that I put in my mouth and the mouths of my children by the numberless privations that are necessary to procure my abundance? Or is it to be certain that my piece of bread only belongs to me when I know that every one else has a share, and that no one suffers because of it.

It is only necessary to understand that, thanks to our social organization, each one of our pleasures, every minute of tranquillity under our organization of life, is obtained by the sufferings and privations of thousands held down by violence—it is only necessary to understand this to know what is conformable to human nature; not to our animal nature alone, but the animal and spiritual nature which constitutes man. When we once understand Christ's law in all its significance, with all its consequences, we shall understand that His teaching is not contrary to human nature; but that its sole object is to supplant the unnatural and chimerical law of the resistance of evil which makes their lives so unhappy.

Christ's teaching regarding the non-resistance of evil vain![1] How about the life of those in whose hearts love and compassion for their kind were originally planted—but who make ready for their fellow-men punishment at the stake, by the knout, the wheel, the rack, chains, compulsory labor, the gibbet, solitary confinement, prisons for women and children, the slaughter of tens of thousands in war, or bring about periodical revolutions and Pugachof rebellions; of those who carry these horrors into execution; of those who benefit by these horrors; of those who try to avoid these sufferings and take their revenge for them,—is not such a life vain?

We need only understand Christ's teaching to understand that this world,—not the world which God gave for the happiness of man, but the world men have organized to their own hurt,—that such an existence is a vanity, the most savage and horrible of vanities, a

[1] *Metchta*, a dream, illusion, vanity.

veritable delirium of madness, from which, when once we have been awakened, we do not again return to such a horrible delusion!

God descended to earth; the Son of God, one person of the Trinity, became incarnate, redeemed Adam's sin, and (so we were taught to believe) this God said many mysterious and mystical things which are difficult to understand — which it is not possible to understand except by the aid of faith and grace — and suddenly the words of God are found to be so simple, so clear, and so reasonable! God said, Do no evil to one another, and evil will cease to exist. Was the revelation from God really so simple — nothing but that? It would seem that we all might understand it, it is so simple!

The prophet Elijah, a fugitive from men, took refuge in a cave, and was told that God would appear to him. There came a great wind, — the trees were uprooted. Elijah thought that this was God, and he looked, but the Lord was not in the wind. After the wind came tempest; the thunder and the lightning were terrific and Elijah went to see if God was there; but God was not there. Then came an earthquake: the earth belched forth fire, the rocks were shattered, the mountains were rent; Elijah looked for the Lord, but God was not in the earthquake. Then it became calm; a gentle breeze came to the prophet, bearing the freshness of the fields; and Elijah looked, and God was there. Such are these simple words of God — "*Resist not evil.*"

They are very simple, but, nevertheless, they express God's law and man's law, one and eternal. This law is to such a degree eternal that if there has been in history a progressive movement for the suppression of evil, it is due to the men who understood the doctrine of Jesus — who endured evil and resisted not evil by violence. The advance of humanity toward righteousness is due, not to the tyrants, but to the martyrs. As fire cannot extinguish fire, so evil cannot suppress evil. Only good, confronting evil and resisting its contagion, can overcome evil. And in the inner world of the human soul, the law is as absolute as was even the law of Galileo, more absolute, more clear, more immutable. Men may turn aside from it, they may hide its truth from others; but the progress of humanity toward righteousness can be attained only in this way. Every forward step must be taken only in the name of the non-resistance of evil. A disciple of Christ may say now, with greater assurance than did Galileo, in spite of misfortunes and threats: "And yet it is not violence, but good, that overcomes evil." If the progress is slow, it is because Christ's teaching (which, through its clearness, simplicity, and wisdom, appeals so inevitably to human nature), has been most cunningly and dangerously hidden from the majority of mankind under an entirely different teaching falsely called His.

CHAPTER V

THE true meaning of Christ's teaching was revealed to me; everything confirmed its truth. But for a long time I could not accustom myself to the strange idea, that after the eighteen centuries during which Christ's law had been professed by milliards of human beings, after thousands of men had consecrated their lives to the study of this law, I had discovered it for myself as something new.

But strange as it seemed, so it was. Christ's teaching regarding the non-resistance of evil was to me wholly new, something of which I had never before had the slightest conception. I asked myself how this could be; I must certainly have had a false idea of Christ's teaching to cause such a misunderstanding. And a false idea of it I unquestionably had.

When I began to read the Gospel, I was not in the condition of a man who, having heard nothing of Christ's teaching, becomes acquainted with it for the first time; on the contrary, I had a preconceived theory as to the manner in which I ought to understand it. Christ did not appear to me as a prophet revealing the divine law, but as one who continued and amplified the absolute divine law which I already knew; for I had very definite and complex notions about God, about the creation of the world and of man, and about the commandments of God given to men through the instrumentality of Moses.

In the Gospels I came to the words, "*It has been said to you, An eye for an eye, and a tooth for a tooth: But I say unto you, That you resist not evil.*" These words, "*An eye for an eye, and a tooth for a tooth,*" was the law given by God to Moses; the words, "*But I say unto you, That you resist not evil,*" was a new law which denied the first.

If I had simply referred to Christ's teaching without the theological theory that I had imbibed with my mother's milk, I should simply have understood the simple meaning of Christ's words. I should have understood that Christ abrogated the old law, and gave His new law. But I had been taught that Christ did not abrogate the law of Moses, but that, on the contrary, He confirmed it to the slightest iota, and that He made it more complete.

Verses 17–20 of the fifth chapter of Matthew in which this was included had always impressed me, when I read the Gospel, by their obscurity, and they plunged me into doubt. I knew the Old Testament, particularly the last books of Moses, very thoroughly, and recalling certain passages in which minute doctrines, often absurd and even cruel in their purport, are preceded by the words, "And the Lord said unto Moses," it seemed to me very singular that Christ should confirm all these injunctions; I could not understand why He did so. But I allowed the question to pass without solution, and accepted with confidence the explanations inculcated in my infancy, — that the two laws were equally inspired by the Holy Spirit, that they were in perfect accord, and that Christ confirmed the law of Moses while completing and amplifying it.

I never gave myself any clear account as to the method by which this fulfilment should come about, how the contradictions apparent throughout the whole Gospel, in verses 17–20 of the fifth chapter, and in the words, "*But I say unto you,*" should be reconciled.

Now that I understood the clear and simple meaning of Christ's teaching, I saw clearly that the two laws are directly opposed to one another; that they can never be harmonized; that, instead of supplementing one by the other, we must inevitably choose between the two; and that the received explanation of the verses, Matthew v. 17–20, which had impressed me by their obscurity, must be incorrect.

When I now came to read once more the verses that had before impressed me as so obscure, I was astonished at the clear and simple meaning which was suddenly revealed to me. This meaning was revealed, not by any combination and transposition, but solely by rejecting the artificial explanations with which the words had been encumbered. Christ said: —

"*Think not that I am come to destroy the law or* (the teaching of) *the prophets: I am not come to destroy, but to fulfil. For verily I say unto you, sooner shall heaven and earth pass, than one jot or one tittle shall pass from the law, till all be fulfilled.*" [1]

And in verse 20 He added: —

"*For I say unto you, That except your righteousness shall exceed the righteousness of the scribes and Pharisees, you shall in no case enter into the kingdom of heaven.*"

Christ said: —

I am not come to destroy the eternal law of whose fulfilment your books and prophecies foretell. I am come to teach you the fulfilment of the eternal law; not of the law that your scribes and Pharisees call the divine law, but of that eternal law which is less subject to change than the earth and the heavens.

I have expressed the idea in other words in order to detach the thoughts of my readers from the traditional false interpretation. If this false interpretation had never existed, the idea expressed in the verses could not be rendered in a better or more definite manner.

The view that Jesus did not abrogate the old law

[1] Matt. v. 17, 18.

arises from the arbitrary conclusion that "law" in this passage signifies the written law instead of the law eternal, the reference to the iota — jot and tittle — perhaps furnishing the grounds for such an opinion. But Christ was not speaking of the written law. If Christ in this place had been speaking of the written law, He would have used the expression "the law and the prophets," which He always employed in speaking of the written law; here, however, He uses a different expression, — "the law *or* the prophets." If Christ had meant the written law, He would have used the expression, "the law and the prophets," in the verses that follow and that continue the thought; but He says, briefly, "the law," and without any addition as it stands in this verse. Moreover, according to the Gospel of Luke, Christ made use of the same phraseology, and the context renders the meaning inevitable. According to Luke, Jesus is speaking to the Pharisees, who assumed the justice of their written law. He says: —

"*You justify yourselves before men; but God knows your hearts: for that which is highly esteemed among men is abomination in the sight of God. The law and the prophets were until John: since that time the kingdom of God is preached, and every man presses into it. And it is easier for heaven and earth to pass, than one tittle of the law to fail.*"[1]

In the words, "*The law and the prophets were until John*," Jesus abrogated the written law; in the words, "*And it is easier for heaven and earth to pass, than one tittle of* the law *to fail*," Christ confirmed the law eternal. In the first passage cited He said, "the law *and* the prophets," that is, the written law; in the second He said "the law" simply, therefore the law eternal. It is clear, then, that the eternal law is opposed to the written law,[2] exactly as in the context of Matthew, where the eternal law is defined by the phrase, "the law *or* the prophets."

[1] Luke xvi. 15–17.

[2] More than this, as if to do away with all doubt as to which law He referred, Jesus cites immediately, in connection with this passage, the most

The history of the variants of the text of these verses is quite worthy of notice. The majority of manuscripts have simply "the law," without the addition, "and the prophets." By such a reading there can be no misinterpretation that it signifies the written law. In other manuscripts, notably Tischendorf's, and the canonical, we find the word "prophets" used, not with the conjunction "and," but with the conjunction "or,"—"the law *or* the prophets,"—which also excludes any question of the written law, and indicates the law eternal.

In several manuscripts, not countenanced by the Church, we find the word "prophets" used with the conjunction "and," not with "or"; and in these versions every repetition of the words "the law" is followed by the phrase, "and the prophets." So that the sense as expressed in this transformation would indicate that Christ spoke only of the written law.

These variants furnish a history of the commentaries on the passage. The only clear meaning is that authorized by Luke,—that Christ spoke of the eternal law. But among the copyists of the Gospels were some who desired that the written law of Moses should continue to be regarded as obligatory. They therefore added to the words "the law" the phrase "and the prophets," and changed the sense.

Other Christians, not recognizing the books of Moses, either suppressed the added phrase, or replaced the particle *καί*, "and," with *ἤ*, "or"; and with this substitution the passage was admitted to the canon. Nevertheless, in spite of the unequivocal clearness of the text as thus written, the commentators perpetuated the interpretation supported by the phrase which had been rejected in the canon. The passage evoked innumerable comments, which stray from the true signification in proportion to the lack, on the part of the commen-

decisive instance of the negation of the law of Moses by the eternal law, the law of which not the smallest jot is to fail: "*Whosoever puts away his wife, and marries another, commits adultery*" (Luke xvi. 18). That is, according to the written law divorce is permissible; according to the eternal law it is a sin.—AUTHOR'S NOTE.

tators, of fidelity to the simple and obvious meaning of Christ's teaching, and the majority of them recognize the apocryphal reading rejected by the canonical text.

To be absolutely convinced that in these verses Christ spoke only of the eternal law, we need only examine the true meaning of the word that has given rise to so many false interpretations. The word "law" (in Greek νόμος, in Hebrew תּוֹרָה, *torah*) has in all languages two principal meanings: one, law in the abstract sense, independent of formulæ; the other, the written statutes which men generally recognize as law.

In the Greek of Paul's Epistles the distinction is indicated by the use of the article. Without the article Paul uses νόμος the most frequently in the sense of the eternal law of God.

By the ancient Hebrews, in the prophets, in Isaiah, תּוֹרָה, *torah*, is always used in the sense of an eternal, ineffable revelation, God's own teaching. Not till the time of Esdras, and later in the Talmud, was "Torah," the law, used to distinguish the five books of Moses, just as with us the word "Bible" is used — with this difference, that while we have words to distinguish between the Bible and the law of God, the Jews employed the same word to express both meanings.

And so Christ, using the word law, "torah," sometimes uses it as Isaiah and the other prophets use it, in the sense of the law of God which is eternal, in this case sanctioning it; and sometimes in the sense of the written law of the Pentateuch, rejecting it. But to distinguish the difference, He always, in speaking of the written law to reject it, adds "and the prophets," or prefixes the word "your," — "your law."

When He says, "*Therefore all things whatsoever you would that men should do to you, do you even so to them: for this is the law and the prophets,*"[1] He speaks of the written law. The entire written law, He says, may be reduced to this one expression of the eternal law, and by these words He abrogated the written law. When He says, "*The law and the prophets were until John the*

[1] Matt. vii. 12.

Baptist,"[1] He speaks of the written law, and by these words denies its obligatoriness. When He says, "*Did not Moses give you the law, and yet none of you keeps the law,*"[2] or "*It is also written in your law,*"[3] or "*that the word might be fulfilled that is written in their law,*"[4] He speaks of the written law, the law whose authority He denied, the law that condemned Him to death: "*The Jews answered him, We have a law, and by our law he ought to die.*"[5] It is plain that this Jewish law, which authorized condemnation to death, was not the law which Christ taught. But when Christ says, "*I am not come to destroy the law, but to teach you the fulfilment of the law; for nothing of this law shall be changed, but all shall be fulfilled,*" then He is speaking, not of the written law, but of the divine and eternal law, and sanctions it.

But let us grant that all this is merely formal proof; let us grant that I have carefully combined contexts and variants, and excluded everything contrary to my theory; let us grant that the commentators of the Church are clear and convincing, that, in fact, Christ did not abrogate the law of Moses, but upheld it in all its force, — let us grant this: but even then what were Christ's teachings?

According to the interpretations of the Church, He taught that He was the second person of the Trinity, the Son of God the Father, and that He came into the world to atone by His death for Adam's sin. But every one who has read the Gospels knows that Christ taught nothing of the sort, or at least spoke but very vaguely on these topics. Let us even grant that we cannot read correctly and that He does speak of this. Well, in any case, the passages in which Christ affirms that He is the second person of the Trinity, and that He was to atone for the sins of humanity, form the most inconsiderable and obscurest portion of the Gospels.

In what, then, does the rest of Christ's teaching consist? It is impossible to deny, and all Christians have

[1] Luke xvi. 16.
[2] John vii. 19.
[3] John viii. 17.
[4] John xv. 25.
[5] John xix. 7.

always recognized the fact, that the chief aim of Christ's teaching is to regulate men's lives, — how they ought to live with regard to one another. But to realize that Jesus taught men a new way of life, we must have some idea of the condition of the people to whom His teachings were addressed.

When we examine into the social development of the Russians, or the English, or the Chinese, or the Indians, or even the savages living on islands, we find that each people invariably has certain practical rules or laws of life; consequently, if any one would inculcate a new law of life, he must by this very teaching abolish the former law of life; if he did not abolish it, he could not teach. So it would be in England, in China, or in Russia; in any race or nation this would be inevitable. Laws that we are accustomed to regard as precious, as almost sacred, he would assuredly abrogate; with us, perhaps, it might happen that a reformer who taught a new law would abolish only our civil laws, the official code, our administrative customs, without touching what we consider as our divine laws, although it is difficult to believe that such could be the case.

But with the Jewish people, who had but one law, and wholly divine, — and embracing life in all its minutest details, — what could a reformer reform if he declared in advance that the existing law was inviolable?

But even if we grant it, this is no proof. Let those that interpret Christ's words as an affirmation of the entire Mosaic law explain to their own satisfaction who it was that Christ denounced during the whole of His ministry, who it was He opposed, calling them Pharisees, scribes, doctors of the law? Who were they that rejected Christ's teaching, and, their high priests at their head, crucified Him? If Christ approved the law of Moses, where were the faithful followers of that law, who practised it sincerely, and must thereby have obtained Christ's approval? Is it possible that there was not one such?

The Pharisees, we are told, constituted a sect. The

Hebrews do not say so; they say the Pharisees were the true performers of the law. But let us grant they were a sect. The Sadducees also were a sect. Where, then, were those that did not belong to a sect, the genuine ones?

In the Gospel of John all of Christ's enemies are spoken of directly as "the Jews." They agree with Christ's teaching, and they are hostile to Him because they are Jews. But in the Gospels not only the Pharisees and the Sadducees are shown as the enemies of Jesus: the doctors of the law, those that interpret the law, the elders, those that are always considered as representatives of the people's wisdom, are also called Christ's enemies.

Christ said, "*I am not come to call the righteous, but sinners to repentance*," to change their way of life (*μετάνοια*). But where were the righteous? Was Nicodemus the only one? He is represented as a good but misguided man.

We are so habituated to the singular opinion that Christ was crucified by the Pharisees and a few wicked Jews, that it never occurs to us to ask the simple question, "Where were the true Jews, the good Jews, the Jews that practised the law?" When we have once propounded this query, everything becomes perfectly clear. Christ, whether he was God or man, brought His teaching to a people possessing a law, called the law of God, governing their whole existence. How must Christ have comported Himself toward that law?

Every prophet, every founder of a religion, in revealing the law of God to men, inevitably meets with what these men regard as the law of God; and he cannot avoid a double use of the word "law," one expressing what his hearers wrongfully consider the law of God — "your law;" and the other the law he has come to proclaim, the true, the eternal, law of God. A reformer not only cannot avoid this double use of the word; often he does not wish to avoid it, but purposely confounds the two ideas, thus indicating that, in the law confessed by those whom he would convert, there are still some eternal truths, and every reformer takes these, laws such as embody the truth, as the basis of his teaching.

This is precisely what Christ did among the Hebrews, by whom the two laws were alike called "torah." Christ recognized that the Mosaic law, and still more the prophets, especially the writings of Isaiah, whose words He constantly quotes, contained divine and eternal truths in harmony with the eternal law, and these — as, for instance, love to God and your neighbor — He takes as the basis of His own teaching.

Christ many times expresses this thought. Thus He said, "*What is written in the law? how readest thou?*"[1] Even in the law one can find eternal truth, if one reads it aright. And more than once He affirms that the commandments of the Mosaic law, to love the Lord and one's neighbor, are also commandments of the eternal law. At the conclusion of all the parables by which Christ explained the meaning of His teaching to His disciples, He pronounced words which have a bearing upon all that precedes: —

"*Therefore every scribe instructed in the truth is like a householder who brings forth out of his treasure* (altogether without distinction) *things new and old.*"[2]

The Church universal understands these words just exactly as they were understood by St. Irenæus; but, at the same time, in defiance of the true signification, it arbitrarily attributes to them the meaning that everything old is sacred. The manifest meaning is this: —

He who seeks for the good, takes not only the new, but also the old; and because a thing is old, he does not therefore reject it. By these words Christ meant that He did not deny what was eternal in the old law. But when they spoke to Him of the whole law, or of the formalities exacted by the old law, His reply was that new wine should not be put into old bottles. Christ could not affirm the whole law; neither could He deny the entire teachings of the law and the prophets, — the law in which it says, "*love thy neighbor as thyself,*" and the prophets whose words He often used to express His

[1] Luke x. 26. [2] Matt. xiii. 52.

own thoughts. And yet, in place of this clear and simple explanation of Christ's simple words, we are offered a vague interpretation which introduces needless contradictions, which reduces the doctrine of Jesus to nothingness, and which reëstablishes the doctrine of Moses in all its savage cruelty.

Commentators of the Church, particularly those that have written since the fifth century, tell us that Christ did not abolish the written law, but sanctioned it. But in what way did He sanction it? How can Christ's law harmonize with the law of Moses? To this there is no reply. The commentators all make use of a verbal juggle and say that Christ fulfilled the law of Moses, and that the prophecies were fulfilled in His person, and that Christ fulfilled the law as our mediator by our faith in Him. And only the essential question for every believer — How to harmonize two conflicting laws, each designed to regulate the lives of men? — is left without any attempt at explanation. Thus the contradiction between the verse where it is said that Christ did not come to destroy the law, but to fulfil the law, and the verse where it says, "*You have heard .... But I say unto you,*" — the contradiction between the spirit of the teaching of Moses and the teaching of Christ, — is left in all its force.

Let any one interested in this question look through the Church commentaries touching this passage from the time of John Chrysostom to our day. After a perusal of these long explanations, he will be convinced not only that there is no solution for the contradiction, but that there is an artificially introduced contradiction where there had been none before.

The impossible attempts to reconcile the irreconcilable prove that this reconciliation is not an error of thought, but that the reconciliation has a clear and definite object, that it is necessary. And it is evident why it is necessary.

Here is what John Chrysostom says in reply to those that reject the law of Moses: —

"Further testing the old law, wherein it is commanded to extort an eye for an eye and a tooth for a tooth, the objection is instantly made: 'How can he be blessed who says that? What shall we say to that?' This: that, on the contrary, it is the greatest sign of divine philanthropy.

"He made this law, not that we might strike out one another's eyes, but that fear of suffering by others might restrain us from doing any such thing to them. As, therefore, He threatened the Ninevites with overthrow, not that he might destroy them (for had that been His will, He ought to have been silent), but that He might by fear make them better, and so quiet His wrath: so also hath He appointed a punishment for those who wantonly assail the eyes of others, that if good principle dispose them not to refrain from such cruelty, fear may restrain them from injuring their neighbors' sight.

"And if this be cruelty, it is cruelty also for the murderer to be restrained, and the adulterer checked. But these are the sayings of senseless men, and of those that are mad to the extreme of madness. For I, so far from saying that this comes of cruelty, should say that the contrary to this would be unlawful, according to men's reckoning. And whereas thou sayest, 'Because He commanded to pluck out *an eye for an eye*, therefore He is cruel'; I say that if He had not given this commandment, then He would have seemed, in the judgment of most men, to be that which thou sayest He is."

John Chrysostom clearly recognized the law, *An eye for an eye,* as divine, and the contrary of that law, that is, the Christ's teaching about the non-resistance of evil, as an iniquity "For let us suppose," says Chrysostom further:—

"For let us suppose that this law had been altogether done away, and that no one feared the punishment ensuing thereupon, but that license had been given to all the wicked to follow their own dispositions in all security, to adulterers, and to murderers, to perjured persons, and to parricides; would not all things have been turned upside down? would not cities, market-places and houses, sea and land, and the whole world, have been filled with unnumbered pollutions and murders? Every one sees it. For if, when there are laws, and fear, and threatening, our evil dispositions are hardly checked; were even this security taken away, what is there to prevent men's choosing vice? and what degree of mischief would not then come reveling upon the whole of human life?

"The rather, since cruelty lies not only in allowing the bad to do what they will, but in another thing too quite as much, — to overlook, and leave uncared for, him who hath done no wrong, but who is without cause or reason suffering ill. For tell me; were any one to gather together wicked men from all quarters, and arm them with swords, and bid them go about the whole city, and massacre all that came in their way, could there be anything more like a wild beast than he? And what if some others should bind, and confine with the utmost strictness, those whom that man had armed, and should snatch from those lawless hands them who were on the point of being butchered; could anything be greater humanity than this?"

St. John Chrysostom does not say what would be the estimate of these others in the opinion of the wicked. And what if these others were themselves wicked and cast the innocent into prison? Chrysostom continues: —

"Now then, I bid thee transfer these examples to the Law likewise; for He that commands to pluck out *an eye for an eye* hath laid the fear as a kind of strong chain upon the souls of the bad, and so resembles him who detains those assassins in prison; whereas he who appoints no punishment for them, doth all but arm them by such security, and acts the part of that other, who was putting the swords in their hands, and letting them loose over the whole city." [1]

If John Chrysostom had understood the law of Jesus, he would have said, Who is it that strikes out another's eyes and casts men into prison? If He who commanded to take an eye for an eye — in other words, if God Himself did such things, then there would be no contradiction; but men must do this, and the Son of God has said to these men that they must not do it. God commanded

[1] "Homilies on the Gospel of St. Matthew," xvi.

to strike out teeth and the Son of God commanded not to strike them out! We must accept one commandment or the other; and John Chrysostom, and since his day the whole Church, has accepted the commandment of God-the-Father, that is, of Moses, and denied that of God-the-Son, in other words, of the Christ, whose teaching it nevertheless claims to believe!

Christ abolished the Mosaic law, and gave His own law in its place. To one who really believes in Christ there is not the slightest contradiction; such an one will pay no attention to the law of Moses, but will believe in Christ's law and put it into practice. To one who believes in the law of Moses there is also no contradiction. The Jews regard Christ's words as foolish, and believe in the law of Moses. The contradiction is only for those who would live according to the law of Moses, but persuade themselves and others that they believe in Christ's law — for those whom Christ denounced as hypocrites, as a generation of vipers.

Instead of recognizing as divine truth the one or the other of the two laws, the law of Moses or Christ's, both are considered divine.

But when the question touches the acts of everyday life, Christ's law is rejected and that of Moses is followed. And in this false interpretation, when we realize its importance, is the source of that terrible, that horrible, drama of the struggle between evil and good, between darkness and light.

Christ made His appearance among the Jewish people, trained to the innumerable formal regulations instituted by the Levites in the rubric of divine laws, each preceded by the words, "And the Lord said unto Moses." He found everything, to the minutest detail, prescribed by rule; not only the relation of man with God, but his sacrifices, his feasts, his fasts, his social, civil, and family duties, the details of personal habits, circumcision, the purification of the body, of domestic utensils, of clothing, — all these regulated by laws recognized as God's command and therefore as God's law.

What could any prophet, even the most ordinary

teacher — I don't say the Christ-God — do in establishing his own doctrines among such a people, but abolish the law by which all these details were regulated? Christ, like all the prophets, selected from what men considered as the law of God the portions that were really the law of God; He took what served His purpose, rejected the rest, and on this foundation established His revelation of the eternal law. It was not necessary to abolish all, but inevitable to abrogate much that was looked upon as obligatory.

This Christ did, and was accused of destroying what was considered the law of God; for this He was condemned and put to death. But His teaching remained among His disciples, traversed the centuries, and is transmitted to other peoples. Under these conditions there have grown up again on this new teaching a crop of similar commentaries and explanations, and pitiable human sophisms have replaced the divine revelation. For the formula, "And the Lord said unto Moses," we substitute "Thus saith the Holy Spirit." And again the letter hides the spirit.

Most astounding of all, Christ's teaching is amalgamated with all that "torah," with the written law, the authority of which He was forced to deny. This "torah," this written law, is declared to have been inspired by the Holy Spirit, the spirit of truth; and thus Christ is taken in the snare of His own revelation — and all His doctrine is reduced to nothingness.

This is why, after eighteen hundred years, it so singularly happened that I discovered the meaning of Christ's teaching as some new thing.

But no, I did not discover it; I did simply what all men have done and must do who seek after God and His law; I found what is the eternal law of God amid all that men call by that name.

CHAPTER VI

When I understood Christ's law as Christ's law, and not as the law of Moses and of Christ, when I understood the commandment of this law which directly abrogated the law of Moses, then the Gospels, so obscure, diffuse, and contradictory before, blended for me into a harmonious whole, the substance of whose doctrine, until then incomprehensible, I found to be formulated in terms simple, clear, and accessible to every searcher after truth.[1]

Throughout the Gospels it speaks of Christ's commands and the necessity of practising them. All the theologians discuss Christ's commands; but I did not know before what these commands were. I thought that Christ's command consisted in loving God, and one's neighbor as one's self. I did not see that this could not be Christ's command, since it was given by the ancients (Deuteronomy and Leviticus). The words: —

"*Whosoever therefore shall break one of these least commandments, and shall teach men so, he shall be called the least in the kingdom of heaven: but whosoever shall do and teach them, the same shall be called great in the kingdom of heaven,*"[2] — these words I believed to relate to the Mosaic law. But it never had occurred to me that Christ's new commands were clearly and precisely formulated in Matthew v. 21–48, and I did not see that in the passage where Christ says, "*Ye have heard that it was said .... But I say unto you,*" He formulated a series of very definite commands — five entirely new, counting as one the two references to adultery. I had heard of the beatitudes and of their number; their explanation and enumeration had formed a part of my religious instruction; but I had never heard anything about Christ's commands spoken of. To my astonishment, I was forced to discover them for myself. And this is how I discovered them. In the fifth chapter of Matthew I found these verses: —

[1] Matt. v. 21–48, especially 38.

[2] Matt. v. 19.

"*You have heard that it was said by them of old time, Thou shalt not kill; and whoever shall kill shall be in danger of the judgment:*[1] (22) *But I say unto you, That whoever is angry with his brother without cause shall be in danger of the judgment: and whosoever shall say to his brother, Raca, shall be in danger of the Sanhedrim: but whosoever shall say, Thou fool, shall be in danger of the fiery Gehenna.* (23) *Therefore if thou bring thy gift to the altar, and there rememberest that thy brother hath aught against thee;* (24) *Leave there thy gift before the altar, and go away; first be reconciled to thy brother, and then come and offer thy gift.* (25) *Agree with thine adversary quickly, while thou art in the way with him; lest at any time the adversary deliver thee to the judge, and the judge deliver thee to the officer, and thou be cast into prison.* (26) *Verily I say unto thee, Thou shalt by no means come out thence, till thou hast paid the uttermost farthing.*"

When I understood the command about non-resistance of evil, it seemed to me that these verses must have a meaning as clear and practical as has the command about resistance of evil. The meaning I had formerly given to the passage was, that every one ought to avoid angry feelings against others, ought never to utter abusive language, and ought to live in peace with all men, without exception. But there was in the text a phrase which excluded this meaning, "Whosoever shall be angry with his brother *without cause*" — the words could not then be an exhortation to absolute peace.

These two words[2] perplexed me, and I turned to the commentators, the theologians, for the removal of my doubts. To my surprise I found that the commentaries of the Church Fathers were chiefly occupied with the endeavor to define under what conditions anger was permissible and when it was not permissible. All the commentators of the Church dwelt on the qualifying phrase "*without cause,*" and explained the meaning to be that one must not be offended without a reason, that one must not be abusive, but that anger is not always

[1] Is. xx. 13.
[2] One in Russian, *naprasno.*

wrong; and, to confirm their view, they quoted instances of anger on the part of saints and apostles.

I could not help acknowledging that the explanation, that anger "for the glory of God" according to their expression, is not reprehensible, although entirely contrary to the spirit of the Gospel, was based on the phrase, "without cause," in the twenty-second verse. These words changed the meaning of the whole passage.

Be not angry without cause. Christ exhorts us to pardon every one, to pardon without limit. He pardoned all who did Him wrong, and chided Peter for being angry with Malchus when Peter sought to defend his Master at the time of the betrayal, when, if at any time, it would seem that it was not without cause. And yet this same Christ in His instructions to all men said, "Be not angry without a cause," and thereby sanctioned anger for a cause. Christ enjoined peace upon all simple men, and suddenly in the phrase, "without a cause," interpolates the reservation that this rule does not apply to all cases; that there are circumstances under which one might be angry with a brother! In the commentaries it says that anger is sometimes expedient!

But who is to decide, I asked, when anger is expedient? I never have as yet encountered an angry person who thought his wrath unjustifiable. All think their anger legitimate and serviceable. The phrase "without cause" destroys the entire force of the verse!

And yet there were the words in the sacred text, and I could not efface them. The effect was the same as if the word "good" had been added to the phrase. "Love thy neighbor"—love thy good neighbor, the neighbor that agrees with thee!

The entire signification of the passage was changed for me by the phrase, "without cause." Verses 23 and 24, which exhort us to be reconciled with all men before we pray, also lost their direct and imperative meaning, and acquired a conditional import through the influence of the foregoing qualification.

It had seemed to me that Christ must forbid all anger, all ill will, and, that it might cease, exhorted us before entering into communion with God to ask ourselves if there were any person who might be angry with us.

If such were the case, whether this anger were with cause or without cause, He commanded us to be reconciled. In this manner I had interpreted the passage; but it now seemed, according to the commentators, that the injunction must be taken as a conditional affirmation.

The commentators all explained that we ought to try to be at peace with all men; but, they added, if this is impossible, if, actuated by evil instincts, any one is at enmity with you, try to be reconciled with him in spirit, in idea, and then the enmity of others will be no obstacle to divine communion.

Moreover that he who said "raca," and "thou fool,"[1] was so terribly guilty always seemed to me strange and absurd. If we are forbidden to be abusive, why were examples chosen of abuse so feeble and almost free from abuse; why this terrible threat against any one who utters abuse so feeble as that implied in the word *raca,* which means a good-for-nothing? All this was obscure to me.

I was convinced that I had before me a problem similar to that which had confronted me in the words, "*Judge not.*" I felt that here again what was simple, serious, precise, and practical had been transferred to the domain of the foggy and the vague. I felt that Christ, in saying, "*be reconciled to thy brother,*" could not have meant, "be reconciled in thought," as they explained it. What does "reconciled in thought" mean? I understood what Jesus meant when, using the words of the prophet, He said, "*I will have mercy, and not sacrifice;*" that is, love to men. If you wish to please God, then, before offering prayer morning and evening, at mass or at the vesper service, remember who is angry with you, and go and arrange it so that he will no longer be angry with you, and then pray if you desire. But how about this phrase, "be reconciled in thought"?

[1] Russian, *bezumnui*, foolish, senseless.

I felt that what seemed to me the only clear and direct meaning of the verse was destroyed by the phrase "without cause." If I could eliminate that, the meaning would be plain. But all the commentators were united against my understanding of it; against it was the canonical text with the phrase, "without cause." If I dropped the words in this case, I might do the same in other cases arbitrarily, and others might follow my example. The whole difficulty lay in one word. If it were not for that one word everything would be clear. So I tried to explain it philologically so that it would not conflict with the sense of the entire passage.

I consulted the lexicons. In ordinary Greek, the word εἰκῇ means "heedlessly, inconsiderately." I tried to find some term that would not destroy the sense; but the words, "without a cause," plainly had the meaning attributed to them. In New Testament Greek the signification of εἰκῇ is exactly the same. I consulted the concordances. The word occurs but once in the Gospels, namely, in this passage. In the Epistles it is used several times. In the first epistle to the Corinthians, xv. 2, it occurs in exactly the same sense. It was impossible to interpret it otherwise; we must acknowledge that Christ said, *Be not angry without cause.* I had to acknowledge that for me to admit that Christ could utter in such vague words a command easily so construed as to be of no effect seemed to me equivalent to rejecting the entire Gospel.

There remained one *last hope!*—is the word to be found in all the manuscripts? I consulted Griesbach, where all variants are recorded—that is to say, how, in what manuscripts, and in which of the Fathers any given expression is employed. I consulted this authority, and discovered to my joy that in this passage there are marginal notes, there are variants. I examined further the variants. All refer to the word εἰκῇ. In most of the Gospel texts and the citations of the Fathers this word does not occur. That proved that the majority were on my side. I consulted Tischendorf for the most ancient reading; the word εἰκῇ did not appear. I looked into

Luther's version whereby I might get hold of this, the shortest way — here again this word does not occur.

So then this word, which destroyed the whole meaning of Christ's teaching, is a fifth century interpolation which had not crept into the best copies of the Gospel. Some copyist added the word; others approved it and undertook its explanation.

Christ did not utter, could not have uttered, this horrible word; and the primary, simple, direct meaning of the whole passage which impressed me and impresses every one is the true one.

But, moreover, now that I understand that Christ's words forbid all anger, whatever the cause, against any one whatever, the formerly confusing prohibition of the words "raca" and "fool," took on a meaning quite distinct from any prohibition with regard to the utterance of abusive epithets. The strange Hebrew word, *raca*, which is not translated in the Greek text, gave me that meaning. *Raca* means, literally, "vain, empty, that which does not exist." It was much used by the Hebrews to express exclusion. *Raca* signifies a man who is scarcely considered as a man. It is employed in the plural form, *rekim*, in Judges ix. 4, where it means "the lost," "the worthless." This word Jesus forbids us to apply to any one, as He forbids us to use the word "fool," which, like "raca," relieves us of all human obligations to a neighbor. We get angry, we do evil to men, and then to excuse ourselves we say that the object of our anger is a worthless or foolish man. Precisely such words as these Christ forbids us to use in speaking of men or to men. He exhorts us not to be angry with any one, and not to excuse our anger with the plea that we have to do with one worthless or foolish.

And so in place of insignificant, vague, and uncertain phrases subject to arbitrary interpretation, I found in Matthew v. 21-26 Christ's first commandment: Live in peace with all men. Regard not anger as justifiable under any circumstances. Never regard a human being as worthless or as a fool.[1] Not only refrain from all

[1] Matt. v. 22.

anger yourself, but do not regard the anger of others toward you justified. If any one is angry with you, even without reason, then before praying go and destroy that hostile feeling.[1] Strive first of all to efface the hostility between you and other men, lest animosity prevail to your loss.[2]

The first commandment of Jesus being thus freed from obscurity, I was able to understand the second, which also begins with a reference to the ancient law: —

"*Ye have heard that it was said by them of old time, Thou shalt not commit adultery:*[3] *But I say unto you, That whosoever looketh on a woman to lust after her hath committed adultery with her already in his heart. And if thy right eye offend thee, pluck it out, and cast it from thee: for it is better for thee that one of thy members should perish, and not that thy whole body should be cast into gehenna. And if thy right hand offend thee, cut it off, and cast it from thee: for it is better for thee that one of thy members should perish, and not that thy whole body should be cast into gehenna. It hath been said, Whoever shall put away his wife, let him give her a writing of divorcement,*[4] *but I say unto you, Whoever puts away his wife, saving for the sin of fornication, causes her to commit adultery: and whoever shall marry her that is divorced commits adultery.*[5]

The significance of these words struck me thus: A man ought not, even in imagination, to admit that he could approach any woman save her to whom he had once been united, and her he might never abandon to take another, although permitted to do so by the Mosaic law.

In the first commandment, that against anger, the advice is given to extinguish anger at the very first, and the advice was illustrated by the parable of the man who is delivered to the judges; so here also Christ declares that debauchery arises from the fact that men and women regard one another as objects of lust. That this may

[1] Matt. v. 22, 23.
[2] Matt. v. 25, 26.
[3] Ex. xx. 14, 28.
[4] Deut. xxiv. 1.
[5] Matt. v. 27–32.

not be so, we ought to put aside everything that may incite to lust, to avoid all that awakens lust, and, once united to a woman, never to abandon her on any pretext, for the abandonment of women leads also to divorce. Women thus abandoned seduce other men, and so debauchery is introduced into the world.

The wisdom of this commandment impressed me. It would suppress all the evils in the world that result from the sexual relations. Convinced that license in the sexual relations leads to contention, men, in obedience to this injunction, would avoid every cause for voluptuousness, and, knowing that the law of humanity is to live in couples, would so unite themselves, and never destroy the bond of union. All the evils arising from dissensions caused by sexual attraction would be suppressed, since there would be neither men nor women deprived of married life.

But now I was much more surprised, as I read the Sermon on the Mount, with the words, which had always surprised, "*saving for the cause of fornication*," which permitted a man to repudiate his wife in case of infidelity. To say nothing of the lack of dignity in the very form in which this thought was expressed, of the fact that here, side by side with what seemed to me the profoundest truths of the Sermon on the Mount, stood, like a note in a criminal code, this strange exception to the general rule, an exception which was diametrically opposed to the fundamental idea.

I consulted the commentators; all, Chrysostom[1] and the others, even learned theological critics like Reuss, recognized the meaning of the words to be that Christ permitted divorce in case of infidelity on the part of the woman, and that, in the exhortation against divorce in the nineteenth chapter of Matthew, the words, *saving for the cause of fornication*, had the same signification. I read the thirty-second verse of the fifth chapter again and again, and it seemed to me that this could not signify sanction to divorce. To verify my doubts I consulted the various contexts, and I found in Matthew xix.,

[1] p. 365.

Mark x., Luke xvi., and in the first epistle of Paul to the Corinthians, affirmation of the doctrine of the indissolubility of marriage without any saving clause. In Luke xvi. 18 it is said:—

"*Whoever puts away his wife, and marries another, commits adultery: and whoever marries her that is put away from her husband commits adultery.*"

In Mark x. 5–12 the doctrine is also proclaimed without any exception whatever:—

"*For the hardness of your heart he wrote for you this command. But from the beginning of the creation God made them male and female. For this cause shall a man leave his father and mother, and cleave to his wife; And they twain shall be one flesh: so then they are no more twain, but one flesh. What therefore God has joined together, let not man put asunder. And in the house his disciples asked him again of the same matter. And he said unto them, Whoever shall put away his wife, and marry another, commits adultery against her. And if a woman shall put away her husband, and be married to another, she commits adultery.*"

The same idea is expressed in Matt. xix. 4–9. Paul, in the first epistle to the Corinthians, vii. 1–11, develops systematically the idea that the only way of preventing debauchery is that every man have his own wife, and every woman have her own husband, and that they mutually satisfy the sexual instinct; then he says, without equivocation, that husband or wife shall in no case abandon each other for the sake of intercourse with any one else.[1]

According to Mark and Luke and Paul, divorce is forbidden. It is forbidden by the assertion repeated in two of the Gospels, that husband and wife are one flesh whom God hath joined together. It is forbidden in the teaching of Christ, who exhorts us to pardon every one, without excepting the adulterous woman. It is forbidden by the general sense of the whole passage, which explains

[1] "*Let not the wife depart from her husband: But and if she depart, let her remain unmarried, or be reconciled to her husband: and let not the husband put away his wife.*"

that divorce is provocative of debauchery, and for this reason that divorce with an adulterous woman is prohibited.

On what, then, is based the opinion that divorce is permissible in case of a woman's infidelity. On the words which had so impressed me in Matt. v. 32; the words every one takes to mean that Jesus permits divorce in case of adultery by the woman; the words, repeated in Matt. xix. 9, in many manuscripts of the Gospel, and by many Fathers of the Church, — the words, "*unless for the cause of adultery.*"

I studied these words carefully anew. For a long time I could not understand them. It seemed to me that there must be a defect in the translation, an exegesis; but I could not find where the source of the error was. The error was very plain.

In opposition to the Mosaic law, which declares that if a man take an aversion to his wife he may write her a bill of divorcement and send her out of his house — in opposition to this law Christ says: "*But I say unto you, That whoever shall put away his wife, saving for the sin of fornication, causes her to commit adultery.*"

I saw nothing in these words to allow us to affirm that divorce was either permitted or forbidden. It is only said that whoever shall put away his wife causes her to commit adultery, and then an exception is made with regard to a woman guilty of adultery. This exception, which throws the guilt of marital infidelity entirely upon the *woman* is, in general, strange and unexpected; but here, in relation to the context, it is simply absurd, for even the very doubtful meaning which might otherwise be attributed to it is wholly destroyed. Whoever puts away his wife exposes her to the crime of adultery, and yet a man is permitted to put away a wife guilty of adultery, as if a woman guilty of adultery would no more commit adultery after she were put away.

But this is not all; when I had examined this passage attentively, I found it also to be lacking in grammatical meaning. The words are, "*Whoever shall put away his wife, except for the fault of adultery, exposes her to the commission of adultery,"* — and the proposition is complete. It is said of a husband, that he, in putting away his wife, exposes her to the commission of the crime of adultery; what, then, is the purport of the qualifying phrase, "*except for the fault of adultery*"? If the proposition had been put in this form, "The husband that puts away his wife is guilty of adultery, unless the wife herself has been unfaithful," it would be grammatically correct.

But as the passage now stands, the subject, "The husband that puts," has no other predicate than the word "exposes." How then can the phrase "except for the fault of adultery" be connected with it? It is impossible to expose except for the adultery of the wife. Even if to the words "except for the fault of adultery," the words "on the wife's part" or "her part" were added, which they are not, even then these words could have no relation to the predicate, "exposes." These words, according to the received exegesis, relate to the predicate, "*Whoever puts away;*" but "whoever puts away" is not the principal predicate, the principal predicate is "exposes." What signifies then the phrase, *except for the fault of adultery.* It is plain that whether for or without the fault of adultery on the part of the woman, the husband who puts away his wife exposes her to the commission of adultery.

The proposition is analogous to the following sentence: Whoever deprives his son of food, except for the fault of cruelty, exposes him to the possibility of being cruel. This sentence evidently cannot mean that a father may refuse food to his son if the son is cruel. If it has any sense, it can only mean that a father who refuses food to his son, besides being cruel toward his son, exposes his son to the possibility of becoming cruel. And in the same way, the Gospel proposition would have a meaning if we could replace the words, "the fault of adultery," by libertinism, debauchery, or something analogous, expressing not an act but a quality.

And so I asked myself if the meaning here was not simply that whoever puts away his wife, besides being himself guilty of libertinism (since no one puts away his wife except to take another), exposes his wife also to the commission of adultery? If, in the original text, the word translated "adultery" or "fornication" had the meaning of libertinism, the meaning of the passage would be clear. And then I met with the same experience that had happened to me before in similar instances. The text confirmed my suppositions so that I could no longer have any doubt about it.

The first thing that struck my eyes in reading the text was that the word *πορνεία*, translated in common with *μοιχᾶσθαι*, "adultery" or "fornication," is an entirely different word from the latter. Could it not be that these two words are synonyms or used so in the Gospels? I consulted all the lexicons — the general lexicons and those of the New Testament Greek — and found that the word *πορνεία*, corresponding to *zanah* in Hebrew, to *fornicatio* in Latin, to *hurerei* in German, to *rasputsro* in Russian, has a very precise meaning, and that it never in any lexicons has signified, and never can signify, the act of adultery, *adultère*, *Ehebruch*, as it has been translated. It signifies a state of depravity, — a quality, and never an act, — and never can be properly translated by "adultery" or "fornication." I found, moreover, that "adultery" is expressed throughout the Gospel, as well as in the passage under consideration, by the word *μοιχεύω*. I had only to correct the false translation, which had evidently been made intentionally, to render absolutely inadmissible the meaning attributed by commentators to this passage and to the context of the nineteenth chapter, and the sense in which the word *πορνεία* is related to the husband in the sentence would become perfectly plain.

A person acquainted with Greek would construe as follows: *παρεκτός*, "except, outside," *λόγου*, "the cause, the sin," *πορνείας*, "of libertinism," *ποιεῖ*, "obliges," *αὐτήν*, "her," *μοιχᾶσθαι*, "to commit adultery" — which rendering gives, word for word, Whoever puts away his wife, besides the fault of libertinism, obliges her to be an adulteress.

We obtain the same meaning from Matt. xix. 9. When we correct the unauthorized translation of πορνεία, by substituting "libertinism" for "fornication," we see at once that the phrase εἰ μὴ ἐπὶ πορνείᾳ cannot apply to "wife." And as the words παρεκτὸς λόγου πορνείας could signify nothing else than the fault of libertinism on the part of the husband, so the words εἰ μὴ ἐπὶ πορνείᾳ, in the nineteenth chapter, can have no other than the same meaning. The phrase εἰ μὴ ἐπὶ πορνείᾳ is, word for word, "if not for libertinism," not "on account of libertinism."

The meaning then becomes clear. Christ replies to the theory of the Pharisees, who held that a man who abandons his wife to marry another without the intention of giving himself up to libertinism does not commit adultery — Christ replies to this theory that the abandonment of a wife, that is, the cessation of sexual relations, even if not for the purpose of libertinism, but to marry another, is none the less adultery.

Thus we come at the simple meaning of this commandment — a meaning which accords with the whole doctrine, with the words of which it is the complement, with grammar, and with logic. This simple and clear interpretation, harmonizing so naturally with the doctrine and the words from which it was derived, I discovered after the most careful and prolonged research. In fact, read these words in German, or in French, where it is directly said, *pour cause d'infidelité*, or *à moins que cela ne soit pour cause d'infidelité*, and see if you can find any other meaning. The word παραδεκτὸς in all lexicons, signifying *excepté*, *ausgenommen*, *krome*, *except*, is translated by the whole proposition *à moins que cela ne soit* — "except it be for." The word πορνείας is translated *infidelité*, *Ehebruch*. And here, on this premeditated alteration of the text, had been based an exegesis which destroyed the moral, and the religious, and the logical, and the grammatical meaning of Christ's words.

And thus once more I found a confirmation of the

awful and joyous truth that the meaning of Christ's teaching is simple and clear, that its affirmations are emphatic and precise, but that the commentaries upon the doctrine, inspired by a desire to sanction existing evil, have so obscured it that determined effort is demanded of him who would know the truth. It became evident to me that if the Gospels had come down to us half burned or effaced, it would have been easier to restore the true meaning of the text than to find that meaning now, beneath the accumulations of fallacious comments which have apparently no purpose save to conceal the doctrine they are supposed to expound. With regard to the passage under consideration, it is even more evident than before that to justify the divorce of some Joann the Terrible this ingenious pretext was employed to obscure the teaching about marriage. When we have thrown aside the commentaries, we escape from the fog and the uncertainty, and Christ's second command becomes precise and clear. "Give not yourself up to the pleasure arising from sexual lust. Let every man, unless he be a eunuch, that is, if he be justified in entering into the sexual relation, have one wife and one wife only, and every wife one husband and one husband only, and under no pretext whatever let this union be violated by either."

Immediately after the second commandment is another reference to the ancient law, followed by the third commandment: —

"*Again, you have heard that it has been said by them of old time, Thou shalt not forswear thyself, but shalt perform unto the Lord thine oaths:*[1] *But I say unto you, Swear not at all; neither by heaven; for it is God's throne:* (35) *Nor by the earth; for it is his footstool: neither by Jerusalem; for it is the city of the great king.* (36) *Neither shalt thou swear by thy head, because thou canst not make one hair white or black.* (37) *But let your communications be, Yea, yea; Nay, nay: for whatever is more than these comes of evil.*"[2]

[1] Levit. xix. 12; Deut. xxiii. 21, 34.

[2] Matt. v. 33–37.

This passage had always troubled me when I read it. It did not trouble me by its obscurity, like the passage about divorce; or by conflicting with other passages, like the authorization of anger for cause; or by the difficulty in the way of obedience, like the command to turn the other cheek, — it troubled me, on the contrary, by its very clearness, simplicity, and practicality. Side by side with rules the profundity and importance of which had filled me with awe and humiliation, was this saying, which seemed to me superfluous, frivolous, weak, and without consequence to me or to others. I naturally did not swear, either by Jerusalem, or by heaven, or by anything else, and it cost me not the least effort to refrain from doing so; on the other hand, it seemed to me that whether I swore or did not swear could not be of the slightest importance to any one. And desiring to find an explanation of this rule, which troubled me through its very simplicity, I consulted the commentators. In this case they helped me.

The commentators all found in these words a confirmation of the third commandment of Moses, — not to swear by the name of the Lord; they explained that Christ, like Moses, forbade employing God's name at all; but, moreover, the commentators still further explained that Christ's will not to take an oath was not always obligatory, and had no reference whatever to the oath which every citizen is obliged to take before the authorities. And they brought together Scripture citations, not to support the direct meaning of Christ's command, but to prove when it ought and ought not to be obeyed.

They claimed that Christ had Himself sanctioned the oath in the courts of justice by His reply, "*Thou hast said*," to the high priest's words, "*I adjure thee by the living God;*" it is said that the apostle Paul invoked God to witness the truth of his words, which invocation was evidently equivalent to an oath; it is said that oaths were prescribed by the law of Moses, but the Lord did not forbid these oaths; it is said that only false oaths, the oaths of Pharisees and hypocrites, are forbidden.

As soon as I understood the sense and object of these

comments, I understood that Christ's regulation regarding the taking of oaths was not so insignificant, superficial, and easy as I had supposed, when, in the number of oaths forbidden by Christ, I had not reckoned the oath of fidelity to the State.

And I asked myself the question, Does not this passage contain an exhortation to abstain also from that oath of allegiance which the commentators of the Church are so zealous to justify? Does it not forbid us to take the oath indispensable to the assembling of men into political groups and the formation of a military caste? The soldier, that special instrument of violence, goes in Russia by the nickname of *prisyaga* (sworn in). If I had asked the grenadier how he solved the contradiction between the Gospels and military code, he would have replied that he had taken the oath, that is, that he had sworn on the Gospels. Such replies soldiers have always made to me. The oath is so indispensable to the organization of that terrible evil produced by war and armed coercion that in France, where Christianity is out of favor, nevertheless the oath remains in full force. If Christ had not said this, had not said in so many words, "Do not take an oath to any one," He ought to have said it! He came to suppress evil, and, if He did not condemn the oath, He left a terrible evil untouched.

It may be said, perhaps, that in Christ's time this evil was unperceived; but this is not true. Epictetus and Seneca declare against the taking of oaths of allegiance to any one. A similar rule is among the laws of Mani. The Jews in Christ's time made proselytes, and obliged them to take the oath.

How then can I say that Christ did not perceive this evil when He forbade it in clear, direct, and explicit terms? He said, "*I say unto you, Swear not at all.*" This expression is as simple, clear, and absolute as the expression, "*Judge not, condemn not,*" and is as little subject to explanation; moreover, He added to this, "*Let your communication be, Yea, yea; Nay, nay: for whatsoever is more than these comes of evil.*"

You see, if obedience to Christ's teaching is always to fulfil God's will, how can a man swear to fulfil man's will? God's will cannot coincide with man's will. And this is precisely what Christ says in the same place. He says[1]:—

"*Swear not by thy head, because not only thy head but every hair on it is in God's power.*"

And the apostle James in his epistle says exactly the same thing.

In his epistle, toward the end, as if it were the summing up of everything, James says[2]:—

"*But above all things, my brethren, swear not, neither by heaven, neither by earth, neither by any other oath: but let your yea be yea; and your nay, nay; lest ye fall into condemnation.*"

The apostle tells us clearly why we must not swear: the oath in itself may not be culpable, but by it men are condemned, and so we ought not to swear at all. How could the saying of Christ and His apostles be more clearly expressed?

My ideas had become so confused that for a long time I kept asking myself: Can it mean what it means? How can we all swear on the Gospels? It cannot be.

But, after having read the commentaries attentively, I saw that the impossible was a fact. The explanations of the commentators were in harmony with those they had offered concerning the other commands: judge not, be not angry, do not violate the marital bonds.

We have organized a social order which we cherish and regard as sacred. Christ, whom we recognize as God, comes and tells us that our social organization is wrong. We recognize Him as God, but we are not willing to renounce our social institutions.

What, then, are we to do? Add, if we can, the words "without a cause" to render void the command against anger; wherever it is possible, mutilate the sense of another law, just as dishonest and unjust judges have done; so reverse the meaning of the law that it shall say precisely the opposite; instead of the command abso-

[1] Matt. v. 36. [2] James v. 12.

lutely forbidding divorce insert phraseology which permits divorce; and if there is no possible way of deriving an equivocal meaning, as in the case of the commands, "*Judge not, condemn not*," and "*Swear not at all*," then with the utmost effrontery openly violate the rule while affirming that we obey it.

In fact, the principal obstacle to a comprehension of the truth that the Gospel forbids all manner of oaths, and particularly the oath of allegiance, exists in the fact that pseudo-Christian commentators themselves, with unexampled audacity, take oath upon the Gospel itself. They make men swear by the Gospel, that is to say, they do just contrary to the Gospel. Why does it never occur to the man who is made to take an oath upon the cross and the Gospel, that the cross was made sacred only by the death of one who forbade all oaths, and that in kissing the sacred book he perhaps is pressing his lips upon the very page where is recorded the clear and direct commandment, "*Swear not at all*"?

But this audacity now no longer troubled me. I saw clearly that in Matt. v. 33–37 was the plain declaration of the third commandment, that we should take no oath, since all oaths are imposed for evil.

After the third commandment comes the fourth reference to the ancient law and the enunciation of the fourth commandment: —

"*It has been said to you, An eye for an eye and a tooth for a tooth:* (39) *But I say unto you, Resist not evil: but whoever shall smite thee on thy right cheek, turn to him the other also.* (40) *And if any man will sue thee at the law, and take away thy coat, let him have thy cloak also.* (41) *And whoever shall compel thee to go a mile, go with him twain.* (42) *Give to him that asks thee, and from him that would borrow of thee turn not thou away.*" [1]

I have already spoken of the direct and precise meaning of these words; I have already said that we have no reason whatever for basing on them an allegorical ex-

[1] Matt. v. 38–42, Luke vi. 29, 30.

planation. The commentaries on these words from the time of John Chrysostom to our day are really surprising. The words are pleasing to every one, and they inspire all manner of profound reflections save one, — that these words have the very meaning that they have. The Church commentators, not at all awed by the authority of one whom they recognize as God, boldly distort the meaning of His words. They say: —

"Of course all these commands about enduring offences and refraining from reprisals are directed against the vindictive character of the Jews; they not only do not exclude all general measures for the repression of evil and the punishment of evil-doers, but they exhort every one to individual and personal effort to sustain justice, to apprehend aggressors, and to prevent the wicked from inflicting evil upon others, — for otherwise these spiritual commands of the Saviour would become, as they became among the Jews, a dead letter, and would serve only to propagate evil and to suppress virtue.

"The love of the Christian should be patterned after the divine love; but divine love limits and punishes evil only so far as it is more or less harmless toward the glory of God and the safety of His servants. In the contrary case we must limit evil and punish it, — which is the special duty of authorities." [1]

Christian scholars and free-thinkers are equally unembarrassed by the meaning of Christ's words, and they correct it. They say the sentiments here expressed are very noble, but are completely inapplicable to life; for if we practised to the letter the command, "*Resist not evil,*" we should destroy the entire social fabric which we have arranged so beautifully. Renan, Strauss, and all the liberal commentators say this.

If, however, we take Christ's words as we would take the words of any one who speaks to us, and admit that He says exactly what He does say, the necessity for all these profound circumlocutions is done away with.

[1] This citation is taken from the "Commentaries on the Gospel," by the Archimandrite Michael, a work based upon the writings of the Fathers of the Church.

Christ says, "I find your social system absurd and wrong. I propose to you another." And then He utters the teachings reported by Matthew.[1] It would seem that before correcting them one ought to understand them; now this is exactly what no one wishes to do. We decide in advance that the social order in which we live, and which is abolished by these words, is the sacred law of humanity.

I did not consider our social order either wise or sacred; and that is why I have understood this command when others have not. And when I had understood these words just as they are written, I was struck with their truth, their lucidity, and their precision.

Christ said, "You wish to suppress evil by evil; this is not reasonable. To abolish evil, cease to do evil." And then He enumerates all the instances where we are in the habit of returning evil for evil, and says that in these cases we ought not so to do.

This fourth command of Christ was the one I first understood; and it revealed to me the meaning of all the others. This simple, clear, and practical fourth commandment says: —

"Never resist evil by force, never return violence for violence: if any one beat you, bear it; if one would deprive you of anything, yield to his wishes; if any one would force you to labor, labor; if any one would take away your property, give it up to him."

After the fourth commandment we find a fifth reference to the ancient law, followed by the fifth command: —

It has been said to you, Thou shalt love thy neighbor and hate thine enemy.[2] *But I say unto you, Love your enemies, bless them that curse you, do good to them that hate you, and pray for them that despitefully use you and persecute you;* (45) *That ye may be the children of your Father which is in heaven: for he makes his sun to rise on the evil and on the good, and sends rain on the just and*

[1] Matt. v. 38–42.
[2] See Levit. xix. 17, 18.

on the unjust. (46) *For if you love them that love you, what reward have you? do not even the publicans the same?* (47) *And if you salute your brethren only, what do you more than others? do not even the heathen so? Be therefore perfect, even as your Father who is in heaven is perfect.*"[1]

These verses I had formerly regarded as a continuation, an exposition, an enforcement, I might almost say an exaggeration, of the words, "*Resist not evil.*"

But as I had found a simple, precise, and practical meaning in each of the passages beginning with a reference to the ancient law, I anticipated a similar experience here. After each reference of this sort had thus far come a command, and each command had been important and distinct in meaning; it ought to be so now.

The closing words of the passage, repeated by Luke, which are to the effect that God makes no distinction of persons, but lavishes His gifts upon all, and that we ought to be like God in this respect, and not make distinctions between persons and ought not to do as the heathen do, but ought to love all men and to do good to all,— these words were clear; they seemed to me to be a confirmation and exposition of some definite law— but what this law was I could not for a long time understand.

To love one's enemies?— this was something impossible. It was one of those sublime thoughts that we must look upon only as an indication of an unattainable moral ideal. It was too much or nothing. We might, perhaps, refrain from doing injury to our enemies— but to love them!— impossible; Christ did not prescribe the impossible. And besides, in the most ancient words, in the reference to the ancient law, it was said: "*It has been said to you, Thou shalt.... hate thine enemy,*" there was cause for doubt. In other references Christ cited textually the terms of the Mosaic law; but here He introduces words which had never been said before. He seems to calumniate the law.

As with regard to my former doubts, so now the

[1] Matt. v. 43-48.

commentators gave me no explanation of the difficulty. They all agreed that the words "*hate thine enemy*" were not in the Mosaic law, but they offered no suggestion as to the meaning of the unauthorized phrase. They spoke of the difficulty of loving one's enemies, that is, wicked men (thus they emended Christ's words); and they said that while it is impossible to love our enemies, we may refrain from wishing them harm and from inflicting injury upon them. Moreover, they insinuated that we might and should "convince" our enemies, that is, resist them; they spoke of the different degrees of this kind of benevolence which we might attain — from all of which the final conclusion was that Christ, for some inexplicable reason, quoted as from the law of Moses words not to be found therein, and then uttered a number of sublime phrases which at bottom are impracticable and meaningless.

It seemed to me this could not be so. In this passage, as in the passages containing the first four commandments, there must be some clear and precise meaning. To find this meaning, I set myself first of all to discover the purport of the words containing the inexact reference to the ancient law: "*It has been said to you, Thou shalt .... hate thine enemy.*" Christ had some reason for introducing each of His commands with words from the law, "*Do not kill, do not commit adultery,*" and the rest; they serve as the antitheses of His own teaching. If we do not understand what is meant by the citations from the ancient law, we cannot understand what He proscribed. The commentators say frankly (it is impossible not to say so) that He in this instance made use of words not to be found in the Mosaic law, but they do not tell us why He did so or what this unveracious reference means.

It seemed to me above all necessary to know what Christ meant by introducing words not to be found in the law, and I asked myself what these words inaccurately introduced by Christ from the law could mean. In all of Christ's other references to the law, only a single rule from the ancient law is cited: "*Thou shalt not kill*" — "*Thou shalt not commit adultery*" — "*Thou shalt not forswear thyself*" — "*An eye for an eye, a tooth for a tooth*" — and taking each as a text He propounds His own.

Here He cites two contrasting rules: "*It has been said, Thou shalt love thy neighbor and hate thine enemy,*" — from which it would appear that the contrast between these two rules of the ancient law, relative to one's neighbor and one's enemy, should be the basis of the new law.

To understand more clearly what this contrast was, I asked myself what is the meaning of the word "neighbor" and the word "enemy," as used in the Gospel text. After consulting lexicons and Biblical texts, I was convinced that "neighbor" in the Hebrew language invariably meant only a Hebrew. The same meaning of "neighbor" is expressed in the Gospel parable of the Samaritan. According to the notion of the Jewish scribe[1] who asked, "*And who is my neighbor?*" the Samaritan could not be his neighbor. The word "neighbor" is used with the same meaning in Acts vii. 27. "Neighbor," in Gospel language, means a compatriot, a person belonging to the same nationality. And so, having come to the conclusion that the antithesis used by Christ in the citation, "*love thy neighbor, hate thine enemy,*" must be in the distinction between the words "compatriot" and "foreigner," I asked myself what was the Jewish understanding of "enemy," and I found my supposition confirmed. The word "enemy" is nearly always employed in the Gospels in the sense, not of a personal enemy, but, in general, of a "hostile people."[2] The singular number in which the word "enemy" is used, in the phrase "*hate thine enemy,*" convinced me that the meaning is a "hostile people." In the Old Testament, the conception "hostile people" is nearly always expressed in the singular number.

As soon as I understood this, the difficulty immedi-

[1] Luke x. 29.
[2] Luke i. 71, 74; Matt. xxii. 44; Mark xii. 36; Luke xx. 43, etc.

ately resolved itself in this way: why and how could Christ, who had before quoted the authentic words of the law, here cite the words, "*It has been said to you, hate thine enemy,*" words which had not been said? We have only to understand the word "enemy" in the sense of "hostile people," and "neighbor" in the sense of "compatriot," and the difficulty is completely solved. Christ is speaking of the manner in which, according to the law of Moses, the Hebrews were directed to act toward "hostile peoples." The various passages scattered through the different books of the Old Testament, prescribing the oppression, slaughter, and extermination of other peoples, Jesus summed up in one word, "hate," .... to do evil to the enemy. And He says: —

"It has been said to you that you must love those of your own race, and hate foreigners; but I say unto you, Love every one without reference to the nationality to which they may belong."

When I had understood these words in this way, another principal difficulty was immediately done away with — how to understand the phrase, "*Love your enemies.*"

It is impossible to love one's personal enemies; but it is perfectly possible to love the citizens of a foreign nation equally with one's compatriots. And for me it became evident that in saying, "*It has been said, Love thy neighbor, and hate thine enemy. But I say unto you, Love your enemies,*" Jesus is speaking of the fact that men are in the habit of looking upon compatriots as neighbors, and foreigners as enemies; and He commands them not to do this. He says: "According to the law of Moses there is a difference between the Hebrews and non-Hebrews — the national enemy; but I say unto you, Make no such distinction." And then, according to Matthew and Luke, after giving this command, He says that with God all men are equal, all are lighted by the same sun, on all falls the same rain. God makes no distinction among peoples, and lavishes His gifts on all men; men ought to act exactly in the same way toward one another, without distinction of nationality, and not like the heathen, who divide themselves into distinct nationalities.

Thus once more I found confirmed on all sides the simple, clear, important, and practical meaning of Christ's words. Once more, in place of a sentence from a cloudy and obscure philosophy, appeared a clear, precise, important, and practical rule. To make no distinction between compatriots and foreigners, and to abstain from all the results of such distinction, — from hostility toward foreigners, from war, from all participation in war, from all preparations for war; to establish with all men, of whatever nationality, the same relations granted to compatriots.

All this was so simple and so clear, that I was astonished that I had not perceived it from the first.

The cause of my error was the same as that which had perplexed me with regard to the passages relating to judgments and the taking of oaths. It is very difficult to understand that tribunals which are opened with Christian services by professed Christians, blest by those that consider themselves the guardians of Christ's law, could be incompatible with Christ's command; could be, in fact, diametrically opposed to it! It is still more difficult to believe that the very oath which we are obliged to take by the guardians of Christ's law, is directly repudiated by this law! To admit that everything in life that is considered essential and natural, as well as what is considered the most noble and grand, — love of country, its defence, its glory, battle with its enemies, and the rest, — to admit that all this is not only an infraction of Christ's law, but is directly denounced by Jesus, — this, I say, is awfully difficult.

Our life is now so far away from Christ's teaching that this very estrangement constitutes now the chief difficulty in understanding its meaning. We have been so deaf and so forgetful of all that He said to us about our lives — not only when He commands us not to kill, but when He warns us against anger, when He commands us not to resist evil, but to turn the other cheek, to love our enemies; we are so accustomed to speak of a body of men especially organized for murder, as a Christian army, we are so accustomed to hear prayers addressed to Christ for the assurance of victory over our enemies, we have put our pride and glory in slaughter, we have made the sword, that symbol of murder, an almost sacred object (so that a man deprived of this symbol, of his sword, is a dishonored man); we are so accustomed, I say, to this, that now it seems to us that Christ did not forbid war, that if He had forbidden it, He would have said so more plainly.

We forget that Christ could never have foreseen that men having faith in His doctrine of humility, love, and universal brotherhood could, with calmness and premeditation, organize themselves for the murder of their brethren.

Christ could not have foreseen this, and so He could not forbid a Christian to participate in war, just as a father who exhorts his son to live honestly, never to wrong any person, and to give all that he has to others, would not forbid his son to cut people's throats on the highway.

None of the apostles, none of Christ's disciples during the first centuries of Christianity, could have realized the necessity of forbidding a Christian that form of murder which we call war.

Here, for example, is what Origen says in his reply to Celsus[1]: —

"In the next place, Celsus urges us 'to help the king with all our might, and to labor with him in the maintenance of justice, to fight for him; and, if he requires it, to fight under him, or lead an army along with him.'

"To this, our answer is that we do, when occasion requires, give help to kings, and that, so to say, a divine help, 'putting on the whole armor of God.' And this we do in obedience to the injunction of the apostle, 'I exhort, therefore, that first of all, supplications, prayers, intercessions, and giving of thanks, be made for all men, for kings, and for all that are in authority;' and the more any one excels in piety, the more effective

[1] "Contra Celsum," Book VIII., chap. lxxiii.

help does he render to kings, even more than is given by soldiers, who go forth to fight and slay as many of the enemy as they can.

"And to those enemies of our faith who require us to bear arms for the commonwealth, and to slay men, we can reply: —

"'Do not those who are priests at certain shrines, and those who attend on certain gods, as you account them, keep their hands free from blood, that they may, with hands unstained and free from human blood, offer the appointed sacrifices to your gods? and even when war is upon you, you never enlist the priests in the army. If that, then, is a laudable custom, how much more so, that while others are engaged in battle, these too should engage as the priests and ministers of God, keeping their hands pure, and wrestling in prayers to God on behalf of those who are fighting in a righteous cause, and for the king who reigns righteously, that whatever is opposed to those who act righteously may be destroyed!'"

And at the close of the chapter, in explaining that Christians, through their peaceful lives, are much more helpful to kings than soldiers are, Origen says: —

"And none fight better for the emperor than we do. *We do not, indeed, fight under him, although he require it; but we fight on his behalf, forming a special army, — an army of piety, — by offering our prayers to God.*"

This is the way in which the Christians of the first centuries regarded war, and such was the language that their leaders addressed to the rulers of the earth at a period when martyrs perished by hundreds and by thousands for having confessed the Christian religion.

But now? Now there is no question as to whether a Christian may or may not go to war! All young men, brought up according to the doctrine of the Church called Christian, are obliged, at a specified date during every autumn, to report at the bureaus of conscription, and, under the guidance of their spiritual directors, deliberately to renounce Christ's law.

Not long ago there was a peasant who refused military service on the plea that it was contrary to the Gospel. The doctors of the Church explained to the peasant his error; but, as the peasant had faith, not in them, but in Christ, he was thrown into prison, where he remained until he was ready to renounce the law of Christ! And all this happened eighteen hundred years after our God had laid down for us Christians the clear and definite command: "Do not consider men of other nations as enemies, but consider all men as brethren, and treat them as you treat compatriots; and therefore refrain not only from killing those who are called enemies, but love them and do them good."

When I had thus understood these simple and definite commands of Christ undistorted by commentaries, I asked myself:—

"What would be the result if the Christian world believed in them, not in the way of reading and chanting them for the glory of God, but of obeying them for the good of men? What would be the result if men believed in the observance of these commands at least as seriously as they believe in saying their prayers every day, in going to church every Sunday, in fasting every Friday, in preparing for the sacraments every year? What would be the result if the faith of men in these commands were as strong as their faith in the requirements of the Church?"

And then I saw in imagination a Christian society living according to these commands and educating the younger generation to follow their precepts. I tried to picture the results if we taught our children from infancy, not what we teach them now,—to maintain personal dignity, to uphold personal privileges against the encroachments of others (which we can never do without humiliating or offending others),—but to teach them that no man has a right to privileges, and can neither be above nor below any one else; that only he who tries to stand higher than others is below others and more ignominious; that there is no more contemptible condition for a man than when he is angry with another; that what may seem to me foolish and despicable in another cannot justify me in anger against him or in enmity with him.

Instead of the whole arrangement of our social organization as it now is, from the show-cases of shops to theaters, novels, and women's finery meant to stimulate sensuous desire, — I tried to imagine the results if we taught our children by precept and by example that the reading of lascivious novels and attendance at theaters and balls are the vulgarest of all pastimes, and that every act having for its object the adornment of the body or its exposure is most low and disgusting.

Instead of our present arrangement of society whereby it is considered right and indispensable for a young man to be a libertine up to the time of his marriage, instead of a life which separates husbands and wives being considered most natural, instead of giving to women the legal right to practise the trade of prostitution, instead of countenancing and sanctioning divorce, — I imagined, instead of all this, we taught by words and actions that the state of celibacy, the solitary existence of a man properly endowed for, and who has not renounced, the sexual relation, is a monstrous and opprobrious wrong; and that the abandonment of wife by husband, or of husband by wife, for the sake of another, is not only an unnatural act, but also an act cruel and inhuman.

Instead of our entire existence being based on violence so that every one of our amusements is provided and maintained by force; so that each of us from childhood to old age is by turns victim and executioner, — I tried to picture the results if we taught by word and deed that vengeance is the lowest of animal feelings, that not only is violence debasing, but that it deprives us of true happiness; that the only joy of life is that not maintained by force; and that our greatest consideration ought to be bestowed, not upon those that accumulate riches to the injury of others, but upon those who best serve others and give most to them.

If instead of regarding it as noble and lawful for every man to take an oath of allegiance and to give his most precious possession, that is to say his whole life, to some unknown person, — I tried to imagine what would be the result if we taught that the enlightened will of man is to the highest degree sacred, so that no one can give it up to any one else; and that if a man place himself at the disposition of any one, and promise by oath anything whatever, he renounces his rational manhood and outrages his most sacred right. I tried to imagine the results, if, instead of the national hatred with which we are inspired under the name of "love for fatherland"; if, in place of those laudations of murder which we call war, which from earliest childhood has been held up to us as the most brilliant achievement of men, we were taught, on the contrary, horror and contempt for all the means — military, diplomatic, and political — which serve to divide men; if we were educated to look upon the division of men into political states, and a diversity of codes and frontiers, as an indication of barbaric ignorance; and that to wage war, that is, to massacre foreigners, strangers to us, without any cause, is a most horrible crime, to be perpetrated only by a depraved and misguided man, who has fallen to the lowest level of the brute. I imagined all men coming to these convictions, and I asked myself what would be the result.

Up to this time I asked myself, What will be the results of Christ's teaching, as I understood it? and the involuntary reply was, Nothing. We shall all continue to pray, to partake of the sacraments, to believe in the redemption and salvation of ourselves and the world through Christ, — and yet hold that salvation will come, not by our efforts, but because the end of the world will come. At the appointed time Christ will appear in His glory to judge the quick and the dead, and the kingdom of heaven will be established independent of what our lives are.

Now Christ's teaching, as I understood it, had an entirely different meaning; the establishment of the kingdom of God on earth depended on us. The practice of Christ's teaching, propounded in the five commands, instituted this kingdom of God. The kingdom of God on earth consists in this, that all men should be at peace with one another. Peace among men is the greatest blessing that men can attain on this earth. Thus the Hebrew prophets conceived of the rule of God. This ideal has been, and is, in every human heart. The prophets all brought to men the promise of peace. Christ's whole teaching has but one object, to establish peace — the kingdom of God — among men.

In the Sermon on the Mount, in the interview with Nicodemus, in the instructions given to His disciples, in all His teachings, He spoke only of this, of the things that divided men, that kept them from peace, that prevented them from entering into the Kingdom of God. All the parables are only a description of what the kingdom of heaven is, and they show us the only way of entering therein is to love our brethren, and to be at peace with all. John the Baptist, the forerunner of Christ, proclaimed that the kingdom of God was at hand, and declared that Christ was to bring it upon earth. Christ Himself said that His mission was to bring peace: —

"*Peace I leave with you, my peace I give unto you: not as the world gives give I unto you. Let not your heart be troubled, neither let it be afraid.*"[1]

And the observance of His five commands will bring peace upon the earth. All five have but one object, — the establishment of peace among men. If men will only believe in Christ's teaching, and practise it, the reign of peace will come upon earth, — not that peace which is the work of man, partial, precarious, and at the mercy of chance; but the peace that is all-pervading, inviolable, and eternal.

The first command says: Be at peace with every one; consider none as foolish or unworthy. If peace is violated, then all our endeavors are to be employed in reëstablishing it. Serving God is in the extinction of enmity among men.[2] We are to be reconciled without delay, that we may not lose that inner peace which is the true life. Everything is comprised in this command; but Christ knew the worldly temptations that prevent peace among men, and gives a second com-

[1] John xiv. 27. [2] Matt. v. 22–24.

mand against the temptation of the sexual relations, so perilous to peace. Look not on the body as an instrument of lust; avoid in advance this temptation. Let each man have one wife, and each woman one husband, and one is never to forsake the other, under any pretext.[1]

The second temptation is that of the oath, which draws men into sin; know beforehand that this is wrong, and give no such promises.[2]

The third temptation is that of vengeance, which we call human justice; this we are not to resort to under any pretext; we are to endure offenses, and never to return evil for evil.[3]

The fourth temptation is that arising from difference in nationalities, from hostility between peoples and states; know that all men are brothers, and children of the same Father, and disturb not the peace with any one in the name of national ends.[4]

If men abstain from practising any one of these commands, peace will be violated. Let men practise all these commands, and peace will be established upon earth. These commands exclude all evil from the lives of men. The practice of these five commands would realize the ideal of human life existing in every human heart. All men would be brothers, each would be at peace with others, enjoying all the blessings of earth to the limit of years accorded by the Creator. Men would beat their swords into plowshares, and their spears into pruning-hooks, and then would come the kingdom of God, — that reign of peace foretold by all the prophets, which was foretold by John the Baptist as near at hand, and which Christ proclaimed in the words of Isaiah: —

"*The Spirit of the Lord is upon me, because he anointed me to preach the gospel to the poor; he sent me to heal the broken-hearted, to preach deliverance to the captives, and recovering of sight to the blind, to set at liberty them that are bruised, to preach the acceptable year*

[1] Matt. v. 28–32.
[2] Matt. v. 34–37.
[3] Matt. v. 38–42.
[4] Matt. v. 43–48.

of the Lord.[1] .... *And he began to say unto them, To-day hath this Scripture been fulfilled in your ears.*"[2]

The commands for peace given by Jesus, — those simple and clear commands, foreseeing all possibilities of discussion, and anticipating all objections, — these commands proclaimed the kingdom of God upon earth. Jesus, then, was, in truth, the Messiah. He fulfilled what had been promised. But we have not fulfilled the commands we must fulfil if the kingdom of God is to be established upon earth, — that kingdom which men in all ages have earnestly desired, and have sought for continually, all their days.

CHAPTER VII

Why have men not done as Christ commanded them, and thus secured the greatest happiness within their reach, the happiness they have always longed for and still desire?

And from all sides I hear one and the same reply, although expressed in different words: "Christ's teaching is very beautiful, and it is true that if we practised it, the kingdom of God would be established on earth; but it is difficult, and consequently impracticable." Christ's teaching how men should live is divinely beautiful, and brings men happiness, but it is difficult for men to practise it. We repeat this, and hear it repeated so many, many times, that we do not observe the contradiction contained in these words.

It is the quality of human nature to do what is best. And any instruction about the life of men is only an instruction as to what is best for men. If men are shown what is best for them to do, how can they say that they would like to do what is best, but cannot? Men can not only do what is bad for them, but they cannot help doing what is best for them.

The reasonable activity of man, since man began, has been applied to finding what is best among the contra-

[1] Isaiah lxi. 1, 2. [2] Luke iv. 18, 19, 21.

dictions with which the life of the individual man and of all men is filled.

Men fight for the soil, for objects which are necessary to them; then they arrive at the division of goods, and call this property; they find that this arrangement, although difficult to establish, is best, and they maintain ownership. Men fight for the possession of women, they abandon their children; then they find it is best for each to have his own family; and although it is difficult to sustain a family, they maintain the family, as they do ownership and many other things.

As soon as they discover that a thing is best, however difficult of attainment, men do it. What does it mean, then, when we say that Christ's teaching is beautiful, that a life according to Christ's teaching would be better than the life which men now lead, but that we cannot lead this better life because it is difficult?

If the word "difficult," used in this way, is to be understood in the sense that it is difficult to renounce the fleeting satisfaction of sensual desires that we may obtain a greater good, why do we not say that it is difficult to plow so that we may have bread, to plant apple trees that we may have apples? Every being endowed with even the slightest spice of reason knows that he must endure difficulties to procure any good. And yet we say that Christ's teaching is lovely, but impossible of practice, because it is difficult! Now it is difficult, because in following it we are obliged to deprive ourselves of many things of which we had never been deprived before. Have we never heard that it is far more to our advantage to endure difficulties and privations than to have no privations and always satisfy all our desires?

A man may be a beast and no one will reproach him for it, but a man cannot argue about his desire to be a beast. From the moment that he begins to reason, he is conscious of being endowed with reason, and this consciousness stimulates him to distinguish between the reasonable and the unreasonable. Reason does not prescribe; it only enlightens.

In searching for a door in the darkness, I kept bruising my hands and knees. A man came with a light, and I saw the door. I ought no longer to hit the wall when I see the door; much less ought I to affirm that I see the door, that it is best to go out through the door, but that I find it is difficult to do so, and that, consequently, I prefer to bruise my knees against the wall.

In this marvelous argument that the Christian teaching is beautiful, and gives the world true happiness, but that men are weak, men are sinful, they would like to do what is best but they do the worst, and so cannot do the best, — there is an evident misapprehension; there is something else besides defective reasoning; there must be also a fallacious idea. Only a fallacious idea that there is something where there is nothing, and nothing where there is something, could lead men to such a strange denial of the possibility of practising that which by their own avowal would be for their true welfare.

The fallacious idea which has reduced men to this condition is that which is called dogmatic Christian religion, as it is taught from childhood through the various catechisms, Orthodox, Catholic, and Protestant, to all who profess the Christianity of the Church.

This religion, according to the definition of it given by its followers, consists in accepting as real that which does not exist — these are Paul's words,[1] and they are repeated in all the theologies and catechisms as the best definition of faith. It is this faith in the reality of what does not exist that has led men to make the strange affirmation that Christ's teaching is beautiful for men, but will not do for men. Here is an exact epitome of what this religion teaches: —

A personal God, eternally existing — one of three persons — decided to create a world of spirits. This God of goodness created the world of spirits for their happiness, but it so happened that one of the spirits became spontaneously wicked and therefore unhappy. A long time passed, and God created another world, a material world,

[1] Heb. ii. 2. Literally, "Faith is the *support* of the hoped for, the *conviction* of the unseen." — Tr.

created man for man's own happiness, created man happy, immortal, and sinless. The felicity of man consisted in the enjoyment of life without toil; his immortality was due to the promise that this life should last forever; his innocence was due to the fact that he knew not evil.

Man was beguiled in paradise by that spirit of the first creation who had become spontaneously wicked, and from that time dates the fall of man, who engendered other men fallen like himself, and from that time men began to undergo toil, sickness, suffering, death, the physical and moral struggle for existence; that is to say, the imaginary man preceding the fall became real, as we know him to be, as we have no right or reason to imagine him not to be. The state of man who toils, who suffers, who chooses the good and rejects evil, who dies,—this state, which is the real and only conceivable state, is not, according to the doctrine of this religion, the normal state of man, but a state which is unnatural and temporary.

Although this state, according to the doctrine, has lasted for all humanity since the expulsion of Adam from paradise, that is, from the commencement of the world until the birth of Christ, and has continued since Christ's birth under exactly the same conditions, the faithful are asked to believe that this is an abnormal and temporary state. According to this doctrine, the Son of God, the second person of the Trinity, who was Himself God, was sent by God into the world in the garb of humanity to rescue men from this temporary and abnormal state; to deliver them from the pains with which they had been stricken by this same God because of Adam's sin; and to restore them to their former normal state of felicity,—that is, to immortality, innocence, and idleness. Christ, the second person of the Trinity (according to this doctrine), by suffering death at the hands of man, atoned for Adam's sin, and put an end to that abnormal state which had lasted from the commencement of the world. And from that time onward, the men who have had faith in Christ have returned to the state of the first man in paradise; that is, have become immortal, innocent, and idle.

The doctrine does not concern itself too closely with the practical result of the redemption, in virtue of which the earth after Christ's coming ought to have become once more, at least for believers, everywhere fertile, without need of human toil; sickness ought to have ceased, and mothers have borne children without pain, — since it is difficult to assure even believers who are worn by excessive labor and broken down by suffering, that it is not hard to toil, and not painful to endure suffering.

But that portion of the doctrine which proclaims the abrogation of death and of sin is asserted with special emphasis. It is asserted that the dead continue to live. And as the dead cannot bear witness that they are dead or that they are living, just as a stone is unable to affirm that it either can or cannot speak, this absence of denial is admitted as a proof, and it is asserted that dead men are not dead. With still more solemnity and assurance it is affirmed that, since Christ's coming, the man who has faith in him is free from sin; that is, that since Christ's coming, it is no longer necessary that man should guide his life by reason, and choose what is best for himself. He has only to believe that Christ has redeemed him from sin and he then becomes sinless, that is, perfectly good. According to this doctrine, men ought to believe that reason is powerless, and that for this cause they are without sin, that is, cannot err.

A faithful believer ought to be convinced that, since Christ's coming, the earth brings forth without labor, that children are born without pain, that diseases no longer exist, and that death and sin, that is, error, are destroyed; in a word, that what is, is not, and what is not, is.

Such is the rigorously logical theory of Christian theology.

This doctrine, by itself, seems to be innocent. But deviations from truth are never inoffensive, and the significance of their consequences is in proportion to the importance of the subject of which the falsehood is spoken. And here the subject of which the falsehood is spoken is the whole life of man.

What this doctrine calls the true life, is a life of personal happiness, without sin, and eternal; that is, a life which no one has ever known, and which does not exist. But the life that is, the only life we know, the life we live and all humanity lives and has lived, is, according to this doctrine, a degraded and evil life, a mere phantasmagoria of the happy life which is our due.

Of the struggle between animal instincts and reason, which takes place in the soul of every man and constitutes the essence of every man's life, this doctrine takes no account. This struggle became a reality which was accomplished in the person of Adam in paradise at the creation of the world. And the question, "Shall I or shall I not eat the apples which tempt me?" does not, according to this doctrine, exist for man. This question was decided, once for all, in the negative, by Adam in paradise. Adam sinned for me; in other words, he did wrong, and all of us have fallen irretrievably; and all our efforts to live by reason are vain and even impious. I am irreparably bad and I ought to know it. My salvation does not depend upon living by the light of reason, and, after distinguishing between good and evil, choosing the good; no, Adam, once for all, sinned for me, and Christ, once for all, has atoned for the wrong committed by Adam; and so I ought, as a looker-on, to mourn over the fall of Adam and rejoice at the redemption through Christ.

All the love for truth and goodness that is inherent in the heart of man, all his efforts to illuminate his spiritual life by the light of reason, all my spiritual life, are not only of slight importance, according to this doctrine, they are a temptation, an incitement to pride.

Life as it is on this earth, with all its joys and its splendors, with all its struggles of reason with darkness, — the life of all men that have lived before me, my own life with its inner struggles and triumphs, — all this is not the true life; it is the fallen life, a life irretrievably bad. The true life, the life without sin, is only in faith, that is, in imagination, that is, in lunacy!

Let any one break the habit contracted from infancy

of believing in all this; let him look boldly at this doctrine as it is; let him endeavor to put himself in the position of a man without prejudice, educated independently of this doctrine, — and then let him ask himself how this doctrine would appear to such a man! It would seem absolute insanity.

Strange and shocking as all this appeared to me, I was obliged to examine into it, for here alone I found the explanation of the objection, so devoid of logic and common sense, that I heard everywhere with regard to the impossibility of practising Christ's teaching: *It is admirable, and would give true happiness to men, but men cannot obey it.*

Only a conviction that reality does not exist, and that the non-existent is real, could lead men to this surprising contradiction. And this false conviction I found in the pseudo-Christian religion which men had been teaching for fifteen hundred years.

The objection that Christ's teaching is excellent but impracticable comes not only from believers, but from skeptics, from those who do not believe, or think that they do not believe, in the dogmas of the fall of man and the redemption. The objection to Christ's teaching that it is impracticable is raised by men of science and philosophers, and in general by men who consider themselves free from all prejudice. They believe, or imagine that they believe, in nothing, and so consider themselves as above such a superstition as the dogma of the fall and the redemption.

It seemed so to me also at first. It seemed to me also that these learned men had serious motives for denying the practicability of Christ's teaching. But when I came to look deeper into the sources of their negation, I was convinced that the skeptics also have a false conception of life; to them life is not what it is, but what they imagine it ought to be, — and this conception rests on the same foundation as does that of the believers. Professing themselves unbelievers, it is true they do believe in God or in Christ or in Adam; but they believe in a fundamental idea which is at the basis of their misconception, — in the rights of man to a life of happiness, — much more firmly than do the theologians.

However privileged science and philosophy boast of their claim to be the arbiters of the human mind, they are not its arbiters, but only its servants. Religion has provided a conception of life, and science travels in the beaten path. Religion reveals the meaning of the life of men, and science only applies this meaning to the different sides of life. And so, if religion gives a false meaning to human life, science, which builds upon this religious philosophy, can only apply this false notion under varying circumstances to the life of man. And this is what has happened with our European-Christian scientific philosophy.

The doctrine of the Church gave a fundamental meaning to the life of men in that man has a right to happiness, and this happiness is not attained by his own efforts, but by something external; and this conception has become the base of all our science and philosophy.

Religion, science, and public opinion, all, with one voice, tell us that the life we now lead is bad, and at the same time they affirm that the doctrine which teaches us how we can become better, and thus succeed in ameliorating life, is impracticable.

Religion says that Christ's teaching, which provides a reasonable method for the improvement of life by our own efforts, is impracticable because Adam fell, and the world was plunged into sin.

Our philosophy says that Christ's teaching is impracticable because human life is developed according to laws independent of the human will. Philosophy and all science, only in other words, say exactly the same as religion says in the dogmas of original sin and the redemption.

There are two fundamental theses at the basis of the doctrine of the redemption: (1) the normal life of man is a life of happiness, but our life on earth is one of misery, and it can never be bettered by man's efforts; (2) our salvation from this life is in faith.

These two theses are the source of the religious conceptions of the believers and the non-believers of our pseudo-Christian society. The second thesis gave birth to the Church and its organization; from the first is derived the received tenets of public opinion and our political and philosophical theories.

All the political and philosophical theories that seek to justify the existing order of things — such as Hegelianism and its offshoots — grow out of this thesis.

Pessimism, which demands of life what it cannot give and therefore denies the value of life, has here also its origin.

Materialism, with its strange and enthusiastic affirmation that man is a development and nothing more, is the legitimate offspring of the doctrine that teaches that life here is a fallen existence.

Spiritism, with its learned adherents, is the best proof we have that the conclusions of philosophy and science are not free, but are based on the religious doctrine of that eternal happiness which should be the natural heritage of man.

This false conception of life has had a deplorable influence on all reasonable human activity. The dogma of the fall and the redemption of man has debarred man from the most important and legitimate field for the exercise of his powers, and has deprived him entirely of the idea that he can of himself do anything to make his life happier or better. Science and philosophy, proudly believing themselves hostile to pseudo-Christianity, only carry out its decrees. Science and philosophy concern themselves with everything except the theory that man can do anything to make himself better or happier. What is called "ethics" — moral instruction — has entirely disappeared from our pseudo-Christian society.

Believers and non-believers do not concern themselves in the least with the problem how we ought to live, how to make use of the reason with which we are endowed, but they ask: —

"Why is our earthly life not what we imagine it ought to be, and when will it become what we wish?"

Thanks only to this false doctrine which has penetrated into the very blood and marrow of our generations, there has arisen the surprising phenomenon that man, as it were, spit out the apple of the knowledge of good and evil, which according to the tradition he ate in paradise, and forgetting that the whole history of man is only a solution of the contradictions between animal instincts and reason, he began to employ his reason in discovering the historical laws that govern his animal nature.

Excepting the philosophical doctrines of the pseudo-Christian world, all the philosophical and religious doctrines of all nations, as far as we know them, — Judaism, the doctrine of Confucianism, Buddhism, Brahmanism, the wisdom of the Greeks, — all aim to regulate human life, and to enlighten men with regard to what each must do to be and to live better. The whole doctrine of Confucius teaches the perfecting of the individual; Judaism, the personal fidelity of every man to an alliance with God; Buddhism, how every man may escape from the evil of life; Socrates taught the perfecting of the individual through reason; the Stoics recognized the independence of reason as the sole basis of the true life.

The reasonable activity of man has always been — it could not be otherwise — to light by the torch of reason his progress toward beatitude. Our philosophy tells us that free-will is an illusion, and then boasts of the boldness of such a declaration. Free-will is not only an illusion; it is a word which has no sense. This word was invented by theologians and experts in criminal law; to refute it is to battle with windmills.

But reason, which illuminates our life and impels us to modify our actions, is not an illusion, and its authority can never be denied. To obey reason in the pursuit of good is the substance of the teachings of all the masters of humanity, and it is the substance of Christ's teaching; it is reason itself, and we cannot deny reason by the use of reason.

Christ's teaching is the teaching about the "son of man," common to all men; in other words, the teaching about the reason common to all men, which illumines man in this endeavor.[1]

Christ's teaching about the "son of man" being the son of God is the basis of all the Gospels, but finds its most complete expression in the interview with Nicodemus. Every man, Christ says, aside from his consciousness of his material, individual life proceeding from his father and his birth in the flesh from his mother's womb, has also a consciousness of a spiritual birth,[2] of an inner liberty, of something within; this comes from on high, from the infinite that we call God;[3] now it is this inner consciousness born of God, the son of God in man, that we must possess and nourish if we would possess true life. The son of man is the son of God with a similar nature (but not the only son).

Whoever elevates within himself this son of God above everything else, whoever believes that life is in this only, will not be at variance with life. Variance from life proceeds only from this, that men do not believe in this light which is within them, the light of which John speaks when he says that "*life is in it; and the life is the light of men.*"

Christ teaches us to lift above everything the son of man, who is the Son of God, and the light of men.

He says, "When you have lifted up (exalted, magnified) the son of man, you will then know that I do not speak of myself personally.[4] The Hebrews did not understand His teachings, and asked, "Who is this son of man we must exalt?"[5] And to this question He answers: —

[1] Count Tolstoï seems to mean that all men have an impulse toward good and toward reason which leads to good. He says in a parenthetical note: —

(It is superfluous to prove that "son of man" signifies son of man. To understand by the words "son of man" anything different from what they signify is to assume that Jesus, to say what He wished to say, intentionally made use of words which have an entirely different meaning. But even if, as the Church says, "son of man" means "Son of God," the phrase "son of man" means also man existent, for Christ Himself called all men "the sons of God.")

[2] John iii. 5, 6, 7.

[3] John iii. 14–17.

[4] John xii. 49.

[5] John xii. 34.

"*Yet a little while is the light in you.*[1] *Walk while you have the light, lest darkness come upon you: for he that walks in darkness knows not whither he goes.*"[2]

To the question, What signifies 'exalt the son of man,' Christ replies: To live in the light that is in men.

The son of man, according to Christ's answer, is the light in which men ought to walk, while the light is in them to illuminate their lives.

"*Take heed therefore, that the light which is in thee be not darkness.*[3] *If the light which is in thee be darkness, how great is that darkness!*"[4] he says in His instructions to all men.

Before Christ and since Christ men have said the same thing: that in man is a divine light descended from heaven, and that this light is reason, which alone should be the object of our worship, since it alone can show the way to true well-being.

This has been said by the Brahmins, by the Hebrew prophets, by Confucius, by Socrates, by Marcus Aurelius, by Epictetus, and by all the true sages, —not by compilers of philosophical theories, but by men who sought goodness for themselves and for all men.[5]

And yet we declare, in accordance with the dogma of the redemption, that it is entirely superfluous to think

[1] In all the translations authorized by the Church, we find here a perhaps intentional error. The words *ἐν ὑμῖν*, *in you*, are invariably rendered *with you*. — AUTHOR'S NOTE.

[2] John xii. 35. [3] Luke xi. 35. [4] Matt. vi. 23.

[5] Marcus Aurelius says: "Reverence that which is best in the universe; and this is that which makes use of all things and directs all things. And in like manner also reverence that which is best in thyself; and this is of the same kind as that. For in thyself, also, that which makes use of everything else, is this, and thy life is directed by this." ("Meditations," v. 21.)

Epictetus says: "From God have descended the seeds not only to my father and grandfather, but to all beings which are generated on the earth and are produced, and particularly to rational beings; for these only are by their nature formed to have communion with God, being by means of reason conjoined with Him." ("Discourses," chap. ix.)

Confucius says: "The law of the great learning consists in developing and reëstablishing the luminous principle of reason which we have received from on high." This sentence is repeated many times, and constitutes the basis of Confucius's doctrine. — AUTHOR'S NOTE.

of the light that is in us, and that we ought not to speak of it at all!

We must, say the believers, study the three persons of the Trinity; we must know the nature of each of these persons, and what sacraments we ought or ought not to perform, for the salvation of men depends, not on our own efforts, but on the Trinity and the regular performance of the sacraments.

We must, say the non-believers, know the laws by which this infinitesimal particle of matter was evolved in infinite space and infinite time; but it is absurd to believe that by reason alone we can secure true well-being, because the amelioration of man's condition does not depend on man himself, but on the general laws we shall discover.

I firmly believe that, a few centuries hence, the history of what we call the scientific activity of this age will be a prolific subject for the hilarity and pity of future generations. For several centuries, they will say, the scholars of the small Western portion of a great continent were the victims of epidemic insanity; they imagined themselves to be the possessors of a life of eternal beatitude, and they busied themselves with divers lucubrations in which they sought to determine in what way this life could be realized, without doing anything themselves, or even concerning themselves with what they ought to do to ameliorate their actual life. And, what to the future historian will seem much more melancholy, it will be found that this group of men had once had a master who had taught them a number of simple and clear rules, pointing out what they must do to render their lives happy, — and that the words of this master had been construed by some to mean that he would come on a cloud to reorganize human society, and by others as admirable, but impracticable, since human life was not what they wished it to be, and consequently was not worthy of consideration; while human reason was obliged to concern itself with the study of the laws of this life, without any relation to the welfare of man.

The Church says Christ's teaching is impracticable, because life here is only a shadow of the true life. It cannot be good, it is all evil. The best way of living this life is to scorn it and to live by faith (that is, by imagination) in a happy and eternal life to come, and to live here as we do live, and to pray.

Philosophy, science, and public opinion say: —

"Christ's teaching is impracticable because the life of man does not depend on the light of reason with which he can illumine life itself, but on general laws; hence it is useless to illumine this life with reason and to live conformably with it; but we must live as we can with the firm conviction that according to the laws of historical and sociological progress, after having lived badly for a very long time, we shall suddenly find that our lives have become very good."

Once there was a farm to which men came; they found there all that was necessary to sustain life, — a house well furnished, barns filled with grain, cellars and storerooms well stocked with provisions, implements of husbandry, horses, sheep, and cattle, — in a word, all that was needed for a life of comfort and ease. Men came from all directions to this farm and began to profit by all they found there, but each for himself, without thinking of others, or of those who might follow. Each wanted the whole for himself, and hastened to seize on all that he could possibly grasp. Then began a veritable pillage; they fought for the possession of the spoils; they slaughtered the milch cow and the unshorn sheep for their flesh; they warmed their stoves with wagons and other implements; they fought for the milk and grain; they wasted and spoiled more than they could use.

No one could eat a morsel in peace. They snapped and snarled at one another; then some one stronger would come and take away the spoils already secured, to surrender them in turn to some one else.

All these people left the farm, exhausted, bruised, and famished.

Thereupon the Master put everything to rights again,

and arranged matters so that men might live there in peace. The farm again became a treasury of abundance. Then came another group of seekers, and the same struggle and tumult was repeated, till these in their turn went away bruised and angry, cursing their comrades and the Master for providing so little and so ill. Still the good Master reorganized the farm so that men might live on it, and again it was the same, and again and again and again!

And here there is found, among the newcomers, a teacher who said to his companions: —

"Brothers, we are not doing the right thing! see how abundantly everything on the farm is supplied, how well everything is arranged! There is enough here for us and for those who will come after us; only let us live in a reasonable manner. Let us not take from one another, but let us help one another. Let us work, plant, care for the dumb animals, and every one will be satisfied."

And it came to pass that some of the company understood what the teacher said; they ceased fighting and robbing one another, and began to work.

But others, who had not heard the teacher's words and distrusted him, did not follow his counsels, but continued to fight as before and to ruin the Master's goods, and then went on their way. Others came, and the same state of things went on. Those who followed the teacher's counsels said to those about them: —

"Cease fighting; do not waste the Master's goods; you will be better off for doing so; do as the teacher says." Still there were many who would not hear and would not believe, and matters went on very much as they did before.

All this was natural, and continued as long as people did not believe what the teacher said. But they tell us the time came when every one on the farm had heard and understood the teacher's words, and realized that God spoke through His lips, and that the teacher Himself was none other than God in person; and all had faith in His words as divine. But they tell us, that even after that, instead of living according to the teacher's advice, each still struggled for his own, and they went on slaying one another, saying: —

"Now we know for a certainty that it must be so and cannot be otherwise."

What does this all mean? There are the cattle — even they live in peace when there is fair grazing for them, so as not to destroy it idly; but men with knowledge, who have learned how they ought to live, who are convinced that God Himself has shown them how to live the true life, follow still their evil ways, because they say, "It is impossible to live otherwise."

These men have imagined something else! Now what have these men at the farm had in mind, if, after having heard the teacher's words, they have continued to live as before, snatching the bread from one another's mouths, fighting, and destroying all that was good and themselves as well? This is what: —

The teacher said to them, "Your life on this farm is bad; live better and your life will become good."

But they imagined that the teacher had condemned their life on the farm, and had promised them another and a better life, not on this farm, but somewhere else. They decided that the farm was only a temporary abiding-place,[1] and that it was not worth while to try to live well there; the important thing was not to be cheated out of the other life promised them elsewhere.

This is the only way in which we can explain the strange conduct of the people on the farm, of whom some believed that the teacher was God, and others that he was a wise man and his words were true, but all continued to live as before in defiance of the teacher's words.

These men heard everything, they understood everything, but they let the one significant truth in the wise man's teachings go in at one ear and out the other, — that they must work out for themselves their own peace and happiness there on the farm, to which they have

[1] *Dvor postoyalui*, an inn. The word translated farm throughout is *dvor*, meaning any residence with the yard and outbuildings.

come, while they imagined that this farm was only a temporary abiding-place, and beyond would be their eternal home.

Here is the origin of the strange declaration that the teacher's precepts were beautiful, even divine, but that they were difficult to practise.

If men would only cease from ruining themselves while waiting for some one to come and aid them: Christ on the clouds with the voice of a trumpet, or an historical law of the differentiation or integration of forces.

No one will come to their aid if they do not aid themselves. And it is easy for them to aid themselves. Only let them expect nothing from heaven or from earth, and cease ruining themselves.

CHAPTER VIII

LET us suppose that Christ's teaching gives the world happiness, that it is reasonable, and that man on the score of reason has no right to reject it, what can a single follower of that teaching do in the midst of a world of men who do not fulfil Christ's law? If all men would suddenly decide to fulfil Christ's teaching, then its practice would be possible. But one man alone cannot go against the whole world. "If, among the world of men who do not practise Christ's teaching," it is commonly said, "I alone obey it; if I give away all that I possess; if I turn the other cheek; if I refuse to take an oath or to go to war, I shall be arrested; if I do not die of hunger, I shall be flogged to death; if I am not flogged, I shall be cast into prison or shot, and all the happiness of my life — my life itself — will be sacrificed in vain."

This plea is founded on the same misunderstanding as forms the basis of all objections to the practicability of Christ's teaching.

This is what is generally said and what I myself thought until I freed myself entirely from the Church dogmas which prevented me from understanding the true significance of Christ's teaching about life.

Christ lays down His teaching about life as a means of salvation from the ruinous life lived by men who do not follow His teaching; and suddenly I declare that I should be very glad to follow His teaching but I fear I may ruin my life! Christ teaches salvation from a ruined life, and I cling to this ruined life! Hence it follows I do not consider this life of mine a ruined life, I consider it a good and profitable possession, something real. In this recognition of my personal worldly life as something real and good and belonging to me lies the misunderstanding that prevented me from comprehending Christ's teaching. Christ knew men's unfortunate tendency to regard their personal, worldly life as real and good, and so, in a series of sermons and parables, He taught them that they had no right to life, that they had no life until they obtain the true life by renouncing the phantom of life which they call their life.

To understand Christ's teaching about "saving" one's life, we must first understand what all the prophets said, what Solomon said, what Buddha said, what all the wise men of the world have said, about the personal life of man. We may, to use Pascal's expression, put it out of our thoughts and carry always before us a screen to conceal the abyss of death, toward which we keep hastening; but it suffices to reflect on the individual personal life of man, to be convinced that this life, in so far as it is personal, is not only of no account to each separately, but that it is a cruel jest to the heart, to the reason, of every man, and to all that is good in every man. And therefore to understand Christ's teaching we must, first of all, return to ourselves, reflect soberly, undergo the *μετάνοια* of which John the Baptist, Christ's predecessor, speaks, when addressing himself to men led astray like ourselves. He said:—

"*First of all, repent;*" in other words, "Reflect, or you will all perish." He said: "*The axe is already laid unto the root of the tree to cut it down. Death and perdition await each one of you. Forget not this, repent!*" Reflect. And Christ at the beginning of His career as a preacher also declared, "*Repent, or else you will all perish.*"

When Christ was told of the death of the Galileans massacred by Pilate, He said: —

"*Do you suppose these Galileans were sinners above all the Galileans, because they suffered such things? I tell you, No: but except you repent, you shall all likewise perish. Or those eighteen on whom the tower in Siloam fell, and slew them, do you suppose they were sinners above all men that dwelt in Jerusalem? I tell you, No: but except you repent, you will all likewise perish.*"[1]

If He had lived in our day, in Russia, He would have said: "Think you that those that were burnt to death in the circus at Berditchevo[2] or that were killed in the railway accident on the embankment of Kukuyevo were sinners above all others? I tell you, No; but you, if you do not repent, if you do not arouse yourselves, if you do not find in your life that which is imperishable, you also will perish. You are horrified by the death of those crushed by the tower, burned in the circus; but lo! your death, equally frightful and inevitable, is here, before you. You strive in vain to forget it; when it comes unexpectedly, it will be only the more horrible."

He said: —

"*When you see a cloud rise out of the west, straightway you say, There comes a shower; and so it is. And when the south wind blows you say, There will be heat; and it comes to pass. You hypocrites, you can discern the face of the sky and of the earth; but how is it that you do not discern this time? And why, even of yourselves, do you judge not what is right?*"[3]

You are able by signs to predict what the weather will be; why, then, do you not see what is before you? Flee from danger, guard your material life as much as you wish, nevertheless, though Pilate may not massacre

[1] Luke xiii. 1–5.

[2] This refers to a wooden building built for public amusement during carnival time in 1883. It caught fire; the doors could not be opened, and nearly all within were burned to death. — ED.

[3] Luke xii. 54–57.

you, a tower may fall on you, but if Pilate or the tower spare you, then you will die in your bed, amidst much greater suffering.

Make a simple calculation, as do worldly-minded men who undertake any enterprise whatever, such as building a house, going to war, or establishing a factory. They contrive and labor with the hope of seeing their calculations realized.

"*For who of you intending to build a tower does not first sit down and count the cost whether he have sufficient to finish it? Lest haply, after he has laid the foundation, and is not able to finish it, all that behold it begin to mock him, saying, This man began to build, and was not able to finish. Or what king, going to make war against another king, does not first sit down and consult whether he be able with ten thousand to meet him that comes against him with twenty thousand?*"[1]

Is it not senseless to labor at what, however much you try, can never be finished? Death will always come before the tower of your worldly prosperity can be completed. And if you know beforehand that, however you may struggle with death, not you, but death, will triumph; is it not an indication that we ought not to struggle with death, or to set our hearts on that which will surely perish, but to seek that which cannot be destroyed by our inevitable death?

"*And he said unto his disciples, Therefore I say unto you, Take no thought for your life what you shall eat; neither for the body, what you shall put on. The soul is more than meat and the body is more than raiment. Consider the ravens: for they neither sow nor reap; which neither have storehouse nor barn; and God feeds them: How much more are you better than the fowls? And who of you with taking thought can add to his stature one cubit? If you then are not able to do that which is least, why take you thought for the rest? Consider the lilies how they grow: they toil not, they spin not; and yet I say unto you that Solomon in all his glory was not arrayed like one of these.*"[2]

[1] Luke xiv. 28–31.

[2] Luke xii. 22–27.

Whatever pains we may take for our nourishment, for the care of the body, we cannot prolong life by a single hour.[1] Is it not folly to trouble ourselves about a thing that we cannot possibly accomplish? You know very well that your material life will end with death, and you take pains to guarantee your life by possessions. Life cannot be guaranteed by property. Understand that this is a ridiculous deception, whereby you only delude yourselves. The significance of life, says Christ, cannot be in what you possess or in what you can accumulate, in what is not yourselves. It must be in something entirely different. He says the life of man, in all its abundance, does not depend on his possessions.

"*The ground of a certain rich man,*" He says, "*brought forth plentifully: And he thought within himself, saying, What shall I do, because I have no room where to bestow my fruits? And he said, This will I do: I will pull down my barns, and build greater; and there will I bestow all my fruits and my goods. And I will say to my soul, Soul, thou hast much goods laid up for many years; take thine ease, eat, drink, and be merry. But God said to him, Thou fool, this night thy soul shall be required of thee: then whose shall those things be, which thou hast provided? So is he that lays up treasure for himself, and is not rich in God.*"[2]

Death always, at every moment, threatens him. Christ says: —

"*Let your loins be girded about, and your lamps burning; and you yourselves like men who wait for their lord, when he will return from the wedding; that when he comes and knocks they may open to him immediately. Blessed are those servants, whom the lord when he comes shall find watching; .... And if he shall come in the second watch, or come in the third watch, and find them so, blessed are those servants. And this know, that if the goodman of the house had known what hour the*

[1] The words of verse 25 are incorrectly translated; the word ἡλικίαν means *age, age of life;* consequently the whole phrase should be rendered can add one hour to his life. — AUTHOR'S NOTE.

[2] Luke xii. 16–21.

thief would come, he would have watched, and not have suffered his house to be broken through. Be therefore ready also: for the son of man comes at an hour when ye think not."[1]

The parable of the virgins waiting for the bridegroom, that of the consummation of the age, and the last judgment, all these places, as the commentators all agree, besides their secondary meaning of the end of the world, are designed to teach that death awaits us at every moment.

Death, death, death, awaits you at every second. Life is passed in sight of death. If you labor for yourselves alone, for your personal future, you know that in the future one thing awaits you, death. And death will destroy all that you have been working for. Consequently, life for itself can have no meaning. If it is a reasonable life, then it must be something else; in other words, it must be a life the object of which is not in a life for itself in the future. The reasonable life consists in living in such a way that life cannot be destroyed by death.

"*Martha, Martha, thou art troubled about many things, but only one thing is needful.*"[2] All the numberless actions which we perform for ourselves in the future will not be necessary for us; it is all a delusion with which we deceive ourselves; one thing only is needful.

From the day of his birth, man is so placed that he is threatened with inevitable ruin, that is a senseless life, and a senseless death, if he does not discover the one thing essential to the true life. This one thing which insures the true life Christ reveals to men. He does not invent this, He promises nothing through His own divine power; He simply reveals to men that, together with this personal life, which is an undoubted delusion, must be that which is the truth and not delusion.

In the parable of the husbandmen[3] Christ explains the cause of that blindness in men which conceals the truth

[1] Luke xii. 35–40.
[2] Luke x. 41.
[3] Matt. xxi. 33–42.

from them, and which impels them to take the apparent for the real, their personal life for the true life.

Men, living in a proprietor's cultivated garden, imagined that they were its owners. And from that erroneous fancy springs a series of foolish and cruel actions, which ends in their expulsion, their exclusion from life. Exactly so we have imagined that the life of each one of us is his own personal property, that we have the right to enjoy it as we wish, without recognizing any obligation to others.

And for us who imagine this there must inevitably be a similar series of senseless and cruel actions followed by exclusion from life. And as the husbandmen killed the householder's messengers and son, thinking that the more cruel they were the better able they would be to gain their ends, so we imagine that we shall obtain the greatest security by means of violence.

As the inevitable end for the husbandmen for not having given any one the fruits of the garden is that the proprietor will drive them out, in exactly the same way will the end be for men who imagine that the personal life is the true life. Death will expel them from life, replacing them by others, not as a punishment, but simply because these men have misconceived the meaning of life. Exactly as the residents of the garden either forgot, or did not wish to remember, that they had received a garden already hedged about and provided with a driven well, and that some one had labored for them and expected them to labor in their turn for others; so men who would live for themselves have forgotten and wish to forget all that has been done for them before they were born, and is done for them all the days of their lives, and that therefore something is expected of them. They wish to forget that all the blessings of life which they enjoy have been given to them and are given to them, and therefore ought to be shared with others.

This correction of our view of life, this *μετάνοια*, or repentance, is the corner-stone of Christ's teaching. According to Christ's teaching, just as the vine-dressers living in the vineyard which had not been cultivated by them should have understood and felt that they owed an unpaid debt to the master; so should men understand and feel that from the day of their birth to the day of their death they owe an unpaid debt to those that lived before them, and to those that are living now, and to those that are to live henceforth, as well as to Him that was and is and is to be the end of all. They ought to understand that every hour of their life during the time of which they do not cut this kind of life short, they increase this obligation, and that a man, therefore, who lives for himself, and denies this obligation connecting him with life and its first principle, deprives himself of life, and so forfeits life. He should remember that in living thus, striving to save his own life, his personal life, he ruins it, as Christ so many times said.

The only true life is the life that continues the past life, that promotes the happiness of the present and the happiness of the future. To take part in this true life, man should renounce his personal will so as to fulfil the will of the Father of Life who gave it to the son of man.

The slave that performs his own will and not his master's will shall not dwell forever in the master's house, says Christ, expressing the same thought in another place;[1] only the son who observes the will of the father shall have eternal life.

Now, the will of the Father of Life is the life, not of an individual man, but of the only son of man living among men; and so a man saves his life when he looks on his life as a pledge, as the talent confided to him by the Father for the profit of all, when he lives not for himself, but for the son of man.

A master gave each of his slaves a certain proportion of his property, and, without saying anything to them, left them to themselves. Some of the slaves, though they had not received explicit directions from their master how to employ their part of the lord's property, understood that the property was not theirs, but still belonged to the master, and that it ought to increase,

[1] John viii. 35.

and they labored for their master. And the servants who had labored for the master became partakers in the master's life, while the others, who had not so labored, were despoiled even of what they had received.[1]

The life of the son of man has been given to all men, and they have not been told why it was given to them. Some men understand that life is not for their personal use, but was given them as a gift, that they must use it for the good of the son of man, and thus live; others, feigning not to understand the true object of life, refuse to serve life: and those that labor for the true life will be united with the source of life; those that do not so labor will lose the life they already have. And here, from verse thirty-one to forty-six, Christ tells us in what the service of the son of man consists and what will be the recompense of that service. The son of man, according to Christ's expression, like a king, will say: —

"*Come you blessed of my Father, inherit the kingdom because you have fed me, given me drink, clothed and received me, because I am the same in you and in the smallest of those whom you have pitied and benefited. You have not lived the personal life, but the life of the son of man, and therefore you have the life eternal.*"

According to all the Gospels, Christ teaches nothing else but this life eternal; and, strange as it may seem to say this of Christ, Christ, who arose again in person, and promised that all should rise again, — Christ not only said nothing in affirmation of individual resurrection and individual immortality beyond the grave, but even attributed to that restoration of the dead in the kingdom of the Messiah conjectured by the Pharisees a significance which allowed no such notion as a personal resurrection.

The Sadducees controverted the restoration of the dead. The Pharisees accepted it just as the orthodox Hebrews accept it now. According to the idea of the Hebrews, the restoration of the dead — but not the resurrection, as this word is incorrectly rendered — is to be accomplished at the time of the coming of the age of the

[1] Matt. xxv. 14-46.

Messiah and the establishment of the kingdom of God on earth. And here Christ, meeting with this superstition of a temporal, local, and physical resurrection, denies it, and in its place establishes His teaching concerning the restoration of the eternal life in God.[1]

When the Sadducees, who denied the restoration of the dead, supposing that Christ believed with the Pharisees in the resurrection, asked Him to which of the seven brethren the woman should belong, He replied with clearness and precision concerning this and the other idea. He said:[2] "*You err, knowing neither the Scriptures nor the power of God.*" And refuting the argument of the Pharisees, He said: The restoration from the dead will be neither physical nor personal. Those that attain restoration from the dead, He said, will become the sons of God, and will live like the angels — the sons of God — in heaven, that is, with God; and such personal questions as "whose wife will she be," cannot exist for them because they, united with God, cease to be persons.

Touching the restoration of the dead He said, replying to the Sadducees, who recognized one earthly life and nothing besides an earthly life in the flesh: —

"*Have you not read what was said to you by God? In the Scriptures it says that in the bush God spoke to Moses, saying, I am the God of Abraham, and the God of Isaac, and the God of Jacob.*"[3] If God said to Moses

[1] The following sentences appear in the French translation, apparently from another manuscript from that used in the Elpidin edition: —

[Every time that Christ met with this superstition (introduced at this period into the Talmud, and of which there is not a trace in the records of the Hebrew prophets), He did not fail to deny its truth. The Pharisees and the Sadducees were constantly discussing the subject of the resurrection of the dead. The Pharisees believed in the resurrection of the dead, in angels, and in spirits (Acts xxiii. 8), but the Sadducees did not believe in resurrection, or angel, or spirit. We do not know the source of the difference in belief, but it is certain that it was one of the polemical subjects among the secondary questions of the Hebraic doctrine that were constantly under discussion in the synagogues. And Christ not only did not recognize the resurrection, but denied it every time He met with the idea.]

[2] Matt. xxii. 29–32; Mark xii. 24–27; Luke xx. 34–38.

[3] Ex. iii. 6.

that He was the God of Jacob, then Jacob is not dead for God, because "*He is not the God of the dead, but the God of the living. For God all are living.*"[1] And so if there is a living God, then also that man is living who has entered into community with the eternally living God.

Against the Pharisees Christ said that the restoration of life could not be physical and personal. Against the Sadducees He said that, apart from the personal and temporal life, there is still another life in union with God.

While Christ denies the personal resurrection in the flesh, He acknowledges the restoration of life in this sense, that man transfers his life to God. Christ teaches salvation from a personal life, and places this salvation in the exaltation of the son of man and life in God. Combining this teaching of His with the teaching of the Hebrews concerning the coming of the Messiah, He speaks to the Hebrews about the restoration of the son of man from the dead, meaning by this, not the physical and personal restoration of the dead, but the awakening of life in God. Of the personal resurrection in the flesh He never speaks. The best proof that Christ never preached the resurrection of men is given by the only two passages which theologians adduce as proofs that He taught the doctrine of the resurrection. These two passages are as follows: Matt. xxv. 31–46, and John v. 28, 29. In the first He is speaking of the coming, that is, the restoration, the exaltation, of the son of man — just exactly as it says in Matthew x. 23; and then the greatness and power of the son of man are compared to a king's. In the second place it speaks of the restoration of the true life here on earth, as this is expressed also in the twenty-fourth verse preceding.

It only requires to reflect on the meaning of Christ's teaching about the eternal life in God, it requires to reëstablish in one's imagination the teaching of the Hebrew prophets, to understand that if Christ had wished to promulgate the teaching about the resurrec-

[1] Mark xii. 26, 27.

tion of the dead, which was at that time only just beginning to get into the Talmud and becoming an object of controversy, then He would have clearly and definitely made this His teaching.

On the contrary, He not only did not do this, but even disclaimed it, and in all the Gospels it is impossible to find a single passage which would support this teaching. And the passages adduced above signify something entirely different. Strange as it may appear to those who have never carefully studied the Gospels for themselves, Christ said nothing whatever about His personal resurrection.

If, as the theologians teach, the foundation of the Christian faith is Christ's resurrection, it would seem the least thing to be desired that Christ, knowing that He was to rise again, knowing that in this would consist the principal dogma of faith in Him, should speak of the matter at least once, in clear and precise terms. Now, according to the canonical Gospels, He not only did not speak of it in clear and precise terms, He did not speak of it at all, not once, not a single word.

Christ's teaching consisted in the elevation of the son of man, that is, the essence of the life of man, man's recognizing himself as the son of God. In His own individuality Jesus personified the man who has recognized His sonship to God.[1] He asked His disciples, who men said that He, the son of man, was. His disciples replied that some took Him for John the Baptist miraculously raised from the dead, others for a prophet, and some for Elijah descended from heaven. "*But who say you that I am?*" He asked. And Peter understanding Christ exactly as He understood Himself, answered, —

"*Thou art the Messiah, the son of the living God.*"

And Christ responded: —

"*Flesh and blood have not revealed it unto thee, but my Father which is in heaven;*" in other words, "thou hast understood, not through faith in human concordances, but because, feeling thyself to be the son of God, thou

[1] Matt. xvi. 13–20.

hast understood me." And after having explained to Peter that the true faith is founded upon this sonship to God, Christ charged His other disciples that they should tell no man that He, Jesus, was the Messiah.

After this, Christ told them that although He should suffer and be put to death, the son of man claiming to be the son of God would be restored and would triumph over all. And these words are interpreted as a prophecy of His resurrection. Here are the fourteen passages[1] which are interpreted as Christ's prophecies of His own resurrection; in three of these passages it refers to Jonah in the whale's belly, in another to the rebuilding of the temple. In the other ten it says the son of man cannot be destroyed; but there is not a word about the resurrection of Jesus Christ.

In none of these passages is the word "resurrection" found in the original text. Ask any one who is ignorant of theological interpretations, but who knows Greek, to translate all these places, and he will never translate them as they stand translated. In the original we find two different words, one ἀνίστημι, the other ἐγείρω; one of these words means to "reëstablish"; the other, in the middle voice, means "to awaken, to rise up, to arouse one's self." But neither the one nor the other can ever, in any case, mean to "resuscitate" — to raise from the dead. In order to be fully convinced that these Greek words and the corresponding Hebrew word, *qum*, cannot mean to "rise from the dead," we have only to examine the scriptural passages where these words are employed, as they very frequently are, to see that in no case is the meaning "to resuscitate" admissible. The word for *voskresnut'*, *auferstehn*, *ressusciter* — "to resuscitate" — did not exist in the Greek or Hebrew tongues, for the reason that the conception corresponding to this word did not exist. To express the idea of resurrection in Greek or in Hebrew, it is necessary to employ a periphrasis, it is necessary to say "is arisen" or "has awakened" from the

[1] John ii. 19, 22; Matt. xii. 40; Luke xi. 30; Matt. xvi. 4; Matt. xvi. 21; Mark viii. 31; Luke ix. 22; Matt. xvii. 23; Mark ix. 31; Matt. xx. 19; Mark x. 34; Luke xviii. 33; Matt. xxvi. 32; Mark xiv. 25.

dead. Thus, in the Gospel of Matthew, xiv. 2, where reference is made to Herod's belief that John the Baptist had been resuscitated, we read, *αὐτὸς ἠγέρθη ἀπὸ τῶν νεκρῶν*, "has awakened from the dead." In the same manner, in Luke xvi. 31, at the close of the parable of Lazarus, it says that even if any one arose from the dead, men would not believe him, and there also it says *ἐάν τις ἐκ νεκρῶν ἀναστῇ*, "if one arose from the dead." But, if in these passages the words "from the dead" were not added to the words "arose" or "awakened," these words "arise" or "waken," never signified and never could signify resuscitation. When Christ spoke of Himself, in all these places, He did not once use the words "among the dead" in any of the passages quoted in support of His prophecy of His own resurrection.

Our conception of the resurrection is so entirely foreign to the Hebrews' conception of life, that we cannot even imagine how Christ would have been able to talk to them of the resurrection, and of an eternal, individual life, which should be the lot of every man. The idea of a future eternal life comes neither from Jewish doctrine nor from Christ's teachings, but it made its way into the ecclesiastical doctrine from an entirely different source. Strange as it may seem, it cannot be denied that belief in a future life is a primitive and crude conception based upon a confused idea of the resemblance between death and sleep, — an idea common to all savage races.

The Hebraic doctrine (and much more the Christian doctrine) was far above this conception. But we are so convinced of the elevated character of this superstition, that we use it as a proof of the superiority of our doctrine to that of the Chinese or the Hindus, who do not believe in it at all. Not the theologians only, but the free-thinkers, the learned historians of religions, such as Tiele, and Max Müller, make use of the same argument, In their classification of religions, they give the first place to those that recognize the superstition of the resurrection, and declare them to be far superior to those not professing that belief. The free-thinker Schopenhauer boldly denounced the Hebraic religion as the most despicable — *die niederträchtigste* — of all religions because it contains not a trace of — *keine Idee* — of the immortality of the soul. Actually not only the idea itself, but the word for it, were wanting to the Hebraic religion. Eternal life is the Hebrew *chayē ôlam.*[1] By *ôlam* is meant the infinite, that which is permanent in the limits of time; *ôlam* also means "world" or "cosmos." Universal life, and much more, "eternal life," *chayē ôlam*, is, according to the Jewish doctrine, the attribute of God alone. God is the God of life, the living God. Man, according to the Hebraic idea, is always mortal. God alone is always living. In the Pentateuch, the expression "eternal life" is twice met with; once in Deuteronomy and once in Genesis. God is represented as saying: —

> "*See now that I, even I, am he,*
> *And there is no god but me:*
> *I kill, and I make alive;*
> *I have wounded, and I heal:*
> *And there is none that can deliver out of my hand.*
> *For I lift up my hand to heaven,*
> *And say, I live forever.*"[2]

The other time in the book of Genesis: —

"*And Jehovah said, Behold, the man is become as one of us, to know good and evil: and now, lest he put forth his hand, and take also of the tree of life, and eat and live forever.*"[3]

These two are the only instances of the use of the expression "eternal life" in the Pentateuch or in the whole of the Old Testament (with the exception of another instance in the apocryphal book of Daniel), and they determine clearly the Hebraic conception of the life in general and the life eternal. Life itself, according to the Hebrews, is eternal, is in God; but man is always mortal: it is his nature to be so.

Nowhere in the Old Testament does it say as we

[1] The phrase occurs only once in the Old Testament, Dan. xii. 2.

[2] Deut. xxxii. 39, 40.

[3] Gen. iii. 22.

are taught by the sacred histories that God breathed an immortal soul into man, or that the first man, until he sinned, was immortal. According to the first recital in the Book of Genesis,[1] God created man exactly like the animals, exactly like them male and female created he them, and commanded them likewise to increase and multiply. As it is not said in regard to animals that they are immortal, so it is not said of men that they are immortal. In the second chapter it tells how man learned to distinguish good and evil. But of life it says categorically that God drove man out of paradise and denied him access to the tree of life. Man, therefore, did not taste the fruit of the tree of life; therefore he did not acquire *chayē òlam*, in other words, eternal life, and remained mortal.

According to the doctrine of the Hebrews man is man, exactly as he is — in other words, he is mortal. Life is in him only as life perpetuated from one generation to another, in a race. According to the doctrine of the Hebrews only one nation possesses in itself the possibility of life.

When God said, "Ye shall live, and not die," he addressed these words to the people. The life that God breathed into man is mortal for each separate human being; this life is perpetuated from generation to generation, if men fulfil the covenant with God, that is, obey the conditions imposed by God. After having propounded the Law, and having told them that this Law was to be found not in heaven, but in their own hearts, Moses said to the people: —

"*See, I have set before you this day life and good, and death and evil; in that I command you this day to love the Eternal, to walk in his ways, and to keep his commandments, that you may live. .... I call heaven and earth to witness against you this day, that I have set before you life and death, the blessing and the curse: therefore choose life, that you may live, you and your seed: to love the Eternal, to obey his voice, and to cleave*

[1] i. 26.

unto him: for from him is your life, and the length of your days."[1]

The principal difference between our conception of human life and that possessed by the Jews is, that while we believe that our mortal life, transmitted from generation to generation, is not the true life, but a fallen life, a life temporarily depraved, — the Jews, on the contrary, believed this life to be the true and supreme good, given to man on condition that he will obey the will of God. From our point of view, the transmission of the fallen life from generation to generation is the transmission of a curse; from the Jewish point of view, it is the supreme good to which man can attain, on condition that he accomplish the will of God.

On this Hebraic conception of life Christ founded His doctrine of the true or eternal life, which He contrasted with the personal and mortal life. Christ said to the Jews: —

"*Search the Scriptures; for in them you think you have eternal life.*"[2]

The young man asked Christ what he must do to have eternal life. Christ said in reply: —

"*If thou wilt enter into life, keep the commandments.*" He did not say "eternal life," but simply "life."[3] To the same question propounded by the scribe, the answer was, "*This do, and thou shalt live*";[4] here also, He says "live" simply, and does not add "forever." From these two instances, we know what Christ meant by eternal life; whenever He made use of the phrase in speaking to the Jews, He employed it in exactly the same sense in which it was expressed in their own law, — the accomplishment of the will of God is the eternal life.

In contrast with a temporary, isolated, and personal life, Christ taught of the eternal life which in Deuteronomy God promised to Israel, — with this difference, that while according to the notion of the Jews the

[1] Deut. xxx. 15–19
[2] John v. 39.
[3] Matt. xix. 17.
[4] Luke x. 28.

eternal life was to be perpetuated solely by them, the chosen people, and that whoever wished to possess this life must follow the exceptional laws given by God to Israel, according to Christ's teaching the eternal life is perpetuated in the son of man, and that to obtain it we must practise Christ's commands, which express the will of God for all humanity.

As opposed to the personal life, Christ taught us, not of a life beyond the grave, but of a universal life united with the life of humanity, past, present, and to come, the life of the son of man.

According to the teaching of the Hebrews, the personal life could be saved from death only by accomplishing the will of God as propounded in the Mosaic law. On this condition only the life of the Hebrews would not perish, but would pass from generation to generation of the chosen people of God.

According to Christ's teaching, the personal life is saved from death likewise by the accomplishment of the will of God as propounded in Christ's command. Only on this condition, according to Christ's teaching, the personal life does not perish, but becomes eternal and immutable in the son of man. The difference is, that while the worship of God as established by Moses was worship of one people's God, Christ's worship of the Father is the worship of the God of all men. The perpetuity of life in the posterity of a people is doubtful, because the people itself may disappear, and perpetuity depends upon a posterity in the flesh. Perpetuity of life, according to Christ's teaching, is indubitable, because life, according to His teaching, is transferred to the son of man who lives in harmony with the will of the Father.

But let us grant that Christ's words concerning the last judgment and the consummation of the age, and other words reported in the Gospel of John, are a promise of a life beyond the grave for the souls of mortal men, — it is none the less true that His teachings in regard to the light of life and the kingdom of God have the same meaning for us that they had for His hearers eighteen centuries ago; that is, that the only real life is the life of the son of man according to the Father's will.

It is easier to admit this than to admit that the doctrine of the true life, according to the Father's will, contains the conception of immortality and a life beyond the grave.

Perhaps it is fairer to presuppose that man, after this terrestrial life passed in the satisfaction of personal desires, will enter upon the possession of an eternal personal life in paradise, with all imaginable enjoyments; perhaps this is fairer, but to believe that this is so, to endeavor to persuade ourselves that for our good actions we shall be recompensed with eternal felicity, and for our bad actions punished with eternal torments, — to believe this, does not aid us in understanding Christ's teaching, but, on the contrary, deprives Christ's teaching of its chief foundation.

All Christ's teaching goes to persuade His disciples who recognize the illusoriness of the personal life to renounce it, and merge it in the life of all humanity, in the life of the son of man. Now the doctrine of the immortality of the individual soul does not impel us to renounce the personal life; on the contrary, it affirms the continuance of individuality forever.

According to the notion of the Jews, the Chinese, the Hindus, and all men who do not believe in the dogma of the fall and the redemption, life is life as it is. A man is united with a woman, engenders children, cares for them, grows old, and dies. His children grow up, and his life continues, it passes on from one generation to another without interruption, like everything else in the world, — stones, metals, earth, plants, animals, stars. Life is life, and we must make the best of it.

To live for self alone is not reasonable. And so men, from their earliest existence, have sought for some reason for living aside from the gratification of their own desires; they live for their children, for their families, for their nation, for humanity, for all that does not die with the personal life.

On the other hand, according to the doctrine of our Churches, human life, the supreme good that is known to us, is but a very small portion of another life of which we are deprived for a season. Our life, according to this conception, is not the life that God intended or was obliged to give us. Our life is degenerate and fallen, a mere fragment, a mockery of life, compared with the real life which we think God ought to give us. The principal object of our life, according to this theory, is not to try to live this mortal life conformably to the will of the Giver of Life; or to render it eternal in the generations of men, as the Hebrews believed; or to identify ourselves with the will of the Father, as Christ taught; no, it is to believe that after this unreal life the true life will begin.

Christ did not speak of the imaginary life that God ought to give us, and that God for some unexplained reason did not give us. The theory of the fall of Adam, of eternal life in paradise, of an immortal soul breathed by God into Adam, was unknown to Christ; He never spoke of it, never by one word made the slightest allusion to its existence.

Christ spoke of life as it is, as it always will be; we speak of an imaginary life which has never existed. How, then, can we understand Christ's teaching.

Christ did not anticipate such a singular change of view in His disciples. He supposed that all men understood that the destruction of the personal life is inevitable, and He revealed to them an imperishable life. He offers true peace to those that suffer; but to those that believe that they are certain to possess more than Christ gives, His doctrine cannot give anything. I am going to exhort a man to toil, assuring him that in return for it he will receive food and clothing; and suddenly this man is persuaded that he is already a millionaire. Evidently he will pay no attention to my exhortations. So it is with regard to Christ's teachings. Why should I toil for bread when I can be rich without labor? Why should I trouble myself to live this life according to the will of God, when without doing so I am sure of a personal life for all eternity?

We are taught that Christ, as the second person of the Trinity, as God made manifest in the flesh, was the salvation of men; that He took upon himself the penalty for the sin of Adam and the sins of all men; that He atoned to the first person of the Trinity for the sins of humanity; that He instituted the Church and the sacraments for our salvation — believing this, the Church says, we are saved, and shall possess a personal, immortal life beyond the grave. But meanwhile we cannot deny that Christ saved and still saves men by revealing to them their inevitable ruin, showing them that He is the way, the truth, and the life, the true way of life instead of the false way of the personal life that men had heretofore followed.

If there are any who doubt the life beyond the grave and salvation based upon redemption, no one can doubt the salvation of all men, and of each individual man, if they will accept the evidence of the destruction of the personal life, and follow the true way to safety by bringing their personal wills into harmony with the will of God. Let each man endowed with reason ask himself, What is life? and What is death? and let him try to give to life and death any other meaning than that revealed by Christ.

Every notion of a personal life not based on the renunciation of self, the service of humanity, of the son of man, is a phantom which vanishes at the first application of reason. I cannot doubt that my personal life will perish, but the life of the world according to the will of the Father will not perish, and that only identification with it gives me the possibility of salvation. It is not much in comparison with the sublime belief in the future life! It is not much, but it is sure.

I am lost in a snowstorm. Some one assures me — and it seems to him so — that he sees a light in the distance, that it is in the village, but it only seems so to him and to me because we want to have it so; we strive to reach this light, but we never can find it. Another plows through the snow; he seeks and finds the road, and he cries to us, "Go not that way, the lights you see are false, you will wander to destruction; here is the hard road, I feel it beneath my feet; it will bring us home." It is very little. When we had faith in those lights that gleamed in our deluded eyes, there seemed to be somewhere yonder a village, a warm izba, deliverance, rest; and now in exchange for it we have nothing but the solid road. But if we continue to travel toward the imaginary lights we shall perish; if we follow the road, we shall surely escape.

What, then, ought I to do, if I alone understood Christ's teaching, and I alone had trust in it among a people who neither understand it nor obey it?

What was I to do — to live like the rest of the world, or to live according to Christ's teaching? I understood Christ's teaching as expressed in His commands, and I saw that the practice of these commands would bring happiness to me and to all men in the world. I understood that the fulfilment of these commands is the will of that first cause from which my life sprang.

More than this, I saw that whatever I did I should die like a brute after a senseless life if I did not fulfil the will of the Father, and that the only chance of salvation lay in the fulfilment of His will.

Doing as all men do, I unquestionably act contrary to the welfare of all men, I unquestionably act contrary to the will of the Giver of Life, I unquestionably forfeit the sole possibility of bettering my desperate condition. Doing as Christ commands me, I continue the work common to all men who had lived before me; I contribute to the welfare of all men now living and of those who will live after me; I obey the command of the Giver of Life; I do the only thing that can save me.

The circus at Berditchevo is in flames. All are pressing and suffocating one another, struggling before the door, which opens inward.

"Back, stand back from the door; the closer you press against it, the less the chance of escape; stand back, and you will be able to get out and save yourselves!"

Whether I am alone in hearing this command, or whether many also hear and believe it, is all the same; but from the moment I have heard and understood, what can I do but fall back from the door, and call upon every one to obey the voice of the savior? I may be suffocated, I may be crushed beneath the feet of the multitude, I may perish, but my sole chance of safety is to go where the only exit is. And I can do nothing else. A savior should be a savior, that is, one who saves. And Christ's salvation is the true salvation. He appeared, He spoke, and humanity is saved.

The circus has been burning an hour, and it is necessary to make haste, otherwise the men inside may have no time to escape. But the world has been burning for eighteen hundred years; it has been burning ever since Christ said, "*I am come to send fire on the earth;*" and I suffer as it burns, and it will burn until men are saved. Do not men exist? was not this fire kindled that men might have the felicity of salvation?

Understanding this, I understood and believed that Jesus is not only the Messiah, the Christ, but that He is in truth the Saviour of the world.

I know that He is the only way, that there is no other way for me or for those that are tormented with me in this life. I know that for all and for me there is no other safety than to fulfil Christ's commands, which give to all humanity the greatest conceivable sum of benefits.

Even if I shall have greater trials to endure, even if, by fulfilling Christ's teaching, I shall the sooner die, still it does not alarm me. This might seem frightful to any one who does not realize the nothingness and absurdity of an isolated personal life, and who believes that he will never die. But I know that my life, considered in relation to my individual happiness, is, taken by itself, a stupendous farce, and that this meaningless existence will end in a stupid death, and therefore this cannot be frightful to me. I shall die as all die, even those that have not observed the doctrine; but my life and my death will have a meaning for myself and for others. My life and my death will have added something to the life and salvation of others, and this is what Christ taught.

CHAPTER IX

If all men practised Christ's teaching, the kingdom of God would have come upon earth; if I alone practise it, I shall do what is best for all men and for myself. There is no salvation without the fulfilment of Christ's teaching.

But who will give me the strength to practise it, to follow it without ceasing, and never to fail? "*Lord, I believe; help thou mine unbelief.*" The disciples called upon Jesus to strengthen their faith.

"*When I wish to do good,*" says the apostle Paul, "*I do that which is evil.*" "It is difficult to be saved," is what is commonly said and thought.

A man is drowning, and calls for aid. A rope, which is the only thing that can save him, is thrown to him, but the drowning man says: "Strengthen my belief that this rope will save me. I believe that the rope will save me; but help my unbelief."

What is the meaning of this? If a man will not seize upon his only means of safety, it is plain that he does not understand his condition.

How can a Christian who professes to believe in Christ's divinity and His doctrine, whatever may be the meaning that he attaches thereto, say that he wishes to believe, and that he cannot believe? God comes upon earth, and says, "Eternal torments, fire, absolute darkness, await you; and here is your salvation — fulfil my doctrine." A believing Christian cannot help believing and profiting by the salvation thus offered to him; he cannot possibly say, "Help my unbelief."

For a man to say this, it must be that he not only

does not believe in his perdition, but he must be certain that he shall not perish.

Children have fallen from a boat into the water. They are kept floating by the current, by their still unsoaked clothes, and their feeble struggles, and they do not realize their danger. Those in the boat throw out a rope. They warn the children against their peril, and urge them to grasp the rope, — the parables of the woman and the piece of silver, the shepherd and the lost sheep, the marriage feast, the prodigal son, all have this meaning, — but the children do not believe; they refuse to believe, not in the rope, but that they are in danger of drowning. Children as frivolous as themselves have assured them that they can continue to float gaily along, even when the boat is far away. The children do not believe that their clothes will soon be saturated, the strength of their little arms exhausted, they will suffocate, sink, and perish. This they do not believe, and so they do not believe in the rope of safety.

Just as the children fallen from the boat will not grasp the rope that is thrown to them, persuaded that they will not perish, so men who believe in the immortality of the soul, convinced that there is no danger, do not practise Christ's commands, God's commands. They do not believe in what it is impossible not to believe, simply because they believe in what it is impossible to believe. And so they cry to some one, "Strengthen our faith, lest we perish."

But this is impossible. To have the faith that they will not perish, they must cease to do what will lead them to perdition, and they must begin to do something for their own safety, — they must grasp the rope of safety.

Now this is exactly what they do not wish to do; they wish to persuade themselves that they will not perish, although they see their comrades perishing one after another before their very eyes. This desire to believe in what does not exist they call faith! It is plain that they never have enough faith, and they wish for more.

When I understood Christ's teaching, I saw that what

these men call faith is that false faith denounced by the apostle James in his epistle:[1]—

"*What does it profit, my brethren, if a man believe he has faith, but has not works? can that faith save him? If a brother or sister be naked and in lack of daily food, and one of you say unto them, Go in peace, be ye warmed and filled; and yet you give them not the things needful to the body; what does it profit? Even so faith, if it have not works, is dead in itself. But some one will say, Thou hast faith, and I have works: Shew me thy faith which is without works, and I, by my works, will shew thee my faith. Thou believest that God is one; thou dost well: the demons also believe, and tremble. But wilt thou know, O vain man, that faith without works is dead? Was not Abraham our father justified by works when he offered up Isaac his son upon the altar? Thou seest that faith wrought with his works, and by works was faith made perfect.*[2]*.... Ye see that by works a man is justified, and not only by faith. .... For as the body without the spirit is dead, so faith is dead without works.*"[3]

James says that the only indication of faith is the acts that it inspires, and consequently that a faith which does not result in acts is of words merely, with which one cannot feed the hungry, or justify belief, or obtain salvation. A faith without acts is not faith. It is only a disposition to believe in something, a vain affirmation of belief in something in which one does not really believe.

Faith, according to this definition, is what originates works, and works are what completes faith, in other words, what makes faith faith.

The Jews said to Christ: "*What signs shewest thou then, that we may see, and believe thee? what dost thou work?*"[4]

This they said to Him when He was on the cross:

[1] The epistle of James was not accepted for a long time by the Church, and when it was accepted was subjected to various alterations: certain words are omitted, others are transposed, or translated in an arbitrary way. I have retained the accepted translation, correcting the defective passages after the Tischendorf text.—AUTHOR'S NOTE IN TEXT.

[2] Gen. xv. 6.

[3] James ii. 14–26.

[4] John vi. 30.

"Let him now come down from the cross that we may see and believe."[1]

"He saved others; himself he cannot save. If he is the king of the Israelites, let him now come down from the cross and we will believe on him."[2]

To such demands for the strengthening of their faith Christ told them that their desire was vain, and that they could not be made to believe what they did not believe. "*If I tell you,*" he said, "*you will not believe;*"[3] "*I told you and you believed not. .... But ye believe not because you are not of my sheep.*"[4]

The Jews asked exactly what is asked by Church Christians; they asked for some outward sign which should make them believe in Christ's teaching. And He explained that this was impossible, and He told them why it was impossible. He told them that they could not believe because they were not of His sheep; that is, they did not follow the road of life He had pointed out to His sheep. He explained the difference between His sheep and others, He explained why some believed, and why others did not believe, and what the foundation of faith really was.

He said: *How can you believe who receive your doctrine* (δόξα[5]) *one of another, and seek not the doctrine that comes only from God?*"[6]

To believe, says Christ, we must seek for the doctrine that comes from God alone.

"*He that speaks of himself seeks his own doctrine* (δόξαν τὴν ἰδίαν), *but he that seeks the doctrine of him that sent him, the same is true, and no untruth is in him.*"[7]

The doctrine of life, δόξα, is the foundation of faith.

All actions result spontaneously from faith. All kinds of faith spring from δόξα in the sense which we attribute to life. There may be an endless number of actions;

[1] Mark xv. 32.
[2] Matt. xxvii. 42.
[3] Luke xxii. 67.
[4] John x. 25, 26.
[5] Here, as in other passages, δόξα has been incorrectly translated "honor"; δόξα, from the verb δοκέω, means "manner of seeing, judgment, *doctrine.*" — AUTHOR'S NOTE.
[6] John v. 44.
[7] John vii. 18.

there also may be many different kinds of faith. But there are only two doctrines of life (δόξα). Christ repudiates the one and affirms the other.

One of these doctrines, the one that Christ repudiates, consists of the idea that the individual life is one of the essential and real attributes of man. This doctrine has been followed, and is still followed, by the majority of men; it is the source of all the divergent beliefs and acts of men.

The other doctrine, taught by Christ and by all the prophets, affirms that our personal life has no meaning save through fulfilment of God's will.

If a man confess the δόξα or doctrine that his own individuality is more important than anything else, he will consider that his personal welfare is the most important thing and desirable in life, and having an eye therefore on what he supposes is the chief good, — the accumulation of an estate, the attainment of distinction or glory, or the satisfaction of his lusts, — he will have a faith in accordance with this view of life, and all his acts will always correspond with his faith.

If a man's δόξα is different, if he finds the essence of life in fulfilling God's will as Abraham understood it and Christ taught it, then having an eye on what he supposes to be God's will, his faith will accord with his principles, and his acts will flow from his faith.

This is why those that believe that true happiness is to be found in the personal life can never have faith in Christ's teaching. All their efforts to believe in it will be always vain. To believe in it they must change their view of life. And as long as they do not change it their actions will always coincide with their faith and not with their desires and their words.

The desire to believe in Christ's teaching on the part of those who asked Him to perform miracles and of believers in our day does not and cannot correspond with their lives, however arduous their efforts may be. They may pray to Christ as God, and observe the sacraments, and give in charity, and build churches, and convert others; they may do all this, but cannot do Christ's works because their acts flow from a faith based on an entirely different doctrine — δόξα — from that which they confess. They could not sacrifice on the altar an only son as Abraham was ready to do, although Abraham had no hesitation whatever as to whether he should or should not sacrifice his son to God, to that God who alone gave the meaning and blessedness of his life. And exactly the same way Christ and His disciples could not help giving their lives for others, because such action alone constituted for them the true meaning and blessedness of their life.

This incapacity of understanding the substance of faith explains the strange desire of men to act in such a way that, while they believe it is better to live in accordance with Christ's teaching, still they endeavor with all the powers of their souls to live in opposition to this doctrine, conformably to their belief that the personal life is a sovereign good.

The basis of faith is the meaning of life, wherefrom flows the valuation which we put upon the important and good, or the trivial and corrupt, in life. Faith is the valuation of all the phenomena of life. And as now, men with a faith based on their own doctrines never can succeed at all in harmonizing this faith with the faith inspired by Christ's teaching, so it was with the early disciples.

This misapprehension is frequently referred to in the Gospels in clear and decisive terms. Several times Christ's disciples asked Him to strengthen their faith in His words.[1] After the message, so terrible to every man who believes in the personal life and who seeks his happiness in the riches of this world, after the words, "*How hardly shall they that have riches enter into the kingdom of God,*" and after words still more terrible for men who believe only in the personal life, that, whoever does not abandon everything, and life itself according to Christ's will, will not be saved; Peter asked, "*Behold, we have forsaken all and followed thee; what shall we have therefore?*" Then, according to Mark, James and

[1] Matt. xx. 20–28; Mark x. 35–48.

John, and according to the Gospel of Matthew, theii mother, asked Him that they might be allowed to sit one on each side of Him when He should be in glory. They asked Him to strengthen their faith with a promise of future recompense. To Peter's question Christ replies with a parable;[1] to James He replies:—

"You know not what you ask; that is, you ask what is impossible; you do not understand my doctrine. My doctrine means a renunciation of the personal life, while you ask for personal glory, a personal recompense. To drink the cup I drink of (that is, live as I live) is in your power; but to sit on my right hand and on my left — that is, to be my equals — is in no one's power." And then Christ adds that only in the worldly life the great of this world had their profit and enjoyment of glory and personal power;" but you, my disciples, ought to know that the true meaning of human life is not in personal happiness, but in ministering to others, in being humiliated before all men. Man does not live to be ministered unto, but to minister, and to give his personal life a ransom for all."

In reply to the unreasonable demands which revealed their slowness to understand His doctrine, Christ did not command His disciples to have faith in His doctrine, that is, to modify that valuation of the good and evil things of life which flowed from their own doctrine — He knew that to be impossible — but He explained to them the meaning of that life which is the basis of true faith, that is, taught them how to discern good from evil, the important from the unimportant.

To Peter's question, "What shall we receive?" what reward for our sacrifices? Jesus replies with the parable of the laborers engaged for various periods and receiving all the same compensation.[1] Christ explains to Peter that failure to understand the doctrine is the cause of lack of faith. Christ says that only in a personal and senseless life is remuneration in proportion to the amount of work done important.

This faith in remuneration for work according to the

[1] Matt. xx. 1–16.

measure of the work is derived from the doctrine of the personal life. This faith is based upon the presumption of certain imaginary rights; but a man has a right to nothing, nor can he have. He is under obligations for the good he has received, and so he can exact nothing. Even if he were to give up his whole life to the service of others, he could not pay the debt he has incurred, and therefore the Master cannot be unjust to him. If a man sets a value upon his rights to life, if he keeps a reckoning with the First Cause from whom he has received life, he proves simply that he does not understand the meaning of life.

Men having received happiness demand something more. These men were standing in the bazaar idle and unhappy; they were not living. The householder took them and gave them the supreme welfare of life, — work. They accepted the benefits offered, and were dissatisfied. They were dissatisfied because they had no clear conception of their position. They went to the work, with their false doctrine that they had a right to their life and their work, and that consequently their work ought to be remunerated. They did not understand that this work is the highest good that is granted them, and that they should be thankful for the opportunity to work, and should not demand remuneration. And so all men who have an uncertain conception of life, as these laborers had, never can have a right and true faith.

This parable of the master and the workman returning from the field, related in response to a direct request by the disciples that He should strengthen, that He should enlarge, their faith, shows more clearly than ever the basis of the faith that Christ taught.

When Jesus told His disciples that they must forgive a brother who trespassed against them not only once, but seventy times,[1] the disciples were overwhelmed at the difficulty of observing this injunction, and said, "Yes, but.... we must believe in order to fulfil that; strengthen, increase, the faith in us." Just as a little while

[1] Luke xvii. 3-10.

before they had asked, "What shall we get in return for this?" So now they ask about this same thing, and so do in exactly the same way so-called Christians even nowadays.

I wish to believe, but cannot; "strengthen our faith that the rope of salvation may save us;" they say: "make us believe" (as the Jews said to Jesus when they demanded miracles); "either by miracles or promises of recompense, make us to have faith in our salvation."

The disciples said what we all say: "How pleasant it would be if we could live our selfish life, and at the same time believe that it would be far better to practise God's teaching by living for others." This disposition, contrary to all the spirit of Christ's teaching, is common to us all; and yet we are astonished at our lack of faith.

This radical misapprehension which existed then just as it exists now, He met with a parable illustrating true faith. Faith cannot come of confidence in what He said; faith comes only of a consciousness of our condition; faith is based only upon the rational consciousness as to what is best to do in a given situation. He showed that this faith cannot be awakened in others by promises of recompense or threats of punishment, that this can only arouse a feeble confidence which will fail at the first trial; but that the faith that removes mountains, the faith that nothing can shatter, is inspired by the consciousness of our inevitable destruction, and of the only salvation that is possible in this situation.

To have faith, we must not count on any promise of reward; we must understand that the only way of escape from a ruined life is a life conformable to the will of the Master. Every one who understands this, will not ask to be strengthened in his faith, but will work out his salvation without the need of any exhortation.

In reply to His disciples' request, to confirm them in their faith, Christ said: The householder, when he comes from the fields with his workman, does not ask the latter to sit down at once to dinner, but directs him first to attend to the cattle and to wait upon him, the master, and then to take his place at the table and dine.

This the workman does without any sense of being wronged; he does not boast and he does not demand gratitude or recompense, but he knows that so it must be, and that he is doing only what he ought to do, that this labor is the inevitable condition of his existence and the true welfare of his life. So says Christ: When you have done all that you are commanded to do, be assured that you have only fulfilled your duty. He who understands his relations to his master will understand that he has life only as he obeys the master's will; he will know in what his welfare consists, and he will have a faith for which nothing is impossible.

This is the faith Christ taught. Faith, according to Christ's teaching, has for its foundation a rational consciousness of the true meaning of life.

The foundation of faith according to Christ's teaching is light: —

"*That was the true light which lights every man that comes into the world. He was in the world, and the world was made by him, and the world knew him not. He came unto his own, and his own received him not. But as many as received him, to them gave he the right to become the children of God, even to them that believe on his name.*"[1]

"*And this is the condemnation,*[2] *that light is come into the world, and men loved darkness rather than light, because their deeds were evil. For every one that does ill hates the light, and comes not to the light, lest his works should be reproved. But he that does the truth comes to the light, that his works may be made manifest, because they have been wrought in God.*"[3]

He who understands Christ's teaching will not ask to be strengthened in his faith. Faith, according to Christ's teaching, is founded on the light, on the truth. Christ never called for faith in Himself; He called only for faith in the truth. To the Jews He said: —

[1] John i. 9–12.

[2] *Sud*, *κρίσις*, condemnation, judgment, does not mean *sud*, but *razdeleniye*, division, separation. — AUTHOR'S NOTE.

[3] John iii. 19–21

"*You seek to kill me, a man who has told you the truth which I have heard from God.*"[1]

He said: —

"*Which of you convicts me of sin? If I say the truth, why do you not believe me?*"[2]

"*To this end have I been born, and to this end am I come into the world, that I should bear witness unto the truth. Every one that is of the truth hears my voice.*"[3]

To His disciples He said: —

"*I am the way, and the truth, and the life.*"[4]

"*The Father,*" He said to His disciples, in the same chapter, ... "*shall give you another Comforter, and he will be with you forever, even the Spirit of truth: whom the world cannot receive; for it beholds him not, neither knows him: you know him; for he abides with you, and shall be in you.*"[5]

He says that all His teaching, that He Himself, is truth.

Christ's teaching is the teaching about the truth. And therefore faith in Christ is not belief in anything concerning Jesus, but it is knowledge of the truth. No one can be persuaded to believe in Christ's teaching, no one can be bribed to practise it. He who understands Christ's teaching will have faith in Him, because His teaching is the truth. He who knows the truth indispensable to his happiness must believe in it, just as a man who knows that he is really drowning cannot help grasping the rope of safety.

Thus the question, What must I do to believe? is an indication Christ's teaching is not understood.

CHAPTER X

We say, It is difficult to live according to Christ's teaching. And why should it not be difficult, when all our lives long we carefully hide from ourselves our true

[1] John viii. 40.
[2] John viii. 46.
[3] John xviii. 37.
[4] John xiv. 6.
[5] John xiv. 16, 17.

situation; when we endeavor to persuade ourselves that our situation is not at all what it is, but that it is something else? And this confidence, which we call faith, we regard as sacred, and we endeavor by all possible means, by threats, by flattery, by falsehood, by stimulating the emotions, to attract men to its support. In this demand for belief in what is contrary to sense and reason, we go so far that we take as an indication of truth the very unreasonableness of the object in behalf of which we solicit the confidence of men. It was a Christian who said "*Credo quia absurdum*," and other Christians have enthusiastically repeated this, supposing that the absurd is the best medium for teaching men the truth?

Not long ago a man of intelligence and great learning said to me that the Christian teaching had no importance as a moral rule of life. Morality, he said, must be sought in the teachings of the Stoics and the Brahmins, and in the Talmud. The essence of the Christian doctrine is not in morality, he said, but in the theosophical doctrine propounded in its dogmas.

According to this I ought to prize in the Christian teaching, not what is eternal and common to humanity, not what is indispensable to life and reasonable; but the most important element of Christianity is that portion of it which cannot be understood, and is therefore useless,—and this in the name of which millions of men have perished.

We have formed a false conception of our life and the life of the world, a conception based upon wrongdoing, and inspired by selfish passions, and we consider our faith in this false conception (which we have in some way attached to Christ's teaching) as most important, and necessary for life. If men had not for centuries maintained confidence in a lie, the lie of our conception of life and the truth of Christ's teaching would long ago have been shown forth.

It is a terrible thing to say, but it sometimes seems to me that if Christ's teaching, and the Church teaching which has grown out of it, had never existed, those who to-day call themselves Christians would be much nearer than they are now to the truth of Christ's teaching; that is, to the reasonable doctrine of the good of life. The moral doctrines of all the prophets of the world would not then be closed to them. They would have their own minor preachers of the truth, and would believe in them. Now, all truth has been revealed, and this absolute truth seemed so terrible to those whose deeds were evil that they have perverted it into a lie, and men have lost confidence in the truth.

In our European society, Christ's testimony that "To this end he had come into the world, that he should bear witness unto the truth, and that every one that was of the truth would hear his voice," — has been for a long time met with Pilate's question, "*What is truth?*" These words, expressing such a deep and melancholy irony against a Roman, we have taken seriously, and have made an article of faith.

All in our world live not only without truth, not only without the least desire to know truth, but with the firm conviction that, among all useless occupations, the most useless is the endeavor to find the truth that governs human life.

The rule of life, the doctrine which all peoples, excepting our European societies, have always considered as the most important thing, the rule of which Christ spoke as the one thing needful, is the one thing excluded from our life and from all human activity. It is turned over to a special institution called the Church, in which no one, not even those that belong to it, really believes.

The only window for the light to which the eyes of all who think and suffer are turned is shut. To the question, What am I? what ought I to do? can I not alleviate my life according to the teaching of that God who, if your words are true, came to save? the answer is: —

"Obey the authorities, and believe in the Church."

"But why do we live so ill in this world?" asks a despairing voice. "Why so much evil? May I not abstain from taking part in all this evil? Is it impossible to lighten this heavy load of wrong?"

The reply is that "It is impossible. Your desire to live well and to help others to live well is only a temptation of pride; the only thing possible is to save one's soul for the future life. If you do not wish to take part in the evil of the world, go out of it!"

This way is open to all, says the doctrine of the Church; but remember, if you choose this path, you can have no part in the life of the world; you will cease to live, and slowly kill yourself.

There are only two ways, our teachers tell us: To believe in and obey the powers that be, to participate in the organized evil about us; or to forsake the world and take refuge in a monastery, — not to sleep and not to eat, or mortify the flesh on a pillar, or to bow down and straighten up again, and to do nothing for men; either to declare Christ's teaching impracticable and accept the iniquity of life sanctioned by the Church, or to renounce life, which is equivalent to slow suicide.

However surprising it may seem to one who accepts Christ's teaching, the error whereby it is claimed that Christ's teaching is excellent for men, but impracticable, the error that he who wishes to practise this doctrine, not in word, but in deed, must retire from the world, is still more surprising. This error, that it is better for a man to retire from the world than to expose himself to the temptations of the world, existed amongst the Hebrews of old, but is entirely foreign, not only to the spirit of Christianity, but also to Judaism. Against this error, long before Christ's time was written the story of the prophet Jonah, which Jesus so loved and cited so often. The idea of the story from beginning to end is a unity. The prophet Jonah wishes to be the only righteous man, and retires from perverse men. But God shows him that he is a prophet, that for that very reason he ought to communicate to misguided men his knowledge of the truth, and so ought not to fly from misguided men, but ought rather to live in communion with them.

Jonah despises the depraved Ninevites and flees from them; but in spite of his efforts to shirk his vocation,

God brings him back by means of the whale, and the will of God is accomplished; the Ninevites receive the words of God through Jonah, and their lives are made better. But instead of rejoicing that he has been made the instrument of God's will, Jonah is angry and jealous of God's favor shown the Ninevites. He would have liked to be the only rational and righteous man. He goes out into the desert and bewails his fate and reproaches God. Then a gourd comes up over Jonah in one night and protects him from the sun, but the next night a worm devours the gourd. Jonah still more despairingly reproaches God because the gourd so dear to him has withered. Then God says to him: —

"Thou art sorry for the gourd thou callest thine own. It came up in a night, and perished in a night; and should I not have pity on a great people which was perishing, living like the beasts, unable to discern between their right hand and their left hand? Thy knowledge of the truth was needed only that thou mightest give it to those that had it not."

Christ knew this story and often referred to it, but moreover in the Gospels we find it related how Christ, after the interview with John, who had retired into the desert, was Himself subjected to the same temptation before beginning His mission; and how He was led by the Devil (deception) into the wilderness and there tempted; and how He triumphed over this deception and in the strength of the Spirit returned to Galilee; and how from that time forth He mingled with the most depraved men, and passed His life among publicans, Pharisees, and sinners, teaching them the truth.[1]

[1] Christ is led by Deception into the desert to be tempted there. Error suggests to Christ that He is not the Son of God if He cannot make stones into bread. Christ replies: "I can live without bread. I am alive by that which is breathed into me by God." Then Error says, "If Thou livest by that which is breathed into Thee by God, then throw Thyself from the height; Thou wilt kill the flesh, but the spirit breathed into Thee by God will not perish." Christ replies: "My life in the flesh is the will of God; to destroy my flesh is to go contrary to the will of God, to tempt God." Then Error says: "If this be so, serve the flesh, like the rest of the world, and the flesh will reward Thee." Christ replies: "I am powerless over the flesh; my life is in the spirit, but I cannot destroy the flesh because the

Even according to the teaching of the Church, Christ, as God in man, gave us an example of life. All of His life that is known to us was passed in the very vortex of life: with publicans, with the downfallen of Jerusalem, and with Pharisees. Christ's chief commands are that His followers shall love others and spread His doctrines. Both exact constant intercourse with the world. And yet the deduction is made that according to Christ's teaching it is necessary to retire from the world, to have nothing to do with others, and to stand on a pillar. That is, to imitate Christ we must do exactly contrary to what He taught and what He did Himself.

According to the Church commentators Christ's teaching offers itself to men of the world and to dwellers in monasteries, not as a rule of life for making it better, for oneself and others, but as a doctrine which teaches men of the world how, while living an evil life, to be saved in the other life, and monks how to render existence still worse than it is.

But Christ did not teach this.

Christ taught the truth, and if abstract truth is the truth, it will remain such in practice. If life in God is the only true life, and is in itself blessed, then it is so here in this world in spite of all the possible accidents of life. If a life here did not confirm Christ's teaching about life, then His teaching would not be true.

Christ did not ask us to pass from better to worse, but, on the contrary, from worse to better. He had pity upon men, who seemed to Him like scattered sheep perishing without a shepherd, and He promised them a shepherd and a good pasturage. He said that His disciples would be persecuted for His doctrine, and that they must bear the persecutions of the world with fortitude. But He did not say that those that followed His teaching would suffer more than those that followed the world's teaching; on the contrary, He said that those that followed the world's teaching would be wretched,

spirit is lodged in my flesh by God's will, and because as I live in the flesh I can serve only God, my Father." And Christ then leaves the desert and returns to the world. (Matt. iv. 1–11; Luke iv. 1–13.)

and that those who followed His doctrine would be blessed. Christ did not teach salvation by faith or by asceticism, that is, by a deceit of the imagination or voluntary tortures in this life, but He taught us a way of life which, while saving us from the ruinousness of the personal life, would give us, even here in this life, less of suffering and more of joy than by living the personal life. Christ in unfolding His doctrine told men that in practising it among those that did not practise it they would be, not more unhappy, but, on the contrary, much more happy than those that did not practise it. Christ says there is one infallible rule, and that was to have no care about the worldly life.

In Mark, Peter began to say to Him: —

"*Lo, we have forsaken all, and followed thee; what then shall we have?*" Jesus replied: "*Verily, I say unto you, There is no man that has left house, or brethren, or sisters, or mother, or father, or children, or wife, or lands, for my sake, and for the gospel's sake, but he shall receive a hundred fold more in this time, houses, and brethren, and sisters, and mothers, and children, and lands, with persecutions; and in the age to come eternal life.*"[1]

Christ declared, it is true, that those that follow His doctrine must expect to be persecuted by those that do not follow it, but He did not say that His disciples will be losers for that reason; on the contrary, He said that His disciples would have, here, in this world, greater happiness than will fall to the lot of those that do not follow Him.

That Christ said and thought this is beyond a doubt, as the clearness of His words on this subject, the meaning of His entire doctrine, His life and the life of His disciples, plainly show.

But is this true?

When we examine the abstract question as to which of the two conditions would be the better, that of Christ's disciples or that of the disciples of the world, we are obliged to conclude that the condition of Christ's dis-

[1] Mark x. 28–30.

ciples must be the better, since Christ's disciples, in doing good to all men, would not arouse the hatred of men. Christ's disciples, doing evil to no one, would be persecuted only by the wicked. The disciples of the world, on the contrary, are likely to be persecuted by every one, since the law of the disciples of the world is the law of each for himself, the law of struggle; that is, of persecution of one another. The chances of suffering would be the same for both with only this difference, that Christ's disciples will be prepared for suffering, while the disciples of the world will use all possible means to avoid suffering; Christ's disciples will feel that their sufferings are useful to the world, but the disciples of the world will not know why they suffer. On abstract grounds, then, the condition of Christ's disciples must be more advantageous than that of the disciples of the world.

But is it so in reality?

To answer this, let each one call to mind all the painful moments of his life, all the physical and moral sufferings that he has endured, and let him ask himself if he has suffered these calamities in the name of the world or in the name of Christ. Let every sincere man recall his past life, and he will find that he has never once suffered for practising Christ's teaching; while the greater part of the misfortunes of his life have resulted from following the doctrines of the world in opposition to his own impulses. In my own life (an exceptionally fortunate one from a worldly point of view) I can reckon up as much suffering caused by following the doctrine of the world as many a martyr has endured in the name of Christ. All the most painful moments of my life, — from the orgies and drunkenness in which I took part as a student, to the duels and wars in which I have participated, the diseases that I have endured, and the abnormal and insupportable conditions under which I now live, — all this is only martyrdom in the name of the doctrine of the world. But I speak of a life exceptionally happy from a worldly point of view. How many martyrs have suffered and are now suffering for the doctrine of the world torments that I should find difficulty in enumerating!

We do not realize the difficulties and dangers entailed by the practice of the doctrine of the world, simply because we are persuaded that all we endure for it is unavoidable.

We are persuaded that all the calamities we inflict upon ourselves are the inevitable conditions of our life, and we cannot understand that Christ's teaching teaches us how we may rid ourselves of these calamities and render our lives happy.

To be able to reply to the question, Which of these two conditions is the happier? we must, at least for the time being, get rid of this false conception and take a careful survey of our surroundings.

Mingle with a great crowd, especially in our cities, and observe the emaciated, sickly, and distorted specimens of humanity to be found therein, and then recall your own existence and that of all the people with whose lives you are familiar; recall the instances of violent deaths and suicides of which you have heard, — and then ask yourself for what cause all this suffering and death, this despair that leads to suicide, has been endured. You will find, strange as it may seem at first, that nine-tenths of all human suffering endured by men is useless, and ought not to exist, that, in fact, the majority of men are martyrs to the doctrine of the world.

One rainy autumn Sunday, in Moscow, I rode on the tramway through the bazaar of the Sukharof Tower. For half a verst the vehicle forced its way through a compact crowd which quickly re-formed its ranks. From morning till night these thousands of men, the greater portion of them starving and in rags, tramped angrily through the mud, venting their hatred in abusive epithets and acts of violence. The same sight may be seen in all the bazaars of Moscow. Their evenings these people spend in taverns and public houses; their nights in their nooks and kennels. Sunday is the best day in their week. Monday, in their pestiferous kennels, they again take up their disgusting work.

Think of the lives of all these people, of the position in which they live in order to choose that in which they have placed themselves; think of the incessant labor which they voluntarily undergo, — men and women, — and you will see that they are true martyrs.

All these people have forsaken houses, lands, parents, often wives and children; they have renounced everything, even life itself, and they have come to the city to acquire that which according to the gospel of the world is indispensable to every one. And all of them, not to speak of the tens of thousands of unhappy people who have lost everything, and who eke out a wretched subsistence on the garbage and vodka in cheap lodging-houses, all, from factory workman, cab-driver, sewing girl, and prostitute, to rich merchants and government officials and their wives, all endure the most painful and abnormal life without being able to acquire what, according to the doctrine of the world, is indispensable to each.

Seek among all these men, from beggar to millionaire, one who would be contented with what he has earned toward what he considers necessary and indispensable according to the teaching of the world, and you will not find one such in a thousand. Each one spends all his strength to obtain what is not necessary for him, but is demanded of him according to the teaching of the world, and the absence of which constitutes his unhappiness; and scarcely has he obtained one object of his desires when he strives for another, and still another, in that endless labor of Sisyphus which destroys the lives of men.

Take the scale of income, ranging from three hundred rubles to fifty thousand rubles a year, and you will rarely find a person who is not jaded and tormented with working to gain four hundred rubles if he have three hundred, five hundred if he have four hundred, and so on endlessly. Among them all you will scarcely find one who, with five hundred rubles, is willing to adopt the mode of life of him who has only four hundred. Even if such an instance occurs, it is not inspired by a desire to make life more simple, but to amass money and lock it up.

Each strives continually to make the heavy burden of existence still more heavy, by giving himself, his soul, without reserve to the practice of the doctrine of the world. To-day we must buy an overcoat and galoshes, to-morrow, a watch and chain; the next day we must install ourselves in an apartment with a sofa and a lamp; then we must have carpets in the drawing-room and velvet gowns; then a house, horses and carriages, pictures in gilt frames, and decorations, and then — then we fall ill of overwork and die. Another continues the same task, sacrifices his life to this same Moloch, and then dies also, without realizing why he has done all this.

But possibly this existence is in itself attractive? Compare it with what men have always called happiness, and you will see that it is hideously unhappy. For what, according to the general estimate, are the principal conditions of earthly happiness, those concerning which there can be no dispute? One of the first and most generally acknowledged conditions of happiness is a life in which the link between man and nature shall not be severed, that is, a life under the open sky, in the sunshine, the pure air, communion with the earth, animals, plants. Men have always regarded it as a great unhappiness to be deprived of all these things. Men shut up in prisons feel this deprivation more keenly than any one else. Look at the life of those men who live according to the doctrine of the world? The greater their success according to the doctrine of the world, the more they are deprived of these conditions of happiness. The greater their worldly success, the less they see of the sunlight, the fields, and woods, and of wild and domestic animals. Many of them — including nearly all the women — arrive at old age without having more than two or three times seen the sun rise or the morning, without having seen the fields or a forest except from a seat in a carriage, or a railway train, without ever having sown or planted anything, and without having reared or fed a cow or a horse or a hen, and without having the least idea how animals are born, grow, and live.

These people, surrounded by artificial light instead of sunshine, look only upon fabrics and stone and wood, fashioned by the hand of man; they hear only the roar of machinery, the roll of vehicles, the thunder of cannon, the sound of musical instruments; they smell perfumes and tobacco smoke; under their feet and hands they have nothing but fabrics, stone and wood, Because of the weakness of their stomachs and their depraved tastes, they eat food not fresh but tainted. When they move about from place to place, they are not saved from the same privations, they travel in closed carriages. Even in the country or abroad when they take journeys they have the same fabrics and wood beneath their feet; the same draperies shut out the sunshine; and the same lackeys, coachmen, dvorniks, cut off all communication with the men, the earth, the vegetation, and the animals about them. Wherever they go, they are like so many captives shut out from the conditions of happiness. As prisoners sometimes console themselves with a blade of grass that forces its way through the pavement of their prison yard, or make pets of a spider or a mouse, so these people sometimes amuse themselves with sickly house plants, a parrot, a poodle, or a monkey, which, however, they do not themselves tend.

Another inevitable condition of happiness is work: first, congenial and free work; secondly, physical work which gives an appetite and tranquil and sound sleep.

Here, again, the greater the prosperity that falls to the lot of men according to the doctrine of the world, the more such men are deprived of this second condition of happiness. All the prosperous people of the world, the dignitaries and the wealthy, either, like prisoners, are deprived of the advantages of work, and struggle unsuccessfully with the disease caused by the lack of physical exercise, and still more unsuccessfully with the ennui which pursues them — I say unsuccessfully, because labor is a pleasure only when it is necessary, and they have need of nothing; or else they undertake work that is odious to them, like the bankers, solicitors, administrators, and government officials, and their wives, who plan receptions and routs, and devise toilettes for themselves and their children. I say odious, because I never yet met any person of this class who was contented with his work or took as much satisfaction in it as the dvornik feels in shoveling away the snow from before their doorsteps. All these favorites of fortune are either deprived of work or are obliged to work at what they do not like, after the manner of criminals condemned to hard labor.

The third undoubted condition of happiness is the family. But the more men are enslaved by worldly success, the less do they obtain this happiness. The majority of them are libertines, who deliberately renounce the joys of family life and retain only its cares. If they are not libertines, their children are not a source of pleasure, but a burden, and all possible means, sometimes even the most painful, are employed to render marriage unfruitful. If they have children, they make no effort to cultivate the pleasures of companionship with them. According to their laws they are compelled to leave their children almost continually to the care of strangers, confiding them first to the instruction of persons who are usually foreigners, and then sending them to public educational institutions, so that of family life they have only the sorrows, and the children from infancy are as unhappy as their parents and, as far as their parents are concerned, have only one feeling — a wish for their parents' death that they may become the heirs.[1] These people are not confined in prisons, but the consequences of their way of living as regards their

[1] The justification of this existence often heard from parents is very curious. "I need nothing for myself," the father says; "this way of living is very distasteful to me; but, because of affection for my children, I do this for them." In other words: "I know for a certainty by experience that our way of living is unhappy, consequently I am training my children to be as unhappy as I am. For love of them, I bring them into a city permeated with physical and moral miasma; I give them into the care of strangers, who regard the education of the young as a lucrative enterprise;

families are more painful than the deprivation of family inflicted on prisoners.

The fourth condition of happiness is sympathetic and unrestricted intercourse with all classes of men. And the higher a man is placed in the social scale, the more certainly is he deprived of this essential condition of happiness. The higher he goes, the narrower becomes the circle of men with whom it is possible for him to associate; the lower sinks the moral and intellectual level of those few that constitute the charmed circle wherefrom there is no escape.

The peasant and his wife are free to enter into friendly relations with a whole world of men, and if a million men do not care to associate with them, there remain eighty millions of laboring people like themselves with whom they may enter into the most intimate brotherly relations, from Arkhangelsk to Astrakhan, without waiting for a ceremonious visit or an introduction.

A chinovnik and his wife will find hundreds of people who are their equals; but the clerks of a higher rank will not admit them to a footing of social equality, and they, in their turn, are excluded by others. For the wealthy society man and his wife, there are dozens of society families. From all the rest of the world they are separated. For the cabinet minister and the millionaire and their families there are only a dozen people as rich and as important as themselves. For kings and emperors, the circle is still more narrow.

Is not the whole system like a great prison where each inmate is restricted to association with two or three jailers?

Finally, the fifth condition of happiness is bodily health and a painless death. And once more the higher men ascend the social scale, the more they are deprived of this condition of happiness. Take a moderately wealthy man and his wife, and an average peasant and his wife, and notwithstanding all the hunger and exces-

I surround my children with physical, moral, and intellectual corruption." And this reasoning has to serve as a justification of the unreasonable existence led by the parents themselves. — AUTHOR'S NOTE.

sive toil which the peasantry endure through no fault of their own, but through the cruelty of men, and compare them: and you will see that the lower they are the healthier they are, and the higher they are the more sickly they are, both men and women. Recall to mind the rich men and women whom you know and have known, and you will see most of them are invalids. A person of that class whose physical disabilities do not oblige him to take a periodical course of hygienic and medical treatment is as rare as is an invalid among the laboring classes. All these favorites of fortune without exception are the victims and practitioners of sexual vices that have become a second nature, and they are toothless, gray, and bald at an age when a workingman is in the prime of manhood. Nearly all are afflicted with nerves, indigestion, or sexual diseases arising from excesses in eating, drunkenness, dissipation, and medicines; and those that do not die young, pass half of their lives under the influence of morphine or other drugs, as melancholy wrecks of humanity incapable of self-support and able to live only as parasites, or those ants which are nourished by their slaves.

Examine the manner of their dying: one has blown out his brains, another has rotted away with syphilis; this old man has died of a "konfortative," this young man has died of a castigation self-administered for the sake of excitement; one has been eaten alive by lice, another by worms; one died of drunkenness, another of gluttony, another from morphine, another from an induced abortion. One after another they perished, in the name of the doctrine of the world. And a multitude presses on behind them, like an army of martyrs, to undergo the same sufferings, the same perdition.

One life after another is cast under the chariot of this god. The juggernaut advances, crushing out their lives, and new and ever new victims with groans and sobs and curses wallow underneath it.

To follow Christ's teaching is difficult! Christ said: —

"Whoever wishes to follow me let him forsake house,

and lands, and brethren, and follow me, his God, and he shall receive in this world a hundred-fold more houses, and lands, and brethren, and besides all this, eternal life." And no one is willing even to make the experiment.

In the doctrine of the world it is commanded: "Leave house and lands and brethren; forsake the country for the filthy towns, live all your life long as a naked bath-rubber, soaping the backs of others in the steam; as a clerk in a little underground shop passing life in counting other men's kopeks; as a public prosecutor spending your days in court or immersed in documents, helping to make the fate of unhappy wretches still more unhappy; as a cabinet minister perpetually signing unnecessary papers, as the head of an army, killing men. Live this hideous life, ending in a cruel death, and you shall receive nothing in this world, and you will receive no eternal life." All listen and obey. Christ said: —

"Take up the cross and follow me," or in other words, "Bear submissively the lot awarded to thee, and obey me, God."

And no one responds.

But let the first worthless man in epaulets, a man fitted only to kill his fellows, take it into his head to say: —

"Take, not your cross, but your knapsack and gun, and march to all sorts of suffering and certain death."

And all set forth. Leaving families, parents, wives, and children, clad in grotesque costumes, subject to the will of the first comer of a higher rank, famished, benumbed, and exhausted by forced marches; they go, like a herd of cattle to the slaughter-house, not knowing where, — and yet these are not cattle, they are men. They cannot help knowing that they are driven to the slaughter-house. With the insoluble question "Why?" and with despair in their hearts they move on, to die of hunger, or cold, or contagious diseases, or, if they survive, to be brought within range of a storm of bullets and commanded to kill men whom they know not. They kill and are killed, none of them knows why or to what end.

The Turks roast them alive in the fire, flog them, disembowel them. And the next day some one whistles, and again all rush forth to meet terrible sufferings, death, and visible evil. And yet no one finds this to be difficult. Neither those that suffer nor their fathers and mothers find that this is difficult. Parents even encourage their children to go. It seems to them not only that such thing should be, but that they could not be otherwise, and that they are altogether admirable and moral.

If the practice of the doctrine of the world were easy, agreeable, and without danger, we might, perhaps, believe that the practice of Christ's teaching is difficult, frightful, and cruel. But the doctrine of the world is much more difficult, more dangerous, and more cruel, than is Christ's teaching.

Formerly, we are told, there were martyrs for Christ; but they were exceptional. We cannot count up more than about three hundred and eighty thousand of them, voluntary and involuntary, in the whole course of eighteen hundred years; but who shall count the martyrs to the doctrine of the world? For each Christian martyr there have been a thousand martyrs to the doctrine of the world, and the sufferings of each one of them have been a hundred times more cruel than those endured by the others. The number of the victims of wars in our century alone amounts to thirty millions of men. These are the martyrs to the doctrine of the world, who would have escaped suffering and death if they had merely refused to follow the doctrine of the world, to say nothing of following Christ's teaching.

All a man has to do is to do as he pleases, and refuse to go to war, and, though they might send him to dig trenches, they would not torment him at Sevastopol and Plevna. All he has to do is not to believe in the teaching of the world, and not think it indispensable to wear galoshes and a chain, to maintain a useless salon, or to do the various other foolish things the teaching of the world demands, and he will never know overwork or suffering or perpetual anxiety, or labor without rest or result; he will remain in communion with nature; he will not be deprived of communion with nature, he will not be deprived of the work he loves, or of his family, or of his health, and he will not perish by a senseless and cruel death.

Christ never taught that martyrdom in His name was necessary. He teaches us to cease tormenting ourselves in the name of the false doctrine of the world.

Christ's teaching has a profound metaphysical meaning; Christ's teaching has a universal meaning; Christ's teaching has also, for the life of every man, a very simple, very clear, and very practical meaning. This meaning may be thus expressed: Christ teaches men not to do foolish things. This is the simple meaning of Christ's teaching, and it is accessible to all.

Christ says:—

"Be not angry; do not consider any one as lower than yourselves—that is stupid; if you are angry and offend others, so much the worse for you."

Again He says:—

"Do not run after women, but choose one woman, and live with her—it will be better for you."

Once more He says:—

"Bind not yourselves to any one by promises or oaths, else you may be compelled to commit foolish and wicked actions."

Again He says:—

"Return not evil for evil, or the evil will return upon you still worse than before, like the log suspended above the honey to kill the bear."

And again He says:—

"Do not consider men as foreigners simply because they dwell in another country and speak a language different from yours. If you consider them as enemies, they will consider you as enemies; and it will be the worse for you. And so if you do none of these foolish things it will be better for you."

"Yes," men say in reply to this, "but the world is so organized that to go against it is much more calamitous than to live in accordance with it. If a man refuses military service he will be shut up in a fortress, and possibly will be shot. If a man will not do what is necessary for the support of himself and his family, he and his family will starve."

Thus argue men who strive to defend the arrangement of the world; but they do not believe so. They say this only because they cannot deny the truth of Christ's teaching, which they profess, and because they must justify themselves in some way for their failure to practise it. They not only do not believe so; they have never thought over the matter at all. They have faith in the doctrine of the world, and they only make use of the plea they have learned from the Church, — that much suffering is inevitable for those who would practise Christ's teaching; and so they have never tried to practise Christ's teaching at all.

We see countless sufferings endured by men in the name of the doctrine of the world, but in these times we hear nothing of suffering in behalf of Christ's teaching. Thirty millions of men have perished in wars, fought in behalf of the doctrine of the world; thousands of millions of beings have perished, crushed by a social system organized on the principle of the doctrine of the world; but I know not of a million, a thousand, a dozen, or a single man, who has died a cruel death, or has even suffered from hunger and cold, in behalf of Christ's teaching. This is only a ridiculous excuse, proving how little we really know of Christ's teaching. We not only do not follow it; we do not even take it seriously. The Church has explained it in such a way that it seems to be, not the doctrine of life, but a bugbear.

Christ calls men to drink of a well of living water, which is close at hand. Men are parched with thirst, they have eaten of filth and drunk one another's blood, but their teachers have told them that they will perish if they come to the fountain shown them by Christ, and men believe them and suffer torments and die of thirst within two steps of the water, not daring to approach it. All we have to do is to believe Christ, believe that He brought good upon earth, believe that He gives us thirsty ones a fountain of living water, and go to it, to see how cunning has been the deception of the Church, and how senseless our sufferings are when salvation is so near. All we have to do is to accept Christ's teaching, frankly and simply, for the horrible error in which we each and all live to become plain to us.

Generation after generation of us struggles to maintain our lives by means of violence, and the assurance of our property. We believe that the happiness of our life is in the greatest possible power, and abundance of property. We are so accustomed to this that Christ's teaching that man's happiness does not depend on fortune and power and that the rich cannot be happy appears to us a demand for sacrifice in the name of future bliss. Christ, however, did not think of calling us to sacrifice; on the contrary, He teaches us not to do what is worse, but to do what is the best for ourselves here in this present life.

Loving men, Christ taught them to refrain from maintaining themselves by violence, and not to seek after riches, just as we teach the common people to abstain, for their own interest, from quarrels and intemperance. He said that if men lived without defending themselves against violence, and without property, they would be more happy; and He confirms His words by the example of His life. He said that a man who lives according to His doctrine must be ready at any moment to endure violence from others, and, possibly, to die of hunger and cold, and must not count on a single hour of life. This seems to us a terrible demand for sacrifices, but it is simply a statement of the conditions under which every man will always continue to exist.

A disciple of Christ must be prepared at every moment for suffering and death. But is not the disciple of the world in the same situation? We are so accustomed to our deception that everything we do for so-called security of life, — our armies, fortresses, provisions, our wardrobes, our medical treatments, all our goods, and our money, — seems to us like something actual, seriously guaranteeing our existence.

We forget what is evident to every one — what happened to the man who resolved to build storehouses to provide an abundance for many years: he died that very night! Everything that we do to make our existence secure is like what the ostrich does when he stands and hides his head in order not to see how they will kill him. We do worse than the ostrich. To establish the uncertain security of an uncertain life in an uncertain future, we certainly sacrifice a certain life in a certain present.

The illusion is in the false persuasion that our existence can be made secure by our competition with others. We are so accustomed to the deception in what we call security of our existence and our property, that we do not realize what we lose by striving after it. We lose everything — we lose life itself. Our whole life is swallowed up in anxious care for personal security, with preparations for living, so that we really never live at all.

All it requires is to get rid of this habit for a moment, and study our lives from one side, and we shall see that all we do in behalf of the so-called security of existence is not done at all for the assurance of security, but simply to help us to forget that existence never has been secure and never can be secure. Not only do we deceive ourselves and spoil our true life for an imaginary life in this attempt to attain security, but we often destroy what we wish to preserve.

The French took up arms in 1870 to make their national existence secure, and the attempt resulted in the destruction of hundreds of thousands of Frenchmen. All nations who take up arms undergo the same experience.

The rich man believes that his existence is secure because he possesses money, but his money attracts a thief who kills him.

The hypochondriac makes his life secure by medical treatment, and the medical treatment slowly kills him; if it does not kill him, at least it deprives him of life, till he is like the impotent man who for thirty-five years did not live, but waited at the pool for an angel. Christ's teaching that we cannot possibly make life secure, but that we must be ready to die at any moment, is unquestionably better than the doctrine of the world, which obliges us to struggle for the security of existence. It is preferable because the impossibility of escaping death, and the impossibility of making life secure, is the same for Christ's disciples as it is for the disciples of the world; but, according to Christ's teaching, life itself is not swallowed up in the idle attempt to make existence secure, but is free, and can be devoted to the end for which it is worthy,—its own welfare and the welfare of others.

Christ's disciple will be poor, but he will always enjoy the gifts God has given him. He will not ruin his own existence. We make the word poverty, which is really happiness, a synonym for calamity, but the fact is not changed thereby. The poor man: it means that he will not live in the city, but in the country, he will not sit idly at home, but will work out of doors, in the woods and fields; he will see the sunshine, the sky, the animals; he will not rack his brains thinking what to eat to stimulate appetite, and what to do in order to be regular. He will be hungry three times a day, will not toss on soft pillows thinking what will save him from insomnia, but he will sleep; he will have children, and live with them, he will be in free relations with all men, and, above all, he will not do anything he does not wish to do, he will have no fear for anything that may happen to him. He will be ill, will suffer, will die, like the rest of the world; but his sufferings and his death will probably be less painful than those of the rich; and he will certainly live more happily. To be poor, to be humble, to be a tramp,—πτωχός signifies *brodyaga*, vagabond,—this is what Christ teaches; without this it is impossible to enter the kingdom of God, without this it is impossible to be happy here on earth.

"But no one will feed you, and you will die of hunger," they say. To this objection, that a man living in accordance with Christ's teaching will die of hunger, Christ replies in a short sentence, which has been interpreted to justify the idleness of the clergy. He said:—

"*Get you no gold, nor silver, nor brass in your purses; no wallet for your journey, neither two coats, nor shoes, nor staff: for the laborer is worthy of his food.*"[1]

"*And into whatever house you shall enter, ... in that same house remain, eating and drinking such things as they give: for the laborer is worthy of his hire.*"[2]

The laborer is worthy of (ἀξιός ἐστιν means, word for word, can and ought to have) his food. It is a very short sentence, but he who understands it as Christ understood it, can never argue that a man, even though he has no property, will die of hunger.

To understand the true meaning of these words we must first of all get entirely rid of that idea, quite too common amongst us, developed from the dogma of the redemption, that man's felicity consists in idleness. We must get back to that point of view natural to all uncorrupted men, that work, and not idleness, is the indispensable condition of happiness for every human being; that man cannot help working, that it is as irksome, wearisome, and difficult for him not to work as it is irksome and wearisome for the ant, the horse, or any other animal not to work. We must rid ourselves of the savage superstition that a man who has an income from a place under the government, from landed property, or from stocks and bonds, giving him the possibility of living in idleness, is in a natural and happy position. We must restore to our consciousness the idea of work possessed by undegenerate men, the idea that Christ had when He said that the laborer is worthy of his food. Christ did not imagine that men would regard work as a curse, and consequently He did not have in mind a man who would not work, or desired not to work. He always supposed that His disciples would work, and so He said, If a man works, his work shall feed him. He who makes use of the labor of another will provide food for him who labors, simply because he profits by that labor. And so he who works will always

[1] Matt. x. 10. [2] Luke x. 5, 7.

have food; he may not have property, but as to food, there need be no uncertainty whatever.

The difference between Christ's teaching and the doctrine of the world, in regard to work, is that according to the doctrine of the world, work is a special merit in a man, whereby he makes agreements with others, and supposes that he has the right to a sustenance large in proportion to his work. According to Christ's teaching, labor is the inevitable condition of human life, and food is the inevitable consequence of labor. Labor produces food, and food produces labor. This is the eternal circle; the one is the cause and consequence of the other. However bad the employer may be, he will always feed his workman, as he will always feed the horse which works for him; he feeds him that he may get all the work possible; in other words, he will coöperate in the very thing which constitutes the welfare of the workman.

"*For verily the son of man came not to be ministered unto, but to minister and to give his life a ransom for many.*"

According to Christ's teaching, every individual man, independently of what the world may be, will have a happier life if he understands that his vocation consists, not in exacting service from others, but in ministering to others, in giving his life for the ransom of many. A man who does this will be worthy of his food — in other words, he cannot fail to have it. By the words, a man does not live in order that men may work for him, but that he may work for others, Christ established a principle which would undoubtedly insure the material existence of man; and by the words, "*the laborer is worthy of his food,*" Christ sets aside once for all the too common objection that a man who should practise Christ's teaching in the midst of those who do not practise it would perish from hunger and cold. [Christ practised His own doctrine amid great opposition, and He did not perish from hunger and cold.] He showed that a man does not insure his own subsistence by amassing worldly goods at the expense of others, but by rendering himself useful and indispensable to others. The more necessary he is to others, the more will his existence be made secure.

In the present organization of the world there are men who do not fulfil Christ's teachings, but who possess no property and minister unto others, but they do not die of hunger. How, then, can we object to Christ's teaching, that those that practise it by working for others will perish for want of food? A man cannot die of hunger while the rich have bread. In Russia at any given minute there are always millions of men who possess no property but live entirely by their own toil.

Among pagans a Christian would be as secure as among Christians. He labors for others; consequently, he is necessary to them, and therefore he will be fed. Even a dog, if he be useful, is fed and cared for; and shall not a man be fed and cared for whose service is necessary to all?

But a sick man, a man with a family, with children, is not needed, he cannot work, and they will cease to feed him, say those who seek by all possible means to prove the justice of the worldly life. They say so, and they will continue to say so; but they themselves do not see that even while they say this and are desirous of acting in conformity to it, they cannot do so, and they act in an entirely different way. These same people, who will not admit that Christ's teaching is practicable, practise it themselves. They do not cease to feed a sheep, an ox, or a dog, when it is sick. They do not kill an old horse, but they give him work in proportion to his strength. They feed their families, their lambs, their pigs, their puppies, expecting a profit from them; and can it be that they will not care for a useful man who has fallen ill, that they will not find work suited to the strength of the old man and the child, that they will not bring up those who later on will be able to work for them in return.

Not only will they do this, but as it is they do it. Nine-tenths of men, the *chornui narod,* the "black people," the laboring classes, are cared for by the other tenth, like so many cattle. And however great the error in which this one-tenth live, however mistaken their views in regard to the other nine-tenths of humanity, the tenth, even if they could, would not deprive the other nine-tenths of food. They will never deprive the poor of what they need in order to multiply and work. Recently this tenth has worked purposely that the nine-tenths might be regularly maintained, in other words, that the latter might furnish the maximum of work, and multiply, and bring up a new supply of workers. Ants care for the increase and welfare of their little milch cows. Shall not men do the same? and cause those whose labor they find necessary to increase? Laborers are necessary. And those that profit by labor will always be careful that their laborers are not destroyed.

The objection concerning the practicability of Christ's teaching, that if I do not acquire something for myself and keep what I have acquired, no one will feed my family, is true, but only in regard to idle, useless, and therefore obnoxious people, such as make up the majority of our opulent class. No one, except foolish parents, will care for lazy people, because lazy people are of no use to any one, not even to themselves; but the worst men will feed and support the laborer. Men rear calves, but man, as a beast of burden, is much more useful than an ox, as the tariff of the slave-mart always shows. This is why children will never be left without support.

Man does not live to be worked for, but to work for others. He who will labor will be fed.

These are truths confirmed by the life of the whole world.

Now, always, and everywhere, the man who labors receives the means of bodily subsistence just as every horse receives fodder. This subsistence is assured to him who works against his will; for such a workman desires one thing: to relieve himself of the necessity of work, and to acquire all that he possibly can in order that he may take the yoke from his own neck and place it upon the neck of the man who has sat on his neck.

A workman like this — envious, grasping, toiling against his will — will never lack for food and will be happier than one who without labor lives on the labor of others. How much happier, then, will that laborer be who labors in obedience to Christ's teaching with the object of accomplishing all the work of which he is capable and wishing for it the least possible return? How much more desirable will his condition be, when around him there will be at least a few, and possibly many, who will follow his example.

Christ's teaching with regard to labor and the fruits of labor is expressed in the story of the five and seven thousand fed with two fishes and five loaves. Humanity will enjoy the highest possible welfare when men will cease trying to grasp all that they can, and using what they have for their personal pleasure, and will do as Christ taught them by the borders of the sea.

Thousands had to be fed. One of Christ's disciples told Him that there was a man who had a few fishes; some of the disciples had also a few loaves. Jesus understood that some of the people coming from a distance had brought provisions with them and that some had not. That many had provisions with them is proved by the fact related in all the four Gospels that at the end of the meal twelve basketfuls of fragments were picked up. If no one but the lad had brought anything, how could so much have been left after so many were fed?

If Christ had not done what He did, that is, performed the miracle of feeding thousands of people with five loaves, the people would have acted as people of the world act now. Those that had food would have eaten what they had, would have compelled themselves to eat it all up, so that nothing might have been left. The mean ones, maybe, would have taken what was left to their homes. Those that had nothing would have been famished, and would have looked at their more fortunate companions with envy and hatred; some of them would perhaps have tried to take food by force from those that had it, and there would have been quarrels and fighting; that is, the multitude would have acted just as people act nowadays.

But Christ knew exactly what He wanted to do. As it says in the Gospels, He commanded all to sit down around Him and told His disciples to give of what they had to those who had nothing, and to request others to do the same. The result was that those that had food followed the example of Christ and His disciples, and offered what they had to others. Then all ate moderately; and when they went round the circle there was sufficient for those that had not eaten at first. And all were satisfied, and so much bread remained that they filled twelve baskets.

Christ teaches men that they ought deliberately to act in this way because such is the law of man and of all eternity.

Work is the inevitable condition of human life, and work gives happiness to man. For this reason, to withhold from others the fruits of their labor or yours hinders the welfare of man.

"If men did not wrest food from others, they would die of hunger," we say. To me it would seem more reasonable to say, "If men wrest their food from one another, some of them will die of hunger," and it is so!

Every man, whether he lives according to Christ's teaching or according to the doctrine of the world, lives only by the labor of others. Others have shielded him and given him to drink and fed him, and they are still shielding him and giving him to drink and feeding him. But according to the doctrine of the world, man has a right to demand that others should continue to support and care for him and for his family. According to Christ's teaching, man is shielded and cared for and supported by others, but in order that other men continue to shield him and give him to drink and support him also, he must not require it of any one else, but must try to serve others, and so render himself useful and indispensable to mankind.

Men of the world will support any one who is useless

who demands support of them, but at the first possible opportunity they cease to feed such a one, and kill him because of his uselessness; but all men always, however wicked they may be, will support and feed the man that labors in their behalf.

Which, then, is surer, the more reasonable, the more joyous life, that according to the doctrine of the world, or that according to Christ's teaching?

CHAPTER XI

CHRIST'S teaching is to bring the kingdom of God on earth. It is wrong to imagine that the practice of this doctrine is difficult; it is not only not difficult, but it is inevitable for the man who has once understood it. This teaching offers the only possible chance of salvation from the certain ruin that threatens the personal life. Finally, the fulfilment of this teaching not only does not call men to endure the privations and sufferings of this life, but it puts an end to nine-tenths of the suffering which we endure in the name of the world's teaching.

When I understood this I asked myself why I had never practised a doctrine which would give me so much happiness and peace and joy; why, on the other hand, I always had practised an entirely different doctrine, and thereby made myself wretched? And the reply could only be one: Because I never had known the truth; it had been concealed from me.

When Christ's teaching was first revealed to me, I did not believe that the discovery would lead me to reject the teaching of the Church. It only seemed to me that the Church had not reached those conclusions that flow from Christ's teaching; but I never thought that this new idea of Christ's teaching which had been revealed to me, and the deductions drawn from it, would separate me from the teaching of the Church. I dreaded this, and in the course of my studies I made no attempt to search out the errors in the teaching of the Church. On the contrary, I sought to close my eyes to propositions that seemed to be obscure and strange, provided they were not in evident contradiction with what I regarded as the essence of the Christian teaching.

But the further I advanced in the study of the Gospels, and the more clearly Christ's teaching was revealed to me, the more inevitable the choice became: either Christ's teaching, reasonable and simple in accordance with my conscience and giving me salvation; or an entirely different teaching, a doctrine in opposition to reason and conscience, offering me nothing except the certainty of my own perdition and that of others. I was therefore forced to reject, one after another, the dogmas of the Church. This I did against my will, struggling with the desire to mitigate as much as possible my disagreement with the Church, that I might not be obliged to separate from the Church, and thereby deprive myself of communion with fellow-believers, the greatest happiness that religion can bestow.

But when I had completed my task, I saw that in spite of al! my efforts to maintain a connecting link with the Church, the separation was complete. Not only nothing remained, but I was convinced that nothing could remain.

Just as I was completing my labors the following incident took place: —

My son, a young lad, one day told me of a discussion which was going on between two domestics (uneducated persons who scarcely knew how to read) concerning a passage in some religious book which maintained that it was not a sin to put criminals to death, or to kill enemies in war. I could not believe that this could be printed in any book, and I asked to see it. The little volume which caused the dispute bore the title of "Prayer Book Explained";[1] third edition; eighth ten thousand; Moscow, 1879. On page 163 of this book I read: —

"What is the sixth commandment of God?

"Thou shalt not kill, shalt do no murder.

"What does God forbid by this commandment?

[1] "Tolkovui Molitvennik."

"He forbids us to kill, to take the life of any man.

"Is it a sin to punish a criminal with death according to the law, or to kill an enemy in war?

"No; that is not a sin. We take the life of the criminal to put an end to the wrong that he commits; we slay an enemy in war, because in war we fight for our sovereign and our native land."

And with these words closes the explanation; the law of God is abrogated! I could scarcely believe my eyes.

The disputants asked my opinion about the subject at issue. To the one that maintained the correctness of what was printed, I said that the explanation was not correct.

"Why, then, do they print what is wrong and contrary to the commandment?" he asked. I could say nothing in reply.

I kept the volume and looked over its contents. The book contained thirty-one prayers with instructions concerning genuflections and the joining of the fingers; an explanation of the *Credo;* certain citations from the fifth chapter of Matthew without any explanation whatever, for some unknown reason headed, "Commands for the Attainment of Bliss"; the ten commandments accompanied by comments that rendered most of them void; and "Troparia" for every saint's day.

As I have said, I not only had sought to avoid condemnation of the religion of the Church; I had done my best to see only its most favorable side; and having, therefore, not sought for its weaknesses, knowing its academic literature well, I was perfectly ignorant of its literature of instruction. This book of devotion, already in 1879 spread broadcast in an enormous number of copies, awakening doubts in the minds of the simplest people, amazed me. I could not believe that a prayer-book so entirely pagan, so wholly out of accord with Christianity, was deliberately spread among the people by the Church. To verify my belief, I bought and read all the books published by the synod or with its "benediction" (*blagoslovenia*), containing brief expositions of the religion of the Church for the use of children and the common people.

Their contents were to me almost entirely new, for at the time when I received my early religious instruction they had not yet appeared. As far as I could remember there were no commandments with regard to the attainment of bliss, and there was no doctrine which taught that it was not a sin to kill. No such teachings appeared in the old catechisms; they were not to be found in the catechism of Peter Mogila, or in the catechisms of Platon, or in that of Belyakof, or the abridged Catholic catechisms. The innovation was introduced by the metropolitan Philaret, who prepared a catechism for the military class, and from this catechism the "Prayer Book Explained" was compiled. Philaret's work is entitled, "The Christian Catechism of the Orthodox Church, for the Use of all Orthodox Christians," and is published, "by order of his Imperial Majesty." [1]

The book is divided into three parts, "Concerning Faith," "Concerning Hope," and "Concerning Love." The first part contains the analysis of the Nicene Creed. The second part is made up of an exposition of the Lord's Prayer, and the first eight verses of the fifth chapter of Matthew, which serve as an introduction to the Sermon on the Mount, and are called for some reason, "Commands for the Attainment of Bliss."

These first two parts treat of the dogmas of the Church, prayers, and the sacraments, but they contain no rules with regard to the conduct of life.

The third part, "Concerning Love," contains an exposition of Christian duties, based, not on Christ's commandments, but upon the ten commandments of Moses. This exposition of the commandments of Moses seems to have been made for the especial purpose of teaching men not to obey them. Each commandment is followed by a reservation which completely destroys its force.

With regard to the first commandment, which enjoins the worship of God alone, the catechism inculcates the

[1] This book has been in use in all the schools and churches of Russia since 1839. — Tr.

worship of angels and saints, to say nothing of the Mother of God and the three persons of the Trinity.[1]

With regard to the second commandment, not to make idols, the catechism enjoins the worship of ikons (p. 108).

With regàrd to the third commandment, "not to swear in vain," the catechism enjoins the taking of oaths as the principal token of legitimate authority (p. 111).

With regard to the fourth commandment, concerning the observance of the Sabbath, the catechism inculcates the observance, not of Saturday, but of Sunday, of the thirteen principal feasts, of a number of feasts of less importance, the observance of Lent, and of fasts on Wednesdays and Fridays (pp. 112–115).

With regard to the fifth commandment, "*Honor thy father and thy mother,*" the catechism prescribes honor to the sovereign, the country, spiritual fathers, all persons in authority,[2] and of these last gives an enumeration in three pages, including "college authorities, civil, judicial, and military authorities, and masters (*sic*) in relation to their servants and serfs" (pp. 116–119).

My citations are taken from the sixty-fourth edition of the catechism, dated 1880. Twenty years have passed since the abolition of serfdom, and no one has taken the trouble to strike out the phrase which, in connection with the commandment of God to honor parents, was introduced into the catechism to sustain and justify slavery.

With regard to the sixth commandment, "*Thou shalt not kill,*" the instructions of the catechism are from the first in favor of murder.

"*Question.* — What is forbidden by the sixth commandment?

"*Answer.* — Manslaughter, or the killing of our neighbor in any manner whatever.

"*Question.* — Is all manslaughter a transgression of the law?

[1] "Special Catechism," pp. 107, 108.

[2] *Natchal's tvuyushchikh f raznuikh otnosheniyakh* (*sic*), those "commanding in various relations."

"*Answer.* — Manslaughter is not a transgression of the law when life is taken in *execution of duty.* For example:

"1st. When a criminal is *punished* by death according to law.

"2d. When we kill our enemies *in war* for the sovereign and our country."

The italics are in the original. Farther on we read: —

"*Question.* — With regard to manslaughter, when is the law transgressed?

"*Answer.* — When any one conceals a murderer or sets him at liberty" (*sic*).

All this is printed in hundreds of thousands of copies, and under the name of Christian doctrine is taught with threats of penalties to every Russian. This is taught to all the Russian people. It is taught to the innocent children, — to the children to whom Christ said, "Suffer them to come unto Him, for of such is the kingdom of God"; to the children whom we must resemble, in ignorance of false doctrines, to enter into the kingdom of God; to the children whom Christ tried to protect in proclaiming woe to him who should offend one of the little ones! And the little children are obliged to learn all this, and are told that it is the only and sacred law of God.

These are not proclamations sent out clandestinely, under fear of penal servitude; they are proclamations which inflict the punishment of penal servitude on all who do not agree with the doctrines they inculcate.

As I write these lines, I experience a painful feeling of dread, simply because I have allowed myself to say that it is impossible to abolish the fundamental law of God inscribed in all laws and in all hearts, by words which explain nothing: "*According to law,*" "*for the sovereign and our country,*" and that this should not be taught to people.

Yes, that has happened of which Christ warned men when he said: [1] —

[1] Luke xi. 33-36; Matt. vi. 23.

"*Look, therefore, whether the light that is in thee be not darkness.*" "*If the light that is in thee be darkness, how great is that darkness.*"

The light that is in us has become darkness; and the darkness of our lives is full of terror.

"*Woe unto you, scribes and Pharisees, hypocrites! because you shut the kingdom of heaven against men: for you enter not in yourselves, neither suffer you others to enter. Woe unto you, scribes and Pharisees, hypocrites! for you devour widows' houses, even while for a pretense you make long prayers: therefore you are still more guilty. Woe unto you, scribes and Pharisees, hypocrites! for you compass sea and land to make one proselyte; and when he is become so, you make him worse than he was. Woe unto you, ye blind guides. ....*

"*Woe unto you, scribes and Pharisees, hypocrites! for you build the sepulchers of the prophets, and garnish the tombs of the righteous, and say, If we had lived in these days when there were prophets, we should not have been partakers in their blood. Wherefore you witness against yourselves, that you are the same as those that slew the prophets. Fill up, then, the measure begun by those like unto you. .... I send unto you prophets, and wise men, and scribes: some of them you will kill and crucify; and some of them you will scourge in your synagogues, and persecute from city to city: that upon you may come all the righteous blood shed on the earth, from the blood of Abel. ....*

"*Every blasphemy* (*calumny*) *shall be forgiven to men; but the blasphemy against the Spirit shall not be forgiven.*"

Of a truth we might say that all this was written but yesterday, not against men who no longer compass sea and land calumniating the Holy Spirit, or converting men to a religion which renders its proselytes worse than they were before, but against men who deliberately force people to embrace their religion, and persecute and bring to death all the prophets and the righteous who seek to expose their falsehoods.

I became convinced that the teaching of the Church,

although it was called "Christian," is the same darkness against which Christ struggled, and against which He commanded His disciples to strive.

Christ's teaching, like all religious teachings, has two sides: first, it is an ethical system which teaches men how to live as individuals, and in relation to one another; second, it is a metaphysical theory which explains why men should live in a given manner and not otherwise. The one is the consequence, and at the same time the cause, of the other.

Man should live in this manner because such is his destiny; or, man's destiny is this, and consequently he should follow it. These two sides of doctrinal expression are common to all the religions of the world. Such is the religion of the Brahmans, of Confucius, of Buddha, of Moses, such is the religion of the Christ. It teaches life — how to live; and it explains precisely why we must live in such a way. But, as has happened to all teachings, Brahmanism, Judaism, Buddhism, so was it with Christ's teaching. Men wander from its teachings of life, and they always find some one to justify their deviations. Those who, as Christ said, sit in Moses' seat, explain the metaphysical side in such a way that the ethical prescriptions of the doctrine cease to be regarded as obligatory, and are replaced by external forms of worship, by ceremonial. This is a condition common to all religions, but it seems to me that this phenomenon has never been manifested with such sharpness as in Christianity; it has been manifested with especial sharpness because Christ's teaching is the most elevated of all doctrines — the most elevated because the metaphysics and ethics of Christ's teaching are so inextricably bound up together and so determine each other that one cannot be separated from the other without destroying the vitality of the whole; and still more because Christ's teaching is in itself Protestantism: that is, it is a denial not only of the ceremonial regulations of Judaism, but of all exterior rites of worship.

Therefore, in Christianity the arbitrary separation of

the metaphysics and ethics could not but disfigure the doctrine, and deprive it of every sort of meaning, and so it was. The separation between the doctrine of life and the explanation of life began with the preaching of Paul, who knew not the ethical teachings set forth in the Gospel of Matthew, and who preached a metaphysico-cabalistic theory entirely foreign to Christ; and this separation was perfected in the time of Constantine, when it was found possible to clothe the whole pagan organization of life in a Christian dress, and without changing it to call it Christianity.

After Constantine, that pagan of pagans, whom the Church for all his crimes and vices admits to the category of the saints, began the councils, and the center of gravity of Christianity was displaced till only the metaphysical portion was left in view. And this metaphysical theory, with its accompanying ceremonial, deviated more and more from its true and primitive meaning, until it has reached its present stage of development, as a doctrine which explains the mysteries of a celestial life beyond the comprehension of human reason, and, with all its complicated formulas, gives *no* religious guidance of this earthly life.

All religions, with the exception of the religion of the Christian Church, demand from their adherents, aside from forms and ceremonies, the practice of certain actions called good, and abstinence from certain actions called bad.

Judaism prescribes circumcision, the observance of the Sabbath, the giving of alms, the year of jubilee, and many other things.

Mohammedanism prescribes circumcision, prayer five times a day, tithes for the poor, pilgrimage to the tomb of the Prophet, and many other things. It is the same with all other religions. Whether these prescriptions are good or bad, they are prescriptions which exact the performance of certain actions. Pseudo-Christianity alone prescribes nothing. The Christian would be under no obligation to do anything at all, and he would be under no obligation to refrain from anything if he did not observe fasts and prayers, which the Church itself does not recognize as obligatory. All that is necessary to the pseudo-Christian is the sacraments. But the sacraments are not performed by the believer; they are administered to him by others. The pseudo-Christian is not obliged to do anything or to abstain from anything for his own salvation, since the Church administers to him everything of which he has need. The Church baptizes him and anoints him, and gives him the eucharist, and confesses him, even after he has lost consciousness, administers extreme unction to him, and prays for him, — and he is saved.

From the time of Constantine the Christian Church has demanded no religious duties of its members. It has never required that they should abstain from anything whatever. The Christian Church has recognized and sanctioned everything that was in the pagan world. It has recognized and sanctioned divorce and slavery and courts of justice and all earthly powers and wars and the death penalty; it has only required at baptism a verbal renunciation of evil, and this only in its early days; later on, when infant baptism was introduced, it no longer required even this.

The Church, though it recognizes Christ's teaching in theory, directly denies it in practice. Instead of guiding the world in its life, the Church, through affection for the world, has expounded Christ's metaphysical doctrine so that no obligation as to the conduct of life might be derived from it, so that it did not prevent men from living differently from the way in which they have been living. The Church has surrendered to the world, and having surrendered, simply follows it. The world does as it pleases, and leaves to the Church the task of justifying its actions with explanations as to the meaning of life. The world has organized its life in absolute opposition to Christ's teaching, and the Church has devised allegories whereby it might be proved that men living contrary to Christ's teaching really live in accordance with it. The result is that the world lives a life which is worse than the pagan life, and the Church not only approves, but maintains that this existence is in exact conformity to Christ's teaching.

But time passed and the light of the true teaching of Christ, which was in the Gospels, notwithstanding that the Church, conscious of its wrong-doing, tried to conceal it — prohibiting the translation of the Bible — time passed and this light reaches the people, even through so-called heretics and free-thinkers, and the falsity of the Church's teaching is shown so clearly that men begin to change the method of living justified by the Church, into one more in accord with Christ's teaching, which has come to them independently of the Church.

Thus men unbeknown to the Church have abolished slavery which the Church justified, have put an end to class privileges, have put an end to the religious punishments justified by the Church, have abolished the divine right of emperors and popes, and are now in turn proceeding to abolish property and the State. And the Church has never forbidden and cannot forbid such action, because the abolition of these iniquities rests on the foundation of the very Christian doctrine, which the Church has preached and still preaches, though it has tried to distort it.

The teaching of human life has been emancipated from the Church, and has remained independent of it.

The Church retains its explanations, but explanations of what? A metaphysical explanation of a teaching has a meaning only when there is a gospel of life which it explains. But the Church has no gospel of life. It has only explanations of that life which it once organized, and which no longer exists. If the Church retains the explanations of that life which at one time existed, like the explanation of the catechism in regard to killing men from duty, no one believes in it. The Church has nothing left but temples and shrines and canonicals and vestments and words.

For eighteen centuries the Church has hidden the light of the Christian gospel of life behind its forms and ceremonials, and wishing to hide it in her robes, has been herself burned in this flame. The world, with its organization sanctioned by the Church, has rejected the Church in the name of the very principles of Christianity which the Church has reluctantly professed, and lives without it. This is an absolute fact and cannot be concealed. Everything that truly lives, not moodily eating out its heart, thus not living, but only preventing others from living, everything that is living in our world of Europe to-day, is detached from the Church, from all churches, and has an existence independent of the Church. Let it not be said that this is true only of the effete Western Europe Our Russia, with its millions of Christian rationalists, civilized and uncivilized, who have rejected the doctrine of the Church, proves incontestably that as regards emancipation from the yoke of the Church, she is, thanks be to God, far more effete than Europe.

Everything that lives is independent of the Church.

The power of the State is based on tradition, on science, on popular suffrage, on brute force, on whatever you will, except on the Church.

Wars, the relation of state with state, are governed by principles of nationality, of the balance of power, but not by the Church.

The institutions established by the State frankly ignore the Church. The idea that the Church can, in these times, serve as a basis for justice or the conservation of property, is simply absurd.

Science not only does not sustain the doctrine of the Church, but is, in its development, entirely hostile to the Church.

Art, formerly entirely devoted to the service of the Church, has wholly forsaken it.

Not only has all life now entirely emancipated itself from the Church; it has no other relation to the Church, except that of contempt as long as the Church does not interfere with human affairs, and hatred when the Church seeks to reassert its ancient privileges. If the form which we call the Church exists, it is simply because men dread to shatter the chalice that once contained something precious. In this way only can we account, in our age, for the existence of Catholicism, of Orthodoxy, and of the different Protestant churches.

All the churches — Catholic, Orthodox, Protestant — are like so many sentinels still keeping careful watch before the prison doors, although the prisoner has long before escaped and is mingling with them and even threatening them. All that whereby the world truly lives at the present time, socialism, communism, politico-economical theories, utilitarianism, the liberty and equality of men and of classes and of women, all the moral principles of humanity, the sanctity of work, the sanctity of reason, science, art, — all these things that make the world progress and show themselves hostile to the Church, are only fragments of the same gospel which, without knowing it, the Church itself promulgated, and which, with Christ's teaching, it has so carefully concealed.

In our day the life of the world goes on its way entirely independent of the teaching of the Church. That teaching is left so far behind, that the men of the world no longer hear the voices of the Church preachers. Indeed there is nothing to hear, because the Church only gives explanations of that organization which the world has already outgrown, and which has either entirely perished or is rapidly falling into irreparable ruin.

Some men were rowing a boat, and a pilot was steering. The men relied on the pilot, and the pilot steered well; but after a time the good pilot was replaced by another, who did not steer at all. The boat moved along rapidly and easily. At first the men did not notice that the new pilot was not steering; and they were only pleased to find that the boat went along so easily. Then they discovered that the new pilot was utterly useless, and they mocked at him, and drove him from his place.

All this would not be so serious, but the misfortune is that the men, under their impulse of indignation against the unskilful pilot, forgot that without a pilot they would not know where they were going.

This very thing has happened with our Christian society. The Church does not steer, it is easy to float, and we have floated a long way, and all the successes of science, of which our nineteenth century is so proud, simply show that we are floating without a helmsman. We are moving onward, not knowing whither. We live and make this life of ours what it is, and really we know not why. But it is impossible to float and row not knowing where you are going, and it is impossible to live and make one's life without knowing why.

If men did nothing of themselves, but were placed by some external force in the situation where they find themselves, they might very reasonably reply to the question, "Why are you in this situation?" — "We do not know; but here we are, and submit." But men make their own positions, and not only for themselves, but also for others, and especially for their children; and so we ask, "Why do you bring together millions of troops, and why do you make soldiers of yourselves, and mangle and murder one another? Why have you expended, and why do you still expend, an enormous sum of treasure and of human energy in the construction of useless and unhealthful cities? Why do you organize childish tribunals, and send people whom you consider as criminals from France to Cayenne, from Russia to Siberia, from England to Australia, when you know that it is senseless? Why do you abandon agriculture, which you like, for work in factories and mills, which you yourselves do not like? Why do you bring up your children in such a way they will be forced to lead an existence which you find worthless? Why do you do this?"

To all these questions you cannot help replying.

If all these things were agreeable, and you liked them, even then you would be compelled to explain why you did them. But as all these things are terribly difficult, and you do them with murmuring and painful struggles, you cannot help reflecting why you do them all. We must either cease to do all this, or we must explain why we do it. Men have never lived and they never can live if this question is left unanswered. And men have always had some answer ready.

The Jew lived as he lived, that is, made war, put criminals to death, built the temple, organized his entire existence in one way and not another, because all this was prescribed in his law, which, he was convinced, God Himself had promulgated. It was the same with the Hindu, with the Chinaman, it was the same with the Roman, and it was the same also with the Mohammedan. It was the same also for the Christian a century ago, and it is the same with the great mass of ignorant Christians now.

To these questions the ignorant Christian makes this reply:

"Military service, wars, tribunals, and the death penalty, all exist in obedience to God's law transmitted to us by the Church. This is a fallen world. All the evil that exists, exists by God's will, as a punishment for the sins of the world, and therefore we cannot palliate this evil. We can only save our own souls by faith, by the sacraments, by prayers, and by submission to God's will as transmitted by the Church. The Church teaches us that all Christians should unhesitatingly obey their rulers, who are the Lord's anointed, and obey also persons placed in authority by rulers; that they ought to defend their property and that of others by force, wage war, inflict the death penalty, and in all things submit to the authorities, who command by the will of God."

Whether these explanations are good or bad, they once sufficed for a believing Christian, as similar explanations satisfied a Jew or a Mohammedan, and men were not obliged to renounce all reason for living according to a law which they recognized as divine. But now the time has come when only the most ignorant people have faith in any such explanations, and the number of these diminishes every day and every hour. It is impossible to check this tendency. Men irresistibly follow those that lead the way, and sooner or later must pass over the same ground as the vanguard. The vanguard are now over an abyss; the vanguard now find themselves in a terrible position; they have organized life to suit themselves, they have prepared the same conditions for those that are to follow, and absolutely have not the slightest idea of why they do what they are doing. No civilized man in the vanguard of progress is able to give any reply now to the direct questions: "Why do you lead the life that you do lead? Why are you doing what you are doing?" I have tried to ask about this, and I have asked hundreds of people, and never have I got from them a direct reply. Instead of a direct reply to the direct question, "Why do you live so and why do you do so?" I have always received an answer, not to my question, but to a question I had not asked.

A believing Catholic, or Protestant, or Orthodox, asked the question why he lives as he lives, that is, contrary to Christ the Lord's teaching, instead of making a direct response, begins to speak of the melancholy state of skepticism characteristic of this generation, of evil-minded persons who spread doubt broadcast among the masses, of the importance of the future of the true Church. But he will not tell you why he does not what his faith commands. Instead of speaking of his own condition, he will talk to you about the general condition of humanity, and of the Church, as if his own life were not of the slightest significance, and his sole preoccupations were the salvation of humanity, and of what he calls the Church.

A philosopher, of whatever school he may be, whether an idealist or a spiritualist, a pessimist or a positivist, to the question why he lives as he lives, that is to say, in disaccord with his philosophical doctrine, always, instead of answering this question, will begin to talk about the progress of humanity, and about the historical law of this progress which he has discovered, and in virtue of which humanity gravitates toward good. But he never will make any direct reply to the question why he himself, in his own life, does not do what he recognizes as reasonable. It would seem as if the philosopher were as preoccupied as the believer, not with his personal life, but with observing the general laws of humanity.

The average man, the immense majority of civilized

half-believers, and who all, without exception, deplore existence, condemn its organization, and predict universal destruction, — the average man, to the question why he continues to lead a life he condemns, without making any effort to ameliorate it, always, instead of a direct reply, begins to talk about things in general, about justice, about the State, about commerce, about civilization. If he be a member of the police or a prosecuting attorney, he asks: —

"And what would become of the State, if I, to ameliorate my existence, were to cease to serve it?"

"What would become of commerce?" he will ask if he be a merchant.

"What of civilization, if I cease to work for it, and seek only to better my own condition?" will be the objection of another.

His response always will be in this form, as if the problem of his life were not in doing the good toward which he strives, but in serving the State, or commerce, or civilization.

The average man replies in just the same manner as does the believer or the philosopher. Instead of making the question personal, he substitutes a general question, and the believer and the philosopher and the average man do this because there is no answer to the personal question of life, because there is no actual teaching concerning life. And he is ashamed.

He is ashamed because he is conscious of being in the humiliating position of a man who has no doctrine of life, for no one has lived or can live without a doctrine of life. Only in our Christian world, instead of a doctrine of life and an explanation of why life is as it is, and is not otherwise, that is, instead of religion, an explanation has been substituted as to why life ought to be what it was once upon a time; and something has been called religion, though it is only a system which is not of the least use to any one, while life itself is made independent of any doctrine, in other words, is left without any definition.

Moreover, as always happens, science has declared this

fortuitous and monstrous condition of our society to be in accordance with a law of all humanity. Learned men, such as Tiele and Spencer, gravely treat of religion, understanding by religion the metaphysical doctrine of the universal principle, and never suspecting that they are not speaking of religion as a whole, but only of one of its phases.

Hence arises the very extraordinary phenomenon that in our day we see learned and intelligent men artlessly believing that they are emancipated from all religion, simply because they do not accept the metaphysical explanation of the universal principle that at some time or other, for some one or other, explained life! It does not occur to them that they must live somehow, that they are living somehow; and that the principle by which they live is their religion. These men imagine they have very elevated convictions, but no faith. Nevertheless, however they talk, they have a faith from the moment they do any reasonable act, for reasonable acts are always determined by a faith. The acts of these men are determined only by the faith that we must always do what we are commanded. The faith of men who do not accept religion is in a religion of obedience to the will of the ruling majority, in a word, submission to established authority.

We may live according to the doctrine of the world, in other words, an animal life, without recognizing any controlling motive more binding than the rules of established authority. But he who lives this way cannot affirm that he lives a reasonable life. Before affirming that we live a reasonable life, we must answer the question: "What doctrine of life do we regard as reasonable?" Alas! wretched men that we are, we have not the semblance of any such doctrine, but we have even lost all perception of the necessity for a reasonable doctrine of life.

Ask the men of our time, believers or skeptics, what theory of life they follow. They will be obliged to confess that they follow but one theory — that based on laws formulated by the functionaries of the second section or by legislative assemblies, and enforced by the police. This is the only theory recognized by Europeans. They know that this doctrine is not from heaven, or from prophets, or from sages; they are continually finding fault with the regulations of these functionaries or legislative assemblies, but nevertheless they recognize this theory, and submit to the police charged with their enforcement, submit without murmuring to the most terrible exactions. The functionaries or the legislative assemblies have decreed that every young man must be ready for outrage and death and for the slaughter of others, and all parents that have adult sons submit to this law, which was drawn up the day before by a mercenary chinovnik, and may be changed the next day.

The idea of a law unquestionably reasonable, and binding upon every one in spirit as well as in letter, has to such a degree become obsolete in our society that the existence among the Hebrews of a law which regulated their whole life, not by forced obedience to its requirements, but by appealing to the conscience of each individual, is considered as the exclusive possession of the Hebrew people. That the Hebrews should have been willing to obey only what they recognized in the depths of their souls as the incontestable truth received directly from God, in other words, that which agreed with their consciences, is considered a national trait of the Jews. But it appears that the natural and normal state of civilized men is to obey what to their own knowledge is decreed by despicable men and enforced by policemen armed with pistols — what each one, or at least the majority of these men, regards as unjust, that is, contrary to their consciences.

I have sought in vain in our civilized society for any clearly formulated moral bases of life. There are none. No perception of their necessity exists. On the contrary, we find the extraordinary conviction that they are superfluous; that religion is nothing more than a few words about God and a future life, and a few ceremonies very useful for the salvation of the soul according to some, and good for nothing according to others: but that life goes of itself and has no need of any fundamental bases or rules, and that we have only to do what we are told to do.

Of what is considered the essence of faith, that is, the doctrine of life and the explanation of its meaning, the first is considered as of very little importance, and as having no relation whatever to faith; the second, that is, the explanation of some bygone life, or speculations and guesses concerning the historical development of life, is considered as of great significance. In all that constitutes the life of man, in all such questions as: how shall he live? shall he go and kill men or shall he not go? shall he judge others or not? shall he educate his children in one way or another? — men of our society give themselves unreservedly to other men, who, like themselves, know not why they live, and compel their fellows to live in one way and not in another.

And men regard an existence like this as reasonable, and have no feeling of shame!

The abyss between the explanation of faith which passes for faith, and faith itself which passes for social and political life, is now as wide as it can possibly be, and the majority of civilized people have nothing to regulate life but faith in the police. This condition would be horrible if it were universal. Fortunately, even in our own time, there are men, the noblest men of our time, who are not contented with such a faith, but have their own faith as to how man ought to live.

These men are regarded as the most malevolent, the most dangerous, and generally as the most unbelieving of all human beings, and yet they are the only believing men of our time, not only believing in general, but believing Christ's teaching, if not as a whole, at least in part.

These men often know nothing at all of Christ's teaching; they do not understand it, and, like their adversaries, they refuse to accept the leading principle of the Christian faith, that of non-resistance to evil; often they hate Christ: but their whole faith with regard to what life ought to be is drawn from Christ's teaching. However much these men may be hounded and persecuted, they are the only ones that do not tamely submit to whatever orders are given, and consequently they are the only men of our society that live a reasonable and not an animal life, the only ones that have faith.

The thread connecting the world and the Church, which gives a meaning to the world, has become weaker and weaker in proportion as the vital juices have been more and more absorbed by the world, and now, when these juices are wholly absorbed, the connecting thread is little more than a hindrance.

This is the mysterious birth process, and it is going on before our eyes. The last bond connecting with the Church will soon be severed, and the process of independent life will begin.

The teachings of the Church, with its dogmas, its councils, and its hierarchy, are undoubtedly united to Christ's teaching. The connecting link is as perceptible as the cord which unites the newly born child to its mother; but as the umbilical chord and the placenta become after parturition useless pieces of flesh, which are carefully buried out of regard for what they once nourished, so the Church has become a useless organ, to hide somewhere out of regard for what it once was.

As soon as respiration and circulation are established, the former source of nutrition becomes a hindrance to life. Vain and foolish would it be to attempt to retain the bond, and to force the child which has come into the light of day to receive its nourishment through the navel string, and not through the mouth and lungs.

But the deliverance of the baby from the mother's womb does not ensure life. The baby's life depends on a new bond of nourishment with its mother.

And so it must be with our Christian world of to-day. Christ's teaching has gestated and given birth to our world. The Church, one of the organs of Christ's teaching, has fulfilled its mission and has become useless, a hindrance. The world cannot be guided by the Church;

but the deliverance of the world from the Church will not ensure life. Life will begin when the world perceives its own weakness and the necessity for a different source of strength. And this is what must take place in our Christian world: it must cry from a consciousness of its helplessness; only this consciousness of its helplessness, a consciousness of the impossibility of depending on its former means of nourishment, and the inadequacy of any other form of nourishment except its mother's milk, will bring it to its mother's breast teeming with milk.

This modern European world of ours, outwardly so self-confident, so bold, so decided, but in the depths of its consciousness so perplexed and despairing, is exactly like a newly born baby: it sprawls, it struggles, it pushes, it gets angry, it cannot tell what to do; it is conscious that its former source of nourishment is exhausted, but it knows not where to seek for a new one.

A newly born lamb uses its eyes and ears, and frisks its tail, and leaps and bounds. It seems to you by its determined look that it knows everything; but, poor thing, it knows nothing! All the impetuosity and energy come from its mother's blood through a medium of transmission which has just been broken, nevermore to be renewed. It is in a blissful, and at the same time a perilous situation. It is full of youth and strength, but it is lost if it cannot get its mother's milk.

And so it is with our European world. Behold what a complex, what an apparently reasonable, and what an energetic life is boiling in this European world! As if all these men knew all that they are doing and why they are doing it all. Behold, with what enthusiasm, what vigor, what youthfulness, do the men of our world do what they are doing! The arts, the sciences, industry, political and administrative details, all are full of life. But this life is only because nourishment once, not so long ago, was furnished through the umbilical cord! There was the Church which transmitted the truth of Christ's teaching to the life of the world. Every manifestation of the world's life has been nourished by it, has grown and developed by it. But the Church has done its work, and has dried up.

All the organs of the world are alive; the fountain from which they formerly received their nourishment has withered away, and they have not yet found another; and they seek everywhere, everywhere but at the breast of the mother from whom they have only just been delivered. Like the lambkin, they still possess the animation derived from nourishment already received, and they do not yet understand that their future nourishment is to be had only from their own mother, but in a different form from what was formerly given to them.

The world must now understand that the period of unconscious nourishment is ended, and that a new process of conscious nutrition must henceforth maintain its life.

This new process consists in consciously accepting those truths of the Christian teaching that were once unconsciously absorbed by humanity through the organism of the Church which still furnishes nutrition for humanity. Men must lift up that light whereby they live, but which has so long remained concealed from them, and carry it high before them and other men, and consciously live by its light.

Christ's teaching, as a religion which governs life and explains to them the meaning of life, is now before the world just as it was eighteen hundred years ago. Formerly the world had the explanations of the Church, which, in concealing the doctrine, seemed in itself to offer a satisfactory interpretation of that old life; but now the time is come when the Church has lost its usefulness, and the world, having no other way of explaining its new life, cannot help feeling its helplessness, and therefore it must go for aid directly to Christ's teaching.

Now, Christ first taught men to believe in the light, and that the light is within themselves. Christ taught men to prize higher than anything else this light of reason, taught them to live conformably with it, and to do nothing that they themselves considered contrary to reason. If you consider it contrary to reason to go out to kill Turks or Germans, do not go; if you consider it contrary to reason to make use of the labor of poor men that you and yours may wear "cylinder" hats and lace yourselves in corsets or live in the height of fashion and maintain a salon, to be a burden to you, why, don't do so; if you consider it contrary to reason to take people already corrupted by idleness and dangerous companionship and shut them up in prison, in other words, in absolute idleness and the most dangerous companionship, do not do so; if you consider it contrary to reason to live in the pestilential air of cities when you can live in a purer atmosphere, if you consider it contrary to reason to teach your children before all and above all the grammatical laws of dead languages, do not do so. Do not do what our whole European world is doing at the present time, — living, and yet not considering its life reasonable; acting, and yet not considering its acts reasonable; but having no confidence in reason, and living in opposition to it.

Christ's teaching is the light. The light shines, and the darkness cannot compass it. Men cannot refuse to accept the light when it shines. They cannot quarrel about it, they cannot help agreeing with it. They must agree with Christ's teaching because it encircles, without coming into collision with, all the errors in which men live, and, like the ether which the physicists tells us about, permeates all things. Christ's teaching is inevitable for every man of our world in whatever situation he may be found. Men cannot help accepting Christ's teaching, not because it is impossible to deny the metaphysical explanation of life which it gives (everything may be denied), but because it alone offers rules for the conduct of life without which humanity has never lived, and never will be able to live; without which no human being has lived or can live, if he would live as man should live, — a reasonable life.

The power of Christ's teaching is not in its explanation of the meaning of life, but in what is deduced from it — in its teaching of life. Christ's metaphysical doctrine is not new; it is that eternal doctrine of humanity inscribed in all the hearts of men, and preached by all the true prophets of the world. The power of Christ's teaching is in the application of this metaphysical doctrine to life.

The metaphysical basis of the ancient doctrine of the Hebrews and Christ is the same: love to God and men. But the application of this doctrine to life, according to Moses, as the Hebrews understood it, demanded the fulfilment of six hundred and thirteen commandments, many of which were absurd and cruel, and all based on the authority of the Scriptures. The teaching of life, according to Christ, springing from the same metaphysical basis, is expressed in five reasonable and beneficent commands, bearing in themselves meaning and justification, and embracing the whole of human life.

Christ's teaching cannot fail to be accepted by those very sincere Jews, Buddhists, Mohammedans, and others who might doubt the truth of their own law; still more must it be accepted by the men of our Christian world who have now no moral law.

Christ's teaching does not quarrel with the men of our world as regards their point of view; to begin with, it is in harmony with it, and while including it in itself, it gives them what they have not now, what is indispensable to their existence, and what they all seek, — it offers them a way of life, not an unknown way, but a way already explored and familiar to all.

You are a sincere Christian, it matters not of what confession. You believe in the creation of the world, in the Trinity, in the fall and redemption of man, in the sacraments, in prayer, in the Church. Christ's teaching is not opposed to your dogmatic belief, and is absolutely in harmony with your theory of the origin of the universe; it only gives you something that you did not possess. While you retain your present religion you feel that the life of the world and your own life are full of evil, and you know not how to remedy it. Christ's teaching (which should be binding upon you since it is the doctrine of your own God) offers you simple and practical rules which will surely deliver you and other men from the evil with which you are tormented.

Believe, if you will, in the resurrection, in paradise, in hell, in the Pope, in the Church, in the sacraments, in the redemption; pray according to the dictates of your faith, attend upon your devotions, sing your hymns, — but all this will not prevent you from practising the five commandments given by Christ for your good: —

Be not angry;
Commit not adultery;
Take no oaths;
Do not defend yourself by violence;
Do not make war.

It may happen that you will break one of these rules; you will perhaps yield to temptation, and violate one of them, just as you violate the rules of your faith, or the articles of the civil code, or the laws of propriety. In the same way you may, perhaps, in moments of temptation, fail of observing all of Christ's commands. But, in your calm moments, do not do as you do now, and so organize your existence as to render it a difficult task not to be angry, not to commit adultery, not to take oaths, not to defend yourself, not to make war; organize rather a life in which it would be difficult to do these things. You cannot help recognizing this because God commands it.

You are an unbeliever, a philosopher of any school. You affirm that the progress of the world is in accordance with a law which you have discovered. Christ's teaching does not oppose your views; it is in harmony with the law that you have discovered. But, aside from this law of yours through which the world will in the course of a thousand years reach a state of felicity, there is still your own personal life to be considered. This life you can use by living in conformity to reason, or you can waste it by living in opposition to reason, and you have now for this, your personal life, no rule whatever, except the decrees drawn up by men whom you do not esteem, and enforced by the police. Christ's teaching offers you rules which are assuredly in accord with your law, for your law of "altruism," or single will, is nothing but a poor paraphrase of this same gospel of Christ.

You are an average man, half believer, half skeptic, having no time to analyze the meaning of human life, and therefore no clearly defined theory of existence. You do what all do. Christ's teaching does not quarrel with you. It says: Very good. You are not capable of reasoning, of verifying the truth of the doctrine taught you; it is easier for you to do as others do. But however modest you may be, you know that you have within you a judge who sometimes approves your acts and sometimes condemns them. However modest your lot, there are occasions when you are bound to reflect and ask yourself, "Shall I do as all do, or in accordance with my own judgment?" Precisely on such occasions, that is, when you are called on to solve some problem with regard to the conduct of life, Christ's commands appeal to you with all their force.

And these commands will surely give answer to your inquiry, because they embrace your whole life, and they will be in accord with your reason and your conscience. If you are nearer to faith than to unbelief, you will, in following these commands, act in harmony with the will of God. If you are nearer to skepticism than to belief, you will, in thus acting, govern your actions by the most reasonable laws existing in the world, and of this you will be convinced because Christ's commands carry their own meaning and their own justification. Christ said: —

"*Now is the judgment of this world: now shall the prince of this world be cast out.*"[1]

"*These things have I spoken unto you, that in me you may have peace. In the world you have tribulation: but be of good cheer; I have overcome the world.*"[2]

And indeed the world, that is, the evil in the world, is overcome.

If the world of evil still exists, it exists only as something dead, it lives only by inertia; it no longer contains the vital principle. For those who have faith in Christ's commands, it does not exist at all. It is vanquished by an awakened conscience of the son of man. A train which has been put in motion continues to move in a

[1] John xii. 31. [2] John xvi. 33.

straight line; but all the intelligent effort of a controlling hand is made manifest, and the movement is reversed.

"*For all things born of God overcome the world; and the victory whereby the world is overcome is your faith.*"[1]

The faith that triumphs over the world is faith in Christ's teaching.

CHAPTER XII

I BELIEVE in Christ's teaching, and this is my faith: —

I believe that my happiness is possible on earth only when all men fulfil Christ's teaching.

I believe that the fulfilment of this teaching is possible, easy, and pleasant.

I believe that even now, when this teaching is not fulfilled, if I should be the only one among all those that do not fulfil it, there is, nevertheless, nothing else for me to do for the salvation of my life from the certainty of eternal loss but to fulfil this teaching, just as a man in a burning house, if he find a door of safety, must go out.

I believe that my life according to the teaching of the world has been a torment, and that a life according to Christ's teaching can alone give me in this world the happiness for which I was destined by the Father of Life.

I believe that this teaching will give welfare to all humanity, will save me from inevitable destruction, and will give me in this world the greatest happiness. Consequently, I cannot help fulfilling it.

"*The law was given by Moses; grace and truth came by Jesus Christ.*"[2]

Christ's teaching is goodness and truth. Formerly, not knowing goodness, I knew not truth. Mistaking evil for good, I fell into evil, and I doubted the lawfulness of my tendency toward good. But I understand and believe now that the good toward which I strive is the will of the Father, is the most lawful essence of my life.

Christ said to me: —

"Live for the good; believe not in those snares and

[1] 1 John v. 4. [2] John i. 17.

temptations ($\sigma\kappa\acute{\alpha}\nu\delta\alpha\lambda\alpha$) which, by enticing thee with the semblance of good, draw thee away from true goodness, and lead thee into evil. Thy welfare is thy unity with all men; evil is the violation of the unity with the son of man. Deprive not thyself of the good which is given thee."

Christ showed me that the unity of the son of man, the love of men for one another, is not as I had formerly supposed, merely an ideal after which men are to strive; but that this unity, this love of men for one another, is their natural condition, the condition into which according to His words children are born, the condition in which all men would live if they were not drawn aside by error, illusions, and temptations.

But Christ has not merely shown me this, He has also enumerated clearly in His commandments, without the possibility of mistake, every one of the temptations that deprive me of this natural condition of unity, love, and good, and insnare me in evil. Christ's commands give me the means of salvation from the temptations that have deprived me of happiness; and so I cannot help believing in these commands. The good of life was given me, and I myself destroyed it. In His commands, Christ has shown me the temptations whereby I destroy my good, and therefore I cannot do what destroys my good. In this, and in this alone, is all my faith.

Christ showed me that the first temptation destructive of my good is my enmity toward men, my anger against them. I cannot help believing this, and so I cannot willingly remain at enmity with others. I cannot, as I could once, foster anger, be proud of it, fan it into flame, justify it, regarding myself as an intelligent and superior man, and others as useless and foolish people. Now, when I give up to anger, I can only realize that I alone am guilty, and seek to make peace with those that are at enmity with me.

But this is not all. While I now see that anger is an abnormal, pernicious, and morbid state, I also perceive the temptation that led me into it. The temptation was in separating myself from other men, recognizing only a few of them as my equals, and regarding all the others as persons of no account (*raka*) or as stupid and uncultivated (*fools*). I see now that this wilful separation from other men, this calling other men *raca* or *fool*, was the principal source of my disagreements. In looking over my past life I see now that I had rarely permitted my anger to rise against those I considered as my equals, and never insulted them. But the least disagreeable action on the part of one whom I considered an inferior inflamed my anger and led me to abusive words or actions, and the more superior I felt myself to be, the more easily I insulted him; sometimes the mere supposition that a man was of a lower social position than myself was enough to provoke me to an outrageous manner.

I understand now that he alone is above others who humbles himself before others and makes himself the servant of all. I understand now why those that are great in the sight of men are an abomination to God, and why woe is threatened the rich and mighty, and why blessedness is promised the poor and humble. Now I understand this truth, I have faith in it, and this faith has transformed my perception of what is right and important, and what is wrong and despicable, in life. Everything that once seemed to me right and important — honors, glory, civilization, wealth, the complications and refinements of life, luxury, rich food, fine clothing, etiquette, — has become for me wrong and despicable. Rusticity, obscurity, poverty, austerity, simplicity of surroundings, of food, of clothing, of manners, all have now become right and important to me.

And therefore if, even now, knowing all this, I may, in a moment of forgetfulness, give myself up to anger and abuse a brother, in my quiet state of mind I cannot yield to the temptation which, raising me above other men, deprived me of my true good, — unity and love; even as a man cannot lay a snare for himself a second time after he has once been caught in one and almost lost.

Now, I can no longer give my support to anything which lifts me above or separates me from others. I cannot, as I once did, recognize in myself or others titles or ranks or qualities aside from the title and quality of man. I cannot seek for fame and glory; I cannot cultivate such sciences as would separate me from others. I cannot avoid striving to get rid of my wealth which separates me from men. In my way of life, my food, my clothing, my manners, I cannot help striving for what will not separate me from others but will unite me to the majority of men.

Christ showed me that the second temptation destructive of my welfare is wanton desire, that is, the desire to possess another woman than her to whom I am united. I cannot help believing in this, and therefore, I cannot, as I did once, consider my passionate temperament as a natural and elevated human quality. I can no longer justify it by my love for the beautiful, or my passionate nature, or my wife's faults. At the first inclination toward wanton desire I cannot fail to recognize that I am in a morbid and abnormal state, and to seek all means to rid myself of this evil.

But, knowing that wanton desire is an evil, I also know the temptation that used to seduce me into it, and so I can avoid it. I know now that the principal cause of this temptation is not that men cannot refrain from lechery, but that the majority of men and women are abandoned by those with whom they were first united. I know now that every desertion of a man or woman when the two have once been united, is that very divorce which Christ forbade, because men and women abandoned by their first companions are the original cause of all the debauchery in the world.

Recalling what led me to debauchery, I see now that besides that barbarous education whereby both physically and intellectually wanton desire was kindled in me and justified by all the subtilities of the mind; the principal temptation that led me astray was in the abandonment of the woman to whom I had first been united, and the situation of the abandoned women on all sides around me. I see now that the principal force of the temptation was not in my carnal desires, but in the fact that those desires were not satisfied in the men and women by whom I was surrounded. I now understand Christ's words:—

"*God created them from the beginning, made them male and female. .... So that they are no more twain, but one flesh. What, therefore, God hath joined together, let not man put asunder.*" [1]

I understand now that monogamy is the natural law of humanity, which cannot with impunity be violated. I now understand perfectly the words declaring that whoever separates from his wife, that is from the woman with whom he was first united, and seeks another, compels her to resort to debauchery, and thus introduces into the world a new evil against himself.

This I believe; and the faith I now have has transformed my opinions with regard to the right and important, and the wrong and despicable, things of life. What once seemed to me the best thing—a refined, elegant life, passionate and poetic love, praised by all poets and artists, now seemed to me wicked and revolting. On the other hand a laborious, indigent, rude life, which moderates the sexual desires, now seemed to me good. The human institutior of marriage, which gives an external seal of legality to the union of man and woman, does not seem to me so lofty and important as the genuine union of man and woman, which, when accomplished, can never be broken without breaking God's will.

If, when in a moment of weakness, I may fall under the promptings of desire, I know the snare that would deliver me into this evil, and so I cannot yield to it as formerly I was accustomed to do. I cannot now desire and seek for physical sloth and luxury, which excite excessive sensuality in me. I cannot now pursue amusements which kindle amorous sensuality, — novels, poetry, music, theaters, balls, — amusements which once seemed to me elevated and refining, but which I now see to be injurious. I cannot abandon my wife, for I know that

[1] Matt. xix. 4–6.

by forsaking her, I set a snare for myself, for her, and for others. I cannot encourage the gross and idle existence of others. I cannot encourage or take part in licentious pastimes, novels, plays, operas, balls, and the like, which are so many snares for myself and for others. I cannot favor the celibacy of persons fitted for the marriage relation. I cannot encourage the separation of wives from their husbands. I cannot make any distinction between unions that are called by the name of marriage, and those that are denied this name. I cannot help considering as sacred and absolute the sole and unique union by which man is once for all indissolubly bound to the first woman with whom he has been united.

Christ showed me that the third temptation destructive to my welfare is the temptation of the oath. I cannot help believing this; consequently, I cannot, as I once did, bind myself by oath to serve any one for any purpose, and I can no longer, as I did formerly, justify myself for having taken an oath because "it would harm no one," because every one did the same, because it is necessary for the State, because the consequences might be bad for me or for some one else if I refused to submit to this exaction. I know now that it is an evil for myself and for others, and I cannot conform to it.

Nor is this all. I now know the snare that led me into evil, and I can no longer yield to it. I know that the snare is in the use of God's name to sanction an imposture, and that the imposture consists in promising in advance to obey the commands of one man, or of many men, while I ought to obey the commands of God alone. I know now that the most terrible evil in its consequences — murders in war, imprisonments, capital punishment — exists only because of the oath, in virtue of which men make themselves instruments of evil, and believe that they free themselves from all responsibility. Remembering now many and many of the evils that have impelled me to hostility and hatred, I see that they all originated with the oath, the engagement to submit to the will of others. I understand now the meaning of the words: —

"*But let your speech be, Yea, yea; nay, nay; and whatever is more than these is of evil.*"[1]

Understanding this, I am convinced that the oath destroys my true welfare and that of others, and this belief changes my estimate of right and wrong, of the important and despicable. What once seemed to me right and important, — the promise of fidelity to the government supported by the oath, the exacting of oaths from others, and all acts contrary to conscience, done because of the oath, — now seem to me wrong and low. Therefore I can no longer evade Christ's command forbidding the oath; I can no longer bind myself by oath to any one, I cannot exact an oath from another, I cannot encourage men to take an oath, or to cause others to take an oath; nor can I regard the oath as necessary, important, or even inoffensive, as many think.

Christ showed me that the fourth temptation destructive of my welfare is the resort to violence for the resistance of evil. I am obliged to believe that this is an evil for myself and for others; consequently, I cannot, as I once did, deliberately resort to violence, and seek to justify my action with the pretext that it is indispensable for the defense of my person and property, or of the persons and property of others. I cannot yield to the first impulse to resort to violence; I am obliged to renounce it, and to abstain from it altogether.

But besides knowing this, I know now the temptation that caused me to fall into this evil. I know now that the snare consisted in the erroneous belief that my life could be made secure by violence, by the defense of my person and property against others. I know now that a great portion of the evils that afflict mankind is due to this, — that men, instead of giving their work for others, deprive themselves completely of the privilege of work, and forcibly appropriate the labor of their fellows. Remembering now all the evil that I caused myself and others and all the evil that others have done, I see that a large part of this evil arises from the fact that we consider it possible by self-defense to guaran-

[1] Matt. v. 37.

tee and better our lives. I also understand now the words:—

"*A man is born not to be worked for, but to work for others,*" and the meaning of the words, "*The laborer is worthy of his food.*"

I believe now that my true welfare, and that of others, is possible only when every man will labor not for himself, but for another, and not only does not withhold his labor from another, but also will give it with joy to any one who has need of it. This faith changed my estimate of what is right and important, and wrong and despicable. What once seemed to me right and important,—riches, private property of every sort, honor, the maintenance of personal dignity and personal privileges, —all this has now become to me low and wrong; all that used to seem to me low and wrong—labor for others, poverty, humility, the renunciation of all property and of all personal privileges—has become good and lofty in my eyes.

If, now, in a moment of forgetfulness, I yield to the impulse to resort to violence, for the defense of my person or property, or of the persons or property of others, I cannot deliberately and calmly use this snare for my own destruction and the destruction of others. I cannot acquire property. I cannot resort to force in any form for my own defense or the defense of another, except in behalf of a child, and then only to deliver from an evil imminently threatening it. I cannot take part with any power which has for an object the defense of men and their property by violence. I cannot be a judge, or take part in a trial, or a nachalnik, or take part in the exercise of any jurisdiction whatever. I can no longer encourage others in the support of tribunals, or in the exercise of authoritative administration.

Christ showed me that the fifth temptation that deprives me of my well-being is the distinction we make between foreigners and compatriots. I cannot help believing this, and consequently, if, in a moment of forgetfulness, I have a feeling of hostility toward a man of another nationality, I am obliged, in quiet moments of reflection, to regard this feeling as wrong. I can no longer, as I did formerly, justify my hostility by the superiority of my own people over others, or by the ignorance, the cruelty, or the barbarism of another race. At the first manifestation of this, I cannot help striving to be even more friendly with a foreigner than with one of my own countrymen.

Not only do I know now that my discrimination among different nations is an evil destructive of my welfare, but I now know the temptation that led me into this evil, and I can no longer, as I once did, deliberately and calmly yield to it. I know now that this temptation consists in the erroneous belief that my welfare is connected only with the welfare of my countrymen, and not with the welfare of all mankind. I know now that my unity with others cannot be shut off by a frontier, or by a government decree which decides that I belong to this or that nation. I know now that all men are everywhere brothers and equals. When I think now of all the evil that I have done, that I have endured, and that I have seen about me, as the consequence of national enmities, I see clearly that it is all due to that gross imposture called patriotism, — love for one's native land. When I think now of my education, I see how these hateful feelings of enmity for other nations, feelings of separation from them, were never inherent in me, but all these evil feelings were artificially inoculated in me by a senseless education. I understand now the meaning of the words: —

"*Do good to your enemies, treat them as you treat your own people. You are all sons of one Father. Therefore be like your Father; in other words, make no distinction between your nation and others; be the same with all.*"

I understand now that true welfare is possible for me only on condition that I recognize my unity with the whole world. I believe this, and this belief has changed my estimate of what is right and wrong, important and despicable. What once seemed to me right and important — love for my country, love for my own nation, for my empire, services rendered at the expense of the welfare of other men, military exploits — now seem to me repulsive and pitiable. What once seemed to me shameful and wrong — renunciation of nationality, and the cultivation of cosmopolitanism — now seem to me right and important. If, now, in a moment of forgetfulness, I can help a Russian more than a foreigner, and desire the success of Russia or of the Russian people, I can no longer in a calm moment yield to this temptation which destroys me and others.

I cannot recognize states or peoples; I can take no part in any quarrels between peoples or states, or any discussion between them, either oral or written, much less in any service in behalf of any particular state. I cannot take part in any of those measures based on divisions between states, — the collection of customs duties, taxes, the manufacture of arms and projectiles, or any act favoring armaments, military service, and still less in any war with other nations, — neither can I help others to do this.

I have learned in what my true welfare consists, I have faith in that, and consequently I cannot do what would inevitably deprive me of that welfare.

I not only believe that I ought to live thus, but I believe that if I live thus, my life will attain its only possible meaning, and be reasonable, pleasant, and indestructible by death.

I believe that my reasonable life, the light I bear with me, was given to me only that it might shine before men, not in words only, but in good deeds, that men may thereby glorify the Father.[1]

I believe that my life and my consciousness of truth is the talent confided to me for a good purpose, and that this talent is a fire which is a fire only when it burns.

I believe that I am a Nineveh with regard to other Jonahs from whom I have learned and shall learn of the truth; but that I am also a Jonah in regard to other Ninevites to whom I am bound to transmit the truth.

I believe that the only meaning of my life is to be at-

[1] Matt. v. 16.

tained by living in the light that is within me, and not putting it under a bushel, but by holding it high before people so that they may see it. This faith gives me renewed strength to fulfil Christ's teaching, and overcomes the obstacles which used to stand in front of me.

All that once sapped within me the truth and the practicability of Christ's teaching, everything that once turned me from it, the possibility of privations, suffering, and death, inflicted by those who know not Christ's teaching, now confirm its truth and draw me into its service.

Christ said, "When you have lifted up the son of man, then shall you be drawn toward me," and I felt that I was irresistibly drawn to Him by the influence of His doctrine. "*The truth*," He says again, "*The truth shall make you free*," and I know that I am in perfect liberty.

An armed enemy will come, or even evil-minded persons attack me, I used to think, and if I do not defend myself they will rob us, and beat us, and torture us, and kill me and my neighbors, those whom I felt bound to protect, and this seemed terrible to me. But this that once troubled me now seems desirable, and confirmed the truth. I know now that the enemy and the so-called malefactors or brigands are all men like myself; that, like myself, they love good and hate evil; that they live, as I live, on the eve of death; and that, with me, they seek for salvation, and will find it only in Christ's teaching. All the evil that they do to me will be evil to them also, and so can be nothing but good for me. But if truth is unknown to them, and they do evil thinking that they do good, I know the truth, only on condition that I reveal it to those that know it not. And this I can do only by refusing to participate in evil, and thereby confessing the truth by my example.

"But hither come the enemy, — Germans, Turks, savages; if you do not make war on them, they will exterminate you!" That is untrue. If there were a society of Christians that did evil to none, and gave of their labor for the good of others, such a society would have no enemies — Germans or Turks or savages — to kill or to torture them. The foreigners would take only what the members of this society would voluntarily give, making no distinction between Russians, Germans, Turks, or savages. But when Christians live in the midst of a non-Christian society which defends itself by war, and calls on the Christians to join in waging war, then the Christians have an opportunity of helping men by revealing the truth to those that know it not. A Christian knows the truth only to bear witness of the truth before those that know it not. He cannot bear witness in any *other* way than by example. He must renounce war and do good to all men, whether they are so-called enemies or compatriots.

"But not merely enemies, but wicked men among his own people will attack a Christian's family, and if he do not defend himself, will pillage and massacre him and his family."

This again is wrong. If all the members of this family are Christians, and consequently hold their lives only for the service of others, no man will be found unreasonable enough to deprive such people of the necessaries of life or to kill them. The famous Miklukha-Maclay lived among the most bloodthirsty of savages, so it is said; they did not kill him, they reverenced him and followed his teachings, simply because he did not fear them, exacted nothing from them, and treated them always with kindness.

But what if a Christian lives in a non-Christian family, accustomed to defend itself and its property by a resort to violence, and is called on to take part in this defense? Then this call is simply an appeal to the Christian to fulfil the duties of his life. A Christian knows the truth only that he may show it to others, more especially to his neighbors and to those who are bound to him by ties of blood and friendship, and a Christian can show the truth only by refusing to join in the errors of others, by taking part neither with aggressors or defenders, but by abandoning all that he has to those who will take it from him, thus showing by his life that he needs nothing save the fulfilment of God's will, and that he fears nothing except disobedience to that will.

But a government cannot permit a member of the society over which it has sway, to refuse to recognize the fundamental principles of governmental order or to decline to fulfil the duties of all citizens. The government exacts from a Christian the oath, jury service, military service, and his refusal to conform to these demands may be punished by exile, imprisonment, and even by death. Then, once more, the exactions of those in authority are only an appeal to the Christian to fulfil the duty of his life. For a Christian, the exactions of those in authority are the exactions of those who do not know the truth. Consequently, a Christian who knows the truth must bear witness of the truth to those that know it not. Exile and imprisonment and death, to which in consequence of this the Christian is subjected, give him the possibility of bearing witness of the truth, not in words, but in acts. All violence — war, brigandage, executions — is not accomplished through the forces of unconscious nature; it is accomplished by men who are blinded, and do not know the truth. Consequently, the more evil these men do to the Christians, the further they are from the truth, the more unhappy they are, and the more necessary it is that they should have knowledge of the truth. Now a Christian cannot make known his knowledge of truth except by abstaining from the errors that lead men into evil; he must render good for evil. In this alone is the whole work of a Christian's life, and its whole meaning, and death cannot destroy it.

Men united by error constitute a compact mass. The compactness of this mass is the evil of the world. All the intellectual activity of humanity is directly destroying the cohesive power of deception.

All revolutions are attempts to shatter the power of evil by violence. Men think that by hammering on the mass it will cease to be a mass, and they pound on it; but, in their efforts to shatter it, they only make it more dense than it was before. The cohesion of the molecules is not destroyed. The disruptive movement must come from within, when molecule releases its hold upon molecule, and the whole mass falls into disintegration.

Error is the force that welds men together; truth is communicated to men only by deeds of truth. Only deeds of truth, by introducing light into the conscience of each individual, can dissolve the cohesion of error, and detach men one by one from the mass united together by the cohesion of error.

This work has been going on for eighteen hundred years.

It began when Christ's commands were first given to humanity, and it will not cease till, as Christ said, "*all things be accomplished.*" [1]

The Church composed of those that sought to unite men in unity by the solemn affirmation that it alone was the truth, has long since fallen to decay.

But the Church composed of men united, not by promises or consecrations, but by deeds of truth and love, has always lived and will live forever. This Church, now as then, is made up not of those that say "*Lord, Lord,*" and work iniquity, but of those that hear the words of truth and reveal them in their lives.

The members of this Church know that life is to them a blessing if they do not destroy the unity of the son of man; and that the blessing will be lost only to those that do not obey Christ's commands. And so the members of this Church cannot help practising Christ's commands and teaching them to others.

Whether this Church be in numbers little or great, it is, nevertheless, the Church that shall never perish, the Church in which all men will be united.

"*Fear not, little flock; for it is your Father's good pleasure to give you the kingdom.*"

MOSCOW, January 22 (O. S.), 1884.

[1] Matt. v. 18.

House of Count L. N. Tolstoï at Yasnaya Polyana.

THE GOSPEL IN BRIEF

AUTHOR'S PREFACE

THIS present book is extracted from a larger work, which exists in manuscript, and cannot be published in Russia.

That work consists of four parts, namely: —

1. An account of that course of my personal life, and of my thoughts, which led me to the conviction that in the Christian teaching lies the truth.

2. An investigation of the Christian teaching — first, according to the interpretation of the Greek Church solely; then, according to the interpretation of the Churches generally, and the interpretation of the apostles, councils, and so-called "Fathers." Also, an exposition of the falsity in these interpretations.

3. An investigation of the Christian teaching, based, not upon the above interpretations, but solely upon the words and deeds ascribed to Christ by the four Gospels.

4. An exposition of the real meaning of the Christian teaching, of the motives for its perversions, and of the consequences to which it should lead.

From the third of these parts this present volume is condensed. I have there effected the fusion of the four Gospels into one, according to the real sense of the teaching. I had no need to digress from the order in which each Gospel is written, so that in my harmonisation the transpositions of verses, rather than being more, are less numerous than in the greater part of those known to me, and in our Grechoulevitch's version of the four Gospels. In my treatment of the Gospel of John there is no transposition, but all stands in the same order as in the original.

My division of the Gospel into twelve chapters (or six, since each pair of the twelve may be taken as one) came about spontaneously from the nature of the teaching. The following is the purport of the chapters: —

1. Man is the son of the Infinite Source of Being; he is the son of this Father, not by the flesh but by the spirit.

2. And therefore, man must serve the Source of his being, in the spirit.

3. The life of all men has a divine Origin. This Origin only is sacred.

4. And therefore, man must serve this Source of all human life. This is the will of the Father.

5. Service of the Will of the Father of Life is life-giving.

6. And therefore, it is not necessary to life that each man should satisfy his own will.

7. This present life in time is the food of the true life.

8. And therefore, the true life is outside time; it is in the present.

9. Time is an illusion in life; the life of the past and the future clouds men from the true life of the present.

10. And therefore, one must aim to destroy the deception arising from the past and future, the life in time.

11. The true life is that now present to us, common to all, and manifesting itself in love.

12. And therefore, he who lives by love now, in this present, becomes, through the common life of all men, at one with the Father, the source, the foundation of life.

So that the chapters, in pairs, are related as cause and effect.

Besides these twelve chapters, this exposition includes —(*a*) The introduction of the first chapter of the Gospel of John, where the writer of the Gospel speaks, in his own name, as to the purport of the whole teaching: and (*b*) a portion of the same writer's Epistle (written probably before the Gospel); this containing the general sense to be derived from the preceding exposition.

These two parts are not essential to the teaching Although the former, as well as the latter of them, might be omitted without loss (the more so as they come in the name of John, and not of Christ), I have, nevertheless, kept them, because, to a straightforward understanding of the whole teaching, these parts, confirming each other and the whole, as against the strange commentaries of the Churches, yield the plainest evidence of the meaning to be put upon the teaching.

At the beginning of each chapter, besides a brief indication of the subject, I had put words from the prayer taught by Jesus to His disciples, such as corresponded with the contents of the chapter.

At the conclusion of my work I found, to my astonishment and joy, that the Lord's Prayer is nothing less than Christ's whole teaching, stated in most concise form, and in that same order in which I had already arranged the chapters, each phrase of the prayer corresponding to the purport and sequence of the chapters, as follows:—

1. Our Father,	Man is the son of the Father.
2. Which art in heaven,	God is the infinite spiritual source of life.
3. Hallowed be Thy name,	May the Source of Life be held holy.
4. Thy kingdom come,	May His power be established over all men.
5. Thy will be done, as in heaven,	May His will be fulfilled, as it is in Himself,
6. So also on earth.	So also in the bodily life.
7. Give us our daily bread	The temporal life is the food of the true life.
8. This day.	The true life is in the present.
9. And forgive us our debts as we forgive our debtors,	May the faults and errors of the past not hide this true life from us,
10. And lead us not into temptation,	And may they not lead us into delusion,
11. But deliver us from evil,	So that no evil may come to us,
12. For Thine is the kingdom, the power, and the glory.	And there shall be order, and strength, and reason.

In that large third part from which this work is condensed, the Gospel according to the four Evangelists is presented in full. But in the rendering now given, all passages are omitted which treat of the following matters, namely, — John the Baptist's conception and birth, his imprisonment and death; Christ's birth, and his genealogy; his mother's flight with him into Egypt; his miracles at Cana and Capernaum; the casting out of devils; the walking on the sea; the cursing of the fig-tree; the healing of sick, and the raising of dead people; the resurrection of Christ Himself; and, finally, the reference to prophecies fulfilled in His life.

These passages are omitted in this abridgment, because, containing nothing of the teaching, and describing only events which passed before, during, or after the period in which Jesus taught, they complicate the exposition. However one takes them, under any circumstance, they bring to the teaching of Jesus neither contradiction nor confirmation of its truth. Their sole significance for Christianity was that they proved the divinity of Jesus Christ for him who was not persuaded of this divinity beforehand. But they are useless to one whom stories of miracles are powerless to convince, and who, besides, doubts the divinity of Jesus as evidenced in His teaching.

In the large work, every departure from the ordinary version, as well as every comment added to the text, and every omission, is made clear, and proved by the comparison of the various versions of the Gospels, from the examination of contexts, and finally, by considerations, philological and other. But in the present abridged rendering, all these arguments and refutations of the false understanding of the Churches, as well as the minute notes and quotations, are omitted; because, however true and exact they may be in their places, they cannot carry conviction as to the true understanding of the teaching. The justness of a conception of this kind is better proved, not by arguing particular points, but by its own unity, clearness, simplicity, fullness, as well as by its harmony with the inner feelings of all who seek truth. Speaking generally, in regard to what divergence there is between my rendering and the Church's authorized text, the reader must not forget that it is a gross error to represent the four Gospels, as is often done, to be books sacred in every verse and in every syllable. The reader must not forget that Jesus never Himself wrote a book, as did, for instance, Plato, Philo, or Marcus Aurelius; that He, moreover, did not, as Socrates did, transmit His teaching to informed and literate men, but spoke to a crowd of illiterate men; and that only a long time after His death men began to write down what they had heard from Him.

The reader must not forget that a great number of such accounts have been written, from which, at first, the Churches selected three, and then another. Moreover, in selecting those which seemed to them the best according to the proverb, "No stick without knots," the Churches, out of the enormous heap of the Christian literature, have been forced to take in with their bargain a great many knots; so that the canonical Gospels contain nearly as many faulty passages as those Gospels rejected as apocryphal.

The reader must not forget that it is the teaching of Christ which may be sacred, but in no way can a certain measure of verses and syllables be so; and that certain verses, from here to here, say, cannot be sacred merely because men say they are so.

Moreover, the reader must not forget that these selected Gospels are, at any rate, the work of thousands of various brains and hands of men; that during centuries the Gospels have been selected, enlarged, and commented upon; that the most ancient copies which have come down to us, from the fourth century, are written straight on without punctuation, so that, even after the fourth and fifth centuries, they have been the subject of the most diverse readings; and that such variations in the Gospels may be counted up to fifty thousand. The reader must have all this present in mind in order to disengage himself from the opinion, so common among us, that the Gospels, in their present shape, have come to us directly from the Holy Spirit. The reader must not forget that, far from it being blamable to dis encumber the Gospels of useless passages, and to illuminate passages the one by the other, it is, on the contrary, unreasonable not to do this, and to hold a certain number of verses and syllables as sacred.

On the other hand, I pray my readers to remember that, if I do not hold the Gospels to be sacred books emanating from the Holy Spirit, I yet less regard the Gospels as mere historical monuments of religious literature. I understand the theological as well as the historical standpoint on the Gospels, but regard the books myself from quite another. I pray the readers of my rendering not to be misled, either by the theological view, or by that other, so usual in our day among educated men, the historical view, neither of which I hold with. I consider Christianity to be neither a pure revelation nor a phase of history, but I consider it as the only doctrine which gives a meaning to life.

And it is neither theology nor history which has won me to Christianity; but just this, that, when fifty years old, having questioned myself, and having questioned the reputed philosophers whom I knew, as to what I am, and as to the purport of my life, and after getting the reply that I was a fortuitous concatenation of atoms, and that my life was void of purport, and that life itself is evil, I became desperate, and wished to put an end to my life. But after recalling to myself how formerly, in childhood, while I still had religious faith, life possessed meaning for me; and that the great mass of men about me, who hold to faith and are uncorrupted by wealth, possess the meaning of life: after all this, I was brought into doubt as to the justness of the reply given to me by the wisdom of men of my own station, and I tried once more to understand what answer it is that Christianity gives to those men who live a life with meaning. And I embarked upon the study of Christianity, as to what in this teaching guides the lives of men. I began to study that Christianity which I saw applied in life, and to make the comparison of this applied Christianity with the sources whence it percolates. The source of the Christian teaching is the Gospels, and there I found the explanation of the spirit which animates the life of all who really live. But along with the flow of that pure, life-giving water I perceived much mire and slime unrightfully mingled therewith; and this had prevented me, so far, from seeing the real, pure water. I found that, along with the lofty Christian teaching, are bound up the teachings of Hebraism and the Church, both of which are repugnant and foreign to the former. I thus felt myself in the position of a man to whom is given a sack of refuse, who, after long struggle and wearisome labor, discovers among the refuse a number of infinitely precious pearls. This man then knows that he is not blameworthy in his distaste for the dirt, and also that those who have gathered these pearls at the same time with the rest of the sackful, and who have preserved them, are no more to blame than himself, but, on the contrary, deserve love and respect.

I knew not the light, and I thought there was no sure truth in life; but when I perceived that only light enables men to live, I sought to find the sources of the light. And I found them in the Gospels, despite the false commentaries of the Churches. And when I reached this source of light I was dazzled with its splendor, and I found there full answers to my questions as to the purport of the lives of myself and others, — answers which I recognized as wholly harmonious with all the known answers gained among other nations, and, to my mind, surpassing all other answers.

I sought a solution of the problem of life, and not of a theological or historical question; and that is why I was indifferent to know whether Jesus Christ is or is not God, and from whom proceeds the Holy Spirit, etc. And it is just as unimportant and unnecessary to know when and by whom such and such a Gospel was written, and whether such and such a parable came from Jesus Himself or not. For me, the only important concern was this light, which, for eighteen hundred years, has shone upon mankind; which has shone upon me likewise, and which shines upon me still. But to know, more than this, how I ought to name the source of this light, what elements compose it, and what kindled it, I in no way concerned myself.

I might end this preface here if the Gospels were newly discovered books, and if the teaching of Jesus had not been, these eighteen hundred years, the subject of a continuous series of false interpretations. But to-day, to rightly understand the teaching of Jesus as He must needs have understood it Himself, it is indispensable to know the chief causes of these false interpretations. The prime cause of such false interpretations, which make it now so difficult for us to recover the true teaching of Jesus, is the fact that, under the cover of the Christian teaching, have been preached the teachings of the Church, which are made up from explanations of most contradictory writings, in which only a small part of the true teaching enters; even that being distorted, and adapted to the commentaries. The teaching of Christ, according to this misinterpretation, is simply one link in the great chain of revelation which began with the world's beginning, and stretches into the Church of our own time.

These misinterpreters call Jesus God; but the recognition of His divinity does not make them recognize a greater importance in His words and teaching than in the words of the Pentateuch, the Psalms, the Acts, the Epistles, the Apocalypse, or even the decisions of the Councils and the writings of the Fathers.

And this false understanding allows no presentment of the teaching of Jesus which does not accord with the revelations which have preceded and followed Him; doing this with the purpose, not to make clear the meaning of the teaching of Jesus, but to harmonize, as far as possible, various writings which contradict each other; such as the Pentateuch, the Psalms, the Gospels, Epistles, Acts, and, generally, all those which pass for sacred.

It is possible, indeed, to make a limitless number of such interpretations, having for object, not truth, but the reconcilement of those two irreconcilables, the Old and the New Testaments. And, in fact, the number of these is unlimited. This is the case with the Epistles of Paul, and with the decisions of the Councils (which last begin with the formula: "It is the will of us and the Holy Spirit"); and such, also, is the case with the decrees of popes and synods, with the teachings of the Khlysty,[1] and with all false interpreters of the thought of Jesus. All recur to the same gross sanctions of the truth of their reconcilements, affirming that these reconcilements are not the result of their personal thought, but a direct witness from the Holy Spirit.

Without entering upon an analysis of these different dogmatic systems, each of which pretends to be the only true one, we may, nevertheless, well see that all of them, beginning by holding sacred the multitude of writings which make up the Old and New Testaments, thereby impose upon themselves an insurmountable barrier to the understanding of the real teaching of Jesus; and out of this confusion necessarily results the possibility, and even the necessity, of an infinite variety of opposed sects.

The reconcilement of all the revelations can be infinitely varied, but the explanation of the teaching of one person, and one looked upon as a God, should, on the contrary, not give rise to any difference of sect. It is impossible there should be conflicting ways of interpreting the teaching of a God come down to earth. If God had so come down to reveal unfailing truth to men, at least He would have revealed it in such a way that all might understand; if, then, this has not been done, that is because it was not God who came; or if, indeed, the truths of God are such that God Himself cannot make them plain to mankind, how can men do so?

If, on the other hand, Jesus was not God, but only a great man, His teaching can still less engender sects. For the teaching of a great man is only great because it explains in a clear, understandable way that which others have set out obscurely, incomprehensibly. That which is incomprehensible in the teaching of a great man is not great. The teaching of a great man can, there-

[1] A Russian sect.

fore, engender no sects. Only, then, this interpretation, which pretends to be a revelation from the Holy Spirit, and to contain the sole truth, raises up antagonisms and gives birth to sects. However much the sects of various religions may assure us that they do not condemn those of other sects, that they pray for union with them, and have no hate to them, it is not true. Never, since the time of Arius, has a single dogma arisen from other cause than the desire to contradict an opposing dogma.

To maintain that a particular dogma is a divine revelation, inspired by the Holy Spirit, is in the highest degree presumption and folly. The highest presumption, because there is nothing more arrogant than for a man to say, "What I tell you, God Himself says through my mouth." And the highest folly, because there is nothing more stupid than to reply to one who says that God speaks by his mouth, "God says quite the opposite, and by mine own mouth." But in this way reason all the Churches; and hence have been born, and are now being born, all the sects and all the evil brought, and being brought, into the world in the name of religion.

And yet deeper than this surface evil, all the sects cherish a second internal vice, which destroys in them any character of clearness, certainty, and honesty. It is this. While these sects present us with their false interpretations, as the last revelation from the Holy Spirit, they are careful never to precisely and decisively determine what is the very essence and purport of this revelation, which they profess is continued through them, and which they call "the Christian teaching."

All the sectarians who accept the revelation from the Holy Spirit, along with the Mohammedans, recognize Moses, Jesus, and Mohammed. The Churchmen accept Moses, Jesus, and the Holy Spirit. But to Mohammedanism, Mohammed is the last prophet, who alone has given the definite explanation of the two preceding revelations, — this is the last revelation, which explains all the preceding; and this one every true believer has before him.

With the religion of the Churches it is quite otherwise. That also, like the Mohammedan, accepts three revelations, but in place of calling their religion by the name of their last revealer, that is, the "religion of the Holy Spirit," they maintain their religion to be that of Jesus, and refer themselves to His teaching. So that, in giving to us what are really their own doctrines, they pretend to rest them upon the authority of Jesus.

Those religions of the Holy Spirit which offer to us the last and most decisive of revelations, whether it be in the writings of the Apostle Paul or the decisions of such and such Councils, or the decrees of popes or patriarchs, ought to say so, and call their faith by the name of him who had the last revelation. And if the last revelation is by the Fathers of the Church, or a decree of the Patriarch of the East, or a papal encyclical, or the syllabus or the catechism of Luther or Philaretus, people should say so, and call their faith by this name; because the last revelation, which explains all the preceding, is always the most important one. But they decline to adorn their dogmatic systems with the names of these authorities, and, continuing to preach quite against Christ's own teaching, they persist in maintaining that Jesus has revealed their doctrine to them. So that, according to their teaching, Jesus declared that He, by His blood, redeemed our humanity, ruined through Adam's sin; that there are three Persons in God; that the Holy Spirit came down upon the apostles, and was transmitted to the priesthood by the laying on of hands; that seven sacraments are necessary to salvation; that communion must be in two kinds; and so on. They would have us believe that all this is part of the teaching of Jesus; whereas we shall there seek in vain even the least allusion to any such matters. The Churches which so pretend would do well in concluding to give all this to us at once as the doctrine of the Holy Spirit, not of Jesus; for, in short, only those are Christians who hold the revelation of Jesus Himself as the decisive one, in virtue of His own saying, that His followers must own no other master than Himself.

It would seem that the matter is so plain that it is not worth thinking about; but however strange it seems to say so, it is none the less true that up till now the teaching of Jesus is not separated, on the one hand, from artificial and unwarrantable connection with the Old Testament, and, on the other hand, from the superadded fantastic notions which have been imposed upon it under cover of the name of the Holy Spirit. Up to now, there are some who, in calling Jesus the second Person of the Trinity, will not conceive of His teaching otherwise than as in accordance with the so-called revelations of the third Person, as these are found in the Old Testament, the decrees of Councils, and the conclusions of the Fathers of the Church; and in preaching the most extravagant things, they affirm these extravagances to be the religion of Christ. Others there are who, in refusing to regard Jesus as a God, similarly conceive of His teaching, not at all as He Himself declared it, but as what Paul and the other interpreters have made of it. Whilst considering Jesus as a man, and not as a God, these learned men deprive Him of a common natural right: the right of being held responsible for His own words only, and not for the words of His misinterpreters. In their endeavors to elucidate the teaching of Jesus, they attribute to Him ideas which He never thought of uttering. The representatives of this school, to begin with Renan, the most popular of them, do not see it their duty to take the trouble of distinguishing between that which bears the stamp of Jesus Himself and that which His interpreters have wrongly ascribed to Him. And, instead of thus troubling to search out the teaching of Jesus Himself a little more deeply than the Churches have done, they have been led to seek in the events of His life, and in the facts of history contemporary with Him, the explanation of His influence and of the diffusion of His ideas.

The problem they are called upon to solve is, in effect, this —

Eighteen hundred years ago a poor wanderer appeared on earth who taught certain things. He was flogged and executed. And since then, although many and many just men have suffered for the belief, millions of people, wise and foolish, learned and ignorant, cannot shake off the conviction that this man, alone among men, was God. Here is a strange phenomenon; how is it to be explained? The Churches explain it by saying that this man, Jesus, was really God, by which everything is explained. But if this man was not God, how are we to explain why this mere man, in particular, has been acknowledged as God?

On this point the learned people of our schools of history gather with extreme care every detail of the life of this man, without noticing that, even though they should succeed in gathering a great number of these details (in truth, they have gathered none); and even though they should succeed in entirely reconstructing the life of Jesus in the smallest details, the supreme question remains unanswered, — the question as to why Jesus, and no one else, exercised such an influence over men. The answer to this is not found in knowledge of the society in which Jesus was born, brought up, and so on; still less is it found in knowledge of the happenings in the Roman world at about this time, or in the fact that the people were inclined to superstitious beliefs. To gain this answer, it is only needful to find what precisely was the especial mark of Jesus which has led so many people to raise Him above the rest of men, and, for eighteen hundred years, to hold Him as a God.

He who would solve this problem, it would seem, must, before all, bring himself to understand the teaching of Jesus: His true teaching, clearly seen, and not the crude interpretations which have been put upon it. But this is just what is neglected. The learned historians of Christianity are so satisfied to think that Jesus was no God, they are so keen to prove that His teaching holds nothing divine, and is, therefore, not binding, that they are not alive to a very plain fact: they do not see that, the more they prove Jesus to have been simply a man, and in nothing divine, the darker and more insoluble they make the problem they have in hand. They are making their full efforts to prove that He was simply a man, that, therefore, His teaching is not obligatory. To see clearly this astonishing error, one has only to remember the last writings of Renan's follower, M. Havet, who remarks, with much simplicity, "Christ was never, in anything, a Christian." And M. Soury, for his part, is altogether ravished with the idea that Jesus was a cultureless man, a simple soul.

The essential thing is: not to prove that Jesus was no God, and His doctrine not divine, any more than to prove He was not a Catholic: but to know what His teaching essentially is; that teaching which has seemed to men so lofty and so precious, that they have again and again owned Him for God who gave it to them.

If the reader belongs to that vast body of educated men who have been brought up in the beliefs of a Church, and who have not renounced its absurdities; if he be a man of reason and conscience (whether retaining love and respect for the Christian teaching, or whether, following the proverb, "Burn the coat now the vermin have got in," he thinks the whole of Christianity a pernicious superstition), I pray him to reflect that that which shocks him, and seems to him a superstition, is not the real teaching of Jesus; and that it were unjust to make Jesus responsible for the follies which have, since His time, incrusted His teaching. It is only necessary to study the teaching of Jesus in its proper form, as it has come down to us in the words and deeds which are recorded as His own. With readers of the kind I have addressed, my book will go to show that Christianity is not only a mixture of things sublime and things base; that it is not only not a superstition, but that, on the contrary, it is the most convincing presentment of metaphysics and morals, the purest and most complete doctrine of life, and the highest light which the human mind has ever reached; a doctrine from which all the noblest activities of humanity in politics, science, poetry, and philosophy instinctively derive themselves.

If, on the other hand, my reader belongs to that small minority of educated men who remain attached to Church doctrines, and who accept religion, not for an outward end, but to gain inward quietude, then I ask such a reader to remember that the teaching of Christ, as set forth herein, is quite other than that teaching as he has been given to understand it; and that, therefore, the question for him is, not as to whether the doctrine here put before him agrees with his beliefs, but, as to which is more in harmony with his reason and his heart — the teaching of his Church composed of reconcilements of many scriptures, or the pure teaching of Jesus. It concerns him only to decide whether he will accept the new teaching, or whether he prefers to retain the teaching of his Church.

If, finally, my reader belongs to the category of men who value and accept outwardly the belief of some Church, not at all for truth's sake, but for the outward consideration of gains that come therefrom, such an one should inform himself that, whatever be the number of his coreligionists, whatever their power, whatever their station, even though monarchs, and whatever lofty personages they can reckon among them, he himself forms one of a party, not of the accusers, but of the accused. Such readers should inform themselves that they are not asked to furnish arguments for their case, because, this long while, all such arguments have been given which can be given; and even should they cite their proofs, they would only prove that which every one of the hundreds of opposing sects proves in its own case.

And, in truth, such people need not to prove anything, but to clear themselves, first, of the sacrilege they commit in putting the teaching of Jesus, whom they hold to be God, upon the same footing as the teachings of Ezra, of the Councils, of Theophylact; and in allowing themselves to distort the sayings of God into agreement with the sayings of men. Again, they must clear themselves of blasphemy in ascribing to God-Jesus all the zealotry which abides in their own hearts, and declaring it to be teaching of Christ. And finally, they must clear themselves of the treason they commit in hiding from men the teaching of God, who has come down to earth to bring us salvation; and by sliding in, to displace this teaching, the tradition of the Holy Spirit, thus depriving thousands of millions of that salvation which Jesus brought for men; and thus, instead of peace and love, bringing in all the diversity of sects, and all the recriminations, murders, and all sorts of misdeeds which follow.

For these readers there are only two issues: either to make humble submission, and renounce their deceits; or, to persecute those who arise to accuse them of the evil they have done and are doing.

If they will not renounce their deceits, it remains for them to take the only other part, that is, to persecute me. For which, in now completing my writing, I am prepared, with joy, and with fear for my own human weakness.

THE GOSPEL IN BRIEF

CHAPTER I

THE SON OF GOD

Man, the son of God, is powerless in the flesh, and free in the spirit

("Our Father")

Mt. i. 18. THE birth of Jesus Christ was thus:—
His mother Mary was betrothed to Jo
seph. But, before they began to live as man
19. and wife, Mary proved with child. But Joseph
was a good man, and did not wish to disgrace
24. her; he took her as his wife, and had nothing
25. to do with her until she had borne her first son,
and called him Jesus.
Lk. ii. 40. And the boy grew and matured, and was
intelligent beyond his years.
41. Jesus was twelve years old; and it happened
42. that Mary and Joseph went to the feast at
43. Jerusalem, and took the boy with them. The
44. feast was over, and they went homeward, and
forgot about the boy. Afterward they recol-
lected, and thought that he had gone off with
45. the children, and they inquired about him along
the road. He was nowhere to be found, and
46. they went back to Jerusalem after him. And
it was the third day before they found the boy
in the temple, sitting with the teachers, ques-
47. tioning them, and listening. And every one
48. wondered at his intelligence. His mother
caught sight of him, and said: "Why have

you done this way with us? Your father and
I have been grieving, and looking for you."
And he said to them: "But where did you Lk. ii. 49.
look for me? Surely you ought to know that
the son must be looked for in his Father's
house?" And they did not understand his 50.
words; they did not understand whom it was
he called his Father.

And after this, Jesus lived at his mother's, 51.
and obeyed her in everything. And he ad- 52.
vanced in age and intelligence. And every iii. 23.
one thought that Jesus was the son of Joseph;
and so he lived to the age of thirty.

At that time the prophet John appeared in Mt. iii. 1.
Judea. He lived in the desert of Judea, on Mk. i. 4.
the Jordan. John's clothes were of camel's Mt. iii. 4.
hair, girt round the waist with a strap; and
he fed on bark and herbs.

He summoned the people to a change of Mk. i. 4.
life, in order to get rid of wickedness; and,
as a sign of the change of life, he bathed people in the Jordan. He said: "A voice calls Lk. iii. 4.
to you: Open a way for God through the wild
places, clear the way for Him. Make it so 5.
that all may be level, that there may be neither
hollows nor hills, neither high nor low. Then 6.
God will be among you, and all will find their
salvation."

And the people asked him, "What are we 10.
to do?" He answered: "Let him who has two 11.
suits of clothes give one to him who has none.
Let him who has food give to him who has
none." And tax-collectors came to him, and 12.
asked: "What are we to do?" He said to 13.
them: "Extort nothing beyond what is ordered." And soldiers asked: "How are we 14.
to live?" He said: "Do no one any harm,
do not deal falsely; be content with what is
served out to you."

And inhabitants of Jerusalem came to him, Mt. iii. 5.

and all the Jews in the neighborhood of the
Mt. iii. 6. Jordan. And they acknowledged their wickedness to him; and, in sign of the change of
life, he bathed them in the Jordan.
7. And many of the orthodox and conventional
religionists also came to John, but secretly. He
recognized them, and said: "You race of vipers!
Have you, also, got wind of it, that you cannot
8. escape the will of God? Then bethink yourselves, and change your faith! And if you
wish to change your faith, let it be seen by
your fruits that you have bethought yourselves.
10. The ax is already laid to the tree. If the
tree produces bad fruit, it will be cut down
11. and cast into the fire. In sign of your change
I cleanse you in water; but, along with this
bathing, you must be cleansed with the spirit.
12. The spirit will cleanse you, as a master cleanses
his threshing-floor; when he gathers the wheat,
but burns the chaff."
13. Jesus came from Galilee to the Jordan to be
bathed by John; and he bathed, and heard
John's preaching.
iv. 1. And from the Jordan he went into the wild
2. places, and there he strove in the spirit. Jesus
passed forty days and nights in the desert,
without food or drink.
Lk. iv. 3. And the voice of his flesh said to him: "If
you were Son of the Almighty God, you might
of your own will make loaves out of stones;
but you cannot do this, therefore you are not
4. Son of God." But Jesus said to himself: "If
I cannot make bread out of stones, this means
that I am not Son of a God of the flesh, but
Son of the God of the spirit. I am alive, not
by bread, but by the spirit. And my spirit is
able to disregard the flesh."

But hunger, nevertheless, tormented him; and the voice of the flesh again said to him: "If you live only by the spirit, and can disre-

gard the flesh, then you can throw off the flesh,
and your spirit will remain alive." And it Lk. iv. 9
seemed to him that he was standing on the
roof of the temple, and the voice of the flesh
said to him: "If you are Son of the God of
the spirit, throw yourself off the temple. You
will not be killed. But an unforeseen force will 10.
keep you, support you, and save you from all
harm." But Jesus said to himself: "I can 11. 12.
disregard the flesh, but may not throw it off,
because I was born by the spirit into the flesh.
This was the will of the Father of my spirit,
and I cannot oppose Him."

Then the voice of the flesh said to him: "If you cannot oppose your Father by throwing yourself off the temple and discarding life, then you also cannot oppose your Father by hungering when you need to eat. You must not make light of the desires of the flesh; they
were placed in you, and you must serve them."
Then Jesus seemed to see all the kingdoms of 5.
the earth, and all mankind, just as they live
and labor for the flesh, expecting gain therefrom. And the voice of the flesh said to him: 6.
"Well, you see, these work for me, and I give
them all they wish for. If you will work for 7.
me you will have the same." But Jesus said 8.
to himself: "My Father is not flesh, but spirit.
I live by Him; I always know that He is in
me. Him alone I honor, and for Him alone I
work, expecting reward from Him alone."

Then the temptation ceased, and Jesus knew 13.
the power of the spirit.

And when he had known the power of the 14.
spirit, Jesus went out of the wild places, and Jn. i. 35.
went again to John, and stayed with him.

And when Jesus was leaving John, John said 36.
of him: "This is the saviour of men."

On account of these words of John, two of 37.
John's disciples left their former teacher and

Jn. i. 38. went after Jesus. Jesus, seeing them following him, stopped and said: "What do you
want?" They said to him: "Teacher! we
wish to be with you, and to know your teach-
39. ing." He said: "Come with me, and I will
tell you everything." They went with him,
and stayed with him, listening to him until the
tenth hour.
40. One of these disciples was called Andrew.
41. Andrew had a brother Simon. Having heard
Jesus, Andrew went to his brother Simon, and
said to him: "We have found him of whom
the prophets wrote, the Messiah; we have
found him who has announced to us our sal-
42. vation." Andrew took Simon with him, and
brought him also to Jesus. Jesus called this
brother of Andrew, Peter, which means a
stone. And both these brothers became disciples of Jesus.
43. Afterward, before entering Galilee, Jesus
met Philip, and called him to go with him.
44. Philip was from Bethsaida, and a fellow-vil-
45. lager of Peter and Andrew. When Philip
knew Jesus, he went and found his brother
Nathanael, and said to him: "We have found
the chosen of God, of whom the prophets and
Moses wrote. This is Jesus, the son of Joseph,
46. from Nazareth." Nathanael was astonished
that he of whom the prophets wrote should be
from the neighboring village, and said: "It
is most unlikely that the messenger of God
47. should be from Nazareth." Philip said: "Come
with me, you shall see and hear for yourself."
48. Nathanael agreed, and went with his brother,
and met Jesus; and, when he had heard him,
49. he said to Jesus: "Yes, now I see that this is
true, that you are the Son of God and the king
51. of Israel." Jesus said to him: "Learn something more important than that. Henceforth
heaven is opened, and people may be in com-

munion with the forces of heaven. Henceforth God will be no longer separate from men."

And Jesus came home to Nazareth; and on Lk. iv. 16.
the Sabbath he went as usual into the synagogue, and began to read. They gave him the 17.
book of the prophet Isaiah, and, unrolling it,
he began to read. In the book was written:—

"The spirit of the Lord is in me. He has 18.
chosen me to announce happiness to the unfortunate and the broken-hearted, to announce
freedom to those who are bound, light to the
blind, and salvation and rest to the weary. To 19.
announce to all men the time of God's mercy."

He folded the book, gave it to the attendant, 20.
and sat down. And all waited to hear what
he should say. And he said: "This writing
has now been fulfilled before your eyes."

CHAPTER II

LIFE IN THE SPIRIT

Therefore man must work, not for the flesh, but for the spirit

("Which art in heaven")

It happened once that Jesus, with his dis- Mt. xii. 1. Mk. ii. 23.
ciples, went through a field on the Sabbath. Lk. vi. 1.
His disciples were hungry, and on the way plucked ears of corn, bruised them in their hands, and ate the grain. But, according to the teaching of the orthodox, God had made an agreement with Moses, that all should observe the Sabbath, and do nothing on that day. According to this teaching of the orthodox, God commanded that he who worked on the Sabbath should be stoned to death. The orthodox Mt. xii. 2
saw that the disciples were bruising ears of corn on the Sabbath, and said; "It is not

right to do so on the Sabbath. One must not
work on the Sabbath, and you are bruising
ears of corn. God ordained the Sabbath, and
commanded the breaking of it should be punished with death." Jesus heard this, and said:
Mt. xii. 7. "If you understand what is the meaning of
God's words, 'I desire love, and not sacrifice,'
you would not attach blame to that which is
8. not blameworthy. Man is more important than
the Sabbath."

Lk. xiii. 10. It happened another time, on a Sabbath, that
11. when Jesus was teaching in the synagogue, a
sick woman came up to him and asked him to
12–14. help her. And Jesus began to cure her. Then
the orthodox church-elder was angry with Jesus
for this, and said to the people: "It is said in
the law of God: There are six days in the week
xiv. 3. on which to work." But Jesus, in reply, asked
the orthodox professors of the law: "Well,
then, in your opinion, may not one help a man
6. on the Sabbath?" And they did not know
5. what to answer. Then Jesus said: "Deceiv-
Lk. xiii. 15. ers! Does not each of you untie his beast
from the manger and lead him to water on the
Mt. xii. 11. Sabbath? And if his sheep falls into a well,
any one will run and drag it out, although even
12. on the Sabbath. And a man is much better
than a sheep. But you say that one must not
Mk. iii. 4. help a man. What, then, in your opinion, must
one do on the Sabbath, good or evil: save a
soul or destroy it? Good must be done always,
on the Sabbath too."

Mt. ix. 9. Jesus once saw a tax-gatherer receiving taxes.
The tax-gatherer was called Matthew. Jesus
began to speak with him, and Matthew understood him, liked his teaching, and invited him
to his house, and showed him hospitality.
10. When Jesus came to Matthew, there came also
Matthew's friends, tax-gatherers and unbelievers, and Jesus did not disdain them, and sat

down, he and his disciples. And the orthodox Mt. ix. 11.
saw this, and said to Jesus' disciples: "How
is it that your teacher eats with tax-gatherers
and unbelievers?" According to the teaching
of the orthodox, God forbade communion with
unbelievers. Jesus heard, and said: "He who 12.
is satisfied with his health does not need a doc-
tor, but he who is ill, does. Understand what 13.
is the meaning of God's words: 'I desire love
and not sacrifice.' I cannot teach a change of
faith to those who consider themselves orthodox, but I teach those who consider themselves
unbelievers."

There came to Jesus orthodox professors of xv. 1. Mk. vii. 1.
the law from Jerusalem. And they saw that Mt. xv. 2. Mk. vii. 2.
his disciples and Jesus himself ate bread with
unwashed hands; and these orthodox began to
condemn him for this, because they themselves 3.
strictly observed, according to church tradition,
how plates and dishes should be washed, and
would not eat unless they had been so washed.
Also, they would eat nothing from the market 4.
unless they had washed it.

And the orthodox professors of the law asked 5.
him: "Why do you live not according to church
tradition, but take and eat bread with unwashed
hands?" And he answered them: "But in Mt. xv. 3.
what way do you break God's commandment,
following your church tradition? God said to Mk. vii. 10, 11.
you: 'Honor your father and mother.' But
you have twisted it so that every one can say:
'I give to God what I used to give my parents.'
And he who so says need not support his father 12.
and mother. Thus, then, you break God's com- 13.
mandment by church tradition. Deceivers!
The prophet Isaiah spoke the truth about you: Mt. xv. 7.
'Because this people only fall down before me 8.
in words, and honor me with their tongue,
while their heart is far from me; and because 9.
their fear of me is only a human law which

they have learnt by heart; therefore I will perform a wonderful, an extraordinary thing upon
this people: The wisdom of its wise men shall
be lost, and the reason of its thinkers shall be
dimmed. Woe to them who take thought to
hide their desires from the Eternal, and who
Mk. vii. 8. do their deeds in darkness.' And so it is with
you: You leave that which is important in the
law, that which is God's commandment, and
observe your human tradition as to the washing of cups!"
14. And Jesus called the people to him, and
15. said: "Hearken all, and understand: There
is nothing in the world that, entering a man,
could defile him; but that which goes forth
from him, this defiles a man. Let love and
mercy be in your soul, and then all will be
16. clean. Try to understand this."
17. And when he returned home, his disciples
18. asked him: "What do these words mean?"
And he said: "Do you also not understand
this? Do you not understand that everything
external, that which is of the flesh, cannot de-
19. file a man? The reason is, it enters not his
soul, but his body. It enters the body, and
20. afterward goes out from it. Only that can
defile a man which goes out from the man
21. himself, from his soul. Because from the soul
of man proceed evil, fornication, impurity, murder, theft, covetousness, wrath, deceit, insolence,
envy, calumny, pride, and every kind of folly.
23. All this evil is out of the soul of man and it
alone can defile a man."
Jn. ii. 13. After this, the Passover came, and Jesus
went to Jerusalem, and entered the temple.
14. In the inclosure of the temple stood cattle,
cows, bulls, rams; and there were cotes full of
pigeons, and money-changers behind their
counters. All this was necessary in order to
make offerings to God. The animals were

slaughtered and offered in the temple. This
was the method of prayer among the Jews, as
taught by the orthodox professors of the law.
Jesus went into the temple, twisted a whip, Jn. ii. 15
drove all the cattle out of the inclosure, and
set free all the doves. And he scattered all 16.
the money, and bade that none of this should
be brought into the temple. He said: "The Mt. xxi. 13.
prophet Isaiah said to you: The house of God Mk. xi. 17.
is not the temple in Jerusalem, but the whole (Isa. lvi. 7. Jer. vii. 4,
world of God's people. And the prophet Jere- 11.)
miah also told you: Do not believe the falsehoods that here is the house of the Eternal.
Do not believe this, but change your life; do not
judge falsely; do not oppress the stranger, the
widow, and the orphan; do not shed innocent
blood, and do not come into the house of God,
and say: Now we may quietly do foul deeds.
Do not make my house a den of robbers."

And the Jews began to dispute, and said to 18.
him: "You say that our piety is wrong. By
what proofs will you show this?" And, turn- 19.
ing to them, Jesus said: "Destroy this temple
and I will in three days awaken a new, living
temple." And the Jews said: "But how will 20.
you at once make a new temple, when this was
forty-six years in building?" And Jesus said Mt. xii. 6.
to them: "I speak to you of that which is
more important than the temple. You would 7.
not say this if you understood the meaning of
the words of the prophet: I, God, do not rejoice
at your offerings, but rejoice at your love to each
other. The living temple is the whole world
of men, when they love each other."

And then in Jerusalem many people believed Jn. ii. 23.
in what he said. But he himself believed in 24.
nothing external, because he knew that everything is within man. He had no need that any 25.
one should give witness of man, because he
knew that in man is the spirit.

Jn. iv. 4. And Jesus happened once to be passing
5. through Samaria. He passed by the Samaritan
village of Sychar, near the place which Jacob
6. gave to his son Joseph. There was Jacob's
well. Jesus was tired, and sat beside the well.
8. His disciples went into the town to fetch bread.
7. And a woman came from Sychar to draw water,
9. and Jesus asked her to give him to drink. And
she said to him: "How is it that you ask me to
give you to drink? For you Jews have no intercourse with us Samaritans."
10. But he said to her: "If you knew me, and
knew what I teach, you would not say this, and
you would give me to drink, and I would give
13. you the water of life. Whoever drinks of the
14. water you have will thirst again. But whoever
shall drink of the water I have shall always be
satisfied, and this water shall bring him ever-
19. lasting life." The woman understood that he
was speaking of things divine, and said to him:
"I see that you are a prophet, and wish to teach
20. me. But how are you to teach me divine things,
when you are a Jew and I a Samaritan? Our
people worship God upon this hill, but you Jews
say that the house of God is only in Jerusalem.
You cannot teach me divine things, because you
have one belief, and we another." And Jesus
21. said to her: "Believe me, woman, the time is
already here, when people, to pray to the Father,
23. will come neither to this hill nor to Jerusalem.
The time has come when the real worshipers
of God will worship the Heavenly Father in
24. spirit and with works. Such are the worshipers the Father needs. God is a spirit, and He
must be worshiped in the spirit and with
25. works." The woman did not understand what
he told her, and said: I have heard that the
messenger of God will come, he whom they call
the anointed. He will then declare every-
26. thing." And Jesus said to her: "It is I, the

same who has spoken with you. Expect nothing more."

After this, Jesus came into the land of Judea, Jn. iii. 22.
and there lived with his disciples, and taught.
At that time John taught the people near Salim, 23.
and bathed them in the river Enon. For John 24.
was not yet put in prison.

And a dispute arose between the disciples of 25.
John and the hearers of Jesus, as to which was
better, John's cleansing in water or Jesus' teaching. And they came to John, and said to him: 26.
"You cleanse with water, but Jesus only teaches,
and all go to him. What have you to say of 27.
him?" John said: "A man of himself can
teach nothing, unless God teach him. Who 31.
speaks of the earth, is of the earth; but whosoever speaks of God, is from God. It is no- 32-34.
wise possible to prove whether the words that
are spoken are from God or not from God. God
is a spirit; He cannot be measured, and He
cannot be proved. He who shall understand
the word of the spirit, by this very thing proves
that he is of the spirit. The Father, loving His 35.
Son, has intrusted all to him. Whoever be- 36.
lieves in the Son has life, and whoever does not
believe in the Son has not life. God is the
spirit in man."

After this there came to Jesus one of the or- Lk. xi. 37.
thodox, and invited him to dinner. Jesus went
in and sat down at table. The host noticed that 38.
he did not wash before dinner, and wondered
thereat. And Jesus said to him: "You ortho- 39-41.
dox wash everything outside; but are you clean
inside? Be well-disposed to men, and all will
be clean."

And while he sat in the house of the orthodox, vii. 37.
there came a woman of the town, who was an
unbeliever. She had learnt that Jesus was in
the house of the orthodox man, and she came
there too, bringing a bottle of scent. And she 38.

knelt at his feet, wept, and washed his feet with
her tears, wiped them with her hair, and poured
Lk. vii. 39 scent over them. The orthodox man saw this,
and thought to himself: "He is hardly a prophet. If he were really a prophet, he would
know what kind of a woman it is that is washing his feet. He would know that this is a
wrong-doer, and would not allow her to touch
40. him." Jesus guessed his thought, and, turning
to him, said: "Shall I tell you what I think?"
41. The host assented. And Jesus said: "Well, it
is this. Two men held themselves debtors to a
certain man of property, one for five hundred
42. pence, the other for fifty. And neither the one
nor the other had anything to pay with. The
creditor pardoned both. Now, in your opinion,
which will love the creditor more, and show him
43. greater attention? And he said: "Of course,
44. he that owed more." Jesus pointed to the
woman, and said: "So it is with you and this
woman. You consider yourself orthodox, and
therefore a small debtor; she considers herself
an unbeliever, and therefore a great debtor. I
came to your house; you did not give me water
to wash my feet. She washed my feet with her
45. tears, and wiped them with her hair. You did
46. not kiss me, but she kissed my feet. You did
not give me oil to anoint my head, but she
47. anoints my feet with precious scent. He who
rests in orthodoxy will not do works of love, but
he who considers himself an unbeliever will do
works of love. And for works of love, all is
48-50. forgiven." And he said to her: "All your
wickedness is forgiven you." And Jesus said:
"All depends upon what each man considers
himself. Whoever considers himself good will
not be good; but whoever considers himself bad
will become good."

xviii. 10. And Jesus said further: "Two men once
came into a temple to pray; one orthodox, and

the other a tax-gatherer. The orthodox man Lk xviii. 11
prayed thus: 'I thank Thee, God, that I am not
as other men, I am not a miser, nor a libertine;
I am not a rogue, not such a worthless fellow as
that tax-gatherer. I fast twice weekly, and give 12.
away a tithe of my property.' But the tax- 13.
gatherer stood afar off, and dared not look up
at the sky, but merely beat his breast, and said:
'Lord, look down upon me, worthless as I am.'
Well, and this man was better than the ortho- 14.
dox, for the reason that whoever exalts himself shall be humbled, and whoever humbles
himself shall be exalted."

After this, disciples of John came to Jesus, v. 33.
and said: "Why do we and the orthodox fast
much, while your disciples do not fast? For,
according to the law, God commanded people
to fast." And Jesus said to them: "While 34
the bridegroom is at the wedding, no one
grieves. Only when the bridegroom is away, 35.
do people grieve. Having life, one must not 36.
grieve. The external worship of God cannot
be combined with works of love. The old
teaching of the external worship of God cannot be combined with my teaching of works
of love to one's neighbor. To combine my
teaching with the old, is the same as to tear
off a shred from a new garment and sew it on
an old one. You will tear the new and not
mend the old. Either all my teaching must
be accepted, or all the old. And having once
accepted my teaching, it is impossible to keep
the old teaching, of purification, fasting, and
the Sabbath. Just as new wine cannot be 37
poured into old skins, or the old skins will
burst and the wine run out. But new wine 38
must be poured into new skins, and both the
one and the other will remain whole."

CHAPTER III

THE SOURCE OF LIFE

The life of all men has proceeded from the spirit of the Father

("Hallowed be Thy Name")

M. xi. 2, AFTER this, John's disciples came to ask
3. Jesus whether it was he of whom John spoke;
whether he was revealing the kingdom of God,
4. and renewing men by the spirit? Jesus answered and said: "Look, listen, — and tell
John, whether the kingdom of God has begun,
and whether people are being renewed by the
spirit. Tell him of what kingdom of God I
5. am preaching. It is said in the prophecies
that, when the kingdom of God shall come,
all men will be blessed. Well, tell him that
6. my kingdom of God is such that the poor are
blessed, and that every one who understands
me becomes blessed."

7. And, having dismissed John's disciples, Jesus
began to speak to the people as to the kingdom of God John announced. He said:
"When you went to John in the wilderness
to be baptized, what did you go to see? The
orthodox teachers of the law also went, but
did not understand that which John announced.
16. And they thought him nothing worth. This
breed of orthodox teachers of the law only
consider that as truth which they themselves
invent and hear from each other, and that as
law which they themselves have devised. But
18. that which John said, that which I say, they
do not hearken to, and do not understand.
Of that which John says, they have understood only that he fasts in the wild places, and
19. they say: 'In him is an evil spirit.' Of that
which I say, they have understood only that

I do not fast, and they say: 'He eats and
drinks with tax-gatherers and sinners — he is
a friend of theirs.' They chatter with each 17.
other like children in the street, and wonder
that no one listens to them. And their wis- 19.
dom is seen by their works. If you went to 8.
John to look at a man attired in rich clothes,
why, such dwell here in palaces. Then, what 9.
did you go to seek in the desert? Did you go
because you think John was the same as other
prophets? Do not think this. John was not
a prophet like others. He was greater than
all prophets. They foretold that which might
be. He has announced to men that which
is, namely, that the kingdom of God was,
and is, on earth. Verily, I tell you, a man has 10.
not been born greater than John. He has
declared the kingdom of God on earth, and
therefore he is higher than all. The law and Lk. xvi. 16.
the prophets, — all this was needful before
John. But, from John and to the present
time, it is announced that the kingdom of God
is on earth, and that he who makes an effort
enters into it."

And the orthodox came to Jesus, and began xvii. 20.
asking him: "How, then, and when, will the
kingdom of God come?" And he answered
them: "The kingdom of God which I preach
is not such as former prophets preached.
They said that God would come with divers
visible signs, but I speak of a kingdom of
God, the coming of which may not be seen
with the eyes. And if any one shall say to
you, 'See, it is come, or it shall come,' or,
'See, it is here or there,' do not believe them.
The kingdom of God is not in time, or in
place, of any kind. It is like lightning, seen 24
here, there, and everywhere. And it has 21
neither time nor place, because the kingdom of
God, the one which I preach, is within you."

Jn. iii. 1. After this, an orthodox believer, one of the
2. Jewish authorities, named Nicodemus, came
to Jesus at night, and said: "You do not bid
us keep the Sabbath, do not bid us observe
cleanliness, do not bid us make offerings, nor
fast; you would destroy the temple. You say
of God, He is a spirit, and you say of the kingdom of God, that it is within us. Then, what
kind of a kingdom of God is this?"
3. And Jesus answered him: "Understand
that, if man is conceived from heaven, then
in him there must be that which is of heaven."
Nicodemus did not understand this, and
said: "How can a man, if he is conceived of
the flesh of his father, and has grown old,
again enter the womb of his mother and be
conceived anew?"
5. And Jesus answered him: "Understand
what I say. I say that man, besides the flesh,
is also conceived of the spirit, and therefore
every man is conceived of flesh and spirit, and
therefore may the kingdom of heaven be in
6. him. From flesh comes flesh. From flesh,
spirit cannot be born; spirit can come only
8. from spirit. The spirit is that which lives in
you, and lives in freedom and reason; it is that
of which you know neither the beginning nor
the end, and which every man feels in him.
7. And, therefore, why do you wonder that I told
you we must be conceived from heaven?"
9. Nicodemus said: "Still I do not believe that
this can be so."
10. Then Jesus said to him: "What kind of a
teacher are you, if you do not comprehend
11. this? Understand that I am not interpreting
some learned points; I am interpreting that
which we all know, I am averring that which
12. we all see. How will you believe in that
which is in heaven if you do not believe in that
which is on earth, which is in you yourself?

"For, no man has ever gone up to heaven, Jn. iii. 13
but there is only man on earth, come down
from heaven, and himself of heaven. Now, 14.
this same heavenly Son in man it is that must
be lifted up, that every one may believe in him 15.
and not perish, but may have heavenly life.
For God gave His Son, of the same essence 16.
as Himself, not for men's destruction, but for
their happiness. He gave him in order that
every one might believe in him, and might not
perish, but have life without end. For He did 17.
not bring forth His Son, this life, into the world
of men in order to destroy the world of men;
but He brought forth His Son, this life, in order
that the world of men might be made alive
through him.

"Whoever commits his life to him does not 18.
die; but he who does not commit his life to
him destroys himself thereby, in that he has
not trusted to that which is life. Death con- 19.
sists in this, that life is come into the world,
but men themselves go away from life.

"Light is the life of men; light came into
the world, but men prefer the darkness to
light, and do not go to the light. He who 20.
does wrong does not go to the light, so that
his deeds may not be seen, and such a one
bereaves himself of life. Whereas he who 21.
lives in truth goes to the light, so that his
deeds are seen; and he has life, and is united
with God.

"The kingdom of God must be understood, not, as you think, in the sense that it will come for all men at some time or other, and in some place or other, but thus, — In the whole world always, some people, those who trust in the heavenly Son of man, become sons of the kingdom, but others who do not trust in him are destroyed. The Father of that spirit which is in man is the Father of those only who acknowledge themselves to be His sons. And, therefore, only those exist to Him who have kept in themselves that which He gave them."

Mt xiii. 3. And, after this, Jesus began to explain to the
people what the kingdom of God is, and he
made this clear by means of parables.
He said: "The Father,—who is spirit,—
sows in the world the life of understanding,
4. as the husbandman sows seed in his field. He
sows over the whole field, without remarking
where any particular seed falls. Some seeds
fall upon the road, and the birds fly down and
5. peck them up. And others fall among stones;
and although among these stones they come
up, they wither, because there is no room for
7. the roots. And others, again, fall among wormwood, so that the wormwood chokes the corn,
8. and the ear springs up, but does not fill. And
others fall on good soil; they spring up, and
make return for the lost corn, and bear ears,
and fill, and one ear will give a hundredfold,
another sixtyfold, and another thirtyfold. Thus,
then, God also sowed broadcast the spirit in
men; in some it is lost, but in others it yields
a hundredfold: these last are they who form
Mk. iv. 26. the kingdom of God. Thus the kingdom is not
such as you think, that God will come to reign
over you. God has only sown the spirit, and
the kingdom of God will be in those who preserve it.
27. "God does not force men. It is as when the
sower casts the seeds in the earth, and himself
28. thinks no more of them; but the seeds of themselves swell, sprout up, put forth leaf, sheath,
29. and ear, and fill with grain. Only when it is
ripened, the master sends sickles to reap the
cornfield. So also God gave His Son, the
spirit, to the world; and the spirit of itself
grows in the world, and the sons of the spirit
make up the kingdom of God.

A woman puts yeast in the kneading trough Mt. xiii. 33
and mixes it with the flour; she then stirs it
no more, but lets it ferment and rise. As long
as men live, God does not interpose in their
life. He gave the spirit to the world, and the
spirit itself lives in men, and men who live by
the spirit make up the kingdom of God. For
the spirit there is neither death nor evil. Death
and evil are for the flesh, but not for the spirit.
The kingdom of God comes in this way. 24.
A farmer sowed good seed in his field. The
farmer is the Spirit, the Father; the field is
the world; the good seeds are the sons of the
kingdom of God. And the farmer lay down 25
to sleep, and an enemy came and sowed darnel
in the field. The enemy is temptation; the
darnel is the sons of temptation. And his 27.
laborers came to the farmer and said: "Can
you have sown bad seed?" Much darnel has
come up in your field. Send us, we will weed 28.
it out." And the farmer said: "You must 29.
not do that, for in weeding the darnel you will
trample the wheat. Let them grow together.
The harvest will come, when I shall bid the 30.
reapers take away the darnel and burn it; and
the wheat I shall store in the barn."

Now, the harvest is the end of man's life, and the harvesters are the power of heaven. And the darnel shall be burnt, but the wheat shall be cleaned and gathered. Thus also, at life's end, all shall vanish which was a guile of time, and the true life in the spirit shall alone be left. For the Spirit, the Father, there is no evil. The spirit keeps that which it needs, and that which is not of it does not exist for it.

The kingdom of God is like a net. The net 47.
will be spread in the sea, and will catch all
kinds of fish. And afterward, when it is 48.
drawn out, the worthless will be set aside and
thrown into the sea. So will it be at the end

of the age; the powers of heaven will take the
good, and the evil will be cast away.
Mt. xiii. 10. And when he finished speaking, the disciples
asked him how to understand these parables?
11. And he said to them: "These parables must
be understood in two ways. I speak all these
parables because there are some like you, my
disciples, who understand wherein is the kingdom of God, who understand that the kingdom
of God is within every man, who understand
how to go into it; while others do not under-
14. stand this. Others look, but see not; they
hearken, and do not understand, because their
15. heart has become gross. Therefore I speak
these parables with two meanings, for both
classes of hearers. To the others I speak of
God, of what God's kingdom is to them, and
they may understand this; while to you I speak
of what the kingdom of God is for you—that
kingdom which is within you.
18. "And see that you understand as you ought
19. the parable of the sower. For you the parable
is this: Every one who has understood the
meaning of the kingdom of God, but has not
accepted it in his heart, to him temptation
comes and robs him of that which has been
20. sown: this is the seed on the wayside. That
which was sown on stones, is he who at once
21. accepts with joy. But there is no root in him,
and he only accepts for a time; but let straits
and persecution befall him, because of the
meaning of the kingdom, and he straightway
22. denies it. That which was sown among the
wormwood is he who understood the meaning
of the kingdom, but worldly cares and the
seductions of wealth strangle the meaning
23. in him, and he yields no fruit. But that which
was sown on good soil is he who understood
the meaning of the kingdom, and accepted it
into his heart; such yield fruit, one a hundred-

fold, another sixtyfold, another thirtyfold. For Mt. xiii. 12
he who retains, to him much is given; while
from him who does not retain, the whole will
be taken.

"And, therefore, take care how you under- Lk. viii. 18.
stand these parables. Understand them so as
not to give way to deceit, wrong, and care;
but so as to yield thirtyfold, or sixtyfold, or a
hundredfold.

"The kingdom of heaven grows and spreads Mt. xiii. 31.
in the soul out of nothing, providing everything. It is like a birch seed, the very smallest of seeds, which, when it grows up, becomes greater than all other trees, and the birds of heaven build their nests in it."

CHAPTER IV

GOD'S KINGDOM

Therefore the will of the Father is the life and welfare of all men

("Thy kingdom come")

AND Jesus went among the towns and vil- Mt. ix. 35.
lages, and taught all men the happiness of fulfilling the Father's will. Jesus was sorry for 36.
men, that they perish without knowing wherein
is the true life, and are driven about and suffer,
without knowing why, like sheep left without
a shepherd.

Once a crowd of people gathered to Jesus, v. 1.
to hear his teaching; and he went up on a hill
and sat down. His disciples surrounded him.

And Jesus began to teach the people as to 2.
what is the Father's will. He said:—

Blessed are the poor and homeless, for they Lk. vi. 20,
are in the will of the Father. Even if they 21.
hunger for a time, they shall be satisfied; and

if they grieve and weep, they shall be com-
Lk. vi. 22. forted. If people look down upon them, and
thrust them aside and everywhere drive them
23. away, let them be glad at this; for the people
of God have ever been persecuted thus, and
they receive a heavenly reward.
24. But woe to the rich, for they have already
got everything they wish, and will get nothing more. They are now satisfied; but they
25, 26. shall be hungry. Now they are merry; but
they shall be sad. If all praise them, woe to
them, because only deceivers get everybody's
praise.

Blessed are the poor and homeless, but
blessed only then, when they are poor, not
merely externally, but in spirit; as salt is good
only when it is true salt; not externally only,
but when it has the savor of salt.

Mt. v. 13. So, you also, the poor and homeless, are the
teachers of the world; you are blessed, if you
know that true happiness is in being homeless
and poor. But if you are poor only externally,
then you, like salt without savor, are good for
14. nothing. You must be a light to the world;
therefore do not hide your light, but show it to
15. men. For when one lights a candle, one does
not put it under a bench, but upon the table,
16. that it may light all in the room. So, you also,
do not hide your light, but show it by your
works, so that men may see that you know the
truth, and, looking at your good works, may
understand your Heavenly Father.
17. And do not think that I free you from the law.
I teach not release from the law, but I teach
18. the fulfilment of the eternal law. As long as
there are men under heaven, there is an everlasting law. There will be no law, only when
men shall of themselves act wholly according
to the eternal law. And now I am giving you
19. the commandments of the eternal law. And

if any one shall release himself, if only from one
of these short commandments, and shall teach
others that they may so release themselves, he
shall be least in the kingdom of heaven; while
he who shall fulfil them, and shall thereby teach
others, shall be the greatest in the kingdom of
heaven. Because if your virtue be not greater Mt. v.
than the virtue of the orthodox leaders, you
will in no way be in the kingdom of heaven.

These are the commandments:—

I

In the former law it was said: "Do not kill." But if any one shall kill another, he must be judged.

But I tell you, that every one is worthy of judgment who gets angry with his brother. And still more to blame is he who abuses his brother.

So that, if you wish to pray to God, remember, first, whether there is no man who may have something against you. If you remember that but one man considers you have offended him, leave your prayer, and go first and make peace with your brother; and then you may pray. Know that God wants neither sacrifice nor prayer, but peace, concord, and love among you. And you may neither pray, nor think of God, if there is but one man to whom you do not bear love.

And so this is the first commandment: Do not be angry, do not abuse; but having quarreled, make peace in such a way that no one may have cause for offense against you.

II

Mt v. 31. In the former law it was said: "Do not
commit adultery; and if you wish to put away
your wife, give her a bill of divorce."
28. But I tell you, if you are drawn by the
beauty of a woman, you are already commit-
29. ting adultery. All sensuality destroys the soul,
and therefore it is better for you to renounce
the pleasure of the flesh than to destroy your
life.
32. And if you put away your wife, then, besides being vicious yourself, you drive her also
into vice, and him who shall have to do with
her.

And therefore, this is the second commandment: Do not think that love toward woman is good; do not admire the beauty of women, but live with the one to whom you have become united, and do not leave her.

III

33. In the former law it was said: "Do not
utter the name of the Lord your God in vain,
do not call upon your God when lying, and do
not dishonor the name of your God. Do not
swear by Me in untruth, so as to profane your
34. God." But I tell you that every oath is a
profanation of God.
35. Therefore, swear not at all. Man cannot
promise anything, because he is wholly in the
36. power of the Father. A man cannot turn one
hair from gray to black; how then shall he
swear beforehand, that he will do this and
that, and swear by God? Every oath is a
profanation of God, for, if a man shall have to
fulfil an oath which is against the will of God,
it must follow that he has sworn to go against

God's will; so that every oath is evil. But Mt. v. 37
when men question you about anything, say:
"Yes," if yes, — "No," if no. Everything
added to this is evil.

Therefore, the third commandment is:
Swear nothing, to any one; say "Yes," when
it is yes, — "No," when it is no; and understand that every oath is evil.

IV

In the former law it was said: "He who de- 38.
stroys life, shall give a life for a life; an eye
for an eye, a tooth for a tooth, a hand for a
hand, an ox for an ox, a slave for a slave,"
and so on.

But I tell you: Do not wrestle with evil by 39.
evil. Not only do not take by law an ox for
an ox, a slave for a slave, a life for a life, but
do not resist evil at all. If any one wishes to 40.
take an ox from you by law, give him another;
if any one wishes to get your coat by law, give
him your shirt also; if any one strikes out your
tooth on one side, turn to him the other side.
If you are made to do one piece of work, do 41.
two. If men wish to take your property, vi. 30.
give it to them. If they do not return your
money, do not ask for it.

And therefore: Do not judge, do not go to 37.
law, do not punish, and you yourself shall not
be judged, nor punished. Forgive all, and you
shall be forgiven, because if you shall judge
people, they will judge you also.

You cannot judge, because you, all men, are Mt. vii. 1.
blind, and do not see the truth. How, with 3.
obstructed eyes, will you discern the mote in
your brother's eye? You must first clear your
own eye. But whose eyes are clear? Can a Lk. vi. 39
blind man lead a blind man? Both will fall

into the pit. Thus, also, they who judge and punish, like the blind, are leading the blind.

Lk. vi. 40. They who judge and condemn people to violent treatment, wounds, maiming, death, wish to teach people. But what else can come from their teaching, than that the pupil will learn his lesson, and will become quite like the teacher? What, then, will he do, when he has learnt his lesson? The same that the teacher does: violence, murder.

Mt. vii. 6. And do not think to find justice in the courts. To seek legal justice, to hand matters over to human courts, is the same as to cast precious pearls before swine; they will trample upon it, and tear you to pieces.

And, therefore, the fourth commandment is: However men may wrong you, do not resist evil, do not judge and do not go to law, do not complain and do not punish.

V

v. 43. In the former law it was said: "Do good
to men of your own nation, and do evil to
strangers."
44. But I tell you, love not only your own
countrymen, but people of other nations. Let
strangers hate you, let them fall upon you,
wrong you; but you speak well of them, and
46. do them good. If you are only attached to
your countrymen, why, all men are thus
attached to their own countrymen, and hence
45. wars arise. Behave equally well toward men
of all nations, and you will be the sons of the
Father. All men are His children, and therefore all are brothers to you.

And, therefore, this is the fifth commandment: Behave equally well toward foreigners, as I told you to behave among yourselves.

Before the Father of all men there are neither different nations nor different kingdoms: all are brothers, all sons of one Father. Make no distinction among people as to nations and kingdoms.

And so: I. Do not be angry, but be at peace with all men. II. Do not seek delight in sexual gratification. III. Do not swear anything to any one. IV. Do not oppose evil, do not judge, and do not go to law. V. Do not make any distinction among men as to nationality, and love strangers like your own people.

All these commandments are contained in Mt. vii. 12
this one: All that you wish people should do
for you, do you even so to them.

Fulfil my teaching, not for men's praise. If vi. 1.
you do it for men, then from men you have
your reward. But if not for men, then your
reward is from the Heavenly Father. So that, 2.
if you do good to men, do not boast about it
before men. Thus hypocrites do, that men
may speak well of them. And they get what
they wish. But if you do good to men, do it 3.
so that no one may see it, so that your left hand
may not know what your right hand is doing.
And your Father will see this, and will give 4.
you what you need.

And, if you wish to pray, do not pray like 5.
the hypocrites. Hypocrites love to pray in
churches, in the sight of men. They do this
for men's sake, and get in return from men
that which they wish.

But, if you wish to pray, go where no one 6.
may see you, and pray to your Father, the
Spirit, and the Father will see what is in your
soul, and will give you that which you wish in
the spirit.

When you pray, do not chatter with your 7.
tongue like the hypocrites. Your Father 8.

knows what you want before you open your lips.

Pray only thus:

Mt. vi. 9. *Our Father, without beginning and without end, like heaven!*

10. *May Thy being only be holy.*

May power be only Thine, so that Thy will be done, without beginning and without end, on earth.

11. *Give me food of life in the present.*

12. *Smooth out my former mistakes, and wipe*
them away; even as I so do with all the mistakes
13. *of my brothers, that I may not fall into temptation, and may be saved from evil.*

Because Thine is the power and might, and Thine the judgment.

Mk. xi. 25. If you pray, above all, bear no one any
26. malice. For if you do not forgive men their wrong-doing, the Father also will not forgive you yours.

Mt. vi. 16. If you fast, and go hungry, do not show it
to men; thus do the hypocrites, that people
may see, and speak well of them. And people
speak well of them, and they get what they
17. wish. But do not you do so; if you suffer
18. want, go about with a cheerful face, that people may not see. But your Father will see, and will give you what you need.

19. Do not lay up store on earth. On earth,
the worm consumes, and rust eats, and thieves
20. steal. But lay up heavenly wealth for yourself.
Heavenly wealth the worm does not gnaw, nor
21. rust eat, nor thieves steal. Where your wealth is, there will your heart also be.

22. The light of the body is the eye, and the
23. light of the soul is the heart. If your eye is dim, then all your body will be in darkness. And if the light of your heart is dim,

then all your soul will be in darkness. You Mt. vi. 24.
cannot serve at one time two masters. You
will please one, and offend the other. You cannot serve God and the flesh. You will either
work for the earthly life or for God. There- 25.
fore, do not be anxious for what you shall eat
and drink, and wherewith you shall be clothed.
Life is more wonderful than food and clothing,
and God gave it you.

Look at God's creatures, the birds. They do 26.
not sow, reap, or harvest, but God feeds them.
In God's sight, man is not worse than the bird.
If God gave man life, He will be able to feed
him too. But you yourselves know that, how- 27.
ever much you strive, you can do nothing for
yourselves. You cannot lengthen your life by
an hour. And why should you care about 28.
clothing? The flowers of the field do not 29.
work and do not spin, but are dressed as Solomon in all his glory never was. Well, then, if 30.
God has so adorned the grass, which to-day
grows and to-morrow is mown, will he not
clothe you?

Do not trouble and worry yourselves; do 31.
not say that you must think of what you will
eat and how you will be clothed. This every 32.
one needs, and God knows this need of yours.
And so, do not care about the future. Live 33.
in the present day. Take care to be in the
will of the Father. Wish for that which alone
is important, and the rest will all come of itself.
Strive only to be in the will of the Father. 34.
And so, do not trouble about the future.
When the future comes, then it will be time to
do so. There is enough evil in the present.

Ask and it shall be given you, seek and you Lk. xi. 9.
shall find, knock and it shall be opened to you.
Is there a father who would give his son a Mt. vii. 9, 10.
stone instead of bread, or a snake instead of a
fish? Then, how is it that we, wicked men, 11.

are able to give our children that which they
need, while your Father in heaven shall not
give you that which you truly need, if you ask
Him? Ask, and the Heavenly Father will
give the life of the spirit to them who ask Him.
Mt. vii. 13. The way to life is narrow, but enter by the
narrow way. The way into life is one only.
It is narrow and strait. About it the plain
lies great and wide, but it is the way of de-
14. struction. The narrow way alone leads to
Lk. xii. 32. life; and few find it. But do not quail, little
flock! The Father has promised you the
kingdom.
Mt. vii. 15. Only, beware of false prophets and teachers;
they approach you in sheepskins, but within
they are ravening wolves.
16. By their fruits will you know them; by that
which they yield. Figs are not gathered from
17. thistles, nor grapes from thorns. But a good
tree brings forth good fruit. And a bad tree
20. brings forth bad fruit. And so you will know
Lk. vi. 45. them by the fruits of their teaching. A good
man, from his good heart, brings forth everything that is good; but a wicked man, from
his evil heart, brings forth everything evil; for
the lips speak from the overflow of the heart.
And therefore, if teachers teach you to do
to others that which is bad for yourselves,—
teach violence, executions, wars,— know that
they are false teachers.
Mt. vii. 21. For it is not he that says: Lord, Lord!
who shall enter the kingdom of heaven, but he
who fulfils the word of the Heavenly Father.
22. The false teachers will say: "Lord, Lord! we
have taught your teaching, and we have driven
23. away evil according to your teaching." But I
will disown them, and say to them: No, I never
acknowledged you, and do not acknowledge
you. Go out of my sight, you are doing that
which is unlawful.

And so, every one who has heard these words Mt. vii. 24.
of mine, and fulfils them, he, like a reasonable
man, builds his house upon a rock. And his 25.
house will stand against all storms. But he 26.
who hears these words of mine, and does not
fulfil them, he, like a foolish man, builds his
house upon sand. When the storm comes, 27.
it will overthrow the house, and all will perish.

And all the people wondered at such teaching; Lk. iv. 32.
because the teaching of Jesus was quite other
than that of the orthodox teachers of the law.
These taught a law which must be obeyed, but
Jesus taught that all men are free. And in Mt. iv. 14.
Jesus Christ were fulfilled the prophecies of
Isaiah: "The people living in darkness, in the 16.
shadow of death, saw the light of life, and he
who furnished this light of truth does no violence nor harm to men, but he is meek and
gentle. He, in order to bring truth into the xii. 19.
world, neither disputes nor shouts; his voice
is never heard raised. He will not break a 20.
straw, and will not blow out the smallest light.
And all the hope of men is in his teaching. 21.

CHAPTER V

THE TRUE LIFE

The fulfilment of the personal will leads to death; the fulfilment of the Father's will gives true life

("Thy will be done")

AND Jesus rejoiced at the strength of the Mt. xi. 25.
spirit, and said: —

"I acknowledge the spirit of the Father, the
source of everything in heaven and earth, Who
has revealed that which was hidden from the
wise and learned, to the simple, solely through

their acknowledging themselves Sons of the
Father.
Mt. xi. 28. "All take care for fleshly happiness, and
have put themselves to a load which they cannot
draw; they have put a yoke upon themselves
which was not made for them.
"Understand my teaching and follow it;
and you shall know rest and joy in life. I
give you another yoke, and another load;
29. namely, the spiritual life. Put yourselves to
that, and you shall learn from me peace and
happiness. Be calm and meek in heart, and
30. you will find blessedness in your life. Because
my teaching is a yoke made for you, and the
fulfilment of my teaching is a light load, with
a yoke made for you."
Jn. iv. 31. The disciples of Jesus once asked him
32. whether he wished to eat. He said: "I
33. have food of which you do not know." They
thought that some one had brought him something
34. to eat. But he said: —
"My food is to do the will of Him who gave
me life, and to fulfil that which He intrusted
35. to me. Do not say 'There is still time,' as the
36. plowman said, waiting for the harvest. He
who fulfils the will of the Father is always satisfied,
and knows neither hunger nor thirst.
The fulfilment of the will of God always satisfies,
bearing its reward within itself. You
must not say, 'I will afterward fulfil the will
of the Father.' While there is life, you always
can, and must, fulfil the will of the Father.
37. Our life is the field which God has sown, and
38. our business is to gather its fruits. And if
we gather the fruits, we get the reward, life
beyond time. True it is, that we do not give
ourselves life; some one else does. And if we
labor to gather in life, then we, like reapers,
get our reward. I teach you to gather in this
life, which the Father has given you."

Once, Jesus came to Jerusalem. And there Jn. v.
was then a bathing-place there. And men said of this bathing-place, that an angel came down into it, and through this the water in the bath would begin to move, and he who first plunged into the water after it was moved got well from whatever he was ailing. And sheds were made around the bath, and under these sheds sick men lay, waiting for the water in the bath to be moved, in order to plunge into it.

And a man was there who had been infirm thirty-eight years. Jesus asked who he was.

And the man told how he had been ailing so long, and was still waiting to get into the bath first, upon the water being moved, in order to be healed; but for these thirty-eight years he had been unable to get in first, others always getting into the bath before him.

And Jesus saw that he was old, and said to him: "Do you wish to get well?"

He said: "I wish to, but I have no one to carry me into the water in time. Some one always will get in before me."

And Jesus said to him: "Awake, take up your bed and walk."

And the sick man took up his bed and walked.

And it was the Sabbath. And the orthodox said: "You must not take up the bed, for to-day is the Sabbath." He said: "He who raised me, bade me also take up the bed." And the infirm man said to the orthodox, that it was Jesus who had healed him. And they became angry, and accused Jesus, because he did such things on the Sabbath.

And Jesus said: "That which the Father always does, I also do. In truth, I say to you, the Son of himself can do nothing. He does only that which he has understood from the Father. What the Father does, he also does.

The Father loves the Son, and by this very
fact has taught him everything which the Son
should know.

Jn. v. 21. "The Father gives life to the dead, and
thus the Son gives life to him who desires it;
because, as the business of the Father is life,
22. so the business of the Son must be life. The
Father has not condemned men to death, but
has given men power, at will, to die or live.
23. And they will live, if they shall honor the
Son as the Father.

24. "I tell you truly, that he who has understood the meaning of my teaching, and has
believed in the common Father of all men,
already has life, and is delivered from death.
25. They who have understood the meaning of
human life, have already escaped from death
26. and shall live forever. Because, as the
Father lives of Himself, so also has He given
27. the Son life within himself. And He has
given him freedom. It is by this, that he is
the Son of Man.

28. "Henceforth all mortals shall be divided
29. into two kinds. They alone, who do good,
shall find life; but they who do evil shall be
30. destroyed. And this is not my decision, but
it is what I have understood from the Father.
And my decision is true, because I thus decide, not in order to do that which I wish, but
in order that all may do that which the Father
of all wishes.

31. "If I were to assure all that my teaching is
true, this would not establish my teaching.
36. But there is that which establishes my teaching; namely, the conduct which I teach. That
shows that I do not teach of myself, but in the
37. name of the Father of all men. And my
Father, He who has taught me, confirms the
truth of my commandments in the souls of
all.

"But you do not wish to understand and to
know His voice. And you do not accept the Jn. v. 38
meaning this voice speaks. That that which
is in you, is spirit descended from heaven, —
this, you do not believe.

"Enter into the meaning of your writings. 39.
You will find in them the same as in my teaching, commandments to live, not for yourself
alone, but for the good of men. Why, then, do 40.
you not wish to believe in my commandments,
which are those that give life to all men? I 43.
teach you in the name of the common Father
of all men, and you do not accept my teaching; but if any one shall teach you in his own
name, him will you believe.

"One cannot believe that which people say 44.
to each other, but one can only believe that in
every man there is a Son like the Father."

And that men may not think that the king- Lk. xix. 11.
dom of heaven is established by anything
visible; but that they may understand that
the kingdom of God consists in the fulfilment
of the Father's will; and understand that the
fulfilment of the Father's will depends on
each man's effort and striving to make people
see that life is given, not for oneself personally, but for the fulfilment of the Father's
will, which alone saves from death and gives
life, — Jesus told a parable. He said: — 12.

"There was a rich man, who had to go
away from his home. Before he went, he 13.
called his slaves, and gave among them ten talents, one to each, and said: 'While I am away,
labor each of you upon what I have given.'
But it happened that, when he was gone, cer- 14.
tain inhabitants of that town said: 'We do not 15.
wish to serve him any more.' When the rich
man came back, he called the slaves to whom
he had given the money, and bade each say
what he had done with his money. The first 16.

came, and said: 'See, master, for your one I
Lk. xix. 17. have earned ten.' And the master said to
him: 'Well done, good servant; you have
been trustworthy in a little, I will place you
over much; be one with me in all my wealth.'
18. Another slave came, and said: 'See, master,
19. for your talent I have earned five.' And the
master said to him: 'Well done, good slave,
20. be one with me in all my estate.' And yet
another came, and said: 'Here is your talent,
I hid it in a cloth and buried it; because I was
21. afraid of you. You are a hard man, you take
where you did not store, and gather where
22. you did not sow.' And the master said to
him: 'Foolish slave! I will judge you by your
own words. You say that, from fear of me,
you hid your talent in the earth, and did not
work upon it. If you knew that I was severe,
and take where I did not give, then why did
Mt. xxv. 26, you not do that which I bade you do? If you
27. Lk. xix. 23. had worked upon my talent, the estate would
have been added to, and you would have fulfilled that which I bade you. But you have
not done that for which the talent was given
you, and, therefore, you must not own it.'
24. And the master bade the talent be taken from
him who had not worked upon it, and given to
25. him who had worked most. And then the
servants said to him: 'Sir, he already has
26. much.' But the master said: 'Give to them
who have worked much, because he who looks
after that which he has, shall receive an increase. As to them who did not wish to be in
Mt. xxv. 30. my power, drive them forth, so that they may
be here no more.'"

Now this master is the source of life, the spirit, the Father. His slaves are men. The talents are the life of the spirit. As the master does not himself work upon his estate, but bids the slaves to work, each by himself, so the spirit of life in men has given them the command to work for the life of men, and then left them alone. They who sent to say that they did not acknowledge the authority of the master, are they who do not acknowledge the spirit of life. The return of the master, and the demand for an account, is the destruction of fleshly life, and the decision of the fate of men as to whether they have yet life beyond that which was given them. Some, the slaves who fulfil the will of the master, work upon that which was given them, and make gain on gain; they are those men who, having received life, understand that life is the will of the Father, and is given to serve the life of others. The foolish and wicked slave, who hid his talent and did not work upon it, represents those men who fulfil only their own will, and not the will of the Father; who do not serve the life of others. The slaves who have fulfilled the master's will, and worked for the increase of his estate, become sharers of the whole estate of the master, while the slaves who have not fulfilled the master's will, and have not worked for him, are bereft of that which was given them. People who have fulfilled the will of the Father, and have served life, becomes sharers in the life of the Father, and receive life, notwithstanding the destruction of the fleshly life. They who have not fulfilled the will, and have not served life, are bereft of that life which they had, and are destroyed. They who did not wish to acknowledge the authority of the master, such do not exist for the master; he drives them forth. People who do not acknowledge within themselves the life of the spirit, the life of the Son of man, such do not exist for the Father.

After this, Jesus went into a desert place. And many people followed him. And he

climbed a mountain, and sat there with his
Jn. vi. 5. followers. And he saw that there was a great
throng, and said: "Whence shall we get bread
7. to feed all these people?" Philip said: "Even
two hundred pence will not suffice, if to each
Mt. xiv. 17. be given but a little. We have only a little
Jn. vi. 9. bread and fish." And another disciple said:
"They have bread; I have seen it. There is
a boy who has five loaves and two small fishes."
10. And Jesus said: "Bid them all lie down on
the grass."

11. And Jesus took the loaves which he had,
and gave them to his disciples, and bade them
give them to others; and so all began to hand
from one to another what there was, and all
were satisfied, yet much was left over.

26. The next day, the people came again to
Jesus. And he said to them: "See, you come
to me, not because you have seen wonders,
but because you have eaten bread and were
27. satisfied." And he said to them: "Work not
for perishable food, but for everlasting food,
such as only the spirit of the Son of Man gives,
sealed by God."

28. The Jews said: "But what must we do, in
order to do the works of God?"

29. And Jesus said: "The work of God is in
this, to believe in that life which He has given
you."

30. They said: "Give us a sign that we may
believe. What are your deeds which can serve
31. as a proof? Our fathers ate manna in the wilderness. God gave them bread from heaven
to eat; and so it is written."

32. Jesus answered them: "The true heavenly
bread is the spirit of the Son of Man, that
33. which the Father gives. Because the nourishment of man is the spirit descended from
heaven. This it is which gives life to the
35. world. My teaching gives true nourishment

to man. He who follows me shall not hunger, and he who believes in my teaching will never know thirst.

"But I have already told you that you have Jn. vi. 36.
seen this, yet do not believe.

"All that life which the Father gave the Son 37.
will be realized through my teaching; and every one who believes will be a sharer in it. I 38.
came down from heaven, not to do that which
I wish, but to do the will of the Father, of Him
who gave me life. But the will of the Father 39.
who sent me is this, that I should keep all that
life which He gave, and should not destroy anything of it. And therefore, herein is the will of 40.
the Father who sent me, that every one who
sees the Son, and believes in him, should have
everlasting life. And my teaching gives life
at the last day of the body."

The Jews were shocked at his saying that his 41.
teaching was come down from heaven. They 42.
said: "Why, this is Jesus, the son of Joseph;
we know his father and mother. How, then,
can he say that his teaching has descended from
heaven?"

"Do not debate as to who I am, and whence 43.
I am come," said Jesus. "My teaching is true, 44.
not because I declare, like Moses, that God
spoke with me on Sinai; but it is true because
it is in you also. Every one who believes my
commandments, believes, not because it is I who
speak, but because our common Father draws
him to Himself; and my teaching will give
him life at the last day. And it is written in 45.
the prophets, that all shall be taught by God.
Every one who shall understand the Father,
and shall learn to understand His will, thereby
yields himself to my teaching.

"That any man has seen the Father, this has 46.
never been, except he who is from God; he has
seen, and sees, the Father.

Jn. vi. 47. "He who believes in me (in my teaching) has
everlasting life.
48, "My teaching is the nourishment of life.
49. Your fathers ate manna, food straight from
50. heaven, and yet they died. But the true nourishment of life, which descends from heaven,
is such, that he who is fed with it will not die.
51. My teaching is this nourishment of life descended from heaven. He who is fed with it
lives forever. And this nourishment which I
teach is my flesh, which I give for the life of
all men."
52. The Jews did not understand what he said,
and began to dispute as to how it was possible
to give one's flesh for the nourishment of men,
and why.
53. And Jesus said to them: "If you shall not
give up your flesh for the life of the spirit,
54. there will be no life in you. He who does not
give up his flesh for the life of the spirit, has
55. not real life. That in me which gives up the
flesh for the spirit, that alone lives.
"And therefore, our flesh is the true food
56. for the real life. That only which in me consumes my body, that which gives up the fleshly
57. life for the true life, that only is I. It is in
me, and I am in it. And as I live in the flesh
by the will of the Father, similarly, that which
lives in me lives by my will."
60. And some of his disciples, when they heard
this, said: "These are hard words, and it is
difficult to understand them."
61. And Jesus said to them: "Your ideas are
so confused, that my sayings as to what man
was, is, and always will be, seem difficult to
63. you. Man is the spirit in the flesh, and the
spirit alone gives life, but the flesh does not
give life. In the words which seem so difficult to you, I have really said nothing more
than that the spirit is life."

Afterward, Jesus chose seventy men out of Lk. x. 1.
his near friends, and sent them into those places
where he himself wished to go. He said to 2.
them:—

"Many people do not know the blessing of
real life. I am sorry for all; and wish to teach
all. But as the master is not enough for the
reaping of his field, so also I shall not suffice.
Go you, then, through the various cities, and 3.
everywhere proclaim the fulfilment of the will
of the Father.

"Say, The will of the Father is in this: Not
to be angered, not to be sensual, not to swear,
not to resist evil, and not to make any distinction between people. And accordingly, do ye
in everything fulfil these commandments.

"I send you like sheep among wolves. Be Mt. x. 16.
wise as snakes, and pure as doves.

"Before everything, have nothing of your Lk. x. 4.
own; take nothing with you, neither wallet, nor
bread, nor money; only clothes upon your body,
and shoes. Further, make no distinction be- 5.
tween people; do not choose your hosts, where
you shall put up. But in whichever house you Mt. x. 12.
shall come first, stay there. When you come
into the house, greet the master. If he welcome you, stay; if not, go into another house.

"For that which you shall say, they will hate 22.
you, and fall upon, and persecute you. And 23.
when they shall drive you out, go into another
village; and if they all drive you out of that,
go yet into another. They will persecute you
as wolves hunt sheep; but do not quail, suffer
to the last hour. And they will take you into
the courts, and will try you, and will flog you,
and will take you before the authorities, that
you may justify yourselves before them. And 19.
when you shall be taken into the courts, be
not afraid; and do not bethink yourselves
what you shall say. The spirit of the Father

will speak through you, what is needful to be
said.
Mt. x. 23. "You will not have passed through all the
towns, before people will have understood your
teachings, and will turn to it.
27. "And so, be not afraid. That which is
hidden in the souls of men will come forth.
26. That which you shall say to two or three will
28. spread among thousands. But chiefly, be not
afraid of those who may kill your body. To
your souls, they can do nothing. And so, do
not fear them. But be afraid lest both your
bodies and souls be destroyed, by your abstaining
from the fulfilment of the will of the
29. Father. That is what you have to fear. Five
sparrows are sold for a farthing, but even they
30. shall not die without the Father's will. And
a hair shall not fall from the head without the
31. Father's will. So then, what need you be
afraid of, seeing you are in the Father's will?
34. "Not all will believe in my teaching. And
they who will not believe, will hate it; because
it bereaves them of that which they love, and
Lk. xii. 49. strife will come of it. My teaching, like fire,
51. will kindle the world. And from it strife must
52, arise in the world. Strife will arise in every
53. house. Father against son, mother against
daughter; and their kin will become haters
of them who understand my teaching, and
xiv. 26. they will be killed. Because, for him who
shall understand my teaching, neither his
father, nor his mother, nor wife, nor children,
nor all his property, will have any weight."
Mk. iii. 22. Then the learned orthodox gathered at
Jerusalem, and went to Jesus. Jesus was in
20. a village, and a crowd of people thronged into
the place, and stood around.
Mt. xii. 24. The orthodox began to speak to the people,
in order that they might not believe in the
teaching of Jesus. They said that Jesus was

possessed; that if they should live by his commandments, there would then be yet more evil among the people than now. They said, that he drove out evil with evil.

Jesus called them to him, and said: "You Mt. xii. 25.
say that I drive out evil with evil. But no 26.
power destroys itself. If it destroys itself,
then it would not be. You would drive out 27.
evil with threats, executions, murders; but
evil, nevertheless, is not destroyed, precisely
because evil cannot make head against itself.
But I drive out evil by other means than you
do; that is to say, not with evil.

"I drive out evil by summoning people to 28.
fulfil the will of the Spirit, the Father, who
gives life to all. Five commandments express
the will of the Spirit which gives happiness
and life. And these commandments destroy 29.
evil. By their doing so, you have a proof
that they are true.

"If men were not sons of one spirit, it would not be possible to overcome evil; as it is not possible to go into the house of a strong man, and rob it. In order to rob the house of a strong man, it is necessary first to bind the strong man. And men are bound thus in the unity of the spirit of life.

"And therefore I tell you, that every mis- 31.
take of men, and every wrong interpretation,
shall escape punishment; but false representa-
tion about the Holy Spirit, which gives life to
all, shall not be forgiven to men. Should any 32.
one say a word against man, that is not important; but should any one say a word against that which is holy in man, against the spirit, this cannot pass unpunished. Gird at me as much as you like, but do not call evil the commandments of life which I have disclosed to you. It cannot pass unpunished, if a man shall call that good which is evil.

Mt. xii. 30. "It is necessary to be at one with the spirit
of life. He who is not at one with it, is against
it. It is necessary to serve the spirit of life
and of good in all men, and not in oneself
33. alone. You must either hold that life and
happiness is good for the whole world, then
love life and happiness for all men, or else
hold life and happiness an evil, and then not
love life and happiness for yourself. You
must either hold a tree good, and its fruit good
or else hold a tree bad, and its fruit bad.
Because a tree is valued by its fruit."

CHAPTER VI

THE FALSE LIFE

Therefore, in order to receive the true life, man must on earth resign the false life of the flesh, and live by the spirit

("On Earth, as in Heaven")

Lk. viii. 19. AND there came once to Jesus his mother
Mt. xii. 46. and brothers, who could in no way get to see
him, because there was a great crowd around
47. him. And a man saw them, and went up to
Jesus, and said: "Your family, your mother
and brothers, are standing without, and wish to
see you."

Lk. viii. 21. And Jesus said: "My mother and my
brothers are they who have understood the
will of the Father, and fulfil it."

xi. 27. And a woman said: "Blessed is the womb
that has brought you forth, and the breasts
that you have sucked."

28. Jesus said to this: "Blessed only are they
who have understood the spirit of the Father,
and keep it."

ix. 57. And a man said to Jesus: "I will follow
you whithersoever you may go."

And Jesus said to him, in answer: "You Lk. ix. 58.
cannot follow me; I have neither house nor
place to live in. Wild beasts have their lairs
and burrows, but man is everywhere at home,
if he lives by the spirit."

And it happened once that Jesus was, with Mk. iv. 35.
his followers, sailing a boat. He said: "Let
us pass over to the other side." A storm arose 37.
upon the lake, and the boat began to fill, so
that it nearly sank. And Jesus lay in the 38.
stern, and slept. They woke him, and said:
"Teacher, is it really all the same to you that
we are perishing?" And, when the storm had 40.
fallen, he said: "Why are you so timid? You
do not believe in the life of the spirit."

Jesus said to a man: "Follow me." Lk. ix. 59.

And the man said: "I have an aged father,
let me first bury him, and then I will follow
you."

And Jesus said to him: "Let the dead bury 60.
the dead, but do you, if you wish to truly live,
fulfil the will of the Father, and make that will
known everywhere."

And again, another man said: "I wish to be 61.
your disciple, and will fulfil the will of the
Father, as you command, but let me first settle
my family."

And Jesus said to him: "If the plowman look 62.
behind, he cannot plow. However strong the
reasons you have to look behind, so long as you
look behind, you cannot plow. You must forget
everything except the furrow you are driving;
then only can you plow. If you consider as
to what will be the outcome for the life of the
body, then you have not understood the real
life, and cannot live by it."

After this, it happened once that Jesus went x. 38.
with his disciples into a village. And a woman
named Martha invited him into her house.
Martha had a sister named Mary, who sat at 39.

the feet of Jesus, and listened to his teaching.
Lk. x. 40. But Martha was busy getting ready the meal.
And Martha went up to Jesus, and said: "Do
you not see that my sister has left me alone to
serve? Tell her to help me in the work."
41. And Jesus said to her in answer: "Martha,
Martha! you trouble and busy yourself with
many things, but only one thing is needful.
42. And Mary has chosen that one thing which is
needful, and which none shall take from her.
For true life the food of the spirit alone is
needful."
ix. 23. And Jesus said to all: "Whoever wishes to
follow me, let him forsake his own will, and
let him be ready for all hardships and sufferings of the flesh at every hour; then only can
24. he follow me. Because he who wishes to take
heed for his fleshly life will destroy the true life.
And he who fulfils the will of the Father, even
if he destroy the fleshly life, shall save the true
25. life. For, what advantage is it to a man if he
should gain the whole world, but destroy or
harm his own life?"
xii. 15. And Jesus said: "Beware of wealth, because
your life does not depend upon your having
more than others.
16. "There was a rich man, who had a great
harvest of corn. And he thought to himself:
17, 18. Let me rebuild my barns. I will erect larger
19. ones, and gather there all my wealth. And I
will say to my soul: 'There, my soul, you
have everything after your desire; rest, eat,
20. drink, and live for your pleasure.' But God
said to him: 'Fool, this very night your soul
shall be taken; and all that you have stored
up shall go to others.'
21. "And thus it happens with every one who
provides for the bodily life, and does not live
in God."
xiii. 2. And Jesus said to them: "Now, you say

that Pilate killed the Galileans. But were
these Galileans any worse than other people,
that this happened to them? In no way. We Lk. xiii. 3
are all such, and we shall all perish likewise,
unless we find salvation from death.
"Or of those eighteen men, whom the tower 4
crushed in falling, were they particularly worse
than all the other dwellers in Jerusalem? In
no wise. If we do not find salvation, sooner 5
or later we shall perish in the same way. If 6
we have not yet perished as they, we must
think of our position, thus:—
"A man had an apple tree growing in his
garden. The master came into the garden,
and saw there was no fruit on the tree. And 7
the master said to his gardener: 'It is now
three years since I have watched this apple
tree, and it is still barren. It must be cut
down, for as it is, it only spoils the place.
And the gardener answered: 'Let us wait yet 8
a little, master; let me dig it round. I will
dung it, and let us see what it will be next
summer. Maybe it will yield fruit. But if it
yields nothing by the summer, well then, we
will cut it down.'

"Likewise we, as long as we live by the flesh, and yield no fruit to the life of the spirit, are barren apple trees. Only by the mercy of some power are we yet left for a summer. And if we do not yield fruit we shall also perish, even like him who built the barn, like the Galileans, like the eighteen men crushed by the tower, and like all who yield no fruit; perishing, dying forever, by death.

"In order to understand this, there is no Lk. xii. 54
need of special wisdom; each one sees this for
himself. For not only in domestic affairs, but
in that also which happens in the whole world,
are we able to reason and to foresee. If the
wind is in the west, we say there will be rain,

Lk. xii. 55. and so it happens. But if the wind is from
the south, we say there will be fair weather,
56. and so it is. How, then, is it that we are able
to foresee the weather, and yet we cannot foresee that we shall all die and perish, and that
the only salvation for us is in the life of the
spirit, in the fulfilment of its will?"

xiv. 25. And a great multitude went with Jesus, and
he once more said to all: —

26. "He who wishes to be my disciple, let him
count for nothing father and mother, and wife
and children, and brothers and sisters, and all
his goods, and let him at every hour be ready
27. for anything. And only he who does as I do,
only he follows my teaching, and only he is
saved from death.

28. "Because every one, before beginning anything, will reckon whether that which he does
is profitable, and if it is profitable, will do it,
but if unprofitable, will abandon it. Every
one who builds a house will first sit down and
reckon how much money is wanted, how much
he has, and whether that will suffice to finish
29. it. He will do this, so that it may not happen
that he should begin to build, and not finish,
for people to laugh at him.

30. "Likewise also, he who wishes to live the
fleshly life must first reckon whether he can
finish that with which he is busy.

31. "Every king, if he wishes to make war, will
first think whether he can go to war with ten
32. thousand against twenty thousand. If he concludes that he cannot, then he will send ambassadors, and make peace, and will not make
war. So also, let every man, before giving
himself over to the fleshly life, bethink him
whether he can wage war against death, or
whether death is stronger than he; and whether
it is not then better for him to make peace beforehand.

"And so, each of you should first examine Lk. xiv. 33
what he considers his own family, money, or
estate. And, when he has reckoned what all
this avails him, and understands that it avails
him nothing, then only can he be my disciple."

And upon hearing this, a man said: "That 25.
is very well, if there be indeed a life of the
spirit. But what if one abandons all, and
there be no such life?"

To this Jesus said: "Not so; every one knows
the life of the spirit. You all know it; but you
do not do that which you know. Not because
you doubt, but because you are drawn away
from the true life by false cares, and excuse
yourselves from it.

"This is like your conduct, like your deeds: 26
A master got ready a dinner, and sent to invite
guests, but the guests began to decline.
One said: 'I have bought land, and I must 18.
go and look after it.' Another said: 'I have 19.
bought oxen, and I must try them.' A third 20.
said: 'I have taken a wife, and am going to
celebrate the wedding.' And the messengers 21.
came and told the master that no one was
coming. The master then sent the messengers
to invite the beggars. The beggars did 22.
not refuse, but came. And when they were
come, there was still room left. And the mas- 23.
ter sent to call in still more, and said: 'Go and
persuade all to come to my dinner, in order
that I may have more people.' And they who
had refused, from want of leisure, found no
place at the dinner.

"All know that the fulfilment of the will of
the Father gives life, but do not go because
the guile of wealth draws them away.

"He who resigns false temporary wealth for
the true life in the will of the Father, does as
did a certain clever steward. There was a man xvi. 1.

who was steward to a rich master. This steward saw that, sooner or later, the master would
drive him away, and that he would remain
Lk. xvi. 3. without food, and without shelter. And the
steward thought to himself: 'This is what I
will do: I will privately distribute the master's
goods to the laborers; I will reduce their debts,
and then, if the master drives me out, the
laborers will remember my kindness, and will
5. not abandon me.' And so the steward did.
He called the laborers, his master's debtors,
6. and rewrote their documents. For him who
owed a hundred he wrote fifty; for him who
owed sixty, he wrote twenty, and similarly for
8. the rest. And the master learned this, and
said to himself: 'Well, he has done wisely;
otherwise he would have had to beg his bread.
To me he has caused a loss, but his own
reckoning was wise.'

"For, in the fleshly life, we all understand
wherein is the true reckoning, but in the life
of the spirit, we do not wish to understand.
9. Thus must we do with unjust, false wealth,—
give it up, in order to receive the life of the
10. spirit. And if we regret to give up such trifles
as wealth for the life of the spirit, then this
11. life will not be given us. If we do not give
up false wealth, then our own true life will not
be given us.

13. "It is impossible to serve two masters at
one time; to serve God and Wealth, the will
of the Father, and one's own will. Either one
or the other."

14. And the orthodox heard this. But loving
wealth, they jeered at him.

15. And he said to them: "You think that,
because men honor you on account of wealth,
you are really honorable. It is not so. God
does not look at the exterior, but looks at the
heart. That which stands high among men, is

abomination in the eyes of God. Now the Lk. xvi. 16
kingdom of heaven is attainable on earth,
and great are they who enter it. But there
enter it, not the rich, but those who have nothing. And this has always been so, both according to your law, and according to Moses,
and according to the prophets also. Listen. 17.
How does it stand with rich and poor in your
way of thinking?

"There was a rich man. He dressed well, 19.
led an idle and amusing life every day. And 20.
there was a vagrant, Lazarus, covered with
sores. And Lazarus came to the yard of the 21.
rich man, and thought there would be leavings
from the rich man's table, but Lazarus did not
get even the leavings, the rich man's dogs ate
up everything, and even licked Lazarus' sores.
And both these died, Lazarus and the rich 22.
man. And in Hades, the rich man saw, far 23.
off, Abraham; and behold, Lazarus, the beggar, was sitting with him. And the rich man 24.
said: 'Father Abraham, see, Lazarus the beggar is sitting with you. He used to wallow
under my fence. I dare not trouble you, but
send Lazarus the beggar to me; let him but
wet his finger in water, to cool my throat, because I am burning in the fire.' But Abraham 25.
said: 'But why should I send Lazarus into
the fire to you? You, in that other world, had
what you wished, but Lazarus only saw grief;
so that he ought now to be happy. Yes, and 26.
though I should like to help you, I cannot,
because between us and you there is a great
pit, and it is impossible to cross it. We are
living, but you are dead.' Then the rich man 27.
said: 'Well, Father Abraham, send Lazarus
the beggar to my home. I have five brothers; 28.
I am sorry for them. Let him tell everything
to them, and show how harmful wealth is; so
that they may not fall into this torture.' But 29.

Abraham said: 'As it is, they know the harm.
They were told of it by Moses, and by all the
Lk. xvi. 30. prophets.' But the rich man said: 'Still, it
would be better if some one should rise from
the dead, and go to them; they would the
31. sooner bethink themselves.' But Abraham
said: 'But if they do not listen to Moses
and the prophets, then, even if a dead man
came to life, they would not listen, even to
him.'"

"That one should share all with one's brother, and do good to everybody; this all men know. And the whole law of Moses, and all the prophets, said only this: 'You know this truth, but cannot do it, because you love wealth.'"

Mk. x. 17. And a rich official among the orthodox went
up to Jesus, and said to him: "You are a good
teacher, what shall I do to receive everlasting
life?"

18. Jesus said: "Why do you call me good?
Only the Father is good. But, if you wish
to have life, fulfil the commandments."

19. The official said: "There are many commandments; which do you mean?"

And Jesus said: "Do not kill, Do not commit adultery, Do not lie, Do not steal. Further, honor your Father, and fulfil His will; and love your neighbor as yourself."

20. But the orthodox official said: "All these
commandments I have fulfilled from my childhood; but I ask, what else must one do, according to your teaching?"

21. Jesus looked at him, at his rich dress, and
smiled, and said: "One small thing you have
left undone. You have not fulfilled that which
you say. If you wish to fulfil these commandments: Do not kill, Do not commit adultery,
Do not steal, Do not lie, and, above all, the
commandment: Love your neighbour as your-

self, — then, at once sell all your goods, and
give them to the poor. Then you will have
fulfilled the Father's will."

Having heard this, the official frowned, and Mk. x. 22
went away, because he was loath to part with
his estates.

And Jesus said to his disciples: "As you 23.
see, it is in no wise possible to be rich, and to
fulfil the Father's will."

The disciples were horrified at these words, 24.
so Jesus once more repeated them, and said:
"Yes, children, he who has his own property, 25.
cannot be in the will of the Father. Sooner Lk. xviii. 25.
may a camel pass through a needle's eye than
he who trusts in wealth fulfil the will of the
Father." And they were still more horrified, 26.
and said: "But, in that case, is it at all possible
to keep one's life?"

He said: "To man it seems impossible to 27.
support one's life without property; but God,
even without property, can support a man's
life."

Once, Jesus was going through the town of xix. 1.
Jericho. And in this town was the chief of 2
the tax-gatherers, a rich man named Zaccheus.
This Zaccheus had heard of the teaching of 3.
Jesus, and believed in it. And when he knew
that Jesus was in Jericho, he wished to see
him. But there were so many people around,
that it was impossible to push through to him.
Zaccheus was short of stature. So he ran 4.
ahead and climbed a tree, in order to see Jesus
as he was going past. And thus, in passing 5.
by, Jesus saw him, and having learnt that he
believed his teaching, said: "Come down from
the tree, and go home; I will come to your
house." Zaccheus climbed down, ran home, 6.
made ready to meet Jesus, and joyfully welcomed him.

The people began to criticize, and to say of 7.

Jesus: "See, he has gone into the tax-gatherer's
house, — the house of a rogue."

Lk. xix. 8. Meanwhile, Zaccheus said to Jesus: "See,
sir, this is what I will do. I will give away half
of my goods to the poor, and out of what is
left I will repay fourfold those whom I have
wronged."

9. And Jesus said: "Now you have saved yourself. You were dead, and are alive; you were
lost, and are found; because you have done as
Abraham did, when he wished to slay his son;
10. you have shown your faith. Therein is the whole
business of man's life; to seek out and save in
his soul that which is perishing. But such sacrifice as yours must not be measured by its
amount."

Mk. xii. 41. It happened once that Jesus and his disciples
were sitting opposite a collecting-box. People
were placing their contributions in the box, for
God's service. Rich people went up to the box,
42. and put in much. And a poor woman, a widow,
came and put in two farthings.

43. And Jesus pointed her out, and said: "See,
now, this poor widow has put two farthings in
44. the box. She has put in more than all. Because they put in that which they did not need
for their own livelihood; while this woman has
put all that she had; she has put in her whole
life."

Mt. xxvi. 6. It happened that Jesus was in the house of
7. Simon the leper. And a woman came into the
house. And the woman had a vase of precious
oil worth fifteen pounds. Jesus said to his disciples, that his death was near. The woman heard
this, and pitied Jesus, and, to show him her love,
wished to anoint his head with the oil. And
she forgot everything, and broke the vase, and
anointed his head and feet, and poured out all
the oil.

8. And the disciples began to discuss among

themselves, thinking that she had done wrong.
And Judas, he who afterward betrayed Jesus,
said: "See how much good stuff has gone for
nothing. This oil might have been sold for fif- Mt. xxvi. 9
teen pounds, with which, how many poor might
have been helped!" And the disciples began
blaming the woman; who was troubled, and did
not know whether she had done well or ill.

Then Jesus said: "You are troubling the 10.
woman without cause. She has, indeed, done a
good work, and you mistakenly think of the poor.
If you wish to do good to the poor, do so; they 11.
are always with you. But why call them to mind
now? If you pity the poor, go with your pity,
do them good. But she has pitied me, and done
real good, because she has given away all that
she had. Who of you can know what is useful,
and what is not necessary? How do you know
that there was no need to pour the oil over me?
She has thus anointed me with oil, and if it
were but to get ready my body for burial, this
was needful. She truly fulfilled the will of the 13.
Father, in forgetting herself and pitying another.
She forgot the reckonings of the flesh and gave
away all that she had."

And Jesus said: "My teaching is the fulfilment of the Father's will; and the Father's
will can be fulfilled by deeds only; not by
mere words. If a man's son, in answer to his xxi. 28.
father's bidding, keeps saying, 'I obey, I
obey,' but does nothing which his father bids,
he then does not fulfil the will of his father.
But if another son keeps saying, 'I do not wish 29.
to obey,' and then goes and does his father's
bidding, he indeed fulfils the father's will.
And so with men: Not he is in the Father's
will who says: 'I am in the Father's will,'—
but he who does that which the Father
wishes."

CHAPTER VII

I AND THE FATHER ARE ONE

The true food of everlasting life is the fulfilment of the Father's will

("Give us our daily bread")

Jn. vii. 1. AFTER this the Jews tried to condemn Jesus
to death, and Jesus went away into Galilee,
and lived with his relations.
The Jewish feast of tabernacles was come.
2. And the brothers of Jesus got ready to go to
3. the feast, and invited him to go with them.
5. They did not believe in his teaching, and said
3. to him: —
"Now, you say that the Jewish service of
God is wrong, that you know the real service
of God by deeds. If you really think that no
one but yourself knows the true service of
God, then come with us to the feast. Many
people will be there, and you can declare before them all that the teaching of Moses is
wrong. If all believe you, then it will be clear
to your disciples also, that you are right. Why
4. make a secret of it? You say that our service is wrong, that you know the true service
of God; well then, show it to all."
6. And Jesus said: "For you, there is a special
time and place in which to serve God; but for
me, there is none. I always and everywhere
7. work for God. This is just what I show to
people. I show to them that their service of
God is wrong, and therefore do they hate me.
8. Go you to the feast, and I will go when I
think fit."
9. And the brothers went, but he remained
10. behind, and only came up at the middle of
11. the feast. And the Jews were shocked at

his not honoring their feast, and delaying to
come. And they discussed his teaching much. Jn vii. 12.
Some said that he spoke the truth, while
others said that he only disturbed the people.

At the middle of the feast, Jesus entered 14.
the temple, and began to teach the people
that their service of God was wrong; that
God should be served not in the temple and
by sacrifices, but in the spirit, and by deeds.
All listened to him and wondered that he 15.
knew the whole of wisdom without having
learnt. And Jesus, having heard that all 16.
wondered at his wisdom, said to them: —

"My teaching is not my own, but His who
sent me. If any one wishes to fulfill the will 17.
of the Spirit which sent us into life, he will
know that I have not invented this teaching,
but that it is of God. Because he who invents 18.
from himself, follows his own mere imaginations; but he who seeks the mind of Him
who sent him, he is right, and there is no
wrong in him.

"Your law of Moses is not the Father's law, 19.
and, therefore, they who follow it do not fulfil
the Father's law, but work evil and falsehood.
I teach you the fulfilment of the will of the 21.
Father alone, and in my teaching there cannot 22.
be contradiction. But your written law of 23.
Moses is all full of contradictions. Do not 24.
judge by outside appearance, but judge by the
spirit."

And some said: "While he has been called 25.
a false prophet, see, he condemns the law, and
no one makes a charge against him. Maybe 26.
in very deed he is a true prophet; maybe even
the authorities have acknowledged him. Only 27.
one reason makes it impossible to believe
him, namely, that it is said, when he who is
sent from God shall come, no one will know

whence he is come; but we know this man's birth and all his family."

The people still did not understand his teaching, and still sought proofs.

Jn. vii. 28. Then Jesus said to them: "You know me,
and whence I am, after the flesh. But you do
not know whence I am, after the spirit. You
do not know Him, from whom I am according
to the spirit; and that is the only needful
29. knowledge. If I had said that I am Christ,
you would have believed me, the Man, but
you would not have believed the Father who
is in me, and in you. But it is necessary to
believe the Father only.

33. "I am here among you for the short space
of my life. I point out to you the way to that
source of life, from which I have come forth.
34. And you ask of me proofs, and wish to condemn me. If you do not know the way, then,
when I shall be no more, you will in nowise
find it. You must not discuss me, but must
follow me. Whoever shall do that which I
say, he shall know whether what I say is true.
He for whom the fleshly life has not become
the food of the spirit, he who follows not the
truth, thirsting for it as for water, cannot
37. understand me. But he who thirsts for the
38. truth, let him come to me to drink. And he
who shall believe in my teaching shall receive the
39. true life. He shall receive the life of the spirit."

40. And many believed in his teaching, and said:
"That which he says is the truth and is of God."
42. Others did not understand him, and still sought
in prophecies for proofs that he was sent from
43. God. And many disputed with him, but none
44. could controvert him. The learned orthodox
45. sent their assistants to contend with him, but
their assistants returned to the orthodox priests
and said: "We can do nothing with him."

And the high priests said to them: "But why

have you not convicted him?" And they an- Jn. vii. 46
swered: "Never did any man speak as he."
Then the orthodox said: "It signifies noth- 47.
ing that it is impossible to controvert him, and
that the people believe in his teaching. We do 48.
not believe, and none of the authorities believe.
But the people is cursed, they were always stu- 49.
pid and unlearned; they believe every one."
And Nicodemus, the man to whom Jesus ex- 50.
plained his teaching, said to the high priests:
"It is impossible to condemn a man without 51.
having heard him to the end, without understanding whither he is leading." But they said 52.
to him: "It is useless to discuss, or pay any attention to this affair. We know that a prophet
cannot come from Galilee."
At another time, Jesus was speaking with the viii. 12.
orthodox, and said to them: "There can be no
proofs of the truth of my teaching, as there cannot be of the illumination of light. My teaching is the real light, by which people tell what
is good and what is bad, and therefore it is impossible to prove my teaching; which itself
proves everything. Whoever shall follow me
shall not be in darkness, but shall have life.
Life and enlightenment, which are one and the
same."
But the orthodox said: "You alone say this." 13.
And he answered them and said: "And if I 14.
alone say this, yet I am right; because I know
whence I came, and whither I go. According
to my teaching, there is reason in life; whereas,
according to yours, there is none. Besides this, 18.
not I alone teach, but my Father, the Spirit,
teaches the same."
They said: "Where is your Father?" 19.
He said: "You do not understand my teaching, and therefore you do not know my Father.
You do not know whence you are and whither 21
you go. I lead you, but you, instead of follow-

ing me, discuss who I am. Therefore you cannot come to that salvation of life to which I
Jn. viii. 24. lead you. And you will perish, if you remain
in this error, and do not follow me."

And the Jews asked: "Who are you?"

26. He said: "From the very beginning, I tell
you, I am the Son of Man, acknowledging the
27. Spirit as my Father. That which I have understood of the Father, the same I tell to the
28. world. And when you shall exalt in yourselves the Son of Man, then you shall know
what I am; because I do and speak, not of
myself, as a man, but I do and speak that
which the Father has taught me. This I say,
this I teach.

29. "And he who sent me is always with me;
and the Father has not left me, because I do
31. His will. Whoever will keep to my understanding of life, whoever will fulfil the will of the
Father, he will be truly taught by me. In
order to know the truth, it is necessary to do
good to men. He who does evil to men, loves
darkness, and goes into it; he who does good
to men, goes to the light; so that, in order to
understand my teaching, it is necessary to do
32. good deeds. He who shall do good, shall know
the truth; he shall be free from evil and death.
34. Because every one who errs becomes the slave
of his error.

35. "And as the slave does not always live in
the house of the master, while the son of the
master is always in the house, so also a man,
if he errs in his life and becomes a slave
through his errors, does not live always, but
dies. Only he who is in the truth remains
always living. The truth is in this, to be not
a slave, but a son. So that, if you err, you will
36. be slaves and die. But if you are in the truth,
then you shall be free sons, and shall be living.

37. "You say of yourselves that you are sons of

Abraham, that you know the truth. But see,
you wish to kill me, because you do not understand my teaching. It comes to this, that I Jn. viii. 38
speak that which I have understood from my
Father, and you wish to do that which you
have understood from your father."

They said: "Our father is Abraham." 39

Jesus said to them: "If you were the sons
of Abraham you would do his deeds. But see, 40.
you wish to kill me because I told you that
which I had learnt from God. Abraham did
not do in that way; therefore you do not serve
God, but serve your father, another one."

They said to him: "We are not bastards, 41.
but we are all children of our Father, all sons
of God."

And Jesus said to them: "If your father 42.
were one with me, you would love me, because
I came forth from that Father. For I was
not born of myself. You are not children of 43.
the one Father with me, therefore you do not
understand my word; my understanding of life
does not find place in you. If I am of the
Father, and you of the same Father, then you
cannot wish to kill me. But if you wish to
kill me, then we are not of one Father.

"I am from the Father of good, from God; 44.
but you are from the devil, from the father of
evil. You wish to do the lusts of your father
the devil, who is always a murderer, and a liar,
with no truth in him. If he, the devil, says
anything, he says what is of himself, and not
common to all, and he is the father of lying.
Therefore you are the servants of the devil
and his children. Now you see how plainly 46.
you are convicted of error. If I err, then convict me; but if there is no error in me, then
why do you not believe in me?"

And the Jews began to revile him, and to 48.
say he was possessed.

Jn. viii 49. He said: "I am not possessed; but I honor
the Father, and you wish to kill me; therefore
you are not brothers of mine, but children of
50. another father. It is not I that affirm that I
51. am right, but the truth speaks for me. Therefore I repeat to you: he who shall comprehend
my teaching and perform it, shall not see death."
52. And the Jews said: "Well, do not we speak
the truth in saying that you are a Samaritan
possessed, and that you convict yourself? The
prophets died, Abraham died; but you say that
he who performs your teaching shall not see
53. death. Abraham died, and shall you not die?
Or are you greater than Abraham?"
54. The Jews were still discussing as to whether
he, Jesus of Galilee, was an important prophet,
or unimportant, and forgot that he had told them
that he said nothing of himself as a man, but
spoke of the spirit that was within him.

And Jesus said: "I do not make myself to
be anything. If I spoke of myself, of that
which only seems to me, then all that I should
say would mean nothing. But there is that
source of everything which you call God; well,
55. it is of Him that I speak. But you have not
known, and do not know the true God. But
I know Him, and I cannot say that I do not
know Him; I should be a liar like you, if I
said that I do not know Him. I know Him,
56. and know His will, and fulfil it. Abraham,
your father, saw and rejoiced over my understanding."
57. The Jews said: "You are only thirty years
old, how were you living at the same time as
Abraham?"
58. He said: "Before Abraham was, there was
the understanding of good, there was that which
I tell you."
59. Then the Jews picked up stones in order to
kill him, but he went away from them.

Jesus said: "My teaching is the awakening Jn. xi. 25.
of life. He who believes in my teaching, notwithstanding that he dies in the flesh, remains
living, and every one who lives and believes in 26.
me shall not die."

And yet a third time Jesus taught the peo- x. 1.
ple; he said: "Men surrender themselves to my teaching, not because I myself prove it. It is impossible to prove the truth. The truth itself proves all the rest. But men surrender to my teaching, because there is no other than it; it is known to men, and promises life.

"My teaching is to men as the shepherd's 2,
familiar voice is to the sheep, when he comes 3.
among them through the door, and gathers
them, to lead them to the pasture. But your 5.
teaching, no one believes; because it is foreign
to them, and because they see in it your own
lusts. It is with men as with sheep, at the
sight of a man who does not enter by the door,
but climbs over the fence. The sheep do not
know him, but feel that he is a robber. My 7.
teaching is the only true teaching; like the one
door for the sheep. All your teachings of the 8.
law of Moses are lies, they are all like thieves
and robbers to the sheep. He who shall give 9.
himself up to my teaching shall find true life;
just as the sheep go forth and find food, if they
follow the shepherd.

"A thief only comes to steal, rob, and de- 10.
stroy, but the shepherd comes to give life. And my teaching alone promises, and gives the true life.

"There are shepherds to whom the sheep 11.
are the chief interest in life, and who give up
their lives for the sheep. These are true 12
shepherds. And there are hirelings who do not care about the sheep, because they are hirelings, and the sheep are not theirs; so that if a wolf comes they abandon their charge and

flee from them, and the wolf devours the sheep.
Jn. x. 13. These are false shepherds. And so there are
false teachers, such as have no concern with
the life of people; while true teachers give up
their lives for the life of men.
14. "I am such a teacher. My teaching is this,
17. —to give up one's life for the life of men.
18. No one shall take my life from me, but I myself freely give it up for men, in order to receive
true life. The commandment to do this I re-
15. ceived from my Father. And as my Father
knows me, so I also know Him; and therefore
17. I lay down my life for men. Therefore the
Father loves me, because I fulfil His commandments.
16. "And all men, not only those here now, but
all men, shall understand my voice; and all
shall come together into one, and all men shall
be one, and their teaching one."
24. And the Jews surrounded him, and said:
"All that you say is difficult to understand,
and does not agree with our writings. Do not
torment us, but simply and straightforwardly
tell us, whether you are that Messiah who,
according to our writings, should come into
the world."
25. And Jesus answered them: "I have already
told you who I am, but you do not believe.
If you do not believe my word, then believe
my works; by them understand who I am,
and wherefore I am come.
26. "But you do not believe me because you do
27. not follow me. He who follows me, and does
28. that which I say, he understands me. And he
who understands my teaching and fulfils it, re-
29. ceives the true life. My Father has united
30. them with me, and no one can disunite us. I
and the Father are one."
31. And the Jews were offended at this, and
took up stones to kill him.

But he said to them: "I have shown you Jn. x. 32.
many good works, and have disclosed the
teaching of my Father. For which, then, of
these good works do you wish to stone me?"
They said: "Not for the good do we wish 33
to stone you; but because you, a man, make
yourself God."
And Jesus answered them: "Why, this is 34
just what is written in your writings, where
it says that God Himself said to the wicked
rulers: 'You are gods.' If He called even 35.
vicious men gods, then why do you consider 36.
it sacrilege to call that the son of God, which
God in His love sent into the world? Every
man in the spirit is the son of God. If I do 37.
not live in God's way, then do not believe that
I am a son of God. But if I live after God's 38.
way, then believe from my life that I am in
the Father, and then you will understand that
the Father is in me and I in Him."
And the Jews began to dispute. Some said 20.
that he was possessed, and others said: "A 21.
man who is possessed cannot enlighten men."
And they did not know what to do with him, 39.
and could not condemn him. And he went 40.
again across the Jordan, and remained there.
And many believed in his teaching, and said 41.
that it was true, as the teaching of John was.
Therefore many believed in it. 42.
And Jesus once said to his disciples: "Tell Mt. xvi. 13.
me how the people understand my teaching
about the son of God and the son of man."
They said: "Some understand it like the 14.
teaching of John, others like the prophecies of
Isaiah; others, again, say that it is like the
teaching of Jeremiah. They understand that
you are a prophet."
"And how do you understand my teaching?" 15.
And Simon Peter said to him: "In my 16.
opinion, your teaching consists in this, that

you are the chosen Son of the God of Life.
You teach that God is the life in man."
Mt. xvi. 17. And Jesus said to him: "Happy are you,
Simon, that you have understood this. No
man could disclose this to you; but you have
understood this, because God in you has disclosed it to you. Not fleshly understanding,
and not I, my words, have disclosed this to
you; but God my Father has directly disclosed
18. it. And upon this is founded that society of
men for whom there is no death."

CHAPTER VIII

LIFE IS NOT TEMPORAL

Therefore true life is to be lived in the present

("This day")

Mt. x. 38. JESUS said: "He who is not ready for all
fleshly sufferings and bereavements, has not
39. understood me. He who shall obtain all that
is best for the fleshly life, shall destroy the true
life; he who shall destroy his fleshly life in fulfilling my teaching, shall receive the true life."
xix. 27. And in answer to these words, Peter said
to him: "See, we have listened to you, have
thrown off all cares and property, and have followed you. What reward shall we have for
this?"
Mk. x. 29, And Jesus said to him: "Every one who
30. has abandoned home, sisters, brothers, father,
mother, wife, children, and his fields, for my
teaching, shall receive a hundredfold more than
sisters and brothers and fields, and all that is
needful in this life; and besides this, he re-
31. ceives life beyond the power of time. There
are no rewards in the kingdom of heaven, the
kingdom of heaven is its own aim and reward.

In the kingdom of God all are equal, there is
neither first nor last.
"Because the kingdom of heaven is like this. Mt. xx. 1.
The master of a house went in the early morning to hire laborers for his grounds. He 2.
hired laborers at a penny a day, and set them
to work in the garden. And he again went at 3.
mid-day and hired more, and sent them into
the garden to work; and at evening he hired
still more, and sent them to work. And with
them all he agreed at a penny. The time 8.
came for the reckoning. And the master
ordered all to be paid alike. First, those who 9.
came last; and afterward, the first. And the
first saw that the last received each a penny.
And they thought that they would receive 10.
more; but the first were also given each a
penny. They took it and said: 'But how is 11.
this? They only worked one shift, and we all 12.
four; why, then, do we receive alike? This 13.
is unjust.' But the master came up, and said:
'What are you complaining about? Have I
offended you? The amount I hired you for, I
have given you. Our agreement was for a 14.
penny, take it and go. If I wish to give to
the last the same as to you, am I not master
of my own will? Or because you see that I 15.
am good, is that the cause of your grudging?'"
In the kingdom of God there is neither first 16.
nor last, for all there are as one.
There came to Jesus two of his disciples, 20.
James and John, and said: "Promise us that Mk. x. 35.
you will do that for us which we shall ask of
you."
He said: "What do you wish?" Mt. xx. 21.
They said: "That we may be equal with
you."
Jesus said to them: "You yourselves do not 22.
know what you ask. You may live just as I
do, and be cleansed from fleshly life like me,

but to make you like myself is not in my
Mt. xx. 23. power. Every man may, by his own effort,
enter the kingdom of his Father, having submitted to His power, and fulfilling His will."
24. When they heard of this, the other disciples
grew angry with the two brothers, because
these wished to be equal to their teacher, and
the first among his disciples.
25. But Jesus called them, and said: "If you
brothers, James and John, asked me to make
you such as I am in order to be first among
my disciples, then you were mistaken; but if
you, my other disciples, are angry with them
because they wish to be your elders, then you
also are mistaken. Only in the world are
kings and officials reckoned by seniority for
governing the people. But among you, there
26. cannot be either elder or younger. Among
you, for one to be greater than another, it is
27. necessary to be the servant of all. Among
you, let him who wishes to be first, consider
28. himself last. Because therein is the will of
the Father as to the Son of Man; who does
not live to be served, but to himself serve all,
and to give up his fleshly life, as a ransom for
the life of the spirit."
xviii. 11. And Jesus said to the people: "The Father
12. seeks to save that which perishes. He rejoices over it, as a shepherd rejoices when he
has found one sheep that was lost. When
one is lost, he leaves the ninety-nine, and goes
Lk. xv. 8. to save the lost one. And if a woman lose a
farthing, she will sweep out the whole hut and
10. seek until she find it. The Father loves the
Son, and calls him to Himself."
xiv. 8. And he told them yet another parable, to
the effect that they who live in the will of
God ought not to exalt themselves. He said:
"If you are invited to dinner, do not seat
yourself in the front corner; some one will

come of more consideration than yourself, and
the master will say: 'Leave your place, and Lk. xiv. 9.
allow him who is better than you to be seated.'
Then you will be put to shame. But do better, 10.
take your seat in the very last place, then the
master will find you, and call you to a place
of honor, and you will be honored.

"So also in the kingdom of God there is no 11.
room for pride. He who exalts himself, by so
doing lowers himself; but he who humbles
himself, and considers himself unworthy, by
this same means raises himself in the kingdom
of God.

"A man had two sons. And the younger xv. 11.
said to his father: 'Father, give me my prop- 12.
erty.' And the father gave him his share.
The younger son took his share, went abroad, 13.
squandered all his property, and began to
suffer want. And abroad, he became a swine- 15.
herd. And he so hungered, that he ate acorns 16.
with the swine. And he bethought himself of 17.
his life, and said: 'Why did I take my share
and leave my father? My father had plenty
of everything; at my father's, even laborers
ate their fill. But I here am eating the same
food as the swine. I will go to my father, fall 18.
at his feet, and say: I am to blame, father,
before you, and am not worthy to be your
son. Take me back even as a laborer.'
So he thought, and he went to his father. 20.
And when he was still far off, his father at
once recognized him, and himself ran to meet
him, embraced him, and began to kiss him.
And the son said: 'Father, I am to blame 21.
before you, I am not worthy to be your son.'
But the father would not even listen, and said 22.
to the laborers: 'Bring quickly the best
clothes and the best boots, to clothe him and
shoe him. And go and bring a fatted calf and 23.
kill it, and we will rejoice that this my son was 24.

dead and is now alive, was lost and is now
Lk. xv. 25. found.' And the elder brother came from
the field, and as he approached he heard the
26. sounds of music in the house. He called a
servant to him, and said: 'Why is there this
merry-making here?' And the boy said:
27. 'Have you not heard that your brother is
returned, and your father is full of joy, and
has ordered a fatted calf to be killed, for joy
28. that his son has returned?' The elder brother
was offended, and did not go into the house.
29. And the father came out and called him. And
he said to his father: 'See, father, how many
years I have worked for you, and have not
disobeyed your command, while you never
30. killed a fatted calf for me. But my younger
brother left the house and squandered all his
property with drunkards, and you have now
killed the calf for him.' And the father said:
31. 'You are always with me, and all mine is
32. yours; and you should not be offended, but
should be glad that your brother was dead and
has become alive, was lost and is found.'

Mk. xii. 1. "A master planted a garden, cultivated it,
arranged it, did everything so that the garden
might yield as much fruit as possible. And
he sent laborers into the garden, that they
might work there, and gather the fruit, and
pay him according to the agreement for the garden. (The master is the Father; the garden,
the world; the laborers, men. The Father
does no more than send His Son, the Son of
Man, into the world, that men may yield fruit
to the Father from the understanding of life
2. which He placed in them.) The time came
when the master sent a servant for the rents.
(The Father, without ceasing, tells men that
3. they must fulfil His will.) The laborers drove
away the messenger of the master with nothing,
and continued to live, imagining that the gar-

den was their own, and that they themselves,
of their own will, were settled on it. (Men
drive away from themselves the declaration of
the will of the Father, and continue to live,
each one for himself, imagining that they live
for the joys of the fleshly life.) Then the Mk. xii. 4-6.
master sent one after another his chosen ones,
then his son, to remind the laborers of their
debt. But the laborers quite lost their reason, 7.
and imagined that if they killed this son of the
master, who reminded them that the garden
was not theirs, they would be left quite in
peace. So they killed him. 8.

"Thus men do not love even a reminder of the spirit which lives in them, and declares to them that it is eternal and they are not eternal; and they have killed, as far as they could, the consciousness of the spirit; they have wrapped in a cloth and buried in the ground the talent that was given them.

"What, then, is the master to do? Nothing Mt. xxi. 40, 41.
else than drive forth those laborers, and send
others.

"What is the Father to do? Sow until there shall be fruit. And this He does.

"People have not understood and do not 42.
understand that the consciousness of the spirit
which is in them, and which they hide because
it troubles them, brings life to them through
understanding it. They reject that stone upon 43.
which everything rests. And they who do not
take as foundation the life of the spirit, do
not enter into the kingdom of heaven, and do
not receive life. In order to have faith, and to
receive life, it is necessary to understand one's
position, and not to expect rewards."

Then the disciples said to Jesus: "Increase Lk. xvii. 5
in us our faith. Tell us that which will make
us more strongly believe in the life of the spirit,
that we may not regret the life of the flesh,

which must be given up wholly for the life of the spirit. For reward, you yourself say there is none."

Lk. xvii. 6. And in answer to this, Jesus said to them: "If you had such a faith as the faith that from a birch seed there springs up a great tree; if, also, you believed that in you there is the germ, the only germ, of the spirit whence springs up the true life, you would not ask me to increase in you your faith.

"Faith does not consist in believing something wonderful, but faith consists in understanding one's position, and wherein lies salvation. If you understand your position, you will not expect rewards, but will believe in that which is intrusted to you.

7. "When the master returns with the laborers
from the field, he does not seat the laborer at
8. his table. But he bids him see to the cattle,
and prepare his supper, and after this only
9. says to the laborer: 'Sit down, drink and eat.'
The master will not thank the laborer for having done what he ought to do. And the laborer, if he understands that he is a laborer, is not offended, but works, believing that he will receive his due.

10. "And so you, also, must fulfil the will of the Father, and think that we are worthless laborers, having only done what we ought to do, and not expect a reward, but be content with receiving that which is due to you.

"There is no need to take care to believe that there will be a reward, and life; this cannot be otherwise; but there is need to take care not to destroy this life, not to forget that it is given us that we may bring forth its fruits, and fulfil the will of the Father.

xii. 35, "And therefore always be ready, like ser-
36. vants awaiting a master, to answer him im-
37, 38. mediately when he comes. The servants do

not know when he will return, either early or
late, and they must always be ready. And
when they meet the master, they have fulfilled
his will, and it is well for them.

"So in life also. Always, every minute of the
present, you must live the life of the spirit, not
thinking of the past or the future, and not saying
to yourself: then or there I will do this or that.

"If the master knew when the thief would Lk. xii. 39.
come, he would not sleep; and so do you also
never sleep; because, to the life of the son of
man time is nothing; he lives only in the present, and does not know when is the beginning
or end of life.

"Our life is the same as that of a slave whom Mt. xxiv. 45, 46.
the master has left as chief in his household.
And well it is for that slave if he does the will
of the master always! But if he shall say, 48.
'The master will not soon return,' and shall forget the master's business, then the master will 50,
return unexpectedly, and will drive him out. 51.

"And so, be not downcast, but always live in Mk. xiii. 33.
the present by the spirit. For the life of the
spirit there is no time.

"Look to yourselves, so as not to weigh your- Lk. xxi. 34.
selves down, and not to blind yourselves with
drunkenness, gluttony, and cares; so as not
to let the time of salvation pass. The time of
salvation, like a web, is cast over all; it is
there always. And therefore always live the
life of the Son of Man.

"The kingdom of heaven is like this. Ten Mt. xxv. 1.
maidens went with lamps to meet the bridegroom.
Five were wise and five foolish. The foolish 2, 3.
ones took lamps but did not take oil; but the 4.
wise took lamps and a store of oil. While they 5.
waited for the bridegroom, they went to sleep.
When the bridegroom was approaching, the 6.
foolish maidens saw that they had little oil, and 7.
went to buy some; and while they were gone, 10.

the bridegroom came. And the wise maidens who had oil went in with him, and the doors were shut. Their business was only this, to meet the bridegroom with lights; and the five foolish ones forgot that it was important, not only that the lights should burn, but that they should burn in time. And in order that they might be burning when the bridegroom came, they must burn without stopping.

"Life is only for this, to exalt the Son of Man, and the Son of Man exists always. He is not in time; and therefore, in serving him, one must live without time, in the present alone.

Lk. xiii. 24. "Therefore make efforts in the present to
25. enter into the life of the spirit. If you do not
make these efforts you shall not enter. You
will say: 'We said so and so.' But there will
be no good works to show, and there will not
Mt. xvi. 27. be life. Because the Son of Man, the one true
spirit of life, will appear in each man, as such
man has acted for the Son of Man.

Mt. xxv. 32. "Mankind is divided according to the way
in which men serve the Son of Man. And
by their works men shall be divided into two
classes, as sheep are divided from goats in
the flock. The one shall live, the other perish.

34. "They who have served the Son of Man,
they shall receive that which belonged to them
from the beginning of the world, that life
which they have kept. They have kept life
by the fact that they have served the Son of
Man. They have fed the hungry, clothed the
naked, welcomed the stranger, visited the prisoner. They have lived in the Son of Man,
felt that he only is in all men, and therefore
they have loved their neighbors.

"Whereas they who have not lived in the Son of Man, they have not served him, have not understood that he alone is in all, and therefore have not joined in him and have lost life in him, and have perished."

CHAPTER IX

TEMPTATIONS

The illusions of temporal life conceal from men the true life in the present

("Forgive us our debts as we forgive our debtors")

Once, children were brought to Jesus. His Mt. xix. 13.
disciples began to drive the children away.
Jesus saw this being done, and was grieved, 14.
and said: —

"You drive the children away without reason. They are better than any, because children all live after the Father's will. They are, indeed, already in the kingdom of heaven.
You should not drive them away, but learn Lk. xviii. 17.
from them; because, in order to live in the Father's will, you must live as children live. Children do not abuse one another, do not bear ill-will to people, do not commit adultery, do not swear by anything, do not resist evil, do not go to law with any one, acknowledge no difference between their own people and foreigners. Therefore are they better than grown
people, and are in the kingdom of heaven. If Mt. xviii. 3.
you do not refrain from all the temptations of the flesh, and become as children, you will not be in the kingdom of heaven.

"Only he who understands that children are 5.
better than we, because they do not break the Father's will, only he understands my teaching. And he who understands my teaching, Lk. ix. 48.
he alone understands the Father's will. We Mt. xviii. 10.
cannot despise children, because they are bet-

ter than we, and their hearts are pure in the sight of the Father, and are always with Him.
Mt. xviii. 14. "And not one child perishes by the Father's will. They perish only as men entice them from the truth. And therefore it behooves us to take care of them, and not to entice them from the Father, and from true life.

"That man does ill who entices them from purity. To entice a child from good, to lead it into temptation, is as bad as to hang a millstone on its neck and throw it into the water. It is hard for it to swim to the surface; it is more likely to drown. It is as hard for a child to get out of temptation into which a grown-up man leads it.

7. "The world of men is unhappy only on account of temptations. Temptations are everywhere in the world, they always were and always will be; and man perishes from temptations.

8. "Therefore give up everything, sacrifice everything, if only you may not fall into temptation. A fox, if it fall into a trap, will wrench off its paw and go away, and the paw will heal and it will remain alive. Do you likewise. Give up everything, if only not to sink into temptation.

Lk. xvii. 3. "Beware of temptation under that first commandment; do not bear ill-will against men, when people offend you, and you would wish to be avenged on them.

Mt. xviii. 15. "If a man offend you, remember that he is
the son of the same Father, and your brother.
If he has offended you, go and persuade him
of it face to face. If he listen to you, then you
have the advantage, you will have found a new
16. brother. If he do not listen to you, then call
to your aid two or three others who may per-
Lk. xvii. 4. suade him. And if he repent, forgive him.
And if he offend you seven times, and seven

times says, 'Forgive me,' then forgive him.
But if he does not listen, then tell the society Mt. xviii. 17
of believers in my teaching, and if he listens
not to them, then forgive him, and have nothing to do with him.
"Because the kingdom of God is like this. 23.
A king began to settle with his tenants. And 24.
there was a man brought to him who owed him
a million, and had nothing to pay him with.
Then the king commanded to sell the man's 25.
estate, his wife, his children, and the man
himself. But the tenant began to beg mercy 26.
of the king. And the king was gracious to 27.
him, and pardoned all his debt. And now, 28.
this same tenant went home, and saw a peasant. This peasant owed him fifty shillings.
The king's tenant seized him, began to strangle
him, and said: 'Give me what you owe me.'
And the peasant fell at his feet, and said: 29.
'Have patience with me, I will pay you all.'
But the tenant showed him no mercy, and put 30.
the peasant into prison, to stay there until he
paid everything. Other peasants saw this, 31.
and went to the king, and told what the tenant had done. Then the king called the 32.
tenant, and said to him: 'Wicked creature,
I pardoned you all your debt, because you
prayed me. And you, also, should have shown 33.
mercy to your debtor, because I showed mercy
to you.' And the king became angry, and gave 34.
the tenant to be made to suffer, until he should
pay all his rent.
"Just so, the Father will do with you, if 35.
you do not forgive, from the bottom of your
heart, all those who are to blame in your sight.
"You know that if a quarrel arise with a v. 25
man, it is better to make it up with him without going to the court. You know this, and
you act so because you know, should it go to
the court, you will lose more. Now, it is the

same with all malice. If you know that malice is a bad thing, and removes you from the Father, then get clear of malice as soon as possible, and make your peace.

Mt. xviii. 18. "You yourselves know that as you become
bound on earth, so you will be before the
Father. And as you free yourselves on earth,
so you will be also free before the Father.
19. Understand that if two or three on earth are
united in my teaching, everything they may
desire they already have from my Father.
20. Because where two or three are joined in the
name of the spirit in man, the spirit of man is
living in them.

Mk. x. 2. "Beware also of temptation under the second commandment; the temptation for men to change their wives."

Mt. xix. 3. There once came to Jesus orthodox teachers, who, trying him, said: "May a man leave his wife?"

4. He said to them: "From the very beginning
man was created male and female. This was
5. the will of the Father. And therefore a man
leaves father and mother and cleaves to his
wife. And husband and wife unite in one
6. body. So that the wife is the same for a
man as his own flesh. Therefore man must
not break the natural law of God, and separate
8. that which is united. According to your law
of Moses, it is said that you may abandon a
wife and take another; but this is untrue.
According to the Father's will, this is not so,
9. and I tell you that he who casts off his wife
drives into immorality both her, and him who
shall have to do with her. And casting off his
wife, a man breeds immorality in the world."

10. And the disciples said to Jesus: "It is too hard to be tied for life, whatever happens, to one wife. If that must be, it were better not to marry."

He said to them: "You may refrain from Mt. xix. 11.
marriage, but you must understand what you
are about. If any one wishes to live without 12.
wife, let him be quite pure, and not approach
women; but he who loves women, let him
unite with one wife and not cast her off, and
not gaze upon others.

"Beware of temptation against the third
commandment; the temptation to force people
to fulfil obligations and to take oaths."

Once, tax-gatherers came to Peter, and asked xvii. 24.
him: "How about your teacher, does he pay
taxes?" Peter said: "No, he does not." 25.
And he went and told Jesus that he had been
stopped, and told that all were bound to pay
taxes.

Then Jesus said to him: "The king does
not take taxes of his sons; and moreover, men
are not bound to pay any one but the king. Is
this not so? Well, so it is with us. If we are
sons of God, then we are bound to no one but
God, and free from all obligations. And if they 27.
demand taxes of you, then pay. But do so,
not because it is your duty, but because you
may not resist evil. Otherwise resistance to
evil will cause a greater evil."

Another time, the orthodox joined with xxii. 16.
Cæsar's officials, and went to Jesus, to entrap
him in his words. They said to him: "You
teach every one according to the truth. Tell 17.
us, are we bound to pay taxes to Cæsar or
not?" Jesus understood that they wished to 18.
convict him of not acknowledging duty to
Cæsar. And he said to them: "Show me 19.
that with which you pay taxes to Cæsar."
They handed him a coin. He looked at the 20.
coin, and said: "What is this here? Whose
effigy and whose signature are these?" They
said: "Cæsar's." And he said: "Well then, 21.
pay Cæsar that which is Cæsar's, but that

which is God's, your soul, give to no one but
to God." Money, goods, your labor, give
everything to him who shall ask it of you.
But your soul, give to none but God.
"Your orthodox teachers go about every-
Mt. xxiii. 15. where, and compel people to swear and vow that
they will fulfil the law. But by this they only
pervert people, and make them worse than
before. It is impossible to promise with one's
16- body for one's soul. In your soul, God is;
22. therefore people cannot promise for God to
men.

"Beware. Temptation under the fourth commandment is the temptation for men to judge and execute people, and call upon others to take part in these judgments and executions."

Lk. ix. 52. The disciples of Jesus once went into a village, and asked for a night's lodging; but they
53. were not admitted. Then the disciples went
54. to Jesus to complain, and said: "Let these
55. people be struck with lightning." Jesus said:
"You still do not understand of what spirit you
56. are. I am teaching, not how to destroy, but
how to save people."

xii. 13. Once a man came to Jesus, and said: "Bid my
14. brother give me my inheritance." Jesus said
to him: "No one has made me judge over you,
and I judge no one. And neither may you
judge any one."

Jn. viii. 3. The orthodox once brought a woman to
4. Jesus, and said: "See, this woman was taken
5. in adultery. Now, by the law she should be
stoned to death. What do you say?"

6. Jesus answered nothing, and waited for them
7. to bethink themselves. But they pressed him,
and asked what he would adjudge to this
woman. Then he said: "He among you who
is without fault, let him be the first to cast a
8. stone at her." He said nothing more.

9. Then the orthodox looked within themselves,

and their consciences smote them; and they
who were in front sought to get behind the
others, and all went away. And Jesus re- Jn. viii. 10.
mained alone with the woman. He looked
round, and saw that there was none else.
"Well," said he to the woman, "has no one
condemned you?" She said: "No one." Then 11.
he said: "And I do not condemn you. Go,
and henceforth sin no more."

Beware. Temptation against the fifth commandment is the temptation for men to consider themselves bound to do good only to their countrymen, and to consider foreigners as enemies.

A teacher of the law wished to try Jesus, Lk. x. 25.
and said: "What am I to do in order to receive
the true life?" Jesus said: "You know, — love 27.
your Father, God, and him who is your brother
through your Father, God; of whatever country
he may be." And the teacher of the law said: 29.
"This would be well, if there were not different nations; but as it is, how am I to love the
enemies of my own people?"

And Jesus said: "There was a Jew who fell 30.
into misfortune. He was beaten, robbed, and
abandoned on the road. A Jewish priest went 31.
by, glanced at the wounded man, and went on.
A Jewish Levite passed, looked at the wounded 32.
man, and also went by. But there came a man 33.
of a foreign, hostile nation, a Samaritan. This
Samaritan saw the Jew, and did not think of
the fact that Jews have no esteem for the
Samaritans, but pitied the poor Jew. He 34.
washed and bound his wounds, and carried
him on his ass to an inn, paid money for him 35.
to the innkeeper, and promised to come again
to pay for him. Thus shall you also behave
toward foreign nations, toward those who
hold you of no account and ruin you. Then
you will receive true life."

Mt. xvi. 21. Jesus said: "The world loves its own, and
hates God's people. Therefore men of the
world — priests, preachers, officials — will harass those who shall fulfil the will of the Father.
And I am going to Jerusalem, and shall be persecuted and killed. But my spirit cannot be
killed, but will remain alive."

Mk. viii. 32. Having heard that Jesus would be tortured
and killed in Jerusalem, Peter was sad, and took
Jesus by the hand, and said to him: "If so,
33. then you had better not go to Jerusalem." Then
Jesus said to Peter: "Do not say this. What
you say is temptation. If you fear tortures and
death for me, this means that you are not thinking of that which is godly, of the spirit, but are
thinking of what is worldly."

34. And having called the people and his disciples, Jesus said: "He who wishes to live according to my teaching, let him forsake his
fleshly life, and let him be ready for all fleshly
suffering; because he who fears for his fleshly
life, shall destroy the true life; he who despises
the fleshly life, shall save the true life."

Mt. xxii. 23. And they did not understand this, and certain
materialists coming, he explained to all what is
the meaning of the true life and the awakening
from death.

The materialists said that after the fleshly
24. death there is no longer any life. They asked:
"How can all rise from the dead? If all were
to rise, then in rising they could in no way have
25. life together. For instance, there were seven
brothers among us. The first married and died.
The wife was taken by the second brother and
28. he died, and she was taken by the third, who
also died, and so on unto the seventh. Well
now, how shall these seven brothers live with
one wife if all arise from the dead?"

Lk. xx. 34. Jesus said to them: "You either purposely
confuse things, or you do not understand what

the awakening to life is. Men in this present
life marry. But they who shall earn everlast- Lk. xx. 35
ing life, and the awakening from death, do not
marry. And that because they can no longer 36
die, but are united with the Father. In your Mt. xxii. 31.
writings, it is said that God said: 'I am the God 32.
of Abraham, Isaac, and Jacob.' And this was said when Abraham, Isaac, and Jacob had died from among men. It follows, that they who have died from among men are alive to God. If God is, and God does not die, then they who are with God are always alive. The awakening from death is, to live in the will of the Father. For the Father, there is no time; therefore in fulfilling the will of the Father, in joining Him, man departs from time and death."

When they heard this, the orthodox no longer 34.
knew what to devise to compel Jesus to hold his tongue; and together they began to question Jesus. And one of the orthodox said: 35.
"Teacher, what, in your opinion, is the chief 36.
commandment in the whole law?"

The orthodox thought that Jesus would get
confused in the answer about the law. But 37
Jesus said: "It is, to love the Lord with all one's soul, in whose power we are. From it the second commandment follows, which is, to love
one's neighbor. Because the same Lord is in 39.
him. And this is the substance of all that is 40.
written in all your books."

And Jesus said further: "In your opinion, 42.
what is Christ? Is he some one's son?" They said: "In our opinion, Christ is the son of
David." Then he said to them: "How, then, 43
does David call Christ his Lord? Christ is neither son of David, nor any one's son after the flesh; but Christ is that same Lord, our Ruler, whom we know in ourselves as our life. Christ is that understanding which is in us."

And Jesus said: "See, beware of the leaven Lk. xii. 1

of orthodox teachers. And beware of the leaven
of the materialists and of the leaven of the gov-
Lk. xii. 5. ernment. But most of all, beware of the leaven
of the self-styled 'orthodox,' because in them
is the chief stumbling-block."
xx. 45. And when the people understood of what he
46. was speaking, he repeated: "Most of all, beware of the teaching of the scholars, of the
Mt. xxiii. 2. self-called 'orthodox.' Beware of them, because they have taken the place of the prophets
who declared the will of God to the people.
They have perversely assumed authority to
preach to the people the will of God. They
preach words, and do nothing. And the result
3. is that they no more than say: 'Do this and
that.' And there is no further result, because
4. they do nothing good, but only talk. And they
tell people to do what is impossible to be done,
5. and they themselves do nothing. They only
labor to keep the teaching in their own hands;
and with this aim they strive to appear imposing; they dress themselves up and exalt them-
8. selves. Know, therefore, that no one should
13. call himself teacher and leader. But the self-
styled orthodox are called teachers, and by this
very thing they hinder you from entering into
the kingdom of heaven, where they themselves
15. do not enter. These orthodox think that people may be brought to God by exterior rites
16. and pledges. Like blind men, they do not see
that the outside show means nothing; that all
23. depends upon the soul of man. They do the
easiest thing, the external thing; that which is
needful and difficult — love, compassion, truth
28. — they leave undone. It suffices them to be
only outwardly in the law, and to bring others
27. outwardly to the law. And therefore they, like
painted coffins, outwardly look clean, but are
30. an abomination within. They outwardly honor
31. the holy martyrs. But in very deed they are the

same as those who torture and kill the saints.
They were before, and are now, the enemies
of all good. From them comes all the evil
in the world; because they hide the good,
and instead of it uphold evil. Most of all to Mk. iii. 28
be feared, therefore, are self-called teachers.
Because you yourselves know every mistake
may be made good. But if people are mis- 29.
taken as to what good is, this mistake can
never be set right. And this is precisely the
condition of self-called leaders."

And Jesus said: "I wished, here in Jeru- Mt. xxiii. 37.
salem, to join all men in one understanding
of true happiness; but the people here are
only capable of putting to death the teachers
of good. And therefore they will remain the 38.
same godless people as they were, and will not
know the true God; until they shall lovingly 39.
welcome the understanding of God." And xxiv. 1.
Jesus went away from the temple.

Then his disciples said to him: "But what
will happen to this temple of God, with all its
embellishments which people have brought
into it, to give to God." And Jesus said: "I 2.
tell you truly, the whole of this temple, with
all its embellishments, shall be destroyed, and
nothing shall remain of it. There is one temple of God; that is, the hearts of men when
they love each other."

And they asked him: "When shall there be 3.
such a temple?" And Jesus said to them: 4.
"That will not be soon. People will yet long
be deceived in the name of my teaching, and
wars and rebellions will be the result. And 12.
there will be great lawlessness, and little love.
But when the true teaching shall spread among 14.
all men, then will be the end of evil and temptations."

CHAPTER X

THE WARFARE WITH TEMPTATION

Therefore, not to fall by temptation, we must, at every moment of life, be at one with the Father

("Lead us not into temptation")

Lk. xi. 53. AFTER this, the orthodox chief priests began
to do all they could to lay traps for Jesus, in
Jn. xi. 47. some way or other to destroy him. They gath-
48. ered in council, and began to consider. They
said: "This man must somehow or other be
put an end to. He so proves his teaching
that, if he be left alone, all will believe in him,
and cast off our belief. Already half of the
people believe in him. But if the Jews believe
in his teaching, that all men are sons of one
Father, and brothers, and that there is nothing
in our Hebrew people different from other peoples, then the Romans will completely over-
whelm us, and the Hebrew kingdom will be no
more."

Lk. xix. 47. And the orthodox high priest and learned
men for long counseled together, and could
48. not think what to do with Jesus. They could
not make up their minds to kill him.

Jn. xi. 49. Then one of them, Caiaphas, the chief priest
of that year, thought of the following device.
50. He said to the others: "You must remember
this: it is expedient to kill one man, that the
whole people may not perish. If we leave this
man alone, the people will perish; this I declare to you. Therefore it is better to kill
52. Jesus. Even if the people do not perish, they
will nevertheless go astray, departing from the
one belief, if we do not kill Jesus. Therefore
it is better to kill Jesus."

53. And when Caiaphas said this, they resolved

that there was no need to discuss, but that
Jesus must be killed without fail.
They would have taken Jesus at once and Jn. xi. 54
killed him, but he withdrew from them into
the desert. But at this time the feast of the 55.
Passover was approaching, when a great multitude always gathered in Jerusalem. And the 56.
orthodox high priests reckoned upon Jesus
coming with the people to the feast. And 57.
they made known to the people that if any one
should see Jesus he should bring him to them.
And it so happened that, six days before the xii. 1.
Passover, Jesus said to his disciples: "Let us xi. 7.
go to Jerusalem." And he went with them.
And the disciples said to him: "Do not go 8.
into Jerusalem. The high priests have resolved
now to stone you to death. If you come they
will kill you."
Jesus said to them: "I can fear nothing, 9.
because I live in the light of understanding.
And as every man, that he may not stumble,
walks by day and not by night, so every man,
that he may doubt nothing and fear nothing,
must live by this understanding. Only he 10.
doubts and fears who lives by the flesh; but
he who lives by understanding, for him there
is nothing doubtful or fearful."
And Jesus came to the village of Bethany, xii. 1.
near Jerusalem, and to the house of Martha
and Mary which was there.
Early in the morning Jesus went into Jeru- 12.
salem. There was a great crowd for the feast.
And when they recognized Jesus, they sur- 13.
rounded him, tore branches from the trees,
and threw their clothes before him on the
road, and all shouted: "Here is our true king,
he who has taught us the true God."
Jesus sat upon an ass's foal, riding, and the 14.
people ran before him and shouted; thus he
rode into Jerusalem. And when he had thus Mt. xxi. 10.

ridden into the town, the whole people were
Mt. xxi. 11. excited, and asked: "Who is he?" They who
knew him answered: "Jesus, the prophet of
Nazareth, in Galilee."

Mk. xi. 15. And Jesus went into the temple, and again
drove out thence all the buyers and sellers.

Jn. xii. 19. And the orthodox high priests saw all this,
and said to each other: "See what this man
is doing. The whole people are following
him."

Mk. xi. 18. But they did not dare to take him straight
from among the people, because they saw that
the people were gathering round him, and they
bethought them how to take him by cunning.

Jn. xii. 20. Meanwhile Jesus was in the temple, and
taught the people. Among the people, besides Jews, there were Greeks and heathen.
The Greeks heard of the teaching of Jesus, and
understood his teaching in this way, namely,
that he taught the truth, not only to Hebrews
21. but to all men. Therefore they wished to be
also his disciples, and spoke about this to
22. Philip. And Philip told this to Andrew.

These two disciples feared to bring Jesus together with the Greeks. They were afraid lest the people should be angry with Jesus, because he did not recognize any difference between Hebrews and other nations, and they long wavered about telling this to Jesus; but afterward both together told him, and hearing that the Greeks wished to be his followers, Jesus was troubled. He knew that the people hated him because he made no difference between the Hebrews and the heathen, but acknowledged himself to be the same as the heathen.

23. He said: "The hour is come to explain
what I understand by the Son of Man, though
I perish because, in explaining this, I destroy
distinction between Jews and heathen. I must

speak the truth. A grain of wheat will only Jn. xii. 24
bring forth fruit when it itself perishes. He 25.
who loves his fleshly life loses the true life, and
he who despises the fleshly life keeps it for the
everlasting life. He who wishes to follow my
teaching, let him do as I do. And he who 26.
does as I do shall be rewarded by my Father.
My soul is now wrestling. Shall I surrender 27.
myself to the compromises of temporary life,
or fulfil the will of the Father, now, at this
hour? And what then? Surely now, when
this hour is come in which I am living, I shall
not say: 'Father, save me from that which I
should do.' I cannot say this for the sake of
my life. And therefore I say: 'Father, show 28.
yourself in me.'"

And Jesus said: "Henceforth the present 31.
society of men is condemned to destruction.
From now that which rules this world shall be
destroyed. And when the Son of Man shall 32.
be exalted above the earthly life, then shall
he unite all in one."

Then the Jews said to him: "We under- 34.
stand from the law what the everlasting Christ
is; but why do you say that the Son of Man
shall be exalted? What is the meaning of
exalting the Son of Man?"

To this Jesus answered: "To exalt the 35.
Son of Man, means to live by the life of understanding that is in you. To exalt the Son 36.
of Man above that which is earthly, means to
believe in the light while there is light, in
order to be a son of understanding.

"He who believes in my teaching believes 44
not in me, but in that spirit which gave life
to the world. And he who understands my 45.
teaching, understands that spirit which gave
life to the world. But if any one hears my 47
words and does not fulfil them, it is not I who
blame him, seeing that I came, not to accuse,

Jn. xii. 48. but to save. He who does not accept my
words is accused, not by my teaching, but by
the understanding which is in himself. This
49. it is which accuses him. I did not speak of
myself, but said what my Father, the living
50. spirit in me, suggested to me. That which I
say, the spirit of understanding has told me,
and that which I teach is the true life."

36. And having said this, Jesus went away, and
again hid from the chief priests.

42. And of those who heard these words of
Jesus, many of the powerful and wealthy
people believed, but were afraid to acknowledge
it to the chief priests, because not one
of these priests believed and acknowledged it.
43. They were accustomed to judge according to
man, and not according to God.

Mt. xxvi. 3. After Jesus had hidden, the high priests and
the elders again met in the court of Caiaphas.
4. And they began to plan how to take Jesus
5. unknown to the people, for they were afraid
14. to seize him openly. And there came to their
council one of the first twelve disciples of
15. Jesus, Judas Iscariot, who said: "If you wish
to take Jesus secretly, so that the people may
not see, I will find a time when there will be
few people with him, and will show you where
he is; and then take him. But what will you
give me for this?" They promised him for
16. this thirty silver coins. He agreed; and from
that time began to seek an opportunity to bring
the chief priests upon Jesus, in order to take
him.

17. Meanwhile Jesus withdrew from the people,
and with him were only his disciples. When
the first feast of unleavened bread approached,
the disciples said to Jesus: "Where, then, shall
18. we keep the Passover?" And Jesus said: "Go
into some village, and enter some one's house,
and say that we have not time to prepare the

feast, and ask him to admit us to celebrate the
Passover." And the disciples did so; they Mt. xxvi. 19
asked a man in the village, and he invited them
in. And they came and sat down to the table, 20
Jesus and the twelve disciples, Judas among
them.

Jesus knew that Judas Iscariot had already Jn. xiii. 11.
promised to betray him to death, but he did
not accuse Judas for this, or show him ill-will,
but as in all his life he taught his disciples
love, so even now he only reproached Judas
lovingly. When they all twelve were seated Mt. xxvi. 21.
at table, he looked at them, and said: "Among Mk. xiv. 18.
you sits he who has betrayed me. Yes, he who Mt. xxvi. 23.
eats and drinks with me shall also destroy me."
And he said nothing more, so that they did not
know of whom he spoke, and they began to sup.

When they began to eat, Jesus took a loaf 26.
and broke it into twelve parts, and gave each
of the disciples a piece, and said: "Take and
eat, this is my body." And he then filled a 27.
cup with wine, handed it to the disciples, and
said: "Drink, all of you, of this cup." And
when they had all drunk, he said: "This is
my blood. I shed it that people may know 28.
my will, to forgive others their sins. For I Lk. xxii. 18
shall soon die, and be no more with you in this
world, but shall join you only in the kingdom
of heaven."

After this, Jesus got up from the table, girt Jn. xiii. 4.
himself with a towel, took a ewer of water, 5.
and began to wash the feet of all the disciples.
And he came to Peter; and Peter said: "But 6.
why will you wash my feet?" Jesus said to 7.
him: "It seems strange to you that I should
wash your feet; but you will know soon why I
do this. Though you are clean, yet not all of 10
you are so, but among you is my betrayer, to
whom I gave, with my own hand, bread and
wine, and whose feet I wish to wash."

Jn. xiii. 12. When Jesus had washed all their feet, he
again sat down, and said: "Do you understand
14. why I did this? It was so that you always
may do the same for each other. I, your
teacher, do this, that you may know how to
17. behave toward those who do you evil. If you
have understood this, and will do it, then you will
18. be happy. When I said that one of you will
betray me, I did not speak of all of you, because
only a single one of you, whose feet I washed,
and who ate bread with me, will betray me."

21. And having said this, Jesus was troubled in
spirit, and yet again said: "Yes, yes, one of
you will betray me."

22. And again the disciples began to look round
at each other, not knowing of whom he spoke.
23. One disciple sat near to Jesus, and Simon
24. Peter signed to him in a way to ask who
25. the betrayer was. The disciple asked. And
26. Jesus said: "I will soak a piece of bread, and
give it to him: and he to whom I shall give it
27. is my betrayer." And he gave the bread to
Judas Iscariot, and said to him: "What you
30. wish to do, do quickly." Then Judas understood that he must go out, and as soon as he had
taken the bread he forthwith went out. And
it was impossible to follow him, as it was night.

31. And when Judas was gone out, Jesus said:
"It is now clear to you what the Son of Man
is. It is now clear to you that in him God is,
to make him as blessed as God Himself.

33. "Children! I have not long now to be with
you. Do not equivocate over my teaching, as
I said to the orthodox, but do that which I do.
34. I give you this, a new commandment. As I
always, and to the end, have loved you all, do
you always, and to the end, love each other.
35. By this only will you be distinguished. Seek
to be only thus distinguished from other
people. Love one another."

And after this, they went to the Mount of Mt. xxvi. 30.
Olives.
And on the way Jesus said to them: "See, 31.
the time is coming when that shall happen
which is written, the shepherd shall be killed,
and all the sheep shall be scattered. And
to-night this shall happen. I shall be taken,
and you will all abandon me, and scatter."
Peter said to him in answer: "Even if all 33.
shall be frightened, and scatter, I will not deny
you. I am ready for prison and for death with
you."
And Jesus said to him: "But I tell you that 34.
this very night, before cock-crow, after I have
been taken, you will deny me, not once, but
thrice."
But Peter said that he would not deny him; 35.
and the other disciples averred the same.
Then Jesus said to the disciples: "Before, Lk. xxii. 35.
neither I nor you had need of anything. You
went without wallet and without change of
shoes, and I so bade you do. But now, if I 36.
am accounted an outlaw, we can no longer do
so, but we must be furnished with everything,
and with swords, that we may not perish in
vain."
And the disciples said: "See, we have two 38.
swords."
Jesus said: "It is well."
And having said this, Jesus went with the fol- Mt. xxvi. 36.
lowers into the garden of Gethsemane. Com- Jn. xviii. 1.
ing into the garden, he said: "Wait you here,
but I wish to pray."
And while near to Peter and the two brothers, Mt. xxvi. 37.
sons of Zebedee, he began to feel weary and sad,
and he said to them: "I feel very sad and my 38.
soul is full of the anguish before death. Wait
here, and be not cast down as I am."
And he went off a little way, lay on the ground 39.
on his face, and began to pray, and said: "My

Father, the Spirit! Let it be not as I will, which
is that I should not die, but let it be as Thou
wilt. Let me die, but for Thee, as a spirit, all is
possible; let it be that I may not fear death, that
I may escape the temptation of the flesh."
Mt. xxvi. 40. And then he arose, went up to the disciples,
and saw that they were cast down. And he
said to them: "How is it you have not strength
for one hour to keep up your spirit even as I!
41. Keep up your spirit, so as not to fall into the
temptation of the flesh. The spirit is strong,
the flesh is weak."
42. And again Jesus went away from them, and
again began to pray, and said: "Father, if I
must suffer, must die, and am about to die, then
43. so let it be. Let Thy will be done." And having said this, he again went up to the disciples,
and saw that they were still more cast down,
and ready to weep.
44. And he again went away from them, and the
third time said: "Father, let Thy will be done."
45. Then he returned to the disciples, and said to
them: "Now be easy, and be calm, because it
is now decided that I shall give myself into the
hands of worldly men."

CHAPTER XI

THE FAREWELL DISCOURSE

The self-life is an illusion which comes through the flesh, an evil. The true life is the life common to all men

("Deliver us from evil")

Jn. xiii. 36. AND Peter said to Jesus: "Whither are you
going?"

Jesus answered: "You will not have the
strength now to go whither I am going; but
afterward you will go the same way."

And Peter said: "Why do you think that I Jn. xiii. 37
have not the strength now to follow whither you
go? I will give up my life for you."
And Jesus said: "You say that you will give 38
up your life for me, and yet even before cock-
crow you shall deny me thrice." And Jesus xiv. 1.
said to the disciples: "Be not troubled and be
not afraid, but believe in the true God of life,
and in my teaching.
"The life of the Father is not only that which 2.
is on earth, but there is another life also. If 3.
there were only such a life as the life here, I
would say to you, that when I die I shall go
into Abraham's bosom, and make ready a place
there for you, and I shall come and take you,
and we shall together live happily in Abraham's
bosom. But I point out to you only the direc- 4.
tion to life."
Thomas said: "But we do not know whither 5.
you go, and therefore we cannot know the way.
We want to know what there will be after death."
Jesus said: "I cannot show you what will be 6.
there; my teaching is the way, and the truth,
and the life. And it is impossible to be joined
with the Father of life otherwise than through
my teaching. If you fulfil my teaching, you 7.
shall know the Father."
Philip said: "But who is the Father?" 8.
And Jesus said: "The Father is He who gives 9.
life. I have fulfilled the will of the Father, and
therefore by my life you may know wherein is
the will of the Father. I live by the Father, 10.
and the Father lives in me. All that I say and 11.
do, I do by the will of the Father. My teaching
is, that I am in the Father and the Father is in
me. If you do not understand my teaching, yet
you see me and my works. And therefore you
may understand what the Father is. And you 12.
know that he who shall follow my teaching may
do the same as I; and yet more, because I shall

Jn xiv. 13. die, but he will still live. He who shall live
according to my teaching, shall have all that he
wishes, because then the Son will be one with
14. the Father. Whatever you may wish that
accords with my teaching, all that you shall
15. have. But for this you must love my teaching.
16. My teaching will give you, in my place, an in-
17. tercessor and comforter. This comforter will be
the consciousness of truth, which worldly men
do not understand; but you will know it in your-
18. selves. You never will be alone, if the spirit of
19. my teaching is with you. I shall die, and
worldly men will not see me; but you will see
me because my teaching lives and you will live
20. by it. And then, if my teaching shall be in you,
you will understand that I am in the Father and
21. the Father in me. He who shall fulfil my teaching, shall feel in himself the Father; and in him
my spirit shall live."

22. And Judas, not Iscariot, but another, said to
him: "But why, then, may not all live by the
spirit of truth?"

23. Jesus said in answer: "Only he who fulfils
my teaching, only him the Father loves, and in
24. him only can my spirit abide. He who does
not fulfil my teaching, him my Father cannot
love, because this teaching is not mine, but the
25. Father's. This is all that I can tell you now.
26. But my spirit, the spirit of truth, which shall
take up its abode in you after I am gone, shall
reveal to you all, and you shall recall and
understand much of that which I have told
27. you. So that you may always be calm in spirit,
not with that worldly calm which men of the
world seek, but with that calm of spirit in
28. which we no longer fear anything. On this
account, if you fulfil my teaching, you have no
reason to grieve over my death. I, as the
spirit of truth, will come to you, and, together
with the knowledge of the Father, will take up

my abode in your heart. If you fulfil my
teaching, then you must rejoice, because instead of me you will have the Father with you
in your heart, and this is better for you.
"My teaching is the tree of life. The Father Jn. xv. 1
is He who tends the tree. He prunes and 2
cherishes those branches upon which there is
fruit, that they may yield more. Keep my 4
teaching of life, and life will be in you. And
as a shoot lives not of itself, but out of the
tree, so do you live by my teaching. My 5
teaching is the tree, you are the shoots. He
who lives by my teaching of life yields much
fruit; and without my teaching there is no
life. He who does not live by my teaching 6
withers and dies; and the dry branches are cut
off and burnt.
"If you will live by my teaching, and fulfil it, 7
then you shall have all that you desire. Be- 8
cause the will of the Father is, that you may
live the true life and have that which you desire. As the Father gave me happiness, so I 9
give you happiness. Hold to this happiness.
I am living, because the Father loves me and 10
I love the Father; do you also live by the
same love. If you will live by this, you shall 11
be blessed.
"My commandment is, that you love one 12
another as I have loved you. There is no 13
greater love than to sacrifice one's life for the
love of one's own, as I have done.
"You are my equals, if you do that which I 14
have taught you. I do not hold you as slaves, 15
to whom orders are given, but as equals; because I have made clear to you all that I have
known of the Father. You do not, of your 16
own will, choose my teaching; but because I
have pointed out to you that only truth by which
you will live, and from which you will have all
that you wish.

Jn. xv. 17. "The teaching is summed up in this — Love
one another.
18. "If the world should hate you, then do not
19. wonder; it hates my teaching. If you were
at one with the world, it would love you. But
I have severed you from the world, and for
20. that it will hate you. If they persecuted me,
21. they will persecute you also. They will do
all this, because they do not know the true
22. God. I explained to them, but they did not
23. wish to hear me. They did not understand
my teaching, because they did not under-
24. stand the Father. They saw my life, and my
25. life showed them their error. And for this
26. they still more hated me. The spirit of truth
which shall come to you will confirm this
27. to you. And you will accept it. I tell you
xvi. 1. this beforehand, so that you may not be
deceived when persecutions shall be upon
2. you. You shall be made outcasts; men shall
think that in killing you they do God's pleas-
3. ure. All this they cannot help doing, because they understand neither my teaching
4. nor the true God. All this I tell you beforehand, so that you may not wonder when it
comes about.
5. "Well then, I now go away to that Spirit
which sent me; and now you understand, you
6. need not ask me whither I go. But before,
you were grieved that I did not tell you whither,
to what place, I depart.
7. "But I tell you truly that it is well for you
that I am going. If I do not die, the spirit of
truth will not appear to you, but if I die, it
8. will take up its abode in you. It will take
up its abode in you, and it will be clear
to you where untruth is, where truth is,
9. and how to make decision. Untruth, in
that people do not believe in the life of the
10. spirit. Truth, in that I am one with the

Father. Decision, in that the power of Jn. xvi. 11.
the fleshly life is at an end.
"I would say yet much more to you, but it 12.
is difficult for you to understand. But when 13.
the spirit of truth dwells in you, it will show
you the whole truth, because it will tell you,
not a new thing of its own, but that which is
of God; and it will show you the way in all
concerns of life. It also will be from the 15.
Father, as I am from the Father; therefore it
also will tell you the same as I tell you.
"But when I, the spirit of truth, shall be in 16.
you, you will not always see me. Sometimes
you will, and sometimes you will not, hear
me."
And the disciples said one to another: 17.
"What does he mean when he says: 'Sometimes you will see me, sometimes you will not
see me.' What means this, 'Sometimes you 18.
will, sometimes you will not'?"
Jesus said to them: "Do you not under- 19.
stand what this means, 'Sometimes you will,
sometimes you will not, see me'? You know 20.
how it always is in the world, that some are
sad and grieved, while others rejoice. And
you will grieve, but your grief will pass into
joy. A woman, when she bears, grieves while 21.
she is in the pangs of childbirth; but when
that is ended, she does not remember the pangs,
for joy that a man is born into the world. And 22.
so you will grieve; anon you will see me, the
spirit of truth will enter into you, and your
grief will be turned into joy. Then you will 23.
no longer ask anything of me, because you will
have all that you wish. Then all which one of
you desires in the spirit, all that he will have
from his Father.
"You formerly asked for nothing for the 24.
spirit; but now ask what you will for the
spirit, and you will have all; so that your

Jn. xvi. 25. bliss will be full. Now I, as a man, cannot
tell you this clearly in words, but when I, as
the spirit of truth, shall live in you, I will
proclaim to you clearly about the Father.
26. Then it will not be I who will give you all you
ask of the Father in the name of the spirit.
27. But the Father will Himself give, because He
loves you for having received my teaching.
28. You have understood that understanding proceeds
from the Father into the world and returns
from the world to the Father."

29. Then the disciples said to Jesus: "Now
we have understood everything, and have
30. nothing more to ask, we believe that you are
from God."

33. And Jesus said: "All that I have said to
you is in order that you may have confidence
and rest in my teaching. Whatever ills may
befall you in the world, fear nothing: my
teaching will conquer the world."

xvii. 1. After this, Jesus raised his eyes to heaven,
and said:

"My Father! Thou hast given Thy Son
the freedom of life in order that he may re-
3. ceive the true life. Life is the knowledge of
the true God of the understanding, Who is
6. discovered to me. I have discovered Thee to
4. men on earth; I have done that work which
Thou hast bidden me do. I have shown Thy
6. being to men on earth. They were Thine
before, but by Thy will I have discovered to
7. 8. them the truth, and they know Thee. They
have understood that all they have, their life,
is from Thee only, and that I have taught
them, not of myself, but as proceeding, I with
9. them, from Thee. But I pray to Thee for
10. 11. those who acknowledge Thee. They have
understood that all that I have is Thine, and
all that is Thine is mine. I am no longer in the
world, for I return to Thee; but they are in

the world, and therefore I pray Thee, Father,
to preserve in them Thy understanding. I do Jn. xvii. 15
not pray Thee to remove them from the world,
but to free them from evil; to confirm them 17, 18.
in Thy truth. Thy understanding is the truth.
My Father! I wish them to be as I am; to 21.
understand as I do, that the true life began
before the beginning of the world. That they
should all be one; as Thou, Father, art in me,
and I in Thee, so they may also be one in me.
I in them, Thou in me, so that all may be one; 23.
so that all men may understand they are not
self-created, but that Thou, in love, hast sent
them into the world as Thou didst send me.
Father of truth! the world did not know Thee, 25.
but I knew Thee, and they have known Thee
through me. And I have made plain to them 26.
what Thou art. Thou art in me, that the
love with which Thou hast loved me may be
in them also. Thou gavest them life, and
therefore didst love them. I have taught them
to know this, and to love Thee; so that Thy
love might be returned from them to Thee."

CHAPTER XII

THE VICTORY OF THE SPIRIT OVER THE FLESH

Therefore, for him who lives, not the self-life, but a common life in the will of the Father, there is no death. Bodily death is for him union with the Father

("Thine is the kingdom, power, and glory")

AFTER this, Jesus said: "Now arise, and Mt. xxvi. 46
let us go; already he is coming who will betray me."

And he had hardly said this, when suddenly 47
Judas, one of the twelve disciples, appeared,
and with him a great throng of people with

Mt. xxvi. 48. sticks and swords. Judas said to them: "I
will bring you where he and his followers are.
and so that you may know him among them
all, he whom I shall first kiss, that is he."
49. And he straightway went up to Jesus, and
said: "Hail, teacher!" and kissed him.
50. And Jesus said to him: "Friend, why are
you here?"

Then the guard surrounded Jesus, and wished to take him.

51. And Peter snatched the sword from the
high priest's servant, and slashed the man's
ear.
52. But Jesus said: "You must not oppose
evil. Cease." And he said to Peter: "Return the sword to him from whom you took
it; he who shall draw the sword, shall perish
with the sword."
55. And after this, Jesus turned to the crowd,
and said: "Why have you come out against
me, as against a robber, with arms? I was
every day among you in the temple, and taught
Lk. xxii. 53. you, and you did not take me. But now is
your hour, and the power of darkness."
Mt. xxvi. 56. Then, having seen that he was taken, all the
disciples ran away.
Jn. xviii. 12. And the officer ordered the soldiers to take
Jesus, and bind him. The soldiers bound him,
13. and took him first to Annas. This was the
father-in-law of Caiaphas, and Caiaphas was
the high priest for that year, and lived in the
14. same house with Annas. This was the same
Caiaphas who planned how to destroy Jesus.
He held that it was good for the sake of the
people to destroy Jesus, because, if that were
not done, it would be worse for the whole peo-
Mk. xiv. 53. ple. And they took Jesus to the house where
this high priest lived.
Mt. xxvi. 58. When they had brought Jesus thither, one
of his disciples, Peter, followed him from afar,

and watched where they were taking him.
When they brought Jesus into the court of the
high priest, Peter went in also, to see how all
would end. And a girl in the yard saw Peter, Mt. xxvi. 69
and said to him: "You, also, were with Jesus
of Galilee." Then Peter was afraid that they 70.
would accuse him also, and he said aloud before all the people: "I do not know what you
are talking about." Afterward, when they 71.
had taken Jesus into the house, Peter also
entered the hall, with the people. In the hall,
a woman was warming herself at the fire, and
Peter approached. The woman looked at Peter,
and said to the people: "See, this man is likely
to have been with Jesus of Nazareth." Peter 72.
was still more frightened, and swore that he
never was with him, and did not even know
what kind of a man Jesus was. A little while 73.
after, the people came up to Peter, and said:
"It is quite clear that you also were among the
disturbers. By your speech one may know that
you are from Galilee." Then Peter began to 74.
swear, and aver that he had never known or
seen Jesus.

And he had hardly said this, when the cock 75.
crew. And Peter remembered those words
which Jesus had said to him, when Peter swore
that if all denied Jesus, he would not deny him:
"Before the cock crow this night, you will deny
me thrice." And Peter went out, and cried
bitterly. Jesus had prayed that he might not
thus fall into temptation. He had fallen into
one temptation, that of strife, when he began
to defend Jesus; and into another temptation,
the fear of death, when he denied Jesus.

And there gathered to the high priest, the Mk xiv. 53.
orthodox chief priests, assistants, and officials.
And when all were assembled, they brought in Jn. xviii. 19
Jesus; and the chief priests asked him, what
was his teaching, and who were his followers.

Jn. xviii. 20. And Jesus answered: "I always said all I
had to say before everybody openly, and so
I speak now; I concealed nothing from any
21. one, and I conceal nothing now. But about
what do you question me? Question those
who heard and understood my teaching. They
will tell you."

22. When Jesus had said this, one of the high
priest's servants struck him in the face, and
said: "To whom are you speaking? Is this
the way to answer the high priest?"

23. Jesus said: "If I spoke ill, say what I spoke
ill. But if I said nothing ill, then there is no
cause to beat me."

Mt. xxvi. 59. The orthodox chief priests strove to accuse
Jesus, and at first did not find any proofs against
him for which it was possible to condemn him.
60, Afterward they found two witnesses. These
61. said about Jesus: "We ourselves heard how
this man said: 'I will destroy this temple of
yours made with hands, and in three days will
build up another temple to God, not made with
59. hands.'" But this evidence, also, was not
62. enough to condemn him. And therefore the
high priest called up Jesus, and said: "Why
do you not answer their evidence?"

63. Jesus held his tongue, saying nothing. Then
the high priest said to him: "Well, say then,
Are you the Christ, and of God?"

64. Jesus answered him, and said: "Yes, I am
the Christ, and of God. You yourselves will
now see that the Son of Man is made like God."

65. Then the high priest cried out: "You blas-
pheme! Now we do not want any evidence.
We all hear, now, that you are a blasphemer."
66. And the high priest turned to the assembly,
and said: "You have yourselves heard that
he blasphemes God. To what do you sentence
him for this?"

And all said: "We sentence him to death."

Then all the people, and the guards, fell Mt. xxvi. 67
upon Jesus, and began to spit in his face, to
strike him on the cheeks, and to tear at him.
They covered his eyes, hit him in the face,
and asked: "Now, prophet, guess who it was 68.
that hit you?"

But Jesus held his peace.

Having abused him, they took him, bound, xxvii. 2.
to Pontius Pilate. And they brought him into Jn. xviii. 28.
the court.

Pilate, the governor, came out to them and 29.
asked: "Of what do you accuse this man?"

They said: "This man is doing wrong, so 30.
we have brought him to you."

And Pilate said to them: "But if he does 31.
wrong, then judge him yourselves according
to your law."

And they said: "We have brought him to
you that you might execute him, for we are
not allowed to kill any one."

And so that happened which Jesus expected. 32.
He said that one must be ready to die on the
cross at the hands of the Romans, more likely
than at the hands of the Jews.

And when Pilate asked, whereof they accused Lk. xxiii. 2.
him, they said, that he was guilty of stirring up
the people, and that he forbade the payment
of taxes to Cæsar, and that he set up himself
as Christ and king.

Pilate listened to them, and bade Jesus be Jn. xviii. 33.
brought to him in the court. When Jesus
came in, Pilate said to him: "So you are king
of the Jews?"

Jesus said to him: "Do you really suppose 34.
that I am a king, or are you repeating only
that which others have told you?"

Pilate said: "I am not a Jew, therefore you 35.
cannot be my king, but your people have
brought you to me. What kind of a man are
you?"

Jn. xviii. 36. Jesus answered: "I am a king; but my kingdom is not an earthly one. If I were an earthly king, my subjects would fight for me, and would not yield to the high priests. But as it is, you see that my kingdom is not an earthly one."

37. Pilate said to this: "But yet, do you not consider yourself a king?" Jesus said: "Not only I, but you also, cannot but consider me a king. For I only teach, in order to discover to all the truth of the kingdom of heaven. And every one who lives by the truth, is a king."

38. Pilate said: "You spoke of truth. What is truth?"

And having said this, he turned, and went to the chief priests. He went out and said to them: "In my opinion, this man has done no wrong."

Mk. xv. 3. But the chief priests insisted upon their opinion, and said that he was doing much evil, and stirring up the people, and had raised the whole of Judea right from Galilee.

4. Then Pilate, in the presence of the chief priests, began to question Jesus. But Jesus did not answer. Pilate then said to him: "Do you hear of what they accuse you? Why do you not justify yourself?"

5. But Jesus still held his tongue, and said not another word, so that Pilate wondered at him.

Lk. xxiii. 6. Pilate remembered that Galilee was in the power of King Herod, and asked: "Ah! he is from Galilee?" They answered: "Yes."

7. Then he said: "If he is from Galilee, then he is under the authority of Herod, and I will send him to him." Herod was then in Jerusalem, and Pilate, in order to rid himself, sent Jesus to Herod.

8. When they brought Jesus to Herod, Herod was very glad to see him. He had heard much

of him, and wished to know what kind of man
he was. So he called Jesus to him, and began Lk. xxiii. 9.
to question him about all he wished to know.
But Jesus answered him nothing. And the 10.
chief priests and teachers, just as with Pilate,
so before Herod, vehemently accused Jesus,
and said that he was a rioter. And Herod 11.
deemed Jesus an empty fellow, and to mock
him, bade them clothe him in red, and send
him back to Pilate. Herod was pleased at 12.
Pilate's showing respect to him, by sending
Jesus for his judgment, and on this account
they became friends, whereas formerly they
had been at variance.

Now, when they brought Jesus again to 13.
Pilate, Pilate called back the chief priests
and Jewish authorities, and said to them:
"You brought this man to me for stirring 14.
up the people, and I have examined him
before you, and do not see that he is a rioter.
I sent him with you to Herod, and now, see, 15.
—nothing wrong is found in him. And, in
my opinion, there is no cause to punish him
with death. Had you not better punish him
and let him go?"

But when the chief priests heard this, all Mt. xxvii. 23.
cried out: "No, punish him in the Roman
fashion! Stretch him on the cross!" Pilate 21.
heard them out, and said to the chief priests:
"Well, as you will! But you have a custom
at the feast of the Passover to pardon one
condemned malefactor. Well, I have lying
in prison, Barabbas, a murderer and rioter.
Which one of the two must be let free:
Jesus or Barabbas?"

Pilate thus wished to save Jesus; but the
chief priests had so worked upon the people,
that all cried out: "Barabbas, Barabbas!"

And Pilate said: "And what shall be done 22.
with Jesus?"

They again cried out: "Roman fashion,—
to the cross, to the cross with him."
Mt.xxvii. 23. And Pilate tried to talk them over. He said:
"Why do you press so hardly on him? He
has done nothing that he should be punished
Jn. xix. 4. with death, and he has done you no harm. I
will set him free, because I find no fault in him."
6. The chief priests and their servants cried
out: "Crucify, crucify him!"
And Pilate said to them: "If so, then take
him and crucify him yourselves. But I see no
fault in him."
7. The chief priests answered: "We ask only
that which our law demands. By our law, he
must be executed for having made himself out
to be Son of God."
8. When Pilate heard this word, he was
troubled, because he did not know what this
9. term "Son of God" meant. And having
returned into the court, Pilate called up Jesus
again, and asked him: "Who are you, and
whence are you?"
But Jesus did not answer.
10. Then Pilate said: "But why do you not
answer me? You surely see that you are in
my power, and that I can crucify you, or set
you free."
11. Jesus answered him: "You have no power.
There is power only from above."
12. Pilate, nevertheless, wished to set Jesus free,
15. and he said to them: "How is it you wish to
crucify your king?"
12. But the Jews said to him: "If you set Jesus
free, you will thereby show that you are a dis-
loyal servant to Cæsar, because he who sets
himself up as king is an enemy to Cæsar.
15. Our king is Cæsar; but crucify this man."
13. And when Pilate heard these words, he
understood that he could now no longer
refuse to execute Jesus.

Then Pilate went out before the Jews, took Mt.xxvii. 24
some water, washed his hands, and said: "I
am not guilty of the blood of this just man."
And the whole people cried out: "Let his 25.
blood be upon us and all our children."

So that the chief priests gained the upper Lk. xxiii. 23.
hand. And Pilate sat in his place of judgment, Jn. xix. 13.
and ordered Jesus to be first flogged. Mt. xxvii. 26.

When they had flogged him, the soldiers, 28,
who had done this, put a crown upon his head 29.
and a rod in his hand, and threw a red cloak
over his back, and fell to reviling him; in
mockery, they bowed down to his feet, and
said: "Hail, king of the Jews!" And others
struck him on the cheeks, over the face, and
spat in his face.

But the chief priests cried: "Crucify him! Jn. xix. 15.
Our king is Cæsar! Crucify him!"

And Pilate bade him be crucified. 16.

Then they stripped Jesus of the red dress, Mt. xxvii. 31.
put on him his own clothing, and bade him
bear the cross to a place called Golgotha, there
to be crucified at once. And he carried his Jn. xix. 18.
cross, and so came to Golgotha. And there
they stretched Jesus on the cross, beside two
other men. These two were at the sides, and
Jesus was in the middle.

When they had crucified Jesus, he said: Lk. xxiii. 34.
"Father! forgive them; they do not know what
they are doing."

And when Jesus was hung on the cross, the 35.
people thronged round him and railed at him.
They came up, wagged their heads at him, and Mk. xv. 29.
said: "So, you wish to destroy the temple of
Jerusalem, and to build it up again in three
days. Well now, save yourself, come down from 30.
the cross!" And the chief priests and leaders 31.
stood there also, and mocked at him, and said:
"He thought to save others, but cannot save
himself. Now show that you are Christ; come 32.

down from the cross, and then we will believe you. He said that he was the Son of God, and that God would not forsake him. But how is it that God has now forsaken him?" And the people, and the chief priests, and the soldiers, railed at him, and even one of the robbers crucified with him, he too railed at him.

Lk. xxiii. 39. One of the robbers, reviling him, said: "If you are Christ, save yourself and us."

40. But the other robber heard this and said:
"Do you not fear God? You who are yourself on the cross, do you even rail at the inno-
41. cent? You and I are executed for our deserts,
but this man has done no harm."

42. And, turning to Jesus, this robber said to him: "Lord, remember me in your kingdom."

43. And Jesus said to him: "Even now you are blessed with me!"

Mt. xxvii. 46. But at the ninth hour, Jesus, worn out, cried aloud: "Eloi, Eloi, lama sabachthani!" This means: "My God, my God! why hast Thou forsaken me?"

47. And when the people heard this, they began to say jeeringly: "He is calling the prophet Elias! Let us see whether Elias will come!"

Jn. xix. 28. Afterward, Jesus cried out: "Let me drink!"

And a man took a sponge, soaked it in vinegar, that stood by, and gave it to Jesus on a reed.

30. Jesus sucked the sponge, and cried out in a
loud voice: "It is finished! Father, I give up
Lk. xxiii. 46. my spirit into your hands!" And, letting his
head fall, he gave up the ghost.

A PROLOGUE

THE UNDERSTANDING OF LIFE

The proclamation of Christ has replaced the belief in an external God by the understanding of life

THE Gospel is the revelation of this truth, that the first source of everything is the understanding of life itself. This being so, the Gospel puts in the place of what men call "God" a right understanding of life. Without this understanding there is no life; men only live in so far as they understand life.

Those who do not grasp this, and who deem that the body is the source of life, shut themselves out from true life; but those who comprehend that they live, not through the body, but through the spirit, possess true life. This is that true life which Jesus Christ came to teach to men. Having conceived that man's life flows from the understanding, he gave to men the teaching and example of a life of the understanding in the body.

Earlier religions were the announcements of law as to what men ought to do, and not to do, for the service of God. The teaching of Jesus, on the other hand, deals only with the understanding of life. No man has ever seen, and no man can see or know, an external God; therefore our life cannot take for its aim the service of such a God. Only by adopting for his supreme principle the inner understanding of life, having for its source the acknowledgment of God, can man surely travel the way of life.

Mk. i. 1. The announcement of salvation of Jesus
Jn. xx. 31. Christ, the Son of God. This is the announcement of salvation; all men who come to know
i. 1. they are sons of God receive true life. The foundation and beginning of all things is the understanding of life. Understanding of life
2. is God. This the announcement of Jesus Christ reveals as the foundation and beginning
3. of everything. All is built upon the understanding of life, without which there can be
4. no living. In this is true life.
5. This understanding is the light of truth. But this light shines amid the darkness, and
9. the darkness is not able to overcome it. The true light has always been in the world, and shines upon all men who come into the world.
10. It has been in the world, and the world existed only because it contained this light; but the
11. world has not adhered to it. This light has appeared in its place, but its place has not retained it.
12. All those who have grasped the understanding of life have received the opportunity of
13. becoming like it through belief in it. Those who have believed that life is in the understanding have become the sons, not of the flesh, but of the understanding.
14. And the understanding of life was united with the flesh in the person of Jesus Christ, and so we were given to know that the offspring of understanding, man in the flesh, is of the same nature as his Father, the original source of life.
15. The teaching of Jesus is the perfect and
16. true faith. In fulfilling the teaching of Jesus, we have understood the new faith which re-

places the old. It was law that Moses gave, Jn. i. 17.
but we come to understand the true faith
through Jesus Christ.

No man has ever seen God; the Son only, 18.
who is in the Father, has shown us the way
of life.

A SUMMARY

THE UNDERSTANDING OF LIFE IS TO DO GOOD

The announcement of blessedness made by Jesus Christ is an announcement of understanding of life

THE understanding of life is this: The source of life is perfect goodness, and therefore human life is perfectly good in its nature. To understand the source of life, it is necessary to believe that our spirit, the life in man, came from this source. The man, formerly not living, is summoned into life by this, his origin. This source of life appoints blessedness for man, because its own being is blessedness.

To keep in harmony with the source of his life, a man must fix himself upon the one characteristic of this source which is comprehensible to him, and which finds blessedness in doing good. Therefore man's life must be devoted to this blessedness; that is, to doing good from love. But we can find no objects of goodness other than men. All our own bodily desires are out of harmony with this principle of blessedness; and therefore they, with all the life of the body, must be surrendered to the principle of blessedness, to active love to mankind.

Love to our fellow-men follows from the understanding of life revealed by Jesus Christ. The confirmations of this understanding of life are twofold. One is, that when not accepted, the source of life seems to be an impostor, who gives to men an unsatisfied craving for life and blessedness. The other is, that man feels in his soul that love and goodness toward his fellow-men is the only true, free, eternal life.

The First Epistle of John the Divine

This is the announcement of the understand- 1 Jn. i. 1-3
ing of life through which men have fellowship
with the Father of life, and therefore have
eternal life.
This is an announcement of blessedness. 4.
The understanding of life is, that God is life 5.
and blessedness, and that in life and blessedness death and evil do not exist.
If we say that we are at one with God, while 6.
we feel we are living in evil and death, then
either we are imposing upon ourselves, or we
are not doing what we ought to do.
Only by living the same life as His, do we 7.
become at one with Him.
As a teacher of this life, we have Jesus ii. 1.
Christ, the right-living. He freed us and all 2.
who will, from wrong-living.
The proof that we know the teaching of 3.
Jesus Christ is, that we carry out his commandments. Any one who says he knows the teach- 4.
ing of Jesus Christ, and does not keep his
commandments, is a liar, and there is no truth
in him. But the man who carries out his 5.
commandments has the love of God in him.
Only through love can we know that we are
at one with God.
He who says he is at one with Jesus Christ, 6.
must also live as Jesus lived.
He who says of himself that he is in life 9-11.
and blessedness, but hates his living brother-
man, is not in life and blessedness, but in

death and evil; and he does not know what
he is doing; he is blind, hating the life which
is in himself also.

1 Jn. ii. 15. To escape this blindness, a man must remember that everything in the world, in the
earthly life, is the desire of the flesh, or vanity,
and that all this is not from God. And that
16. all this passes away, perishes. And that only
17. he who does the will of God, which is love,
endures for ever.

23. Only he who recognizes that his spirit is
the offspring of the Father, is united with the
24. Father. Therefore remain in the knowledge
that you are, in the spirit, sons of the Father,
God, and you will have eternal life.

iii. 1. God gives us the opportunity of being His
sons, and like Himself. So that, in this present
2. life, we become His sons. We do not know
what we are to be, but we know that we
are like Him, and that we are united with
Him.

3. Confidence in this eternal life rids us of our
mistakes, and purifies us to the Father's purity.
4. For whoever commits sin, violates the will of
God.

5. Jesus Christ came to teach us the way to
deliverance from sin, and unity with God.
6. Therefore those who become united with
Him can no longer sin. Only that man will
7. sin who does not know Him. But he who
8. lives in God, acts righteously; and only he
9. who is not united with God, does unright-
eously. He who owns his origin from God,
cannot do any falsehood.

10. Therefore men are of two classes — men of
God, and men who are not of God; men who
know the right and love the brethren, and
men who do not know the right and do not
love the brethren.

11. For, following the teaching of Jesus Christ,

we cannot refrain from loving one another.
Through the teaching of Jesus Christ, we 1 Jn. iii 14.
know that we have passed from death to life,
because we love the brethren, and that he who
does not love his brother is in death. We 15.
know that one who does not love his living
brother does not love life. And he who does
not love life cannot himself possess life.

By this teaching we recognize love, in the 16.
fact that life is given to us; and we know,
therefore, that we also must give up our life
for our brother. So that he who, himself 17.
having the means of life, sees his brother in
need, and does not yield his own life for his
brother's sake, — in him there is no divine
love.

We must love, not by words, but by deeds, 18.
in truth. And he who so loves has a quiet 19.
heart, because he is at one with God.

If our heart is at strife in us, we subdue it 20.
to God. For God is higher than the wishes 21.
of our hearts. But if there is no strife in our
hearts, then we are blessed, and that because 22.
we do all we can, the best deeds, and fulfil all
that is ordained for us.

And this is ordained for us — to believe that 23.
man is the son of God, and to love our brother.
Those who do this are united with God, and iv. 4.
are risen above the world, because that which
is in us is greater, of more consequence, than
all the world.

Therefore let us love one another. Love is 7.
from God, and every one who loves is the son
of God, and knows God. And he who does 8.
not love, does not know God. Because God
is love.

That God is love, we know because He sent 9.
into the world this Spirit, such as He Himself is, and thereby gave us life. We did not 10.
exist, and God was under no compulsion, but

He gave us life and blessedness; therefore
He must love us.
1 Jn. iv. 11. No man can perfectly know God. All we
13. can know of Him is, that He had love toward
us, and because of this love gave us life. And
to be in fellowship with God, we must be like
Him, and do as He does; we must love one
another. If we love one another, God dwells
in us, and we dwell in Him.
16. Having understood the love of God toward
us, we believe that God is love, and that he
17. who loves is united with God. And having
understood this, we do not fear death, because
in this world we become such as God Himself
18. is. Our life becomes love, and is thus freed
from fear and all sufferings.
19. We love, because He loves. And we love
not a God whom no one can love, because no
one sees Him, but our brother-man, whom it is
20. possible to love. He who says he loves God,
and yet hates his brother, is deceiving himself.
Because, if he does not love the brother whom
he sees, how, then, can he love God whom he
21. does not see? For it is ordained to us to love
God in our brother.
v. 3. To love God, is to fulfil His commandments.
And these commandments are not hard for
4. him who, recognizing that his origin is from
5. God, rises above the world. Our faith lifts us
above the world. And our faith in that which
Jesus, the Son of God, taught us, is true. He
has taught us that he lived in the world, not
merely in the way of truth, but by the power
6. of the spirit. And that spirit is in us, and
makes us strong in truth, following out the
teaching.
9. If we believe in what men affirm, why, then,
should we not believe in the spirit that is in
10. ourselves? He who believes in that spirit of
life which is in us, has assurance within him-

self. And he who does not believe that there is a spirit from above us, from the Father, makes God a deceiver.

The spirit in us affirms that our life is eter- 1 Jn. v. 11.
nal. He who knows that this spirit is the off- 12.
spring of the Infinite Spirit, and becomes like
Him, has eternal life. And for him who so 14.
believes, there is no difficulty left in his life,
but everything he desires in the will of the
Father will come to him.

Therefore he who believes himself to be a 18.
son of God, will not live in any deception, but
is free from evil. Because he knows that this 19.
material world is an illusion, and that in man 20.
himself there is the capacity to know that which
has real existence. And only the Spirit, the
Son, the offspring of the Father, really exists.

A RECAPITULATION

CHAPTER I

THE SON OF GOD

Man, the son of God, is powerless in the flesh, and free in the spirit

("Our Father")

JESUS in his childhood called God his Father. There arose in Judea, at this time, a prophet named John. John preached the coming of God upon earth. He said that when men should change their lives, when they should treat one another as equals, when they should cease to injure one another, and, instead of so doing, serve one another, then God would appear upon earth, and His kingdom would be established on earth. Jesus, having heard this declaration, withdrew from among men and went into the wild places, to meditate upon the meaning of human life, and upon his relations to that infinite source of all being, called God. And Jesus accepted as his Father that infinite source of being whom John had called God.

After passing days in the wild places without taking food, Jesus began to suffer hunger. Then he thought to himself, "I am the Son of God the Almighty; I ought, then, to be as He is. But now, I wish to eat, and no bread comes for my need; I am not, then, all-powerful." Then he said to himself, "It is true, I cannot make for myself bread out of stones; but I can overcome the want of bread. So that, though not all-powerful in the body, I am all-powerful in the spirit, and I can quell the body; and thus I am the Son of God, not through the flesh, but through the spirit."

Then he said: "But if I am the Son of the Spirit, I can free myself of the body, and do away with it." But to that he answered, "I am born as spirit, embodied in flesh. Such is the will of my Father, and I cannot set myself against His will."

"But if you cannot satisfy the wants of your body, and if you are no better able to free yourself from your body," he went on to himself, "you ought, then, to labor for the body, and to enjoy all the pleasures it gives you."

But to that he answered, "I cannot satisfy the wants of my body any better than I can rid myself of it; but my life is all-powerful, in that it is the spirit of my Father; and it follows that in my body I must serve the spirit, my Father, and labor for Him only! And becoming convinced that man's life is only in the spirit of the Father, Jesus left the wild places, and began to declare his teaching to men. He said that the spirit dwelt in him, that henceforth heaven was opened, that the powers of heaven were brought to men, that for men a free and boundless life was begun, and that all men, however unfortunate in the body, may be happy.

CHAPTER II

LIFE IN THE SPIRIT

Therefore man must work, not for the flesh, but for the spirit

("Which art in heaven")

THE Jews, holding themselves orthodox, worshiped an external God, whom they regarded as Creator and Lord of the Universe. According to their teaching, this external God had made an agreement with them. According to this agreement, he had promised the Jews to help them, and they had promised to worship Him; and the chief condition of the alliance was the keeping of the Sabbath.

But Jesus said: "The Sabbath is a human institution. That man shall live in the spirit, is more important than all religious ceremonies. Like all external forms of religion, the keeping of the Sabbath includes in itself a delusion. It is impossible to do nothing on the Sabbath. Good actions must be done at any time; and if keeping the Sabbath prevents good action, then the Sabbath is an error."

Another condition in this agreement with God, was the avoidance of the society of infidels. As to this, Jesus said: "God asks for no sacrifice to Himself, but only that men should love one another."

Still another condition related to the following of rules about washing and cleansing; as to which, Jesus said: "God demands, not outside cleanliness, but only, pity and love toward men." He taught that all such external ceremonies were harmful, and that the church tradition itself was an evil. The church tradition causes men to neglect the most important acts of love, as, for instance, love to father and mother. Of all external ceremonies, of all the ritual of the old law, which had for object, as was held, the purification of men, Jesus said: "Know all of you, that nothing from outside can defile a man; only what he thinks, and what he does, defiles him."

After this, Jesus went to Jerusalem, a town considered holy, entered the temple, where the orthodox believed that God dwelt, and there taught: "It is useless to offer God sacrifices; man is of more consequence than a temple; and the only duty is, to love one's neighbor, and help him."

And he taught, further: "Men need not worship God in any particular place, but they must worship Him in spirit and in act. The spirit cannot be seen or shown. The spirit is man's consciousness of his sonship to the Infinite Spirit. No temple is needed. The true temple is the society of men united in love." He said: "All external worship of the divine is not only false and injurious, as with the Jews, among whom it caused murder and admitted neglect of parents, but harmful, because one who goes through external ceremonials, thinks himself made righteous, and free from the need of doing what love demands." He said: "Only that man aims at good, and does good, who feels his own imperfection. To do good deeds, a man must think of himself as imperfect. But external acts of worship lead men into the delusion of self-conceit. All external ceremonies are unnecessary, and must be thrown aside. Deeds of love are incompatible with ceremonial performances, and it is impossible to do good in that form. Man is the son of God by the spirit, and therefore must serve the Father in the spirit."

CHAPTER III

THE SOURCE OF LIFE

The life of all men has proceeded from the spirit of the Father

("Hallowed be Thy Name")

JOHN's disciples asked Jesus what was meant by his "Kingdom of God." He said that the Kingdom of God as preached by him was also that preached by John; and that therein every man, however poor, might be blessed.

And Jesus said to the people: "John was the first who preached to men a Kingdom of God which is not of the external world, but is in the soul of man. The orthodox went to hear John, but understood nothing, because they know only those fictions of their own about an external God, which they preach; and they are astonished when no one pays heed to them. But John preached the truth of the Kingdom of God within men, and therefore he did more than them all. He did so much that, since his time, the law and the prophets, and all external forms of divine worship, are superseded. Since he taught, it is made clear that the Kingdom of God is in the soul of man.

"The beginning and the end of all things is in the soul

of man. Every man, in addition to his bodily life, to the fact which he knows as to his conception from a bodily father through a bodily mother, recognizes in himself a free spirit, intelligent, and independent of the body. This very Spirit, infinite, and proceeding from the infinite, is the origin of all, and is what we call God. We know Him only as we recognize Him within us. This Spirit is the source of our life, and must be ranked above everything; and to Him we must live. By making Him the foundation of our life, we gain the true and infinite life.

"The Father-Spirit, who sends this Spirit into men, cannot have sent Him to deceive men, so that, while conscious of Him, they might come to lose Him. This infinite Spirit being in man, He must have been given to the end that men, through Him, might have infinite life. Therefore the man who conceives of this Spirit as his life, has infinite life. The man who does not so conceive, has no true life. Men can of themselves choose life or death. Life,—in the Spirit; death,—in the flesh. The life of the Spirit is goodness, light. The life of the flesh is evil, darkness. To believe in the Spirit means to do good deeds; to disbelieve, means to do evil deeds. Goodness is life; evil is death.

"God, the Creator, external to us, the beginning of all beginnings, we do not know. Our conception of Him can only be this, that He sowed in men the Spirit; sowing, as a sower does, everywhere, not discriminating, over the field; and the seed, falling on good ground, grows, falling on sterile ground, perishes.

"The Spirit alone gives life, and men are responsible for keeping or losing it. To the Spirit, no evil exists. Evil is but an illusion of life. There are only the two conditions, of living and not-living. Thus the world presents itself to every man; and for every man there is in his soul a consciousness of the Kingdom of Heaven. Each one can, by his own free will, enter, or not enter, that Kingdom. To enter, belief in the life of the Spirit is necessary. He who believes in that life of the Spirit, has infinite life."

CHAPTER IV

GOD'S KINGDOM

Therefore the will of the Father is the life and welfare of all men

("Thy kingdom come")

JESUS pitied men because they did not know true blessedness; therefore he taught them. He said: "Blessed are those who have no property, no position, and who do not care for these; and unhappy are they who seek riches and position. Because such poor and oppressed people are in the Father's will; but the rich and acknowledged people seek only to make gain from men for this temporary life. To carry out God's will, one must not fear to be poor and despised, but must rejoice in this, while showing men what true happiness is.

"To carry out the will of the Father, which gives life and welfare, mankind must fulfil five commandments, namely:—

The First Commandment

To do no ill to any one, and to so act as to rouse evil in no one; because from evil comes evil.

The Second Commandment

Not to follow after women, and not to desert the woman with whom a union has once been formed; because desertion and change of wives causes all the world's dissoluteness.

The Third Commandment

To take no oath of any kind; because nothing can be promised, since man is in the Father's power; and oaths, when taken, are for bad ends.

The Fourth Commandment

Not to fight against evil, but to suffer wrong, and to give even more than men would exact from us; not to condemn, and not to use the law; because every man is himself full of errors, and cannot guide others. By taking revenge, we only teach others to revenge.

The Fifth Commandment

To make no difference between a fellow-countryman and a foreigner; because all men are children of one father.

"The observance of these five commandments is necessary, not to win praise from men, but for oneself, for one's own welfare; therefore there is no propriety in praying and fasting in sight of men.

"The Father knows all that men need, and there is no necessity to pray for particular things; it is simply needful to seek to be in the Father's will. And this is the will of the Father, that a man shall have no anger toward any other. To keep fasts is not essential, for men may fast merely to win praise from men, and such praise ought to be avoided. It is only necessary carefully to conform to the will of God, and the rest will follow of itself. While caring for the body, care cannot be given to the Kingdom of Heaven. Even though a man does not trouble about food and clothing, he will live on. The Father will give life. The needful thing is, at this present moment, to be in the will of the Father. The Father gives to his children what they need. We must desire only the power of the Spirit, which the Father gives.

"The five commandments mark out the road to the Kingdom of Heaven. This narrow path alone leads to eternal life. False teachers — wolves in the skins of sheep — always try to turn men astray from this road; they must be guarded against. False teachers can always be detected, because they teach evil in the name of good. If they teach violence and executions, they are false teachers. By the deeds they teach they may be known.

"Not that man does the Father's will, who calls on the name of God; but he who does good deeds. And he who fulfils these five commandments will have secure and true life, of which nothing can deprive him. But he who does not fulfil them will have an insecure life; one soon to be taken from him, leaving him nothing."

The teaching of Jesus filled the people with admiration and joy, because it offered freedom to every one.

The teaching of Christ was the fulfilment of John's prophecy that God's chosen one should bring light to men, overcome evil, and restore truth, by kindness, meekness, and goodness, but not by violence.

CHAPTER V

THE TRUE LIFE

The fulfilment of the personal will leads to death; the fulfilment of the Father's will gives the true life

("Thy will be done")

The wisdom of life is, the recognition of one's own life as the offspring of the Father's Spirit. Men set before themselves the aims of the bodily life, and in pursuing these aims, they harass themselves and others.

In receiving the doctrine of the spiritual life, and in subjecting and making less of the body, men will find a full satisfaction in the life of the Spirit, in that life which is appointed for them.

Jesus said to his disciples: "The true food of man is the fulfilment of the will of the Father-Spirit. This fulfilment is always possible. Our whole life is a gathering of the fruits of the life sown within us by the Father. Those fruits are the good we are doing among men.

"We ought not to look forward with anxiety for anything. We ought, without ceasing our interest in life, to do good among men."

After this, Jesus happened to be in Jerusalem, where was a bath, beside which lay a sick man, doing nothing but waiting a miracle to cure him. Jesus came, and said to him: "Do not expect a cure by a miracle, but live your life according to your strength, and do not be deluded as to the purpose of life." The invalid obeyed Jesus, got up, and went away.

The orthodox, seeing this, began to reproach Jesus for what he said, and because he had, on the Sabbath, raised an invalid. Jesus said to them: "I did nothing new. I have only the power to act of our common Father, the Spirit. He lives, and gives life to men, and I have done likewise. And to do this is every man's business. Every one is free, and can live, or not live. To live, is to fulfil the will of the Father, which is to do good to others. Not to live, is to fulfil one's own will, not to do good to others. It is in every one's power to do this, or that; to gain life, or to destroy it.

"The true life of man is like this. A master apportioned to his slaves some valuable property, and told each one to work upon what was given to him. Some worked; some did not work, but put out of sight what was given to them. The master demanded an account: and to those who worked, he gave yet more than they had; but from those who did not work, he took away everything."

The portion of valuable property of the master is the Spirit of life in man, who is the son of the Father-Spirit. He who in his life works for the sake of the spirit-life, receives infinite life; he who does not work, is deprived of what was given to him.

The true life is the common life of humanity, and not the life of the individual. Each one must work for the life of others.

After this, Jesus went to a desert place, and many people followed him. At evening, the disciples came, and said: "How shall we feed all these people?" Among the gathering were some who had nothing, and some who had bread and fish. And Jesus said to his disciples: "Give me all the bread you have." He took the loaves, and gave bread to his disciples, who gave to others, who did likewise. So all ate of others' bread, not consuming all there was, and all were satisfied. And Jesus said: "Act just in this way. It is not necessary that each one should get food for himself, but it is needful to do that which the Spirit in man demands, namely, that each shall share to others what supply there is. The true food of man is the Spirit of the Father. Man lives by the Spirit only. Everything in life must be made subservient to this; for life consists in doing, not one's own will, but the will of the Father of life. And that will is, that the perfect life of the Spirit which is given to men, shall remain in them, and that all shall cherish the life of the Spirit within them until the hour of death. The Father, the source of life, is Spirit. Life consists only in carrying out the will of the Father; and to carry out that will of the Spirit, one must surrender the body. The body is the food, the material for the life of the Spirit. Only in giving up the body does the Spirit live."

After this, Jesus chose certain disciples, and sent them everywhere to preach the doctrine of the life of the Spirit. In sending them, he said: "Preach the life of the Spirit, and, consistently therewith, renounce beforehand all fleshly desires, and have nothing of your own. Be ready for persecution, privation, suffering. Those who love the life of the body will hate you, harass and murder you; but do not fear. If you fulfil the will of the Father, then you possess the life of the Spirit, of which no one can deprive you."

The disciples went away, and when they returned, declared that everywhere the teachings of evil were conquered by them.

Then the orthodox told Jesus that his teaching, even if it conquered evil, was in itself an evil, because those who carry it out must of necessity suffer. To this, Jesus answered: "Evil cannot conquer evil. If evil is conquered, it can only be by good. Goodness is the will of the Father-Spirit common to all men. Every man has a knowledge of what benefits himself. If he does similar benefits to others, if he does that which is the will of the Father, then he will do good. Therefore the carrying out of the will of the Father-Spirit results well, even though it be followed with sufferings and deaths of those who fulfil that will."

CHAPTER VI

THE FALSE LIFE

Therefore, in order to receive the true life, man must on earth resign the false life of the flesh, and live by the Spirit

("On earth as in heaven")

To the spiritual life there can be no difference between members of one family and strangers. Jesus said that his mother and his brethren, as such, had no superior claims upon him; only those were near to him who fulfilled the will of the common Father. A man's life and welfare depend, not on family relations, but on the life of the Spirit.

Jesus said: "Blessed are those who retain their understanding of the Father. The man who lives by the Spirit has no home, for, being by the Spirit, he cannot own any special house." And he said that he himself had no fixed abode; that not being needed to enable a man to carry out the will of the Father, which can be done at all times, in all places.

The death of the body cannot be dreadful to a man who gives himself up to the will of the Father, because the life of the Spirit goes on despite the death of the body. Jesus said that he who believes in the life of the Spirit has nothing to fear.

No cares make it impossible for a man to live in his Spirit. When a man said that he would obey the teaching of Christ presently, but that he must first bury his father, Jesus answered: "Only the dead trouble about burial of the dead; but the living live always in fulfilling the will of the Father." Cares about relations and family affairs must not hinder the life of the Spirit. He who troubles about the results to his bodily life from the fulfilment of the Father's will, does as the plowman does, who plows, looking not in front, but behind.

Cares for the pleasures of the bodily life, which seem so important to men, are delusions. The only, the real business of life, is the making plain of the Father's will, attention to it, and fulfilment of it. To Martha's reproach, that she alone troubled about the supper, and that her sister Mary did not help, but listened to his teaching, Jesus said: "You blame her unjustly. Take some trouble, yourself, if you need what comes of it, but let those who do not need pleasures for the body attend to the one essential business of life."

And Jesus said: "He who desires the true life, which comes of fulfilling the Father's will, must first of all give up his own personal desires." He must not only cease to plan out his life to his own wishes, but he must be ready at any moment to bear any privations and sufferings. One who seeks to arrange his bodily life to his own desires, will wreck the true life of fulfilment of the Father's will.

Most ruinous to the life of the Spirit is the love of gain, of getting rich. Men forget that, however much they acquire riches and goods, they may die at any moment, and their property is not an essential of life. Death broods over every one of us. Sickness, killing by men, fatal accidents, may at any minute end life. Bodily death is the unescapable condition of every second of life. While one lives, one must regard every hour of life as a delay granted by the kindness of some power. This we must remember, and not say that we do not know it. We know and foresee in regard to all events of earth and sky, but death, which we know waits on us every moment, we forget. But unless we forget death, we cannot yield ourselves to the life of the body, we cannot build upon it. To follow the teaching of Christ, one has to count up the advantages of serving the bodily life, of serving one's own will, and the advantages of fulfilling the Father's will. Only one who clearly takes account of this can be a disciple of Christ. And he who makes the calculation, will not prefer a visionary benefit and a visionary life to the true good and the true life. The true life has been given to men, and men know it, they hear its summons, but, always swept on by the cares of the moment, they are withheld from it. The true life is as though a rich man gave a feast, and summoned the guests. His call to them is the voice of the Spirit of the Father inviting all men to Himself. But of those invited some are busy in commerce, some in the household, some in family affairs, — none come to the feast. Only the poor, such as have no cares of the body, come to the feast, and gain happiness. So men, distracting themselves with cares for the bodily life, are losing the true life. He who cannot, and that altogether, decline the cares and gains of the bodily life, cannot fulfil the Father's will, because one cannot serve oneself a little, and the Father a little.

A man must calculate, whether it is better to serve the body, whether it is possible to arrange his life according to his own will. He must do as one does who would build a house, or who contemplates war. Such an one will reckon whether he has means to finish building, whether he has means to conquer. And upon seeing that he has not, he will not spend for nothing either labor or armies. Otherwise, he fruitlessly wastes, and will be a laughingstock to men. If one could arrange the bodily life to one's own will, then it might be well to serve the body; but as that is impossible, then better sacrifice the body, and serve the Spirit. Otherwise, one will gain neither one thing nor another; the bodily life will not be gained, and the spiritual life will be lost. So that, to fulfil the Father's will, the bodily life must be quite resigned.

The bodily life is involved in the world's false riches, which we are commissioned to manage in such a way as to gain the true and perfect riches.

If a rich man has a manager who knows that, however he may serve his master, the latter will dismiss him, leaving him with nothing, this manager will do well if, during his management of the other's riches, he treats people well. Then, even though his master dismiss him, those whom he has benefited will receive him and sustain him. So also must men act as to the bodily life. The bodily life is that wealth, not one's own, which is given to one to manage for a time. If men will rightly use this wealth, which is not their own, then they will gain true wealth, really their own.

If we do not give up our falsely held riches, then the true life will not be given to us. The illusory life of the body, and the life of the spirit, cannot both be served. One cannot serve property and God. What is honorable with men, is abomination before God. Riches are evil before God. A rich man is continually guilty, in that he eats abundantly and luxuriously, while at his door the poor starve. And every one knows that the property which one will not share to others is held in non-fulfilment of the Father's will.

Once Jesus was approached by an orthodox and rich ruler, who began to boast that he had fulfilled all the commandments of the law. Jesus reminded him that there is a commandment to love others as oneself, and that this is the Father's will. The ruler said he kept this also. Then Jesus said to him: "That is not true; if you desire to fulfil the Father's will, you would not have property. A man cannot fulfil the will of the Father, if he has a fortune of his own, which he does not give away to others."

And Jesus said to the disciples: "Men think it impossible to live without property, but I tell you, true life is in the giving up of one's own to others."

A man, Zaccheus by name, heard the teaching of Jesus, and believed it, and having invited Jesus to his house, he said to him: "I am giving half my fortune to the poor, and I will restore four times over to those whom I may have wronged." And Jesus said: "Here is a man who fulfils the Father's will; for the fulfilment of that will is not a matter of finding an opportunity, but the whole life must go in fulfilment."

Goodness cannot be measured in any way. It is impossible to say who has done more good, and who less. A widow who gives away her last farthing gives more than a rich man who gives thousands. It is also impossible to measure goodness by utility or inutility.

As an instance of how goodness must be shown, take the woman who pitied Jesus, and in her emotion poured upon him many pounds' worth of costly oil. Judas said she had done foolishly, because many people might have been fed on the price. But Judas was a thief; he spoke untruth, and in talking of the worldly value of the oil, he did not consider the poor. Not utility, not value, comes into the question, but the necessity of always, every minute, loving others, and giving up to them one's own.

CHAPTER VII

I AND THE FATHER ARE ONE

The true food of everlasting life is the fulfilment of the Father's will

("Give us our daily bread")

ANSWERING the Jews' demands for proofs of the truth of his teaching, Jesus said: "The truth of my teaching is proved in the fact that I teach, not in my own name, but in the name of the common Father of all men. I teach that which is good in the sight of the Father of all men, and is therefore good for all men.

"Do as I say; fulfil the five commandments, and you will see that the truth is as I say. Fulfilment of these five commandments will drive away all the world's evil; therefore it must be that they are true and right. Clearly, he who teaches, not his own personal will, but the will of Him who sent him, will teach the truth. The Mosaic law teaches the fulfilment of men's own wills, and is therefore full of contradictions; but my teaching is to fulfil the will of the Father, and therefore in it all is harmonious."

The Jews did not understand him, and looked for external proofs as to whether he himself were the Christ written of in the prophecies. On this he said to them: "Do not inquire who I am, whether it is of me your prophecies speak, but attend to my teaching, to what I say of our common Father. It is not necessary to inquire about outside matters, as to whence I come; but my teaching must be followed. He who will follow my teaching will obtain true life. There can be no proofs of my teaching. It is the light itself, and as you cannot illuminate light, so you cannot prove the truth of truth. My teaching is light; he who sees it has light and life, and has no need of proofs. But he who is in darkness must come to the light."

But again the Jews asked him who he was, as to his bodily personality. He said to them: "I am, as I told you from the first, a man, the Son of the Father of life. Only he who will so regard himself (this is the truth I teach), and will fulfil the will of the common Father, only he will cease to be a slave, and become a free man. Because we are slaves only through the error which considers the bodily life as the real life. He who will understand the truth, that life consists only in the fulfilment of the Father's will, only he will become free and immortal. Just as a bond-servant in a master's house is not there for ever, but the son does remain, so the man who lives the life of a slave of the flesh does not remain in life for ever; but he who in spirit fulfils the Father's will, remains in life for ever. To understand me, you must understand that my Father is not that which is your Father, what you call God. Your Father is a God of the flesh; but my Father is the Spirit of life. Your Father, your God, is a God of revenge, a murderer, one who executes men; but my Father gives life. Therefore we are children of different Fathers.

"I am following the truth, and you wish to kill me for that, to please your God. Your God is the devil, the source of evil; and in serving him, you serve the devil.

"Sheep follow the shepherd, who gives them food and life; and in the same way, men accept my teaching because it gives life to all. And as the sheep do not follow the thief who climbs over into the fold, but throw themselves aside from him, so men, also, cannot accept the doctrines which teach violence and putting-to-death.

"My teaching is a door to the sheep, and all who will follow me shall find true life. As those only are good shepherds who own and like the sheep, and devote their lives to them, while the mere hirelings, who have no liking for sheep, are bad shepherds; so, also, only that teacher is true who does not look after himself, and he is bad who cares only about himself. My teaching is, that a man shall not look after himself, but shall yield up the life of the body for the life of the spirit. This I teach and fulfil."

Still the Jews did not understand, and persisted in looking for proofs as to whether or not Jesus was the Christ, to determine whether they should believe in him or not. They said: "Do not torment us, but tell us frankly, are you the Christ, or not?" Then Jesus answered them: "Belief must be given, not to words, but to deeds. By the deeds I teach you may know whether I teach truth or not. Do as I do, and do not trifle over words. Fulfil the will of the Father, and then you will all join with me and with the Father, because I am a Son of Man, and at one with the Father. And I am that which you call God, and I call Father. God and I are one. Even in your own writings it is said, that God said to men, 'You are gods.' Every one, by his spirit, is son of this Father. And if a man lives fulfilling the will of the Father, then he becomes at one with the Father. If I fulfil the will, the Father is in me, and I am in the Father."

After this, Jesus asked the disciples how they understood his teaching as to the Son of Man. Simon Peter answered him: "Your teaching is that you are the Son of the God of life; that God is the life of the spirit in man." And Jesus said to him: "Not only I am a son, but all men are; and this is revealed to men, not by me, but by the common Father of men. Upon this knowledge is based the true life of man. To this life there is no death."

CHAPTER VIII

LIFE IS NOT TEMPORAL

Therefore true life is to be lived in the present

("This day")

DEALING with the disciples' question as to the recompense for surrendering the life of the body, Jesus said: "To him who enters into the reality of this teaching, no further recompense can be given; because, first, when a man yields up friends and goods for the sake of this teaching, he gains a hundred times more friends and goods; and second, a man who seeks such recompense wants to have something over and above others, which is entirely contrary to the fulfilment of the Father's will." In the Kingdom of Heaven there is neither great nor small; all are equal. Those who look for something extra as reward for their goodness, are like the laborers who claimed a greater payment than that for which they had agreed with their employer; merely because, in their opinion, they were more deserving than other laborers. There are no rewards, punishments, degradations, or exaltations, for him who understands this teaching. No one can be higher or lower, more or less important, than another, according to the teaching of Jesus.

All can equally fulfil the Father's will. Therefore, in so doing, no one becomes superior, truer, or better, than another.

Kings and those who serve them, they only are measured by such standards. By my teaching, said Jesus, there can be no superior rank, because he who would excel must serve everybody; for the teaching is, that life is given to man, not that others may serve him, but that he may give his whole life to serve others; but he who will not do this, but seeks to exalt himself, shall fall lower than he was.

To get rid of all ideas of rewards and of one's elevation, the meaning, purpose, of life must be understood. That lies in fulfilling the will of the Father; and the will of the Father is, that that which He gave shall be returned to Him. As a shepherd leaves his flock, and goes to look for the lost sheep, as a woman will search everywhere to find a lost penny, so also the Father's continual work is manifested to us in His drawing to Himself that which pertains to Him.

We must understand the true life, what it is. The true life is brought to light always in the lost being brought back to where they belong, in the awakening of those who slept. People who have the true life, who are restored to the source of their being, cannot, like worldly men, take account of others as better or worse; but, being sharers of the Father's life, they can take delight only in the return of the lost to their Father. If a son, who has gone astray and left his father, should repent, and return, how then could the other sons of the same father grudge at the father's joy, or themselves not rejoice at the brother's return?

To lead us to believe the teaching, and to alter one's way of living, and fulfil the teaching, we need, not external proofs, not promises of reward, but a clear understanding of what the true life is. If men think they are complete masters of their own lives, and that life is given them for bodily enjoyment, then clearly, any sacrifice made for another will seem to them an act worthy of reward, and without such payment they will yield nothing. A man demands rents from tenants who have forgotten that their ground is theirs on condition that they give up the fruits to the owner; and when he demands the rent again and again, they seek to kill him. So with the men who think themselves masters of their own lives, not discerning that life is given by true understanding; men who demand the fulfilment of their own wills.

Both belief and action are necessary, to learn that a man can do nothing of himself, and if he give up his bodily life to serve goodness, he deserves neither thanks nor reward. We must understand that, in doing good, a man only does his duty, does what he must necessarily do. Only by so understanding his life, can a man have faith to enable him to do deeds of true goodness.

Precisely in such an understanding of life, the Kingdom of Heaven consists. This Kingdom is invisible; it cannot be pointed out as identified with this or that place. The Kingdom of Heaven is in the human understanding. The whole society of the world goes on living as of old; men eat, drink, marry, trade, die, and along with this, in the souls of men, lives the Kingdom of Heaven. It is the understanding of life, growing from itself, like a tree in the spring.

The true life of the fulfilment of the Father's will is not in the life of the past, or of the future, but it is the life of now, the life which all must live at this instant of time. Therefore one must never relax the true life in them. Men are set to watch over life, not of the past or the future, but the life now being lived; and in that, to fulfil the will of the Father of all men. If they let this life escape them, by not fulfilling the Father's will, then they will not receive it back again; just as a watchman, set upon a night-long watch, does not perform his duty if he fall asleep even for a moment; for in this moment a thief may come.

Therefore a man must concentrate his strength in the present hour, for in this hour only can he fulfil the Father's will. And that will is life and blessing for all men. Only those live who are doing good. Good done to men, now, in this hour, is life, life which unites us with the common Father.

CHAPTER IX

TEMPTATIONS

The illusions of temporal life conceal from men the true life in the present

("Forgive us our debts as we forgive our debtors")

MAN is born with knowledge of the true life of fulfilment of the Father's will. Children live by that knowledge; through them we may see what the Father's will is. To understand the teaching of Jesus, one must understand the life of children, and be like them.

Children always live in the Father's will, not breaking the five commandments. They would not come to break them if their elders did not mislead them. In misleading children to break those commandments, men ruin the children. In misleading them, men are doing as they would do by fastening a millstone to a man's neck and throwing him into the water.

If there were no temptations, the world would be happy. The world is unhappy by them only. These temptations are wrong-doing which men enact for imaginary gain to the life in time. Temptations ruin men; therefore it is necessary to give up everything rather than fall into temptation.

Temptation against the first commandment leads men to consider themselves in the right against others, and others as in the wrong, debtors to them. To avoid this temptation, men must remember that all men are always infinitely in debt to the Father, and they can only clear themselves of this debt by forgiving their brother-men.

Therefore men must overlook injuries, and not be deterred though the offender again and again injure them. However many times a man may be injured, he must forgive, and still forgive, not remembering the wrong. For the Kingdom of Heaven is forgiveness.

If we do not forgive, we are doing as the debtor did. This debtor, greatly owing, came to him in whose power he was, and began to ask for mercy. The other forgave him all. The debtor went away, and began himself to squeeze a debtor, who owed him but a little. Now, to gain life, we must fulfil the Father's will. And we pray the Father to forgive us, that we have not duly fulfilled his will, and we hope to be forgiven. What, then, are we doing, if we do not ourselves forgive? We are doing to others what we dread for ourselves.

The will of the Father is well-being, and evil is that which separates us from the Father. Why, then, should we not strive to quench evil right away, when evil ruins us, and takes our life?

Temptation against the second commandment is, to think that woman is created for bodily pleasure, and that in leaving one woman and taking another, heightened pleasure is gained. To avoid this temptation, we must remember that the Father's will is, not that man should amuse himself with woman's charms, but that every man, with his wife, should be one body. The Father's will is, for every man, one wife; for every wife, one husband. If one man keep to one wife, then there is wife or husband for each one who needs. Therefore he who changes the woman he lives with deprives her of a husband, and tempts some other man to leave his wife and take the deserted one. A man may do without a wife, but he must not have more than one, because if he does, he goes against the will of the Father, which is, that one man unite with one woman.

Temptation against the third commandment is, for men to create, for the protection of the temporal life, authoritative powers, and to demand from each other oaths, pledges, to do the deeds those powers demand.

To avoid this temptation, men must remember that they are not indebted for their life to any power but God. The claims of authority must be regarded as violence; and, following the commandment regarding the non-resistance of evil, men must yield what the authorities demand, namely, their goods and labor; but they cannot, either by oaths or promises, pledge their conduct. Oaths, being imposed, make men bad. He who recognizes life in the will of the Father cannot bind his actions by pledges; because for such a man there is nothing more sacred than his own life.

Temptation against the fourth commandment is, for men to hold that, by giving themselves up to animosity and revenge, they can exterminate evil from among themselves. If a man injure another, men think he should be punished, and that justice lies in human judgments. To be free from this temptation, we must remember that men are called, not to judge, but to save each other. To judge of another's injustice is impossible for men, as they themselves are full of wickedness. The only thing open to them is to teach others by example of goodness, forgiveness, and purity.

Temptation against the fifth commandment is, for man to think there is a difference between one's own countrymen and men of other nations; and that it is therefore necessary to make defense against other nations, and to injure them. To avoid this temptation, it is necessary to know that all the commandments are summed up in this one, of fulfilling the will of the Father who gives life and well-being to all men; and therefore it is necessary to do good to all men, without distinction. Even though others still make such distinctions, and though nations who look on each other as aliens are at war, nevertheless, everybody who would fulfil the Father's will must do good to all men, even to those who belong to another nation which is at war.

To avoid falling into any delusions of men, we must not think about bodily affairs, but about spiritual. To him who has understood that life consists in being, at this moment, in the Father's will, neither deprivations, nor suffering, nor death can be dreadful. Only he obtains true life who is, at every moment, ready to give up his bodily life in order to fulfil the Father's will.

And that all may understand the true life to be one in which there is no death, Jesus said: "Eternal life must not be understood to be like this present life. For the true life in the Father's will, there is neither space nor time. Those who are awakened to the true life, live in the will of the Father, for which there is no space nor time ; and they live with the Father. Though they die to us, they live to God. Therefore one commandment includes in itself all others; the commandment, namely, to love, with all our strength, the source of life; and consequently to love all men, each of whom bears in himself this same original."

And Jesus said: "This source of life is that very Christ which you await. The comprehension of this source of life, which knows no distinction of persons, no time, no place, is the Son of Man which I teach. Anything which hides this source of life from men is temptation. There is the temptation of the scribes, bookmen, and of the materialists; do not yield thereto. There are the temptations of authority; do not yield thereto. And there is the most terrible temptation, from the teachers of religion who call themselves orthodox. Beware of this last more than of all others; because just they, these self-ordained teachers, by inventing the worship of a false God, decoy you from the true God. They, instead of serving the Father of life by deeds, substitute words, and they teach words, while they themselves do nothing. Therefore you can learn nothing from them but words. But the Father requires deeds, not words. And they have nothing to teach, because they themselves know nothing; but for their own gain they must parade as teachers. But you know that no man can be the teacher of another. There is one teacher for all — the Lord of life — understanding. And these self-assuming teachers, thinking to teach others, deprive themselves of true life, and prevent others from the understanding of it. They teach that their God will be pleased with external ceremonies; and they think they can bring men to serve religion by vows. They are concerned with appearances only. An outward assumption of religion suffices them, but they do not care what is in the hearts of men. Therefore they are like elaborate coffins, very nice outside, but within full of repulsiveness. They give honor, in words, to saints and martyrs, but they are themselves just the very men who have murdered and tortured in the past, and who murder and torture the saints of to-day. By them come all the world's temptations; because, under the guise of good, they teach evil. The temptation they create is the root of all others, because they defile that which is most sacred. For a long time yet they will not be changed, but will continue their deceptions, and increase evil in the world. But there shall come a time when all the temples will be ruined, with all the external God-worship; when all men will understand, and unite in love, to serve the one Father of life, by fulfilling His will."

CHAPTER X

THE WARFARE WITH TEMPTATION

Therefore, not to fall by temptation, we must, at every moment of life, be at one with the Father

("Lead us not into temptation")

THE Jews saw that the teaching of Jesus would destroy their state, religion, and nationality, and at the same time they saw they could not controvert him; so they decided to kill him. His innocence and justness stood in their way, but the high priest Caiaphas discovered a reason for killing Jesus, though innocent. Caiaphas said: "We need not consider whether this man is just or unjust; we have to determine whether our Jewish people shall remain a separate nation, or whether we shall be broken up and dispersed: the nation will perish, and the people be scattered, if we leave this man alone, and do not put him to death." This argument settled the matter, and the orthodox sentenced Jesus to death. They instructed the people to seize upon him as soon as he might appear in Jerusalem.

Jesus, although he knew about this, nevertheless, on the feast of the Passover, came to Jerusalem. His disciples entreated him not to do so; but he said: "What these orthodox can do to me, and all that other men can do, cannot alter the truth for me. If I have the light, I know where I am, and which way I am going. Only he who does not know the truth can fear anything, or can doubt anything. Only he who cannot see, stumbles." And he went to Jerusalem, stopping on the way at Bethany.

When he left Bethany, and went to Jerusalem, crowds of people met and followed him. This still more convinced the orthodox of the need to kill him. They only wanted an opportunity to seize him. He knew also that the lightest incautious word from him at that time, spoken against the law, would be a reason for his execution; but notwithstanding this, he entered the temple, and declared again that the worship of the Jews, with their sacrifices and libations, was false, and he declared his teaching. But his teaching, based on the prophets, was such that the orthodox could not yet find a palpable breach of the law which would justify them in putting him to death; the more so that the greater part of the lower class was with Jesus.

At the feast were certain heathen, who, having heard of the teaching of Jesus, wished to talk with him about it. The disciples, hearing of this, were afraid, fearing lest Jesus, in talking with them, should betray himself, and excite the people. At first they would not bring Jesus and these heathen together; but afterward they resolved to tell him these men wanted to see him. Hearing this, Jesus was disturbed. He well knew that his speech to the heathen would clearly show his antagonism to the whole Jewish law, would turn the crowd from him, and would give the orthodox a reason to accuse him of being in league with the hated heathen. Jesus became disturbed, knowing this; but he also knew that his mission was to make clear to men, the children of one Father, their real unity, despite differences of religion. He knew that the step he was about to take would end his bodily life, for the sake of giving birth to spiritual results. He said: "He who holds fast to the bodily life is deprived of the true one; and he who is not careful for the bodily life obtains the true life. I am troubled by what is before me, but I have only lived that I might reach this hour; how, then, can I fail to now do what I must do? So let the Father's will be shown through me now."

And turning to the people, heathen and Jews, Jesus declared openly what he had only privately told to Nicodemus. He said: "Men's lives, with all their various religions and organized powers, must be wholly changed. All power and authority must disappear. It is only necessary to understand the nature of man as the son of the Father of life, and this understanding abolishes all division among men, and all ruling power, and makes men one."

The Jews said: "You wholly destroy our religion. Our law looks to the Christ, but you speak only of the Son of Man, and say that he must be set up. What do you mean?" He answered them: "To set up the Son of Man means to live by the light of the understanding which is in men, to follow this light into more light. I teach no new faith, only that which every one may know within himself. Every man knows he has life, given to him and to all men by the Father of life. My teaching is only this, that man must live the life given by the Father to all."

Many of the humbler kind of people believed Jesus. But the notable and official classes disbelieved; because they did not want to consider the universal basis of what he said, but only its immediate and temporary bearings. They saw that he turned the people from themselves, and they wished to kill him; but they were afraid to seize him openly, and did not seek to do so in Jerusalem and in the daytime, but secretly elsewhere.

And one of the twelve disciples, Judas Iscariot, approached the authorities, and him they bribed to take their emissaries to Jesus when he should be away from the people. Judas promised this, and went again to Jesus, awaiting a suitable opportunity to betray him.

On the first day of the feast, Jesus and his disciples kept the Passover. And Judas, thinking Jesus was not aware of his treachery, was with them. But Jesus knew Judas had sold him. And as they all sat at table, Jesus took bread, broke it in twelve pieces, and gave a

But my teaching is, that we are the sons of the Father of life, and that he who believes in my teaching shall not see death."

The Jews asked: "How can a man not die, when all the most God-pleasing men, even Abraham, are dead? How, then, can you say that you, and those that believe your teaching, will not die?" To this Jesus answered: "I speak not by my own authority. I speak of the one source of life, whom you call God, and who is in men. This source I know, I cannot help knowing, and I know His will, and I fulfil it; and of this source of life I say, that it was, and is, and shall be, being deathless."

The demand for proof of Jesus' teaching is like a demand made upon a once-blind man, to give proofs of how and why he sees light. The blind man whose sight was restored, still the same man he was before, can only say, he was blind, but now sees. Just this, and nothing else, can one answer who formerly did not understand the meaning of life, but now does understand. Such a man will say that he did not, before, know the true good in life, but now he knows. The once-blind man, when told he is cured not according to rule, and that he who cured him is the evil-doer, and that he must be cured in another way, can only reply, that he knows nothing as to the correctness of the manner of cure, or as to the faultiness of his healer, or as to their being a better way of cure, but that he knows only, he was blind, and now sees. And just so, he who grasps the meaning of this doctrine, that the true good is to fulfil the Father's will, can say nothing as to the regularity of the teaching, or as to the possibility of gaining something better. He will say: "Formerly I did not see the meaning of life; now I see. I know no more."

And Jesus said: "My teaching is the awakening of the life which has so far slept; he who will believe my teaching, shall awaken to eternal life, and continue to live after death. My teaching is not proved in any way, except that men give themselves up to it, because it alone has the promise of life for men.

piece to each disciple, including Judas with the rest. And not mentioning any name, he said: "Take, eat my body." Then he took the cup with the wine, passed it to them, for them all, including Judas, to drink from, and said: "One of you will shed my blood. Drink my blood."

Afterward Jesus got up, and began to wash the feet of all his disciples, including Judas. And having finished, he said: "I know that one of you will betray me to my death, and shed my blood; but him I have fed, and given to drink, and washed his feet. I have done this to show you how you must act toward those who do you harm. If you will act in this way, you shall be blest." And the disciples went on to ask who the betrayer was. But Jesus did not give his name, so that they might not turn on him. And when it had grown dark, Jesus showed that it was Judas, and at the same time told him to go away. Judas got up from the table and went off, no one hindering him.

Then Jesus said: "This is the meaning of setting up the Son of Man. To set up the Son of Man is to be like the Father, good; and that, not only to those who love us, but to all men, even to those who do us harm. And therefore do not argue over my teaching, do not pick it to pieces as the orthodox did, but do as I have done; do as I have done under your eyes. This one commandment I give you: Love men. My whole teaching is, to love men always, and to the last."

After this, fear came over Jesus, and he went in the dark with his disciples to a garden, to be out of the way. While walking, he said to them: "You are all wavering and timid; if they move to take me, you will all run away." To this, Peter said: "No, I will never leave you; I will defend you even to death." And all the disciples said so. Then Jesus said: "If that be the case, then get ready for defense; take provision, because we must hide, take weapons, to fight for ourselves." The disciples said they had two swords.

When Jesus heard this about the swords, anguish came over him. And going to a vacant place, he began to pray, and entreated his disciples to do the same. But the disciples did not understand his state of mind Jesus said: "My Father, the Spirit, end in me this struggle with temptation. Strengthen me to the fulfilment of Thy will. I do not want my own way. I do not want to defend my bodily life. I want to do Thy will, in not resisting evil."

The disciples still did not understand. And he said to them: "Do not consider the concerns of the body, but try to rise into the spirit; strength is in the spirit, but the flesh is powerless." And a second time he said: "My Father, if suffering must be, then let it come. But even in suffering, I want one thing only: that not my will shall be fulfilled, but thine." The disciples did not understand. And again he struggled with the temptation; and at last conquered it. Coming to the disciples, he said: "It is settled now; you can be at rest. I shall not fight, but shall surrender myself into the hands of the men of this world."

CHAPTER XI

THE FAREWELL DISCOURSE

The self-life is an illusion which comes through the flesh, an evil. The true life is the life common to all men

("Deliver us from evil")

JESUS, finding himself prepared for death, went to give himself up. Peter stopped him, and asked: "Where are you going?" Jesus answered: "I am going where you cannot go. I am ready for death, and you are not yet ready." Peter said: "No, I am even now ready to sacrifice my life for thee." Jesus said to him: "A man cannot promise anything."

And he said to all his disciples: "I know death is before me, but I believe in the life of the Father, and therefore am not afraid of it. Do not be distressed over my death, but believe in the real God, in the Father of life, and then my death will not seem dreadful to you. If I am united with the Father of life, then I cannot be deprived of life. It is true, I do not tell you what and where my life will be, after death, but I point out to you the way to true life. My teaching does not reveal what that life is to be, but it reveals the only true way of life. That is, to be in unity with the Father. The Father is the source of life. My teaching is, that man shall live in the will of the Father, and fulfil His will for the life and well-being of all men.

"Your teacher, when I am gone, will be your knowledge of the truth. In fulfilling my teaching, you will always feel that you are in the truth, that the Father is in you, and you are in the Father. And knowing in yourselves the Father of life, you will experience a peace of which nothing will deprive you. And therefore, if you know the truth and live in it, neither my death nor your own can trouble you.

"Men think of themselves as separate beings, each with his own power of will in life; but this is only an illusion. The only true life is that which recognizes the Father's will as the source of life. My teaching reveals this oneness of life, and represents life, not as separate shoots, but as one tree, on which all the shoots grow. Only he who lives in the Father's will, like a shoot of a tree, only he lives; and he who wishes to live by his own will, dies away like a torn-off shoot.

"The Father gave me life to do good, and I have taught you to live to do good. If you will fulfil my commandment, you will be blessed. The commandment which sums up my whole teaching is no more than this, that all men shall love one another. And love is to sacrifice one's own bodily life for another's sake. Love has no other definition. In fulfilling my commandment of love, you will not fulfil it like slaves, who follow the orders of a master without understanding them; but you will live as free men, as I am, because I have made clear to you the purpose of life, which follows from the knowledge of the Father of life. You have adopted my teaching, not from accidental choice, but because it is the only truth by which men are made free.

"The teaching of the world is to do evil to men; but I teach that men love each other. Therefore the world will despise you, as it has despised me. The world does not understand my teaching, and therefore will persecute you, and do you evil, thinking thereby to serve God. Do not be astonished at this; you must understand that it is necessarily so. The world, not understanding the true God, must persecute you; but you must affirm the truth.

"You grieve because they will kill me; but they kill me for declaring the truth. And therefore my death is necessary for the declaration of the truth. My death, in facing which I do not go back from the truth, will strengthen you, and you will understand the nature of untruth and of truth. You will understand that untruth lies in men's belief in the bodily life, and their disbelief in the life of the spirit; that truth consists in unity with the Father, from which results the victory of the spirit over the flesh.

"Even when I shall not be with you in the bodily life, my spirit will be with you. But you, like all men, will not always feel within you the power of the spirit. Sometimes you will relax and lose strength of spirit; and you will fall into temptation; and at times you will again awaken to the true life. Hours of bondage to the body will come upon you, but for a time only; you will suffer, and again be restored to the spirit, like a woman who suffers birth-pangs, and then has joy because she has brought a human being into the world. So will your experience be, when, after falling under the power of the body, you rise again by the spirit. You will then feel such joy, that nothing will be left for you to desire. Know this, then, beforehand; and in spite of persecution, in spite of internal struggle and casting down of spirit, know that the spirit lives in you, and that the only true God is the knowledge of the Father's will, as I have revealed it."

And addressing the Father, the Spirit, Jesus said·

"I have done that which Thou hast commanded me; I have revealed to men that Thou art the source of everything. And they have understood me. I have taught them that they all come from the source of infinite life, and therefore they are all one; and that as the Father is in me, and I am in the Father, so they, too, are one with me and the Father. I have revealed to them also, that, like Thee, who in love hast sent them into the world, they, too, shall with love live in the world."

CHAPTER XII

THE VICTORY OF THE SPIRIT OVER THE FLESH

Therefore, for him who lives, not the self-life, but a common life in the will of the Father, there is no death. Bodily death is for him union with the Father

("Thine is the kingdom, power, and glory")

WHEN Jesus had ended his discourse to the disciples, he rose, and, instead of running away or defending himself, he went on the way to meet Judas, who was bringing soldiers to take him. Jesus came to Judas, and asked him why he had come. But Judas did not answer, and a crowd of soldiers came round Jesus. Peter threw himself forward to defend his teacher, and, drawing his sword, began to fight. But Jesus stopped him, and said to him, that he who fights with a sword must himself perish with the sword, and ordered him to put up the sword. Then Jesus said to those who had come to take him: "I have up to now gone about among you alone, without fear, and I do not fear now. Do as you choose."

And while all the disciples ran away, Jesus was left alone. The officer of the soldiers ordered Jesus to be bound, and led before Annas. This Annas was a former high priest, and lived in the same house with Caiaphas, who was then high priest. Caiaphas it was who provided the reason upon which they decided to kill Jesus; namely, that if he were not killed the nation would disappear.

Jesus, feeling himself to be in the will of the Father, was ready for death, and did not resist when they took him, and was not afraid when they led him away. But the very Peter who had just promised Jesus that he would not renounce him, but would die for him, this same Peter who wished to protect him,— now, when he saw that they were taking Jesus for execution, and being met with the door-keeper's question, Whether he was not with Jesus? gave up, and deserted him. It was only afterward that, hearing the cock crow, Peter brought to mind all that Jesus had said. Then he understood that there are two temptations of the flesh, fear and fighting; and that it was with these that Jesus struggled when he prayed in the garden, and asked the disciples to pray. And now he, Peter, had fallen before both these temptations of the flesh, of which Jesus had forewarned him; he had wished to fight against evil, and to defend the truth, he had been about to strike and to do evil himself; and now he could not endure the fear of bodily suffering, and had renounced his teacher. Jesus had yielded neither to the temptation to fight, when the disciples got ready two swords for his defense, nor to the temptation to fear before the men of Jerusalem, first, in the case of the heathen, and now before the soldiers, who had bound him and led him to trial.

Jesus was taken before Caiaphas. Caiaphas began to question him about his teaching. But knowing that Caiaphas was examining him, not to find out what his teaching was, but only to convict him, Jesus did not answer, but said: "I have concealed nothing, and now conceal nothing. If you wish to know what my teaching is, ask those who heard and understood it." For saying this, the high priest's servant struck Jesus in the face, and Jesus asked him why he so beat him. But the man did not answer him, and the high priest continued the trial. Witnesses were brought, who deposed that Jesus had boasted that he made an end of the Jewish religion. And the high priest interrogated Jesus; who, seeing they did not examine him to learn anything, but only to make a show of a judicial trial, answered nothing.

Then a priest asked him: "Tell me, are you the Christ, the Son of God?" Jesus said: "Yes, I am the Christ, the Son of God; and now, in torturing me, you will see how a Son of Man is like to God." And the priest was glad to hear these words, and said to the other judges: "Are not these words enough to condemn him?" And the judges said: "That is enough; we sentence him to death." And when they said that, the people threw themselves upon Jesus, and began to beat him, to spit in his face, and insult him. He was silent.

The Jews had no power to punish men with death, and for that needed permission from the Roman governor. Therefore, having condemned Jesus in their court, and having subjected him to ignominy, they took him to the Roman governor, Pilate, that he might execute him. Pilate asked why they wished to kill Jesus. They said, because he was a criminal. Pilate said that if he was so, they must judge him by their own law. They said: "We want you to put him to death, because he is guilty before the Roman Cæsar; he is a rebel, he agitates the people, he forbids payment of taxes to Cæsar, and calls himself the Jewish king."

Pilate summoned Jesus before him, and said: "What is the meaning of this; are you the Jewish king?"

Jesus said: "Do you really wish to know what my kingdom means, or are you only asking for form's sake?"

Pilate answered: "I am not a Jew, and it is the same to me whether you are the Jewish king or not; but I ask you, who are you, and why do they call you king?"

Jesus said: "They say truly, that I call myself a king. I am indeed a king, but my kingdom is not of earth, but of heaven. The kings of the earth war and fight, and have armies; but as for me, — you see they have bound and beaten me, and I did not resist. I am king from heaven: my power is of the spirit."

Pilate said: "Then it is indeed true that you think yourself a king?"

Jesus answered: "You know this yourself. Every one who lives by the spirit is free. I live by this only, and I only teach by showing men the truth, that they are free by the spirit."

Pilate said: "You teach the truth, but nobody knows what truth is, and every one has his own truth."

And having said this, he turned his back on Jesus, and went again to the Jews. Coming out to them, he said: "I find nothing criminal in this man. Why, then, put him to death?"

The priests answered: "He ought to be put to death, because he incites the people."

Then Pilate began to examine Jesus before the priests; but Jesus, seeing it was only a mock inquiry, answered nothing. Then Pilate said: "I alone cannot condemn him; take him to Herod."

At Herod's tribunal, Jesus again answered nothing to the accusations of the priests; and Herod, thinking Jesus to be a common fellow, ordered him, for mockery, to be dressed in red clothes, and sent back to Pilate.

Pilate pitied Jesus, and began to entreat the priests to forgive him, if only on account of the feast. But the priests did not consent, and all — the people with them — cried out to crucify Christ. Pilate tried a second time to persuade them to let Jesus go; but priests and people cried out that he must be executed. They said: "He is guilty of calling himself the Son of God." Pilate again summoned Jesus, and asked him what he meant by calling himself the Son of God. Jesus answered nothing.

Then Pilate said: "Why do you not answer me, seeing that I have power to execute you or to set you free?"

Jesus answered: "You have no authority over me; authority only comes from on high."

And Pilate a third time began to persuade the Jews to set Jesus free. But they said to him: "If you will not execute this man, whom we have exposed as an enemy to Cæsar, then you yourself are not a friend, but an enemy, to Cæsar."

And hearing these words, Pilate gave way, and ordered the execution of Jesus. They first stripped him and flogged him; then they dressed him again in a ridiculous way. And they beat him, mocked him, and insulted him. Then they caused him to carry the cross, and led him to the place of execution, where they crucified him.

And as Jesus hung on the cross, the whole populace mocked him. But to this mockery Jesus answered: "Father! do not call them to account; they do not know what they are doing." And then, as he was now drawing near death, he said: "Father! I yield my spirit into Thy care."

And bowing his head, he breathed his last.

www.ingramcontent.com/pod-product-compliance
Lightning Source LLC
Chambersburg PA
CBHW031821270326
41932CB00008B/490
* 9 7 8 3 3 3 7 3 1 9 5 1 9 *